ONE HUNDRED YEARS *of* HOMOSEXUALITY

This scene might be entitled, "More Than He Bargained For." A vase-painter teases the erotic conventions of male society in classical Athens by depicting an amorous boy responding more enthusiastically than expected to the overtures of an evidently startled adult suitor. Note, however, that the boy is not portrayed as *sexually* aroused by physical contact with the man whom he wishes to encourage: he is shown without an erection. (The J. Paul Getty Museum, The Carpenter Painter, Attic Red-Figure Kylix, ca. 515–510 B.C., terracotta, diameter of rim: 33.5 cm. 85.AE.25)

ONE HUNDRED YEARS *of* HOMOSEXUALITY

AND OTHER ESSAYS ON GREEK LOVE

DAVID M. HALPERIN

ROUTLEDGE
NEW YORK • LONDON

Published in 1990 by

Routledge
An imprint of Routledge, Chapman and Hall, Inc.
29 West 35 Street
New York, NY 10001

Published in Great Britain by

Routledge
11 New Fetter Lane
London EC4P 4EE

Printed in the United States of America

Library of Congress Cataloging in Publication Data

Halperin, David M., 1952–
    One hundred years of homosexuality : and other essays on Greek
love / David M. Halperin.
       p.   cm. — (New ancient world series)
    Bibliography: p.
    ISBN 0-415-90096-4; ISBN 0-415-90097-2 (pbk.)
    1. Homosexuality, Male—Greece—History. 2. Sodomy—Greece—
History. I. Title II. Title: 100 years of homosexuality.
III. Series.
    HQ76.2.G8H35   1989   89–33158
306.76'62'09495—dc20   CIP

British Library Cataloguing in Publication Data
Halperin, David M. *1952–*
    One hundred years of homosexuality. — (New ancient world)
    1. Greece ancient period   Sex relations
    I. Title
    306.7'0938
    ISBN 0-415-90096-4
          0-415-90097-2(pb)

Table of Contents

For
Elaine P. Halperin

Preface

This volume brings together, in revised and expanded form, a number of my previously published essays* on love, sex, and gender in ancient Greece. All of the essays were written in the last three years, and they cluster around a single theme: the erotics of male culture in the ancient Greek world. They do not constitute a comprehensive and systematic treatment of that (large) topic. Rather, they focus on selected aspects of it and explore a variety of issues that have emerged from modern efforts to elucidate it.

The words "Greek love" in my sub-title represent something of a tease. They have traditionally functioned (for example, in the title of a disreputable and fascinating book by J. Z. Eglington, published in 1964, which is hardly about Greece at all) as a coded phrase for the unmentionable term *paederasty*, meaning the sexual pursuit of adolescent males by adult males. Paederasty is, in origin, a Greek word; it names a practice which classical Athenian society not only tolerated but—under certain conditions, at least—actively promoted and even celebrated. As such, paederasty has come to be seen (whether rightly or wrongly, the reader may judge from the essays collected here) as one of the distinguishing, not to say peculiar, features of ancient Greek civilization; it has come to stand for the whole of "Greek love." The present volume, however, contains no essay exclusively devoted to paederasty—although I shall have enough to say about it in the following pages to satisfy, I trust, the curiosity of any reader who approaches this book intrigued by the allusion in the sub-title. Instead, I have inquired into the wider social components and contexts of "Greek love," believing as I do that we may come to a more satisfactory understanding of classical Athenian paederasty if we do not view it as an isolated, and therefore "queer," institution but if we regard it, rather, as merely one strand in a larger and more intricate web of erotic and social practices in ancient Greece, ranging from heroic comradeship to commercial sex. The result of this shift in emphasis, I hope, will be to broaden the scope of the study of the erotics of male culture in ancient Greece, to distance that study from the modern medical/forensic/social-scientific category of homosexuality (with its essentializing, psychologistic implications), and to suggest a number of theoretical direc-

---

* With the exception of "Heroes and their Pals," which appears in print here for the first time.

tions which future practitioners of classical studies, gay studies, and the history of sexuality may find useful to pursue.

The writing and revising of these essays have been generously supported by two Fellowships, both funded by the Andrew W. Mellon Foundation, from the National Humanities Center (in 1985-86) and the Stanford Humanities Center (in 1987-88); the latter grant was matched by a sabbatical leave from the School of Humanities and Social Sciences at the Massachusetts Institute of Technology. Further research monies were provided by the M.I.T. Literature Faculty and by the School of Humanities and Social Sciences at M.I.T. I am most grateful for all the institutional and intellectual support that these grants represent.

Many people have contributed to my thinking about the issues discussed below, and I have tried to record their names, along with my gratitude, in the headnotes to the individual essays which have benefited from their criticisms and suggestions. Here I must acknowledge the three most important intellectual influences on my work, without which this book could not have been written. They are K. J. Dover's *Greek Homosexuality* (1978), the first modern scholarly study of the subject and a triumph of empirical research; Michel Foucault's *L'usage des plaisirs* (1984; translated into English as *The Use of Pleasure* in 1985), the second volume of his unfinished History of Sexuality (Foucault died of AIDS in 1984), notable for the originality of its theoretical approach as well as for the brilliance of its individual insights; and John J. Winkler's *The Constraints of Desire: The Anthropology of Sex and Gender in Ancient Greece* (1990), a collection of essays whose combination of philological mastery, critical tact, methodological sophistication, intellectual range, and human engagement sets a new standard for the interpretation of ancient cultures. I have had the opportunity to read Jack Winkler's essays as they were being written and revised, as well as the advantage of working closely with their author on a related project—a book of essays, co-edited by us with Froma I. Zeitlin, entitled *Before Sexuality: The Construction of Erotic Experience in the Ancient Greek World* (Princeton, 1990). Jack has encouraged me in my work on the present volume from the start and, during a period in which he was learning to meet and to master the challenge of living with AIDS, has freely shared with me his knowledge and his enthusiasm. He does not agree with everything in this book, but the work contained in it owes more than I can say to the inspiration of his personal, political, and intellectual example.

The author and publisher of this volume have arranged to donate half of the author's proceeds from its sale to the San Francisco AIDS Foundation.

D.M.H.

Stanford, California
30 June 1988

Introduction

"Omit: a reference to the unspeakable vice of the Greeks." With those words, uttered in "a flat toneless voice," the Dean of a Cambridge college, in the seventh chapter of E. M. Forster's self-suppressed novel, *Maurice* (originally composed in 1913–14 and first released for publication upon the novelist's death in 1970), interrupts a student who has been dutifully translating aloud from the text of an unnamed classical Greek author. After the class is over, one of the other students in it remarks indignantly to a friend that the Dean ought to lose his fellowship for such hypocrisy: they suspect his affectless tone of concealing a personal sympathy for the unspeakable. If their interpretation is correct, the Dean would seem to have succeeded in imparting to his students, along with a knowledge of classical Greek, not only a sense of scholarly decorum—a heightened sensitivity to what one may say and what one may not say when speaking about the ancient Greeks—but also an exemplary model of self-censorship.

The episode takes on additional significance, and greater poignancy, five chapters later, when the reader learns that the finest classical scholar among the students in the Dean's translation class has been drawn to the study of the classics because he considers that the ancient Greeks gave temperate and exquisite expression to homoerotic feelings identical to his own. Study of the Greeks, especially Plato, has enabled this young man gradually to accept himself and his desires as he had never been able to do in the course of his religious upbringing; the Greeks provided an ideological weapon against the condemnatory reflexes of his own Christian conscience, offering him, in its place, "a new guide for life." Even today, the Greeks continue to perform analogous functions for many of us: as Forster wrote, somewhat guardedly, in a 1934 biography of his mentor at Cambridge, Goldsworthy Lowes Dickinson, "The Greeks—and Plato particularly—understand our political and social confusion, but they are not part of it, and so they can help us."[1] It is not the purpose of this book to deprive anyone of a potentially meaningful "guide for life." But if we are ever to discover who "we" really are, it will be necessary to examine more closely the many respects in which

1

Greek sexual practices *differ* from "our own"—and do not merely confirm current cherished assumptions about "us" or legitimate some of "our" favorite practices. The moment has come to suspend our projects of identification (or disavowal, as the case may be) long enough to devise an interpretation of erotic experiences in classical antiquity that foregrounds the historical and cultural specificity of those experiences. Such, at least, is the aim to which the essays collected here are intended to contribute.

Times have changed since the late 1890's, when Forster studied the classics at Cambridge: the self-censorship which Lowes Dickinson evidently exercised (and which Forster duly reproduced in his biography of the man, where no mention is made of Dickinson's homosexuality) has now become—at least, within the confines of the better American universities—more a matter of personal choice than professional necessity. Within the last two decades, especially, political movements originating outside the academy have so transformed life within it that a classical scholar who studies ancient Greek sexual practices, including paederasty (the "unspeakable vice" at issue in Forster's fictional translation class), can expect not only to be tolerated by the profession but to be materially rewarded by it as well. Little wonder, then, if, in the world of scholarship at least, the love that once (in Alfred Douglas's words) dared not speak its name—either because it was traditionally, in the judicial phrase, "not to be named among Christians" or because at the time Douglas wrote his maudlin lyric it did not quite know by what name to call itself[2]—little wonder if that once-silent love now cannot shut up (as reactionaries are often heard to complain). What was once unspeakable is nowadays so compulsively voluble that Michel Foucault took this apparent reversal in cultural practice as the starting point for his inquiry into the history of sexuality.

Despite all these developments, however, the ban on speaking about ancient sexual attitudes and behaviors had still not been totally lifted when I began to study the classics at an American college in the early 1970's. My fellow students and I read, to be sure, both the obscene and the paederastic poems of Catullus at the insistence of a young and politically engaged classical scholar whom we revered, but we did not translate all of them in class, nor was the meaning of certain Latin words made known to us. The authoritative lexicons of the ancient languages were not much help in that department: they defined the ancient terms for the less mentionable sexual acts in Latin, if the terms were Greek; and in Greek, if the terms were Latin. Standard translations of classical authors in the Loeb Classical Library omitted passages judged to be obscene or left them "in the decent obscurity"[3] of a dead language—translating Greek texts into Latin, allowing Latin texts to stand untranslated, or translating them (bizarrely) into Italian[4]: these strategies effectively served to conceal the meaning of the less common obscenities from even professional scholars while enabling the inquisitive student to locate unerringly the passages in which they occurred. But in certain cases even the obscurity afforded by a dead language proved insufficiently dark and deep for the "indecency" it was intended to conceal: when, in 1930, towards the end of his life, A. E. Housman (the English poet and a leading classical scholar) proposed to clarify the meaning of various sexual acts mentioned in Roman literature and, in particular, to explicate Roman attitudes to sex between males—a topic to which he brought a personal as well as a scholarly interest—he chose to express himself in Latin rather than in English; Housman's intricate Latin style, however, was still too explicit for the Board of Management of the *Classical Quarterly*, which forbade the Editor to publish Housman's essay (the essay had already been set up in type, but that was as far as it got). Housman ultimately published his essay abroad, in the German classical periodical *Hermes*: it appeared in 1931, still in Latin.[5]

To be sure, much lexical knowledge did exist at the time I was in college, but it was scattered and buried in scholarly commentaries or in the notes to learned articles. I eventually discovered that it constituted a body of subterranean lore which circulated informally among classical scholars and was communicated from like-minded professor to student in the course of private conversations outside the classroom. Only within the last fifteen years has that lore begun to emerge into the light of day, facilitating scholarly clarification of the more arcane Greek and Latin obscenities.[6] A telling instance is the Greek verb *laikazein*, an abusive term for fellation, whose meaning was known to Housman and earlier scholars without ever having been definitively established. That verb, along with its derivatives, was in 1980 the subject of an exhaustive and masterly study by H. D. Jocelyn in the *Proceedings of the Cambridge Philological Society* (Forster's fictional classicist would have been pleased); *laikastria* had been discussed, in passing, only two years before, by K. J. Dover, a scholar of immense philological learning and total lack of inhibition, but his remarks indicate that even he, even in 1978, still did not know exactly what the word meant.[7] Even today, much work remains to be done.

Although Forster himself was probably not aware of it, by the time he got to Cambridge "the unspeakable vice of the Greeks" had already embarked upon its career of loquaciousness. In a magisterial and deeply influential study of the Greek "races and cities," first published in 1820–24, Karl Otfried Müller devoted a chapter to a detailed and business-like consideration of the evidence for paederastic initiation rituals in Sparta and Crete, behaviors which Müller took to be inherited from the military pre-history of "the Dorian race" (Müller thereby provided Oscar Wilde's Dorian Gray, more than half a century later, with his un-Christian first name).[8] The earliest published work championing passionate love between men took the form, in 1836, of a tract on "male love" in ancient Greece: it was written by an obscure Swiss pastor, Heinrich Hössli,[9] who used the prestige of Greek culture in his own day to make the dubious argument that Plato must have had a better grasp than most moderns of what was and was not truly "natural" in matters of love. The following year, 1837, witnessed the publication, in a German encyclopaedia, of a scholarly article by M.-H.-E. Meier exclusively devoted to paederasty in the ancient world; this would seem to have been largely a compilation of the relevant ancient texts, if we can judge by the revised and expanded version prepared a hundred years later by L.-R. de Pogey-Castries.[10] As these various literary productions attest, scholarly and political interests in "Greek love" developed side-by-side, if not exactly hand-in-hand, throughout much of the nineteenth century. Karl Heinrich Ulrichs, whose earliest writings date to 1862 and who appears to have been the first political activist for the emancipation of sexual minorities, drew much of his inspiration from classical sources, especially Plato;[11] in the next decade, the first study of "Greek love" in English, by John Addington Symonds, was explicitly designed to promote judicial reform, although many years passed before Symonds's work could be widely circulated: a limited edition of one hundred copies appeared only in 1901—the year Forster completed his studies at Cambridge.[12] The twentieth century has witnessed a veritable explosion of writings on the subject.[13]

A new era in the study of the history of sexuality began in 1978, which would also seem, in retrospect, to have been the high-water mark of the recent political movement for lesbian and gay freedom in the United States. The new era was defined by the appearance of K. J. Dover's *Greek Homosexuality* and by the English publication of the first volume of Foucault's unfinished *History of Sexuality*. Each work deserves an independent description.

It would be difficult to exaggerate the importance, within the field of classical studies, of Dover's long-awaited monograph on homosexual behavior in ancient Greece. Its author was, and is, an eminent political and intellectual historian, a superb philologist, and a brilliant polemicist. At the time he published *Greek Homosexuality*, Dover was President of Corpus Christi College, Oxford (the book had been written while Dover was Professor of Greek at the University of St. Andrews); he had also been President of the Oxford Philological Society and, a year before *Greek Homosexuality* appeared, he had been knighted for his work in Greek history. He subsequently went on to become President of the British Academy. Dover therefore brought to the study of his controversial subject an incomparable, and well-deserved, academic prestige. No less crucial to the reception of Dover's work than his credentials as a scholar were his credentials as a heterosexual, which were equally above suspicion ("I am fortunate in not experiencing moral shock or disgust at any genital act whatsoever, provided that it is welcome and agreeable to all the participants," Dover coolly remarked in the Preface to his book), and both sets of credentials were celebrated by reviewers. Whatever the book's other defects—and it did meet with many hostile and unfair reviews, coming from a variety of perspectives—it could be accused of neither faulty scholarship nor special pleading. In this respect, the reception of Dover's work has differed greatly from that of Foucault's.

Greek Homosexuality turned out, nonetheless, to be in many ways a maddening book to read. It did not pretend to offer a full survey of its subject. As the first modern, systematic, scholarly student of homosexuality in ancient Greece, Dover maintained that the material on which to base a thematic survey was lacking. And so his book took the form of a series of commentaries on selected documents, bringing in other evidence from the whole of Greek antiquity where relevant. Dover's interpretation of "Greek homosexuality" thus emerges *seriatim* from detailed analyses of individual documents: it is not laid out before the reader in a single motion. Dover's discussion of certain topics, such as the question of whether, to what extent, or in what contexts the Greeks acknowledged or tolerated mutual desire between male sexual partners (a matter on which Dover was attacked by a number of reviewers), has to be pieced together from half a dozen different passages in his book: he never deals fully with the issue in its own right. That is why some reviewers and readers misunderstood him: they remembered what Dover said in one context but not how he qualified or explicated his statement in another. Despite these annoyances and frustrations, however, the great value of Dover's work has become even clearer with time. His book richly repays rereading and close study by specialists. Dover's relentlessly empirical approach succeeded in its main purpose, which was to establish once and for all a few basic facts about "Greek homosexuality" in the face of skepticism on the part of traditional classical scholars. Among Dover's main points were (1) that homosexual behavior among Greek males largely took the form of paederastic relations between a man and a youth; (2) that the classical Greeks considered the desire of adult males for sexual pleasure through contact with handsome youths to be normal and natural; (3) that neither Athenian law nor Athenian custom forbade or penalized the sexual expression of such desire, so long as the lovers observed certain conventional decencies; and (4) that paederastic love-affairs which conformed, at least outwardly, to those conventions were regarded by Athenian society as decent, honorable, and—under certain circumstances—even praiseworthy. John Boswell[14] has questioned (1) and David Cohen[15] has tried to refute (2) and (3), but neither has been able to shake the main results of Dover's research, nor is anyone else likely to do so.

Dover was concerned, first and foremost, with establishing the facts of the matter and with getting them right. He worked within a tradition of empirical research whose aims and methods he was prepared to justify, but he was not concerned primarily with theoretical questions. That dimension of the history of sexuality was taken up, with characteristic brilliance and matchless penetration, by the late French philosopher and historian Michel Foucault. Foucault's own field was modern history; he specialized in studying how the various régimes of knowledge and institutional practice had shifted from the end of the Renaissance to the present day. By the time he began his inquiry into the history of sexuality, Foucault had already traced the genealogy of a number of modern institutions (the medical clinic, the insane asylum, the prison, the sciences) along with the systems of knowledge and power that supported them and that were, in turn, constituted by them, plus the human subjects and objects they produced. He initially set out to do the same thing for "sexuality," to trace the evolution of the régimes of power and knowledge that constituted human beings as the conscious subjects of their "sexuality"—and that did so, moreover, by (among other means) requiring them to *speak* about their sexual experiences. Foucault intended to follow this evolution in the institutions and experiences of sexuality from the Christian confessional to the psychoanalyst's couch to the EST weekend seminar. He discovered, however, that he could not pick up the threads of this story in the Renaissance without taking for granted too many aspects of "sexuality" whose specific conditions of emergence needed to be established. So he abandoned his project as he had initially conceived it and devoted himself to the study of Greek and Roman antiquity.

Basing himself on Dover's work, as well as on that of many classical scholars, Foucault produced an analytic interpretation of the formation of sexual experience in the ancient world that stands in marked contrast to Dover's achievement: it is holistic, systematic, comprehensive (in its own, highly specialized, terms), and general. As such, it dramatizes the interpretative perils that Dover, by confining himself to scholarly commentary on the available documents, wisely avoided. Unlike Dover's work, Foucault's is admittedly schematic; it also contains a number of elementary scholarly errors. For all those reasons, it has proved vulnerable to attack from specialists: Foucault-bashing now seems to have become, since the man's death in 1984, the favorite indoor sport of a host of lesser intellectuals on both sides of the Atlantic. For all that, the interpretative gains which Foucault's work on sex in antiquity represents cannot be exaggerated. Foucault's analysis has, in effect, thrown open a window on the articulation of sexual morality in ancient Greece, providing a clear and economical analysis of its basic structure. He thereby allows us to see what, perhaps, we "always" knew but never expressed to ourselves in such simple and elegant terms before; he fits scattered pieces of knowledge into a new and lucid pattern, and he thereby reorients our basic outlook on the material. I shall have a good deal to say about Foucault's approach to the Greek evidence in "Two Views of Greek Love," included in this volume, so I shall limit myself here to the following observation.

The distinctive contribution which the English publication in 1978 of the first volume of Foucault's *History of Sexuality* made to subsequent work can be simply, if baldly, put: Foucault did for "sexuality" what feminist critics had done for "gender."[16] That is, Foucault detached "sexuality" from the physical and biological sciences (just as feminists had detached "gender" from the facts of anatomical sex, of somatic dimorphism) and treated it, instead, as "the set of effects produced in bodies, behaviors, and social relations by a certain deployment" of "a complex political technology."[17] He divorced "sexuality" from "nature" and interpreted it, instead, as a cultural production. He thereby made possible an extremely profitable alliance between certain radical elements in philosophy and anthropology.

In the third section of "One Hundred Years of Homosexuality" I shall argue that Foucault's understanding of "sexuality" is not only helpful as a way of thinking about sex in history and society but is also supported by the ancient evidence. My reason for dwelling on Foucault here is to describe the enormous impetus that Foucault's work gave to anthropological tendencies within the humanities and, specifically, to research into sexuality in all areas of the human sciences. For so long as sexuality, like sex, was thought to be rooted in nature, historians and anthropologists guided by that assumption were bound to unearth merely different "attitudes" to or "expressions" of sexuality—historically or culturally variant responses to the universal "fact" of sexuality, local improvisations on nature's unchanging theme; that theme, moreover, regularly turned out on inspection to be a remarkably familiar one, uncannily recapitulating (and thereby reaffirming) traditional categories and experiences. Thus, historians might show that this or that historical figure was "a homosexual" (Plato, for example) or "a bisexual" (Shakespeare); at a less rudimentary level, historians might measure the social "toleration" of homosexuality or anthropologists note the presence or absence of homosexual behavior in a culture. That some people might not have a sexuality to express, or might have sexual experiences unassimilable to modern sexual categories, was seldom a practicable conclusion to draw from the evidence uncovered in the course of research. But with the appearance of Foucault's work, the pressing questions now became, "How was sexual experience constituted in a given culture?" "In what terms was sexual experience constructed?" "How was sexual experience distinguished from and related to other sorts of experience, and how were the boundaries between these various kinds of experience articulated?" "Were sexual pleasures and desires configured differently for different members of a given society and, if so, according to what principles?" "How did the terms employed by the various members of human living-groups to organize their sexual experiences operate, conceptually and institutionally, so as to constitute human beings as the subjects of sexual experience? What other areas of life were implicated in their operation?" "How did the constitution of sexual subjects relate to the constitution of other social forms? of power? of knowledge?"

Under the impetus provided by Foucault, by feminism, and by the preceding decade or more of empirical research into the history of sexuality, progress in this field since 1978 has been rapid and scholarly activity has been intense. In a period, in other words, when much of western Europe and America seems to have sunk into a reactionary torpor, embracing with a hollow and cynical enthusiasm the comforts of conventional pieties and rushing to rediscover the demagogic possibilities of a self-serving obscurantism, intellectual ferment within the universities has been quietly but inexorably proceeding at an accelerating rate, and research has made great strides. One of the considerable pleasures I have had in the course of writing and revising the essays contained in this book has been that of acquainting myself with the enormous scope and variety of recent work, much of it highly sophisticated and enlightening, in the history of sexuality. One of the purposes of this book, accordingly, is to take stock of our scholarly progress, to consolidate its gains, and to issue an interim report—however spotty and incomplete—on the results of it. If some readers may find my citations of other scholars and my references to their work to be excessive in quantity or complexity, I can only plead my eagerness to tell the scholarly world the good news—to show something of the breadth, scope, and diversity of work that has been carried out in the history of sexuality over the last ten years or so in half a dozen countries. And, in any case, I have tried to restrict those scholarly citations to the notes, lodged at the back of this volume out of the way of the non-scholarly reader, to whom I hope to have something amusing and compelling to say.

From all this recent work on the history of sexuality a certain picture is starting to emerge. Its details are extremely sketchy, and there are large gaps on its surface, some of which perhaps will never be filled in. But let me attempt to convey my impression of it. Homosexuality and heterosexuality, as we currently understand them, are modern, Western, bourgeois productions. Nothing resembling them can be found in classical antiquity. A certain identification of the self with the sexual self began in late antiquity; it was strengthened by the Christian confessional. Only in the high middle ages did certain kinds of sexual acts start to get identified with certain specifically sexual types of person: a "sodomite" begins to name not merely the person who commits an act of sodomy but one distinguished by a certain type of specifically sexual subjectivity which inclines such a person to commit those acts; nonetheless, sodomy remains a sinful act which any person, given sufficient temptation, may be induced to commit. In London and Paris, in the seventeenth and eighteenth centuries, there appear—evidently for the first time, and in conjunction with the rise of companionate marriage—social gathering-places for persons of the same sex with the same socially deviant attitudes to sex and gender who wish to socialize and to have sex with one another. In London, these are the so-called molly-houses, where men dress as women and assume women's names. This phenomenon contributes to the formation of the great nineteenth-century experience of "sexual inversion," or sex-role reversal, in which some forms of sexual deviance are interpreted as, or conflated with, gender deviance. The emergence of homosexuality out of inversion, the formation of a sexual orientation independent of relative degrees of masculinity and femininity, takes place during the latter part of the nineteenth century and comes into its own only in the twentieth. Its highest expression is the "straight-acting and -appearing gay male," a man distinct from other men in absolutely no other respect besides that of his "sexuality." Although this personality type may have been a cherished ideal in earlier periods—as a fantasy image it is memorably realized in the title character of E. M. Forster's *Maurice*, for example—it is the distinctive creation of the period after the Second World War, and as I write it may already be on the wane.

This collection of essays is divided into two parts. Part One is largely theoretical, and the essays contained in it address a number of issues that have to do with scholarly method and current critical practice. Part Two contains examples of practical literary criticism and historical analysis which apply some of the principles argued for in the earlier essays to a series of concrete problems in the interpretation of Greek culture. The six essays are intended to be read as a sequence, but they may be read in any order, although a good deal of what is said in the title essay of the collection is taken for granted in the subsequent essays, and so the reader is encouraged to have a look at it first.

"One Hundred Years of Homosexuality" sounds many of the major themes heard elsewhere in this volume. It represents my best attempt to show not only that our own cultural assumptions are inappropriate to the interpretation of sexual life in ancient Greece but, more importantly, that a radical reinterpretation of sexual life in ancient Greece has the potential to transform our own cultural and sexual self-understanding. In particular, I argue that the study of sexual life in antiquity reveals homosexuality, heterosexuality, and even sexuality itself to be relatively recent and highly culture-specific forms of erotic life—not the basic building-blocks of sexual identity for all human beings in all times and places, but peculiar and indeed exceptional ways of conceptualizing as well as *experiencing* sexual desire. I appeal to the Greek documentary record for evidence that sexual experiences and forms of erotic life are culturally specific, that they are not universal but historical, and I contend that it may be possible to recover some of the indigenous meanings attached to sexual experiences in ancient Greece if only we do not insist on viewing the ancient documents through the prism of modern social and sexual categories. In the latter part of the essay, I provide a sketch of the distinctive ways in which sexual experience was articulated and organized in the ancient Greek world.

It has been my experience, in the course of lecturing to different audiences around the United States, that the thesis I propound in the title essay tends to elicit—quite understandably—a certain amount of skepticism and resistance. The second item in this volume, " 'Homosexuality': A Cultural Construct," takes the form of an interview with the sociologist Richard Schneider; it represents an attempt to answer some of the questions that are typically asked in response to my arguments. I realize that it may not be possible to anticipate all the objections that may be raised to one's line of thinking, and I know it is impossible to state one's own position so clearly and unambiguously that it cannot be misunderstood. My goal in this interview, then, is not to eliminate all misapprehension but rather to make more explicit some of the assumptions and guiding principles that have shaped my work. In the process, I have also tried to make the best theoretical case I can imagine for "constructionism"—for the proposition, that is, that sexual identities are not "given" by nature but are culturally constituted or produced.

"Two Views of Greek Love" is a report on and a critique of current trends in classical scholarship that bear on the study of paederasty in ancient Greece. I look specifically at the work of the German classicist Harald Patzer as well as at that of Michel Foucault. Patzer and Foucault, I find, exhibit contrasting intellectual styles and methods, and so they help to define some of the very different contemporary tendencies in the study of the history of sexuality. In particular, Patzer's approach begins from the assumption that classical Greek paederasty must not be interpreted in the light of modern sexual categories: in that respect, it is highly congenial to my own approach. But it sharply diverges from my interpretation in highlighting the ritual element in Greek paederasty. That emphasis on ritual reflects, moreover, what is now perhaps the dominant intellectual orientation among those classicists who treat paederasty in the light of Dover's evidence for the wide distribution of homosexual behaviors in ancient Greece. Patzer also makes use of some of the same ethnographic data to which I appeal in my exchange with Dr. Schneider and in my concluding essay on the figure of Diotima in Plato's *Symposium*. Thus, by confronting Patzer's work, I am able both to clarify further my own position on the place of comparative ethnographies in the ongoing debate over the cultural articulation of sexual categories and to criticize what has looked for some time to be the emerging orthodoxy about the meaning of paederasty in classical Greece (an orthodoxy, by the way, to which Sir Kenneth Dover himself does not adhere, as he has lately made plain).[18] And by comparing Patzer's interpretative tactics to Foucault's, I hope to demonstrate to classicists, who have been slow to embrace Foucault's methods and insights, some of the advantages of Foucault's approach over that of traditional philology, which Patzer—despite his anthropological interests—largely exemplifies.

"Heroes and their Pals," in Part Two, is a comparative study of three narrative traditions, each of which features a close friendship between two male warriors: the Babylonian Gilgamesh Epic, the Books of Samuel in the Old Testament of the Bible, and Homer's *Iliad*. I examine each of these friendships in order to gauge the extent of the structural and thematic correspondences between them as well as to identify some of the distinctive meanings that cluster about each friendship as it is represented in the different literary traditions. The ultimate purpose of my comparison is to define more precisely the peculiar form of erotic life common to the three friendships and to distinguish it from later Greek paederasty as well as from modern homosexuality.

In "The Democratic Body" I attempt to document the existence and to reconstruct the meaning of male prostitution in classical Athens. In particular, I ask why it was that any male of Athenian parents who had been a prostitute in his youth was subsequently debarred from participating in the communal life of the city. Under what conception of prostitution would prostitution represent a disqualification for citizenship? And under what conception of citizenship would prostitution constitute a violation of civic duty? Treating prostitution and citizenship as complementary functions in the code used to articulate the ideology of social life in classical Athens, I seek an answer to these questions by examining shifts in the cultural definition of manhood in Athens, for it was in that half-articulated definition that social and political practices were often rooted. I try to show that "citizenship," for free Athenian males, was a sexual and gendered concept as well as a political and social one—and, hence, that the boundary between "private" and "public" life was drawn in a radically different way from the way it is drawn now: indeed, it is not even clear whether the Greek distinction between *oikos* and *polis*, between household and community, brought into play anything like the modern notions of "private" and "public," "civil society" and "state."

When I originally set out to write the essay on Diotima, I had intended to establish the extent to which Plato might be considered a "feminist" in comparison to his fellow Athenians. By employing a woman, the prophetess Diotima, to articulate the central tenets of his erotic theory in the *Symposium*, and by casting those tenets in a "feminocentric" form, Plato, I thought, was implicitly criticizing the sexual ethos of his male contemporaries. While I still believe that some version of this thesis is plausible, I became more interested, in the course of writing the paper, in the politics of gender and the politics of representation implicit in Plato's decision to enunciate, in the voice of a woman, what is (in the first instance at least) a doctrine of male homoerotic desire. My thinking led me to inquire into the role of "the feminine" in the social reproduction of male culture and to analyze the characteristic male strategy of speaking *about* women by speaking *for* women. But once I put the problem in those terms, I saw that my own discourse about Plato's Diotima represented an instance of exactly the phenomenon I had set out to expose and to criticize. Moreover, there appeared to be no way that I could escape from that paradox, no "politically correct" stance that I could assume, for the project as a whole was obviously implicated in the same politics of gender and the same politics of representation as Plato's (far more interesting) text: no amount of discursive acrobatics could enable me to talk or write my way out of it. In discussing Plato, then, I found myself condemned to reproduce the very structures of domination that I had set about to make visible in Plato. In my essay on Diotima, therefore, I have attempted to dramatize this paradox and to suggest how the contradictions inherent in it might themselves create further opportunities for a feminist critique.

PART I

1

One Hundred Years of Homosexuality

I

In 1992, when the patriots among us will be celebrating the five-hundredth anniversary of the discovery of America by Christopher Columbus, our cultural historians may wish to mark the centenary of an intellectual landfall of almost equal importance for the conceptual geography of the human sciences: the invention of homosexuality by Charles Gilbert Chaddock. Though he may never rank with Columbus in the annals of individual achievement, Chaddock would hardly seem to merit the obscurity which has surrounded him throughout the past hundred years. An early translator of Krafft-Ebing's classic medical handbook of sexual deviance, the *Psychopathia sexualis*, Chaddock is credited by the *Oxford English Dictionary* with having introduced "homo-sexuality" into the English language in 1892,[1] in order to render a German cognate twenty years its senior.[2] Homosexuality, for better or for worse, has been with us ever since.

Before 1892 there was no homosexuality, only sexual inversion. But, as George Chauncey, who has made a thorough study of the medical literature on the subject, persuasively argues, "Sexual inversion, the term used most commonly in the nineteenth century, did not denote the same conceptual phenomenon as homosexuality. 'Sexual inversion' referred to a broad range of deviant gender behavior, of which homosexual desire was only a logical but indistinct aspect, while 'homosexuality' focused on the narrower issue of sexual object choice. The differentiation of homosexual desire from 'deviant' gender behavior at the turn of the century reflects a major reconceptualization of the nature of human sexuality, its relation to gender, and its role in one's social definition."[3] Throughout the nineteenth century, in other words, sexual preference for a person of one's own sex was not clearly distinguished from other sorts of non-conformity to one's culturally defined sex-role: deviant object-choice was viewed as merely one of a number of pathological symptoms exhibited by those who reversed, or "inverted," their proper sex-roles by adopting a masculine or a feminine style at variance with what was

15

deemed natural and appropriate to their anatomical sex. Political aspirations in women and (at least according to one expert writing as late as 1920) a fondness for cats in men were manifestations of a pathological condition, a kind of psychological hermaphroditism tellingly but not essentially expressed by the preference for a "normal" member of one's own sex as a sexual partner.[4]

This outlook on the matter seems to have been shared by the scientists and by their unfortunate subjects alike: inversion was not merely a medical rubric, then, but a category of lived experience. Karl Heinrich Ulrichs, for example, an outspoken advocate for the rights of sexual minorities and the founder, as early as 1862, of the cult of Uranism (based on Pausanias's praise of Uranian, or "heavenly," paederasty in Plato's *Symposium*), described his own condition as that of an *anima muliebris virili corpore inclusa*—a woman's soul confined by a man's body.[5] That sexual object-choice might be wholly independent of such "secondary" characteristics as masculinity or femininity never seems to have entered anyone's head until Havelock Ellis waged a campaign to isolate object-choice from role-playing and Freud, in his classic analysis of a drive in the *Three Essays* (1905), clearly distinguished in the case of the libido between the sexual "object" and the sexual "aim."[6]

The conceptual isolation of sexuality *per se* from questions of masculinity and femininity made possible a new taxonomy of sexual behaviors and psychologies based entirely on the anatomical sex of the persons engaged in a sexual act (same sex vs. different sex); it thereby obliterated a number of distinctions that had traditionally operated within earlier discourses pertaining to same-sex sexual contacts and that had radically differentiated active from passive sexual partners, normal from abnormal (or conventional from unconventional) sexual roles, masculine from feminine styles, and paederasty from lesbianism: all such behaviors were now to be classed alike and placed under the same heading.[7] Sexual identity was thus polarized around a central opposition rigidly defined by the binary play of sameness and difference in the sexes of the sexual partners; people belonged henceforward to one or the other of two exclusive categories, and much ingenuity was lavished on the multiplication of techniques for deciphering what a person's sexual orientation "really" was—independent, that is, of beguiling appearances.[8] Founded on positive, ascertainable, and objective behavioral phenomena—on the facts of who had sex with whom—the new sexual taxonomy could lay claim to a descriptive, trans-historical validity. And so it crossed the "threshold of scientificity"[9] and was enshrined as a working concept in the social and physical sciences.[10]

A scientific advance of such magnitude naturally demanded to be crowned by the creation of a new technical vocabulary, but, unfortunately, no objective, value-free words readily lent themselves to the enterprise. In 1891, just one year before the inauguration of "homosexuality," John Addington

Symonds could still complain that "The accomplished languages of Europe in the nineteenth century supply no terms for this persistent feature of human psychology, without importing some implication of disgust, disgrace, vituperation."[11] A number of linguistic candidates were quickly put forward to make good this lack, and "homosexuality" (despite scattered protests over the years) gradually managed to fix its social-scientistic signature upon the new conceptual dispensation. The word itself, as Havelock Ellis noted, is a barbarous neologism sprung from a monstrous mingling of Greek and Latin stock;[12] as such, it belongs to a rapidly growing lexical breed most prominently represented by the hybrid names given to other recent inventions—names whose mere enumeration suffices to conjure up the precise historical era responsible for producing them: e.g., "automobile," "television," "sociology."

Unlike the languages of technology (whether of production or of knowledge), however, the new terminology for describing sexual behavior was slow to take root in the culture at large. In his posthumous autobiographical memoir, *My Father & Myself* (1968), J. R. Ackerley recalls how mystified he was when, about 1918, a Swiss friend asked him, "Are you homo or hetero?": "I had never heard either term before," he writes. Similarly, T. C. Worsley observes in his own memoir, *Flannelled Fool* (1966), that in 1929 "The word [homosexual], in any case, was not in general use, as it is now. Then it was still a technical term, the implications of which I was not entirely aware of."[13] These two memoirists, moreover, were not intellectually deficient men: at the respective times of their recorded bewilderment, Ackerley was shortly about to be, and Worsley already had been, educated at Cambridge. Nor was such innocence limited—in this one instance, at least—to the holders of university degrees: the British sociologist John Marshall, whose survey presumably draws on more popular sources, testifies that "a number of the elderly men I interviewed had never heard the term 'homosexual' until the 1950s."[14] The *Oxford English Dictionary*, originally published in 1933, is also ignorant of (if not willfully blind to) "homosexuality";[15] the word appears for the first time in the *OED*'s 1976 three-volume Supplement.[16]

It is not exactly my intention to argue that homosexuality, as we commonly understand it today, didn't exist before 1892. How, indeed, could it have failed to exist? The very word displays a most workmanlike and scientific indifference to cultural and environmental factors, looking only to the sexes of the persons engaged in the sexual act. Moreover, if homosexuality didn't exist before 1892, heterosexuality couldn't have existed either (it came into being, in fact, like Eve from Adam's rib, eight years later),[17] and without heterosexuality, where would all of us be right now?

The comparatively recent genesis of heterosexuality—strictly speaking, a twentieth-century affair—should provide a clue to the profundity of the cultural issues over which, hitherto, I have been so lightly skating. How is it possible that until the year 1900 there was not a precise, value-free, scientific term available to speakers of the English language for designating what we would now regard, in retrospect, as the mode of sexual behavior favored by the vast majority of people in our culture? Any answer to that question must direct our attention to the inescapable historicity of even the most innocent, unassuming, and seemingly objective of cultural representations.[18] Although a blandly descriptive, rigorously clinical term like "homosexuality" would appear to be unobjectionable as a taxonomic device, it carries with it a heavy complement of ideological baggage and has, in fact, proved a significant obstacle to understanding the distinctive features of sexual life in non-Western and pre-modern cultures.[19] It may well be that homosexuality properly speaking has no history of its own outside the West or much before the beginning of our century.[20] For, as John Boswell remarks, "if the categories 'homosexual/heterosexual' and 'gay/straight' are the inventions of particular societies rather than real aspects of the human psyche, there is no gay history."[21]

II

Boswell, of course, argues the contrary. He maintains, reasonably enough, that any debate over the existence of universals in human culture must distinguish between the respective modes of being proper to words, concepts, and experiences[22]: according to this line of reasoning, people who lived before Newton experienced gravity even though they lacked both the term and the concept; similarly, Boswell claims that the "manifest and stated purpose" of Aristophanes's famous myth in Plato's *Symposium* "is to explain why humans are divided into groups of predominantly homosexual or heterosexual interest," and so this text, along with a number of others from classical antiquity, vouches for the existence of homosexuality as an ancient (if not a universal) category of human experience—however new-fangled the word for it may be.[23] Now the speech of Plato's Aristophanes would seem indeed to be a *locus classicus* for the differentiation of homo- from heterosexuality, because Aristophanes's taxonomy of human beings features a distinction between those who desire a sexual partner of the same sex as themselves and those who desire a sexual partner of a different sex. The Platonic passage alone, then, would seem to offer sufficient warrant for positing an ancient concept, if not an ancient experience, of homosexuality. But closer examination reveals that Aristophanes stops short of deriving a distinction between homo- and heterosexuality from his own myth just when the logic of his analysis would seem to have driven him ineluctably to it. That omission is telling, I believe, and worth considering in greater detail.*

According to Aristophanes, human beings were originally round, eight-limbed creatures, with two faces and two sets of genitals—both front and back—and three sexes (male, female, and androgyne). These ancestors of ours were powerful and ambitious; in order to put them in their place, Zeus had them cut in two, their skin stretched over the exposed flesh and tied at the navel, and their heads rotated so as to keep that physical reminder of their daring and its consequences constantly before their eyes. The severed halves of each former individual, once reunited, clung to one another so desperately and concerned themselves so little with their survival as separate entities that they began to perish for lack of sustenance; those who outlived their mates sought out persons belonging to the same sex as their lost complements and repeated their embraces in a foredoomed attempt to recover their original unity. Zeus at length took pity on them, moved their genitals to the side their bodies now faced, and invented sexual intercourse, so that the bereaved creatures might at least put a temporary terminus to their longing and devote their attention to other, more important (if less pressing) matters. Aristophanes extracts from this story a genetic explanation of observable differences among human beings with respect to sexual object-choice and preferred style of life: males who desire females are descended from an original androgyne (adulterers come from this species), whereas males descended from an original male "pursue their own kind, and would prefer to remain single and spend their entire lives with one another, since by nature they have no interest in marriage and procreation but are compelled to engage in them by social custom" (191e–192b, quoted selectively). Boswell, understandably, interprets this to mean that according to Plato's Aristophanes homosexual and heterosexual interests are "both exclusive and innate."[24]

But that, significantly, is not quite the way Aristophanes sees it. The conclusions that he draws from his own myth help to illustrate the lengths to which classical Athenians were willing to go in order to avoid conceptualizing sexual behaviors according to a binary opposition between different- and same-sex sexual contacts. First of all, Aristophanes's myth generates not two but at least three distinct "sexualities" (males attracted to males, females attracted to females, and—consigned alike to a single classification, evidently—males attracted to females as well as females attracted to males). Moreover, there is not the slightest suggestion in anything Aristophanes

---

* Here follows a close reading of two ancient texts. Some readers may wish to skip ahead to section III.

says that the sexual acts or preferences of persons descended from an original female are in any way similar to, let alone congruent or isomorphic with, the sexual acts or preferences of those descended from an original male;[25] hence, nothing in the text allows us to suspect the existence of even an implicit category to which males who desire males and females who desire females *both* belong in contradistinction to some other category containing males and females who desire one another.★ On the contrary, one consequence of the myth is to make the sexual desire of every human being *formally identical* to that of every other: we are all looking for the same thing in a sexual partner, according to Plato's Aristophanes—namely, a symbolic substitute for an originary object once loved and subsequently lost in an archaic trauma. In that respect we all share the same "sexuality"—which is to say that, despite the differences in our personal preferences or tastes, we are not individuated at the level of our sexual being.

Second, and equally important, Aristophanes's account features a crucial distinction *within* the category of males who are attracted to males, an infrastructural detail missing from his description of each of the other two categories: "while they are still boys [i.e., pubescent or pre-adult],[26] they are fond of men, and enjoy lying down together with them and twining their limbs about them, . . . but when they become men they are lovers of boys. . . . Such a man is a paederast and philerast [i.e., fond of or responsive to adult male lovers]"[27] at *different stages of his life* (191e–192b, quoted selectively). Contrary to the clear implications of the myth, in other words, and unlike the people comprehended by the first two categories, those descended from an original male are *not* attracted to one another *without qualification*; rather, they desire boys when they are men and they take a certain (nonsexual) pleasure in physical contact with men when they are boys.[28] Now since—as the foregoing passage suggests—the classical Athenians sharply distinguished the roles of paederast and philerast, relegating them not only to different age-classes but virtually to different "sexualities,"[29] what Aristophanes is describing here is not a single, homogeneous sexual orientation common to all those who descend from an original male but rather a set of distinct and incommensurable behaviors which such persons exhibit in different periods of their lives; although his genetic explanation of the diversity of sexual object-choice among human beings would seem to require that there be some adult males who are sexually attracted to other adult

---

★ To be sure, a certain symmetry does obtain between the groups composed, respectively, of those making a homosexual and those making a heterosexual object-choice: each of them is constituted by Aristophanes in such a way as to contain both males and females in their dual capacities as subjects and objects of erotic desire. Aristophanes does nothing to highlight this symmetry, however, and it may be doubted whether it should figure in our interpretation of the passage.

males, Aristophanes appears to be wholly unaware of such a possibility, and in any case he has left no room for it in his taxonomic scheme.＊

That omission is all the more unexpected because, as Boswell himself has pointed out (in response to the present argument), the archetypal pairs of lovers from whom all homoerotically inclined males are supposed to descend must themselves have been the same age as one another, since they were originally halves of the same being.[30] No age-matched couples figure among their latter-day offspring, however: in the real world of classical Athens— at least, as Aristophanes portrays it—reciprocal erotic desire among males is unknown.[31] Thus, the social actuality described by Aristophanes features an erotic asymmetry absent from the mythical paradigm used to generate it. Now inasmuch as Aristophanes's myth is an aetiological fable, a projection of contemporary practices backwards in time to their imagined point of origin, the meaning of his myth is necessarily determined, in the first instance at least, by its contemporary reference. Even though the myth, in other words, happens to posit as the ancestors of "modern" human beings some pairs of lovers of the same sex and the same age who are animated by mutual desire for one another, and who would therefore seem to qualify as "homosexuals" rather than as either "paederasts" or "philerasts," the myth is clearly *not* intended to explain mutual same-sex desire among coevals in classical Athens, and so we are not entitled read "homosexual" desire into the myth—especially on the basis of a detail in it whose significance is largely the accidental creation of our own cultural preoccupations (if Aristophanes admittedly fails to say anything explicit that would rule out such a reading of his own myth, that is only because Plato did not anticipate the cultural situation of his twentieth-century readership and so did not dream that anyone would ever place upon Aristophanes's words what, to Plato's way of thinking, would surely have been an outlandish interpretation). Those Athenians who allegedly descend from a mythical all-male ancestor are not defined by Aristophanes as male homosexuals but as willing boys when they are young and as lovers of youths when they are old. Despite Boswell, then, neither the concept nor the experience of "homosexuality" is known to Plato's Aristophanes.[32]

A similar conclusion can be drawn from careful examination of the other document from antiquity that might seem to vouch for the existence both of homosexuality as an indigenous category and of homosexuals as a native

---

＊ Nor does Aristophanes make any allowance in his myth for what was perhaps the most widely shared sexual taste among his fellow Athenian citizens—namely, an undifferentiated liking for good-looking women and boys (that is, a sexual preference not defined by an exclusively gender-specific sexual object-choice). Such a lacuna should warn us not to treat Aristophanes's myth (as, most recently, Cantarella, 84–85, treats it) as a simple description or reflection of contemporary experience.

species. Unlike the myth of Plato's Aristophanes, a famous and much-excerpted passage from a classic work of Greek prose, the document to which I refer is little known and almost entirely neglected by modern historians of "sexuality";[33] its date is late, its text is corrupt, and, far from being a self-conscious literary artifact, it forms part of a Roman technical treatise. But despite its distance from Plato in time, in style, in language, and in intent, it displays the same remarkable innocence of modern sexual categories, and I have chosen to discuss it here partly in order to show what can be learned about the ancient world from texts that lie outside the received canon of classical authors. Let us turn, then, to the ninth chapter in the Fourth Book of *De morbis chronicis*, a mid-fifth-century A.D. Latin translation and adaptation by the African writer Caelius Aurelianus of a now largely lost work on chronic diseases by the Greek physician Soranus, who practised and taught in Rome during the early part of the second century A.D.

The topic of this chapter is *molles* (*malthakoi* in Greek)—that is, "soft" or unmasculine men who depart from the cultural norm of manliness insofar as they actively desire to be subjected by other men to a "feminine" (i.e., receptive) role in sexual intercourse. Caelius begins with an implicit defense of his own unimpeachable masculinity by noting how difficult it is to believe that such people actually exist;[34] he then goes on to observe that the cause of their affliction is not natural (that is, organic) but is rather their own excessive desire, which—in a desperate and foredoomed attempt to satisfy itself —drives out their sense of shame and forcibly converts parts of their bodies to sexual uses not intended by nature. These men willingly adopt the dress, gait, and other characteristics of women, thereby confirming that they suffer not from a bodily disease but from a mental (or moral) defect. After some further arguments in support of that point, Caelius draws an interesting comparison: "For just as the women called *tribades* [in Greek], because they practise both kinds of sex, are more eager to have sexual intercourse with women than with men and pursue women with an almost masculine jealousy . . . so they too [i.e., the *molles*] are afflicted by a mental disease" (132–133). The mental disease in question, which strikes both men and women alike and is defined as a perversion of sexual desire, would certainly seem to be nothing other than homosexuality as it is often understood today.

Several considerations combine to prohibit that interpretation, however. First of all, what Caelius treats as a pathological phenomenon is not the desire on the part of either men or women for sexual contact with a person of the same sex; quite the contrary: elsewhere, in discussing the treatment of satyriasis (a state of abnormally elevated sexual desire accompanied by itching or tension in the genitals), he issues the following advice to people who suffer from it (*De morbis acutis*, 3.18.180–181).[35]

> Do not admit visitors and particularly young women and boys. For the attractiveness of such visitors would again kindle the feeling of desire in the patient. Indeed,

even healthy persons, seeing them, would in many cases seek sexual gratification, stimulated by the tension produced in the parts [i.e., in their own genitals].[36]

There is nothing medically problematical, then, about a desire on the part of males to obtain sexual pleasure from contact with males—so long as that desire respects the proper phallocentric protocols (which, as we shall see, identify "masculinity" with an insertive sexual role); what is of concern to Caelius,[37] as well as to other ancient moralists,[38] is the male desire to be sexually penetrated by males, for such a desire represents the voluntary abandonment of a "masculine" identity in favor of a "feminine" one. It is sex-role reversal, or *gender-deviance*, that is problematized here and that also furnishes part of the basis for Caelius's comparison of *molles* to *tribades*, who assume a "masculine" role in their relations with other women and actively "pursue women with an almost *masculine* jealousy." Indeed, the "soft"— that is, sexually submissive—man, possessed of a shocking and paradoxical desire to surrender his masculine autonomy and precedence to other men, is monstrous precisely because he seems to have "a woman's soul confined by a man's body" and thus to violate the ancients' deeply felt and somewhat anxiously defended sense of congruence between a person's gender, sexual practices, and social identity.[39]

Second, the ground of the similitude between Caelius's *molles* and *tribades* is not that they are both homosexual but rather that they are both bisexual (in our terms). The *tribades* "are *more* eager to have sexual intercourse with women *than with men*" and "practise both kinds of sex"—that is, they have sex with both men and women.[40] As for the *molles*, Caelius's earlier remarks about their extraordinarily intense sexual desire implies that they turn to receptive sex because, although they try, they are not able to satisfy themselves by means of more conventionally masculine sorts of sexual activity, including insertive sex with women;[41] far from having desires that are structured differently from those of normal folk, these gender-deviants desire sexual pleasure just as most people do, but they have such strong and intense desires that they are driven to devise some unusual and disreputable (though ultimately futile) means of gratifying them. That diagnosis becomes explicit at the conclusion of the chapter when Caelius explains why the disease responsible for turning men into *molles* is the only chronic disease that becomes stronger as the body grows older (137).

For in other years when the body is still strong and can perform the normal functions of love, the sexual desire [of these persons] assumes a dual aspect, in which the soul is excited sometimes while playing a passive and sometimes while playing an active role. But in the case of old men who have lost their virile powers, all their sexual desire is turned in the opposite direction and consequently exerts a stronger demand for the feminine role in love. In fact, many infer that this is the reason why boys too are victims of this affliction. For, like old men, they do not possess virile powers; that is, they have not yet attained those powers which have already deserted the aged.[42]

"Soft" or unmasculine men—far from having a fixed and determinate sexual identity, a sexual nature oriented permanently in one specific direction (towards other members of their own sex)—are evidently either men who once experienced an orthodoxly masculine sexual desire in the past or who will eventually experience such a desire in the future. They may well be men with a constitutional tendency to gender-deviance, according to Caelius, but they are not homosexuals: being a womanish man, or a mannish woman, after all, is not the same thing as being a homosexual. Moreover, all the other ancient texts known to me which place in the same category both males who enjoy sexual contact with males and females who enjoy sexual contact with females display one or the other of the two taxonomic strategies employed by Caelius Aurelianus: if such men and women are classified alike, it is either because they are both held to *reverse* their proper sex-roles and to adopt the sexual styles, postures, and modes of copulation conventionally associated with the opposite sex or because they are both held to *alternate* between the personal characteristics and sexual practices proper, respectively, to men and to women.[43] No category of homosexuality, defined in such a way as to contain men and women alike, is indigenous to the ancient world.★

III

Plato's testimony and Caelius Aurelianus's testimony combine to make a basic conceptual and historical point. Homosexuality presupposes sexuality, and sexuality itself (as I shall argue in a moment) is a modern invention. Homosexuality presupposes sexuality because the very concept of homosexuality implies that there is a specifically sexual dimension to the human personality, a characterological seat within the individual of sexual acts, desires, and pleasures—a determinate source from which all sexual expression proceeds. Whether or not such a distinct and unified psychophysical entity actually exists, homosexuality (like heterosexuality, in this respect) necessarily assumes that it does: it posits sexuality as a constitutive principle of the self. Sexuality in this sense is not a purely descriptive term, a neutral

---

★ Indeed, as Manuli (1983), 151 and 201n., observes, even the category of anatomical sex, defined in such a way as to be applicable to men and women alike, does not exist in Greek thought: "the notion of sex never gets formalized as a functional identity of male and female, but is expressed solely through the representation of asymmetry and of complementarity between male and female, indicated constantly by abstract adjectives (*to thêly* ['the feminine'], *to arren* ['the masculine'])."

representation of some objective state of affairs. Rather, it serves to interpret and to organize human experience, and it performs quite a lot of conceptual work.

First of all, sexuality defines itself as a separate, sexual domain within the larger field of man's psychophysical nature. Second, sexuality effects the conceptual demarcation and isolation of that domain from other areas of personal and social life that have traditionally cut across it, such as carnality, venery, libertinism, virility, passion, amorousness, eroticism, intimacy, love, affection, appetite, and desire—to name but a few of the older claimants to territories more recently staked out by sexuality. Finally, sexuality generates sexual identity: it endows each of us with an individual sexual nature, with a personal essence defined (at least in part) in specifically sexual terms.[44] Now sexual identity, so conceived, is not to be confused with gender identity or gender role: indeed, one of the chief conceptual functions of sexuality is to distinguish, once and for all, sexual identity from matters of gender—to decouple, as it were, *kinds* of sexual predilection from *degrees* of masculinity and femininity. That is precisely what makes sexuality alien to the spirit of ancient Mediterranean cultures. For as the example of Caelius Aurelianus makes plain, ancient sexual typologies generally derived their criteria for categorizing people not from sex but from gender: they tended to construe sexual desire as normative or deviant according to whether it impelled social actors to conform to or to violate their conventionally defined gender roles.[45]

Sexuality, then, is not, as it often pretends to be, a universal feature of human life in every society. For as the word is used today (outside the life sciences, at least)[46] sexuality does not refer to some positive physical property—such as the property of being anatomically sexed—that exists independently of culture; it does not rightly denote some common aspect or attribute of bodies. Unlike sex, which is a natural fact, sexuality is a cultural production[47]: it represents the *appropriation* of the human body and of its erogenous zones by an ideological discourse. Far from reflecting a purely natural and uninterpreted recognition of some familiar facts about us, sexuality represents a peculiar turn in conceptualizing, experiencing, and institutionalizing human nature, a turn that (along with many other developments) marks the transition to modernity in northern and western Europe. As Robert Padgug, in a classic essay on sexuality in history, puts it,

> what we consider "sexuality" was, in the pre-bourgeois world, a group of acts and institutions not necessarily linked to one another, or, if they were linked, combined in ways very different from our own. Intercourse, kinship, and the family, and gender, did not form anything like a "field" of sexuality. Rather, each group of sexual acts was connected directly or indirectly—that is, formed part of—institutions and thought patterns which we tend to view as political, economic, or social in nature, and the connections cut across our idea of sexuality as a thing, detachable from other things, and as a separate sphere of private existence.[48]

Where there is no such conception of sexuality, there can be no conception of either homo- or heterosexuality—no notion that human beings are individuated at the level of their sexuality, that they differ from one another in their sexuality or belong to different types of being by virtue of their sexuality.[49]

The invention of homosexuality (and, ultimately, of heterosexuality) had therefore to await, in the first place, the eighteenth-century discovery and definition of sexuality as the total ensemble of physiological and psychological mechanisms governing the individual's genital functions and the concomitant identification of that ensemble with a specially developed part of the brain and nervous system; it had also to await, in the second place, the nineteenth-century interpretation of sexuality as a singular "instinct" or "drive," a force that shapes our conscious life according to its own unassailable logic and thereby determines, at least in part, the character and personality of each one of us.[50] Sexuality, on this latter interpretation, turns out to be something more than an endogenous principle of motivation outwardly expressed by the performance of sexual acts; it is a mute power subtly and deviously at work throughout a wide range of human behaviors, attitudes, tastes, choices, gestures, styles, pursuits, judgments, and utterances. Sexuality is thus the inmost part of an individual human nature. It is the feature of a person that takes longest to get to know well, and knowing it renders transparent and intelligible to the knower the person to whom it belongs. Sexuality holds the key to unlocking the deepest mysteries of the human personality: it lies at the center of the hermeneutics of the self.[51]

Before the scientific construction of "sexuality" as a supposedly positive, distinct, and constitutive feature of individual human beings—an autonomous system within the physiological and psychological economy of the human organism—certain kinds of sexual *acts* could be individually evaluated and categorized, and so could certain sexual tastes or inclinations, but there was no conceptual apparatus available for identifying a person's fixed and determinate sexual *orientation*, much less for assessing and classifying it.[52] That human beings differ, often markedly, from one another in their sexual tastes in a great variety of ways (of which sexual object-choice—the liking for a sexual partner of a specific sex—is only one, and not necessarily the most significant one) is an unexceptionable and, indeed, an ancient observation;[53] but it is not immediately evident that differences in sexual preference are by their very nature more revealing about the temperament of individual human beings, more significant determinants of personal identity, than, for example, differences in dietary preference.[54] And yet, it would never occur to us to refer a person's dietary object-choice to some innate, characterological disposition or to see in his or her strongly expressed and even unvarying preference for the white meat of chicken the symptom of a profound psychophysical orientation, leading us to identify him or her in contexts quite removed from that of the eating of food as, say (to continue the practice of combining Greek and Latin roots), a "pectoriphage" or a "stethovore"; nor would we be likely to inquire further, making nicer discriminations according to whether an individual's predilection for chicken breasts expressed itself in a tendency to eat them quickly or slowly, seldom or often, alone or in company, under normal circumstances or only in periods of great stress, with a guilty or a clear conscience, beginning in earliest childhood or originating with a gastronomic trauma suffered in adolescence. If such questions did occur to us, moreover, I very much doubt whether we would turn to the academic disciplines of anatomy, neurology, clinical psychology, genetics, or sociobiology in the hope of obtaining a clear causal solution to them. That is because (1) we regard the liking for certain foods as a matter of taste; (2) we currently lack a theory of taste; and (3) in the absence of a theory we do not normally subject our behavior to intense, scientific or aetiological, scrutiny.[55]

In the same way, it never occurred to pre-modern cultures to ascribe a person's sexual tastes to some positive, structural, or constitutive feature of his or her personality.[56] Just as we tend to assume that human beings are not individuated at the level of dietary preference and that we all, despite many pronounced and frankly acknowledged differences from one another in dietary habits, share the same fundamental set of alimentary appetites, and hence the same "dieticity" or "edility," so most pre-modern and non-Western cultures, despite an awareness of the range of possible variations in human sexual behavior, refuse to individuate human beings at the level of sexual preference and assume, instead, that we all share the same fundamental set of sexual appetites, the same "sexuality." For most of the world's inhabitants, in other words, "sexuality" is no more a fact of life than "dieticity." Far from being a necessary or intrinsic constituent of the eternal grammar of human subjectivity, "sexuality" seems to be one of those cultural fictions which in every society give human beings access to themselves as meaningful actors in their world, and which are thereby objectivated.*

---

* In order to avoid misunderstanding, let me emphasize that I am not saying it would be outlandish to categorize people according to dietary preference; I do not believe my analogy between dietary and sexual object-choice shows that distinctions based on object-choice are absurd and that we should place no more credence in sexual categories than in dietary ones. On the contrary, it is easy to enumerate forms of dietary behavior whose subjects we tend to classify as specific types of human beings; there are many conditions under which we refer a person's dietary behavior, even today, to some constitutive feature of his or her personality: if, for example, I eat so little as virtually to starve myself, I am identified as an "anorectic," which is to say that I become a particular *species* of person, characterologically different from other people, with a peculiar case history, presumed psychology, and so forth—just as if I have sex "too much" or "too often," I am regarded as "sexually compulsive" or, even, as "a sexual compulsive," yet another species of humankind. Whereas some aspects of one's dietary patterns (e.g., preference for white meat) are considered unremarkable, and are therefore not marked,

To say that sexual categories and identities are objectivated fictions is not to say that they are false or unreal, merely that they are not positive, natural, or essential features of the world, outside of history and culture. Homosexuals and heterosexuals do exist, after all, at least nowadays; they actually desire what they do: they are not deluded participants in some cultural charade, or victims of "false consciousness." Moreover, the modern term "homosexual" does indeed refer to any person, whether ancient or modern, who seeks sexual contact with another person of the same sex; it is not, strictly speaking, incorrect to predicate that term of some classical Greeks.[57] But the issue before us is not captured by the problematics of reference: it cannot be innocently reformulated as the issue of whether or not we can accurately apply our concept of homosexuality to the ancients—whether or not, that is, we can discover in the historical record of classical antiquity evidence of behaviors or psychologies that are amenable to classification in our own terms (obviously, we can, given the supposedly descriptive, trans-historical nature of those terms); the issue isn't even whether or not the ancients were able to express within the terms provided by their own conceptual schemes an experience of something approximating to homosexuality as we understand it today.[58] The real issue confronting any

---

others *are* marked, just as only some aspects of sexual behavior (e.g., homosexual object-choice) are marked, whereas others (e.g., preference for persons with blue eyes) remain unmarked. (I wish to thank George Chauncey for supplying me with this formulation of the issue.) Moreover, a growing mass of historical data suggests that dietary categories have indeed provided, in certain times and places, a viable basis on which to construct typologies of human beings: see Bynum (1987), and for an example from relatively recent history of the possible linkage between sexual and dietary morality, see Stephen Nissenbaum, *Sex, Diet, and Debility in Jacksonian America: Sylvester Graham and Health Reform*, Contributions in Medical History, 4 (Westport, CT: Greenwood Press, 1980).

My argument, then, is simply this: (1) there seems to be no way of proving that sexual preferences are more *fundamental* features of the human personality than dietary preferences; (2) dietary preferences don't, for the most part, determine our personal identities nowadays; (3) therefore, sexual preferences should not be thought of as intrinsic constituents of the personality; rather, sexual categories based on preference should be considered culturally contingent. Now contingency is not the same thing as absurdity. To be sure, so long as one's notions of "truth" are connected—as Western notions have tended to be since the Renaissance—to notions of "nature" and "necessity," to what is naturally and necessarily and always the case (whether human beings recognize it to be the case or not), there may be some difficulty establishing that a traditional way of looking at things is grounded in culture rather than in nature without *also* seeming to imply that it is false. But I am not claiming that it is false to categorize people according to sexual object-choice, merely that it is not natural or necessary to do so; such classifications are, instead, just as contingent, arbitrary, and conventional as are classifications of people according to dietary object-choice. Both schemes are possible; neither is inevitable. To maintain that something isn't a fact, in short, is not to maintain that it's a lie. We are concerned here neither with truths nor falsehoods but with representations, and our willingness to accept or believe in representations generally has to do more with their representational power than with their truth.

cultural historian of antiquity, and any critic of contemporary culture, is, first of all, how to recover the terms in which the experiences of individuals belonging to past societies were actually constituted and, second, how to measure and assess the differences between those terms and the ones we currently employ. For, as this very controversy over the scope and applicability of sexual categories illustrates, concepts in the human sciences—unlike in this respect, perhaps, concepts in the natural sciences (such as gravity)—do not merely describe reality but, at least partly, constitute it.[59] What this implies about the issue before us may sound paradoxical but it is, I believe, profound—or, at least, worth pondering: although there have been, in many different times and places (including classical Greece), persons who sought sexual contact with other persons of the same sex as themselves, it is only within the last hundred years or so that such persons (or some portion of them, at any rate) have been homosexuals.

Instead of attempting to trace the history of "homosexuality" as if it were a *thing*, therefore, we might more profitably analyze how the significance of same-sex sexual contacts has been variously constructed over time by members of human living-groups. Such an analysis will probably lead us (and we must be prepared for this) into a plurality of only partly overlapping social and conceptual territories, a series of cultural formations that shift as their constituents change, combine in different sequences, or compose new patterns. The sort of history that will result from this procedure will no longer be gay history as John Boswell tends to conceptualize it (i.e., as the history of gay people), but it will not fail to be gay history in a different, and perhaps more relevant, sense: for it will be history written from the perspective of contemporary gay interests—just as feminist history is not, properly speaking, the history of women but history that reflects the concerns of contemporary feminism.[60] In the following paragraphs I shall attempt to exemplify the approach I am advocating by drawing, in very crude outline, a picture of the cultural formation underlying the classical Athenian institution of paederasty, a picture whose details will have to be filled in at some later point if this aspect of ancient Greek social relations is ever to be understood historically.[61]

IV

Let me begin by observing that the attitudes and behaviors publicly displayed by the citizens of Athens (to whom the surviving evidence for the classical period effectively restricts our power to generalize) tend to portray sex not as a collective enterprise in which two or more persons jointly engage but rather as an action performed by one person upon another.[62] I hasten to emphasize that this formulation does not purport to describe positively what the experience of sex was "really" like for all members of Athenian society but to indicate how sex is *represented* by those utterances and actions of free adult males that were intended to be overheard and witnessed by other free adult males.[63] Sex, as it is constituted by this public, masculine discourse, is either act or impact (according to one's point of view): it is not knit up in a web of mutuality, not something one invariably has *with* someone. Even the verb *aphrodisiazein*, meaning "to have sex" or "to take active sexual pleasure," is carefully differentiated into an active and a passive form; the active form occurs, tellingly, in a late antique list (that we nonetheless have good reason to consider representative for ancient Mediterranean culture, rather than eccentric to it)[64] of acts that "do not regard one's neighbors but only the subjects themselves and are not done in regard to or through others: namely, speaking, singing, dancing, fist-fighting, competing, hanging oneself, dying, being crucified, diving, finding a treasure, having sex, vomiting, moving one's bowels, sleeping, laughing, crying, talking to the gods, and the like."[65] As John J. Winkler, in a commentary on this passage, observes, "It is not that second parties are not present at some of these events (speaking, boxing, competing, having sex, being crucified, flattering one's favorite divinity), but that their successful achievement does not depend on the cooperation, much less the benefit, of a second party."[66]

Not only is sex in classical Athens not intrinsically relational or collaborative in character; it is, further, a deeply polarizing experience: it effectively divides, classifies, and distributes its participants into distinct and radically opposed categories. Sex possesses this valence, apparently, because it is conceived to center essentially on, and to define itself around, an asymmetrical gesture, that of the penetration of the body of one person by the body—and, specifically, by the phallus[67]—of another. Sex is not only polarizing, however; it is also hierarchical. For the insertive partner is construed as a sexual agent, whose phallic penetration of another person's body expresses sexual "activity," whereas the receptive partner is construed as a sexual patient, whose submission to phallic penetration expresses sexual "passivity." Sexual "activity," moreover, is thematized as domination: the relation between the "active" and the "passive" sexual partner is thought of as the same kind of relation as that obtaining between social superior and social inferior.[68] "Active" and "passive" sexual roles are therefore necessarily isomorphic with superordinate and subordinate social status; hence, an adult, male citizen of Athens can have legitimate sexual relations only with statutory minors (his inferiors not in age but in social and political status): the proper targets of his sexual desire include, specifically, women, boys, foreigners, and slaves—all of them persons who do not enjoy the same legal and political rights and privileges that he does.[69] Furthermore, what a citizen does in bed reflects the differential in status that distinguishes him from his

sexual partner: the citizen's superior prestige and authority express themselves in his sexual precedence—in his power to initiate a sexual act, his right
to obtain pleasure from it, and his assumption of an insertive rather than a
receptive sexual role. (Even if a sexual act does not involve physical penetration, it still remains hierarchically polarized by the distribution of phallic
pleasure: the partner whose pleasure is promoted is considered "active,"
while the partner who puts his or her body *at the service* of another's pleasure
is deemed "passive"—read "penetrated," in the culture's unselfconscious
ideological shorthand.) What Paul Veyne has said about the Romans can
apply equally well to the classical Athenians: they were indeed puritans when
it came to sex, but (unlike modern bourgeois Westerners) they were not
puritans about conjugality and reproduction; rather, like many Mediterranean peoples, they were puritans about virility.[70]

When the sexual system of the classical Athenians is described in that
fashion, as though it constituted a separate sphere of life governed by its
own internal laws, it appears merely exotic or bizarre, one of the many
curiosities recorded in the annals of ethnography. But if, instead of treating
Athenian sexual attitudes and practices as expressions of ancient Greek "sexuality" (conceived, in modern terms, as an autonomous domain), we situate
them in the larger social context in which they were embedded, they will at
once disclose their systematic coherence. For the "sexuality" of the classical
Athenians, far from being independent and detached from "politics" (as we
conceive sexuality to be), was constituted by the very principles on which
Athenian public life was organized. In fact, the correspondences in classical
Athens between sexual norms and social practices were so strict that an
inquiry into Athenian "sexuality" *per se* would be nonsensical: such an
inquiry could only obscure the phenomenon it was intended to elucidate,
for by isolating sexual norms from social practices it would conceal the sole
context in which the sexual protocols of the classical Athenians make any
sense—namely, the structure of the Athenian polity.

In classical Athens a relatively small group made up of the adult male
citizens held a virtual monopoly of social power and constituted a clearly
defined élite within the political and social life of the city-state. The extraordinary polarization of sexual roles in classical Athens merely reflects the
marked division in the Athenian polity between this socially superordinate
group, composed of citizens, and various subordinate groups (all lacking
full civil rights, though not all equally subordinate), composed respectively
of women, foreigners, slaves, and children (the latter three groups comprising persons of both sexes). Sex between members of the superordinate
group was virtually inconceivable, whereas sex between a member of the
superordinate group and a member of any one of the subordinate groups
mirrored in the minute details of its hierarchical arrangement, as we have

seen, the relation of structured inequality that governed the lovers' wider social interaction.★

Sex in classical Athens, then, was not a simply a collaboration in some private quest for mutual pleasure that absorbed or obscured, if only temporarily, the social identities of its participants. On the contrary, sex was a manifestation of personal status, a declaration of social identity; sexual behavior did not so much express inward dispositions or inclinations (although, of course, it did also do that) as it served to position social actors in the places assigned to them, by virtue of their political standing, in the hierarchical structure of the Athenian polity. Far from being interpreted as an expression of commonality, as a sign of some shared sexual status or identity, sex between social superior and social inferior was a miniature drama of polarization which served to measure and to define the social distance between them. To assimilate both the senior and the junior partner in a paederastic relationship to the same "(homo)sexuality," for example, would have struck a classical Athenian as no less bizarre than to classify a burglar as an "active criminal," his victim as a "passive criminal," and the two of them alike as partners in crime[71]: burglary—like sex, as the Greeks understood it—is, after all, a "non-relational" act. Each act of sex in classical Athens was no doubt an expression of real, personal desire on the part of the sexual actors involved, but their very desires had already been shaped by the shared cultural definition of sex as an activity that generally occurred only between a citizen and a non-citizen, between a person invested with full civil status and a statutory minor.

The social articulation of sexual desire in classical Athens furnishes a telling illustration of the interdependence in culture of social practices and subjective experiences. It thereby casts a strong and revealing light on the ideological dimension—the purely conventional and arbitrary character—of our own conceptions of sex and sexuality. The Greek record suggests that sexual choices do not always express the agent's individual essence or reveal the profound orientation of the inner life of a person, independent of social

---

★ This account of the principles that structured sexual and social roles in classical Athens does not capture, of course, what the *sensation* of being in love was like: I am interested here not in erotic phenomenology but in the social articulation of sexual categories and in the public meanings attached to sex. Hence, my discussion of the male citizen's social and sexual precedence is not intended either to convey what an erotic relation felt like to him or to obscure the extent to which he may have experienced being in love as a *loss* of mastery—as "enslavement" to his beloved or to his own desire. Such feelings on a lover's part were evidently conventional (see Dover [1974], 208; Golden [1984], 313–16; Foucault [1985], 65–70) and possibly even cherished (see Xenophon, *Symposium* 4.14 and *Oeconomicus* 7.42). Indeed, the citizen-lover could afford to luxuriate in his sense of helplessness or erotic dependency precisely because his self-abandonment was at some level a chosen strategy and, in any case, his actual position of social preëminence was not in jeopardy.

and political life. Quite the contrary: the sexual identities of the classical Athenians—their experiences of themselves as sexual actors and as desiring human beings—seem to have been inseparable from, if not determined by, their social identities, their public standing.[72] If the Greeks thought sex was "non-relational" in character, for example, that is because sex was so closely tied to differentials in the personal status of the sexual actors rather than to the expressive capacities of individual human subjects. Thus, the classical Greek record strongly supports the conclusion drawn (from a quite different body of evidence) by the French anthropologist Maurice Godelier: "it is not sexuality which haunts society, but society which haunts the body's sexuality."[73]

Even the relevant features of a sexual object in classical Athens were not so much determined by a physical typology of sexes as by the social articulation of power.[74] Sexual partners came in two significantly different kinds—not male and female but "active" and "passive," dominant and submissive.[75] That is why the currently fashionable distinction between homosexuality and heterosexuality (and, similarly, between "homosexuals" and "heterosexuals" as individual types) had no meaning for the classical Athenians: there were not, so far as they knew, two different kinds of "sexuality," two differently structured psychosexual states or modes of affective orientation, corresponding to the sameness or difference of the anatomical sexes of the persons engaged in a sexual act; there was, rather, but a single form of sexual experience which all free adult males shared[76]—making due allowance for variations in individual tastes, as one might make for individual palates. This "universal" form of sexual experience could be looked at differently, to be sure, according to whether one viewed it from the perspective of the "active" or the "passive" sexual partner, but its essential nature did not change with such shifts in point of view.

In the Third Dithyramb by the classical poet Bacchylides, the Athenian hero Theseus, voyaging to Crete among the seven youths and seven maidens destined for the Minotaur and defending one of the maidens from the advances of the libidinous Cretan commander, warns him vehemently against molesting *any one* of the Athenian youths (*tin' êïtheôn*: 43)—that is, any girl *or boy*. Conversely, the antiquarian *littérateur* Athenaeus, writing six or seven hundred years later, is amazed that Polycrates, the tyrant of Samos in the sixth century B.C., did not send for any boys *or women* along with the other luxury articles he imported to Samos for his personal use during his reign, "despite his passion for relations with males" (12.540c–e).[77] Now *both* the notion that an act of heterosexual aggression in itself makes the aggressor suspect of homosexual tendencies *and* the mirror-opposite notion that a person with marked homosexual tendencies is bound to hanker after heterosexual contacts are nonsensical to us, associating as we do sexual object-choice with a determinate kind of "sexuality," a fixed sexual nature, but it would be a monumental task indeed to enumerate all the ancient documents in which the alternative "boy or woman" occurs with perfect nonchalance in an erotic context, as if the two were functionally inter-changeable.[78]

A testimony to the imaginable extent of male indifference to the sex of sexual objects,* one that may be particularly startling to modern eyes, can be found in a marriage-contract from Hellenistic Egypt, dating to 92 B.C. This not untypical document stipulates that "it shall not be lawful for Philis-cus [the prospective husband] to bring home another wife in addition to Apollonia or to have a concubine *or boy-lover.* . . ."[79] The possibility that one's husband might decide at some point during one's marriage to set up another household with his boyfriend evidently figured among the various potential domestic disasters that a prudent fiancée would be sure to anticipate and to indemnify herself against. A somewhat similar expectation is articu-lated in an entirely different context by Dio Chrysostom, a moralizing Greek orator from the late first century A.D. In a speech denouncing the corrupt morals of city life, Dio asserts that even respectable women are so easy to seduce nowadays that men will soon tire of them and will turn their attention to boys instead—just as addicts progress inexorably from wine to hard drugs (7.150–152). According to Dio, then, paederasty is not simply a *pis aller*; it is not "caused," as many modern historians of the ancient Mediterranean appear to believe, by the supposed seclusion of women, by the practice (it was more likely an ideal) of locking them away in the inner rooms of their fathers' or husbands' houses and thereby preventing them from serving as sexual targets for adult men. In Dio's fantasy, at least, paederasty springs not from the insufficient but from the superabundant supply of sexually available women; the easier it is to have sex with women, on his view, the less desirable sex with women becomes, and the more likely men are to seek sexual pleasure with boys. Scholars sometimes describe the cultural formation underlying this apparent refusal by Greek males to discriminate categorically among sexual objects on the basis of anatomical sex as a bisexu-ality of penetration[80] or—even more intriguingly—as a heterosexuality indif-ferent to its object,[81]† but I think it would be advisable not to speak of it as

---

* I wish to emphasize that I am *not* claiming that all Greek men felt such indifference: on the contrary, plenty of ancient evidence testifies to the strength of individual preferences for a sexual object of one sex rather than another (see note 53). But many ancient documents bear witness to a certain constitutional reluctance on the part of the Greeks to predict, in any given instance, the sex of another man's beloved merely on the basis of that man's past sexual behavior or previous pattern of sexual object-choice.

† This is not so paradoxical as it may at first appear. Whether the object of a free adult male's desire turns out to be a woman, a boy, a foreigner, or a slave, it remains from his point of view "hetero"—in the sense of "different" or "other": it always belongs to a different social category or status.

a sexuality at all but to describe it, rather, as a more generalized ethos of penetration and domination,[82] a socio-sexual discourse structured by the presence or absence of its central term: the phallus.[83]

If that discourse does not seem to have looked to gender for a criterion by means of which to differentiate permissible from impermissible sexual objects (but to have featured, instead, a gender-blind distinction between dominant and submissive persons), we should not therefore conclude that gender was unimplicated in the socio-sexual system of the ancient Greeks. Gender did indeed figure in that system—not at the level at which sexual *objects* were categorized,* to be sure, but at the level at which sexual *subjects* were constituted.[84] Let us not forget, after all, that the kind of desire described by Greek sources as failing to discriminate between male and female objects was itself *gendered* as a specifically *male* desire. Now, to define the scope of sexual object-choice *for men* in terms independent of gender is almost certainly to construct different subjectivities for men and for women, to do so specifically in terms of gender, and thus to define male and female desire asymmetrically. For women and boys will qualify as equally appropriate sexual targets for adult men only so long as they remain relatively stationary targets (so to speak), only so long as they are content to surrender the erotic initiative to men and to await the results of male deliberation. A *sexual* ethos of phallic penetration and domination, in which the gender of the object does not determine male sexual object-choice, requires the differential *gendering* of both desire and power: if women and boys had the kind of wide-ranging, object-directed desires that men have, and if they had the social authority to act on those desires, they would be more likely to frustrate or to interfere with men's sexual choices.

Desire appears to have been gendered in precisely this way in classical Athens. Neither boys nor women were thought to possess the sort of desires that would impel them to become autonomous sexual actors in their relations with men, constantly scanning the erotic horizon for attractive candidates uniquely adapted to their personal requirements. On the contrary: both women and boys, in different ways and for different reasons, were considered sexually inert. Boys did not (supposedly) experience any erotic desire at all for adult men,[85] whereas women's desire was not directed in the first instance to individual male objects: it did not present itself as a longing for

---

* Even at this level, however, gender had an impact: it can be felt in the male liking for some physical characteristics of boys which Greek culture associated with women (e.g., smooth and hairless skin [for details, see "The Democratic Body," in this volume]); the courtesan Glycera went so far as to claim, according to Clearchus, that "boys are attractive for as long as they resemble a woman" (Athenaeus, 13.605d). Dover (1978), 68–81, however, argues convincingly that in a number of other departments besides hair and skin boyish good looks, as Greek males defined them, included features that qualified as specifically "masculine" by contemporary standards.

one or another man in particular but as an undifferentiated appetite for sexual pleasure; it arose, in other words, out of a more diffuse and generalized somatic need, determined by the physiological economy of the female body, and even then it was fundamentally reactive in character—it appeared in response to a specific male stimulus (whereupon, of course, it immediately became insatiable) and it could be aroused, allegedly, by anyone (even a woman)[86] with the proper phallic equipment.* As Andromache remarks, with pardonable skepticism, in Euripides's *Trojan Women*, "They say that one night in bed dissolves a woman's hostility to sexual union with a man" (665–66).[87]

The *sexual* system of classical Athens, which defined the scope of sexual object-choice for adult men in terms independent of gender, was therefore logically inseparable from the *gender* system of classical Athens, which distributed to men and to women different kinds of desires, constructing male desire as wide-ranging, acquisitive, and object-directed, while constructing female desire (in opposition to it) as objectless, passive, and entirely determined by the female body's need for regular phallic irrigation.[88] Instead of associating different sorts of sexual object-choice with different *kinds* of "sexuality," as we do, the classical Greeks assigned different forms of desire to different genders. The relation between sex and gender in classical Athens, then, was perhaps just as strict as it is in modern bourgeois Europe and America, but it was elaborated according to a strategy radically different from that governing the relation of sex and gender under the current régime of "sexuality."

For those inhabitants of the ancient world about whom it is possible to generalize, "sexuality" obviously did not hold the key to the secrets of the human personality.† The measure of a free male in Greek society was most often taken not by scrutinizing his sexual constitution but by observing how

---

* I must point out, once again, that I am speaking about Greek canons of sexual propriety, not about the actual phenomenology of sexual life in ancient Greece. It would be easy to come up with many counter-examples to the generalizations I am making here in order to show, for instance, that women sometimes were considered capable of pursuing men. Thus, in Euripides's *Hippolytus*, Phaedra becomes erotically obsessed by one man in particular without having ever received much direct encouragement from him; her example, however, far from refuting the picture I have drawn, might actually corroborate it, if we remember that it was precisely by portraying such instances of female "shamelessness" that Euripides earned his ancient reputation for misogyny. His portrait of Phaedra was interpreted by his contemporaries, in other words, not as realism but as slander. Hanson notes, further, that if Phaedra had followed her Nurse's advice and consulted a male doctor (295–96), he would most likely have prescribed phallic penetration (real or simulated) to ease her hysterical symptoms.

† In fact, the very concept of and set of practices centering on "the human personality"— the physical and social sciences of the blank individual—belong to a much later era and bespeak the modern social and economic conditions (urban, capitalist, bureaucratic) that accompanied their rise.

he fared when tested against other free males in public competition. War (and other agonistic contests), not love, served to reveal the inner man, the stuff a free Greek male citizen was made of.[89] A striking example of this emphasis on public life as the primary locus of signification can be found in the work of Artemidorus, a master dream-analyst who lived and wrote in the second century of our era but whose basic approach to the interpretation of dreams does not differ—in this respect, at least—from attitudes current in the classical period.[90] Artemidorus saw public life, not erotic life, as the principal tenor of dreams. Even sexual dreams, in Artemidorus's system, are seldom *really* about sex: rather, they are about the rise and fall of the dreamer's public fortunes, the vicissitudes of his domestic economy.[91] If a man dreams of having sex with his mother, for example, his dream signifies to Artemidorus nothing in particular about the dreamer's own sexual psychology, his fantasy life, or the history of his relations with his parents; it's a very common dream, and so it's a bit tricky to interpret precisely, but basically it's a lucky dream: it may signify—depending on the family's circumstances at the time, the postures of the partners in the dream, and the mode of penetration—that the dreamer will be successful in politics ("success in politics" meaning, evidently, the power to screw one's country), that he will go into exile or return from exile, that he will win his law-suit, obtain a rich harvest from his lands, or change professions, among many other things (1.79). Artemidorus's system of dream interpretation resembles the indigenous dream-lore of certain Amazonian tribes who, despite their quite different socio-sexual systems, share with the ancients a belief in the predictive value of dreams. Like Artemidorus, these Amazonian peoples reverse what modern bourgeois Westerners take to be the natural flow of signification in dreams (from images of public and social events to private and sexual meanings): in both Kagwahiv and Mehinaku culture, for example, dreaming about the female genitals portends a wound (and so a man who has such a dream is especially careful when he handles axes or other sharp implements the next day); dreamt wounds do not symbolize the female genitals.[92] Both these ancient and modern dream-interpreters, then, are innocent of "sexuality": what is fundamental to their experience of sex is not anything *we* would regard as essentially sexual;* it is something essentially outward, public, and social. Instead of viewing public and political life as a dramatization of individual sexual psychology, as we often tend to do, they see sexual behavior as an expression of political and social relations.[93] "Sexuality," for cultures

---

* Note that even the human genitals themselves do not necessarily figure as sexual signifiers in all cultural or representational contexts: for example, Bynum (1986) argues, in considerable detail, that there is "reason to think that medieval people saw Christ's penis not primarily as a sexual organ but as the object of circumcision and therefore as the wounded, bleeding flesh with which it was associated in painting and in text" (p. 407).

not shaped by some very recent European and American bourgeois developments, is not a cause but an effect. The social body precedes the sexual body.

V

If there is a lesson that we should draw from this picture of ancient sexual
attitudes and behaviors, it is that we need to de-center *sexuality* from the focus
of the interpretation of sexual experience—and not only ancient varieties of
sexual experience. Just because modern bourgeois Westerners are so obsessed
with sexuality, so convinced that it holds the key to the hermeneutics of the
self (and hence to social psychology as an object of historical study), we
ought not therefore to conclude that everyone has always considered sexuality a basic and irreducible element in, or a central feature of, human life.
Indeed, there are even sectors of our own societies to which the ideology of
"sexuality" has failed to penetrate. A socio-sexual system featuring a rigid
hierarchy of sexual roles that reflect a set of socially articulated power-
relations rather than the determinate sexual orientations of those involved
has been documented in contemporary America by Jack Abbott, in one of
his infamous letters written to Norman Mailer from a federal penitentiary;
because the text is now quite inaccessible (it was not reprinted in Abbott's
book), and stunningly apropos, I have decided to quote it here at length.

> It really was years, many years, before I began to actually realize that the women
> in my life—the prostitutes as well as the soft, pretty girls who giggled and teased
> me so much, my several wives and those of my friends—it was years before I
> realized that they were not women, but men; years before I assimilated the notion
> that this was unnatural. I still only know this intellectually, for the most part—
> but for the small part that remains to my ken, I know it is like a hammer blow
> to my temple and the shame I feel is profound. Not because of the thing itself,
> the sexual love I have enjoyed with these women (some so devoted it aches to
> recall it), but because of shame—and anger—that the world could so intimately
> betray me; so profoundly touch and move me—and then laugh at me and accuse
> my soul of a sickness, when that sickness has rescued me from mental derangement
> and despairs so black as to cast this night that surrounds us in prison into day.
>   I do not mean to say I never knew the physical difference—no one but an
> imbecile could make such a claim. I took it, without reflection or the slightest
> doubt, that this was a natural sex that emerged within the society of men, with
> attributes that naturally complemented masculine attributes. I thought it was a
> natural phenomenon in the society of women as well. The attributes were feminine
> and so there seemed no gross misrepresentation of facts to call them (among
> us men) "women." . . . Many of my "women" had merely the appearance of
> handsome, extremely neat, and polite young men. I have learned, analyzing my
> feelings today, that those attributes I called feminine a moment ago were not
> feminine in any way as it appears in the real female sex. These attributes seem

now merely a tendency to need, to depend on another man; to need never to become a rival or to compete with other men in the pursuits men, among themselves, engage in. It was, it occurs to me now, almost boyish—not really feminine at all.

This is the way it always was, even in the State Industrial School for Boys—a penal institution for juvenile delinquents—where I served five years, from age twelve to age seventeen. They were the possession and sign of manhood and it never occurred to any of us that this was strange and unnatural. It is how I grew up—a natural part of my life in prison.

It was difficult for me to grasp the definition of the clinical term "homosexual"— and when I finally did it devastated me, as I said.[94]

Gender, for Abbott, is not determined by anatomical sex but by social status and personal style. "Men"* are defined as those who "compete with other men in the pursuits men, among themselves, engage in," whereas "women" are characterized by the possession of "attributes that naturally complement masculine attributes"—namely, "a tendency to need, to depend on another man" for the various benefits won by the victors in "male" competition. In this way "a natural sex . . . emerge[s] within the society of men" and qualifies, by virtue of its exclusion from the domain of "male" precedence and autonomy, as a legitimate target of "male" desire. In Abbott's society, as in classical Athens, desire is sparked only when it arcs across the political divide, when it traverses the boundary that marks out the limits of intramural competition among the élite and that thereby distinguishes subjects from objects of sexual desire. Sex between "men"—and, therefore, "homosexuality"—remains unthinkable in Abbott's society (even though sex between anatomical males is an accepted and intrinsic part of the system), whereas sex between "men" and "women" does not so much implicate both partners in a common "sexuality" as it articulates and defines the differences in status between them.

VI

To discover and to write the history of sexuality has long seemed to many a sufficiently radical undertaking in itself, inasmuch as its effect (if not always

---

* Abbott, of course, uses quotation marks only to surround *women*, not *men*. But one could hardly ask for a better illustration of the post-structuralist doctrine that when meaning is not fixed by reference but is determined solely by the play of differences within a system of signification, all hierarchical binaries are potentially reversible: although Abbott defines "'women'" by reference to "men," as a supplement to the definition of masculinity, and assumes "men" to represent an unproblematic term, it is obvious that his definition of masculinity is a highly specialized, tendentious one whose criteria are determined by opposition to his definition of femininity. Therefore, in discussing Abbott's text, I have placed both *men* and *women* within quotation marks.

the intention behind it) is to call into question the very naturalness of what
we currently take to be essential to our individual natures. But in the course
of implementing that ostensibly radical project many historians of sexuality
seem to have reversed—perhaps unwittingly—its radical design: by preserving "sexuality" as a stable category of historical analysis not only have they
not denaturalized it but, on the contrary, they have newly idealized it.[95] To
the extent, in fact, that histories of "sexuality" succeed in concentrating their
focus on *sexuality*, to just that extent are they doomed to fail as *histories*
(Foucault himself taught us that much), unless they also include as an integral
part of their proper enterprise the task of demonstrating the historicity,
conditions of emergence, modes of construction, and ideological contingen-
cies of the very categories of analysis that undergird their own practice.[96]
Instead of concentrating our attention specifically on the history of sexuality,
then, we need to define and refine a new, and radical, historical sociology
of psychology—an intellectual discipline designed to analyze the cultural
poetics of desire, by which I mean the processes whereby sexual desires are
constructed, mass-produced, and distributed among the various members of
human living-groups.[97] We must acknowledge that "sexuality" is a cultural
production no less than are table manners, health clubs, and abstract expres-
sionism, and we must struggle to discern in what we currently regard as our
most precious, unique, original, and spontaneous impulses the traces of a
previously rehearsed and socially encoded ideological script.[98] We must train
ourselves to recognize conventions of feeling as well as conventions of
behavior and to interpret the intricate texture of personal life as an artefact,
as the determinate outcome, of a complex and arbitrary constellation of
cultural processes. We must, in short, be willing to admit that what seem
to be our most inward, authentic, and private experiences are actually, in
Adrienne Rich's admirable phrase, "shared, unnecessary and political."[99]

   A little less than fifty years ago W. H. Auden asked, "When shall we learn,
what should be clear as day, We cannot choose what we are free to love?"[100]
It is a characteristically judicious formulation: love, if it is to be love, must
be a free act, but it is also inscribed within a larger circle of constraint, within
conditions that make possible the exercise of that "freedom." The task of
distinguishing freedom from constraint in love, of learning to trace the
shifting and uncertain boundaries between the self and the world, is a dizzy-
ing and, indeed, an endless undertaking. I should like to propose the upcom-
ing homosexual centenary as an appropriate deadline to set ourselves for
learning a more modest version of the lesson that Auden has assigned
us, one that three generations of feminist scholars have shown us how
to approach. The project before us has been well articulated, albeit in a
comparatively prosaic idiom, by Jeffrey Weeks: "Social processes construct
subjectivities not just as 'categories' but at the level of individual desires.
This perception . . . should be the starting point for future social and historical studies of 'homosexuality' and indeed of 'sexuality' in general."[101]

2

"Homosexuality": A Cultural Construct

An Exchange with Richard Schneider

Schneider. A conference at Brown University, "Homosexuality in History and Culture, and the University Curriculum," held on 20–21 February 1987, highlighted an ongoing debate between you, John J. Winkler, and others, on the one hand, and John Boswell, on the other, concerning the genesis and cultural articulation of homosexuality. While Boswell argues that "homo-" and "heterosexual" are categories that many (or all) societies implicitly recognize, you contend that this dualism is actually a cultural construction of the last century or two in the West. I wonder if you could clarify this debate.

Halperin. The debate to which you refer reflects a longstanding (and, some would argue, sterile) ideological dispute within social science between "essentialists" and "constructionists." As that controversy applies to sexual categories, it divides those who believe that terms like "gay" and "straight" refer to positive, objective, culturally invariant properties of persons (in the same way as do the terms for different blood-types or genetic traits)* from those who believe that the experiences named by those terms are artefacts of specific, unique, and non-repeatable cultural and social processes. "Essentialists" typically consider sexual preference to be determined by such things as biological forces or hormonal levels, and treat sexual identities as "cognitive realizations of genuine, underlying differences" (to quote Steven Epstein, who devoted an essay in a recent issue of the *Socialist Review* to an exploration and critique of this controversy),[1] whereas "constructionists"

---

* I owe these examples to Edward Stein, who points out to me that genetics may provide the best model for essentialist claims about sexuality, because a specific genetic potentiality may be realized or actuated differently in different environments without itself undergoing any change (the appeal to this genetic model, however, should not be taken to commit essentialists necessarily to the proposition that sexual orientations are "caused" by genetic factors—although some essentialists *may* coincidentally happen to believe that: the genetic model merely provides an illustration of the way that an essentialist argument might work).

41

assume that sexual desires are learned and that sexual identities come to be fashioned through an individual's interaction with others.[2] The debate between essentialists and constructionists largely recapitulates the old "nature/nurture" controversy over the relative influences on the individual of heredity and environment—or, as Boswell prefers, it may represent merely the most recent instance of a long-lived scholastic quarrel between "realists" and "nominalists" over the existence of universals.[3] In any case, it is easy to understand why essentialists are inclined to regard sexual categories as relatively unchanging over time, despite the various social or cultural forms sexual expression may take, whereas constructionists believe that different times and places produce different "sexualities."

My own position is close to that of the constructionists. Anthropological and historical studies have shown to my satisfaction that patterns of sexual preference and configurations of desire vary enormously from one culture to the next. I know of no way to explain why human beings in different cultures grow up, *en masse*, with distinctly different sorts of sexual dispositions, temperaments, or tastes, which they themselves consider normal and natural, unless I am willing to grant a determining role in the constitution of individual desire to social or cultural factors. But even if I am wrong about the *causes* of variation among patterns of human sexual preference, the *extent* of such variation still remains to be gauged, and that can be done only if we do not insist on defining it in advance of actual research, allowing our current presuppositions to fix the contours of what has yet to be discovered. Constructionism may not turn out to be right in all of its preliminary claims, but in the meantime it encourages us to put some distance between ourselves and what we think we "know" about sex. And so, by bracketing in effect our "instinctive" and "natural" assumptions, it makes it easier for us to highlight different historical configurations of desire and to distinguish various means—both formal and informal—of institutionalizing them.

The very least that can be said on behalf of the constructionist hypothesis, in other words, is that it is immensely valuable as a guide for future research. It directs the scholar's attention to the salient particularities of sexual life in a given society, particularities that might have gone unnoticed—or, if noticed, unexamined—in the absence of a research program that called for scrutinizing them. It also helps the interpreter resist the temptation to integrate alien or exotic phenomena into a plausible discourse of the known, into a picture whose appeal derives largely from its familiarity to its viewers. Whether or not the accounts constructionists give of their own methods and aims are cogent, whether or not the conclusions they reach are well-founded, they have certainly turned up enough interesting material to demonstrate the heuristic value of their theories. When they have finished charting the various social and historical constructions of sexual meaning, we shall be in a better position to judge the validity of the constructionist hypothesis and to determine what, if anything, can be said on behalf of its essentializing competitors. In the meantime, it's too soon to close off debate on the theoretical issues: there's too much work to be done.

Now, with respect to the question you raise, constructionists have demonstrated, I believe, that the distinction between homosexuality and heterosexuality, far from being a fixed and immutable feature of some universal syntax of sexual desire, can be understood as a particular conceptual turn in thinking about sex and deviance that occurred in certain sectors of northern and northwestern European society in the eighteenth and nineteenth centuries. The new conceptualization, moreover, seems to coincide with the emergence, in the same period (or in the centuries immediately preceding it), of some new sexual types—namely, the homosexual and the heterosexual, defined not as persons who perform certain acts, or who adhere to one sex-role or another, or who are characterized by strong or weak desires, or who violate or observe gender-boundaries, but as persons who possess two distinct kinds of subjectivity, who are inwardly oriented in a specific direction, and who therefore belong to separate and determinate human *species*. From what I have been able to tell, these new sexual types, the homosexual and the heterosexual, do not represent merely new ways of classifying persons—that is, innovations in moral or judicial language—but new types of desire, new kinds of desiring human beings.

To say that homosexuality and heterosexuality are culturally constructed, however, is not to say that they are unreal, that they are mere figments of the imagination of certain sexual actors. (Constructionists sometimes *sound* as if they are saying something like that, and so there is some justification for Epstein's ascription of such a belief to them, but that is not—or, at least, it ought not to be—the constructionist claim.) Homosexuality and heterosexuality are not fictions inasmuch as there really are, nowadays, homosexual and heterosexual people, individuals whose own desires are organized or structured according to the pattern named by those opposed and contrasting terms. No one, save someone determined to uphold a theory at all costs, would say that homosexuals or heterosexuals are simply imagining things, that they are deluded in supposing that they are attracted to one sex rather than another: they really do desire what they do, and that is a *fact* about them. But if homo- and heterosexuality—within some sectors of our culture, anyway—are not fictions, neither are they pure *facts of life* (as such things used to be called), positive and changeless features of the natural world. Rather, they are among the cultural codes which, in any society, give human beings access to themselves as meaningful subjects of their experiences and which are thereby objectivated—that is, realized in actuality. Hence, we need, as Epstein has written, "a better understanding of the 'collectivization of subjectivity.' We must be able to speak of sexually based group identities without assuming *either* that the group has some mystical or biological unity, *or* that the 'group' doesn't exist and that its 'members' are indulging in a dangerous mystification."[4]

Schneider. Many gay people are predisposed to take up with Boswell's argument, feeling their own homosexuality to be deeply rooted in childhood and thus unconditioned by cultural categories or norms. Your argument seems to contradict what many people claim to "know" intuitively about themselves—does it not?

Halperin. I don't think so. The more we become aware of the contingency of all forms of erotic life, the more we are disinclined to believe in such a thing as a "natural" sexuality, something we are simply born into. Now gay sub-cultures provide abundant evidence for the vast plurality of possible sexual styles. Many gay people must know, therefore, that "sexuality" is not the sort of thing that comes in only two kinds (i.e., "hetero-" and "homo-"). "Nature" is not exhausted by these two possibilities of sexual object-choice. The better we get to know ourselves and our friends, the more we realize—at least, I do—how idiosyncratic and various, how unsystematic sexuality is: is a gay woman into S/M more like a gay woman who is not or a straight woman who is? And to the extent that we define "gayness" as a kind of lifestyle or outlook or set of values rather than as the performance of certain sexual acts, to that extent we acknowledge that it is something more than a sexual reflex.

But perhaps I am dodging your question. Perhaps there is a sense in which the constructionist thesis is not only counter-intuitive but is *necessarily* so. The cultural construction of our sexuality is almost surely bound to be beyond the reach of intuitive recall. For our intuitions about the world and about ourselves are no doubt constituted at the same time as our sexuality itself: both are part of the process whereby we gain access to ourselves as self-conscious beings through language and culture. If we *could* recover the steps by which we were acculturated, we would not have been very securely acculturated in the first place, inasmuch as acculturation consists precisely in learning to accept as natural, normal, and inevitable what is in fact conventional and arbitrary. The arbitrary character of sexual acculturation is perhaps clearest in the case of heterosexuality: the production of a population of human males who are (supposedly) incapable of being sexually excited by a person of their own sex *under any circumstances* is itself a cultural event without, so far as I know, either precedent or parallel, and cries out for an explanation. No inquiry into the origins of homosexuality can therefore be divorced from an inquiry into the origins of heterosexuality. Although the explicit *conceptualization* of homosexuality precedes that of heterosexuality—which was a late and rather hasty appendix to it—the cultural construction of homosexuality is probably a mere reflex of the social processes that produced the (comparatively speaking) strange and distinctively bourgeois formation represented by exclusive heterosexuality.

In other words, I think the cultural production of "the homosexual" is an incidental result of the social changes responsible for the formation of "the heterosexual": in the course of constructing "the heterosexual," of producing sexual subjects constituted according to an exclusive (cross-sex) sexual object-choice, western European societies also created, as a kind of by-product of that imperfect process, other sexual subjects defined by a similarly exclusive, but same-sex, sexual object-choice. Homosexuals are, in this sense, casualties of the cultural construction of exclusive heterosexuality. For that reason, I don't think it makes any sense to ask what "causes" homosexuality while ignoring heterosexuality, and any account that purports to "explain" homosexuality in isolation from heterosexuality is bound to be inadequate and should arouse immediate suspicion on political grounds—as a maneuver designed to reassert the "normativity" of heterosexuality. Homosexuality and heterosexuality are part of the same system; they are equally problematic, and each stands in just as much need of analysis and understanding as the other.[5]

Schneider. In arguing that "homo-" and "heterosexual" are role categories peculiar to modern Western society, are you saying that homosexuality itself does not exist in other societies?

Halperin. My claim is considerably more radical than that. I am claiming that there is no such thing as "homosexuality itself" or "heterosexuality itself." Those words do not name independent modes of sexual being, leading some sort of ideal existence apart from particular human societies, outside of history or culture. Homosexuality and heterosexuality are not the atomic constituents of erotic desire, the basic building-blocks out of which every person's sexual nature is constructed. They just represent one of the many patterns according to which human living-groups, in the course of reproducing themselves and their social structures, have drawn the boundaries that define the scope of what can qualify—and to whom—as sexually attractive. Because they happen to be the dominant organizing principles of sexual pleasure and sexual desire in our culture, homosexuality and heterosexuality also represent those categories of sexual psychology and behavior that we find most obvious and compelling, and so we interpret in terms of them the sexual phenomena that we encounter on our ethnographic excursions through other cultures. Because we do not tend to see our own sexual categories as arbitrary or conventional, and because we regard them accordingly as empty of ideological content, we consider "homosexual" and "heterosexual" to be purely descriptive, trans-cultural, and trans-historical terms, equally applicable to every culture and period. Now there is nothing necessarily wrong in granting those terms a wide application, so long as we recognize that they are not *native* to the pre-modern and non-Western societies to which we apply them, and that if we *do* insist on applying them to those societies we must be careful not to mistake the "data" produced by our research for something we have discovered, rather than something we have put there ourselves.

The dangers of taking our sexual categories for granted are well illustrated by the work of Boswell who, arguing correctly that many societies have contained individuals capable of deriving sexual pleasure from contact with members of their own sex, claims on that basis that homosexuality is universal. To be sure, even Boswell does not regard homosexuality as a *thing*, an item in a cultural inventory whose presence or absence can be simply and positively checked off; he contents himself with the more modest claim that homosexuality takes different forms in different contexts, changing its character according to its cultural environment. But redescribing same-sex sexual contact as homosexuality is not as innocent as it may appear: indeed, it effectively obliterates the many different ways of organizing sexual contacts and articulating sexual roles that are indigenous to human societies— as if one were to claim that, because feudal peasants work with their hands and factory laborers work with their hands, feudal peasantry was the form that proletarianism took before the rise of industrial capitalism![6] Does the "paederast," the classical Greek adult, married male who periodically enjoys sexually penetrating a male adolescent share *the same sexuality* with the "berdache," the Native American (Indian) adult male who from childhood has taken on many aspects of a woman and is regularly penetrated by the adult male to whom he has been married in a public and socially sanctioned ceremony? Does the latter share *the same sexuality* with the New Guinea tribesman and warrior who from the ages of eight to fifteen has been orally inseminated on a daily basis by older youths and who, after years of orally inseminating his juniors, will be married to an adult woman and have children of his own? Does any one of these three persons share *the same sexuality* with the modern homosexual?[7] It would be more prudent to acknowledge that although there are persons who seek sexual contact with other persons of the same sex in many different societies, only recently and only in some sectors of our own society have such persons—or some portion of them—been homosexuals.

Schneider. As a classicist, you have argued that the touted approval of homosexuality in ancient Greece has been misunderstood, that what was being sanctioned was not homosexual love as such, but some other kind of erotic expression. Could you explain your thinking on this question?

Halperin. What was approved, and (in certain contexts) even celebrated,[8] by free classical Athenian males was not homosexuality *per se*, but a certain hierarchical relation of structured inequality between a free adult male and an adolescent youth of citizen status—or a foreigner or slave (the latter combinations being considerably less glamorous). Let me unpack this formulation.

First, the relation had to be hierarchical: for a sexual contact between males to be deemed respectable the persons involved could not stand in a reciprocal or socially symmetrical relation to one another but had to be differentiated from one another in terms of their relative degrees of power or status; every male couple had to include one social superior and one social inferior. Second, the sexual acts performed by a male couple had to be congruent with the power-differential according to which the relation was structured: the superior partner took sexual precedence—he alone, that is, might initiate a sexual act, penetrate the body of his partner, and obtain sexual pleasure; thus, the lack of social reciprocity in the relation was mirrored by a lack of sexual reciprocity (the goods and services exchanged between male lovers were both unlike and unequal in value). So long as a mature male took as his sexual partner a statutory minor, maintained an "active" sexual role vis-à-vis that person, and did not consume his own estate in the process or give any other indication that he was "enslaved" to the sexual pleasure he obtained from contact with his partner, no reproach attached itself to his conduct. That, in brief, is what "the approval of homosexuality in ancient Greece" came down to.

The description I have just offered is, to be sure, highly schematic, and in any case it refers to *the moral conventions* governing sexual relations between males; it is not intended to define the limits of what could actually go on. In fact, there seems to have been a kind of twilight zone between youth and manhood where sexual relations between males of roughly the same age do seem to have occurred and were apparently tolerated.★ Even in that context, however, one youth seems to have been called upon to play an "active," the other a "passive" part, and I know of no evidence suggesting that such lovers took turns or switched roles.[9] It was possible for a youth on the border between adolescence and adulthood to alternate between being "active" and "passive" but only insofar as he was involved in separate relationships with different people; he could not be both "active" and "passive" at once in relation to the same person.[10]

Schneider. It is an axiom of gay liberation that "the 10 percent" is a roughly constant feature of societies worldwide. This claim, if valid, implies that a

---

★ Numerous courting scenes on Greek vases, for example, depict youths of roughly similar age.

homosexual identity emerges regardless of the availability of role categories—or forces every society to create such categories to accommodate the
variant minority. Do you have a sense of the anthropological evidence that
leads you to reject the "universal" argument? Is our existence as a self-
conscious social category truly singular in the annals of history?

Halperin. John J. Winkler has observed that "almost any imaginable configuration of pleasure can be institutionalized as conventional and perceived
by its participants as natural."[11] The notion that there is no such thing as a
purely natural sexuality may be comforting to gay people today, since the
label "unnatural," which has packed such a hefty moral wallop since the
early modern period (though not, as Winkler has shown, in the ancient
world), has so often been applied to gays. But to that comforting thought
there corresponds the further disquieting possibility that the subjectivities
generated by human cultures may vary; some societies may produce sexualities that exclude homosexual desire altogether: a claim to this effect has in
fact been made quite recently in the case of an Amazonian people by Thomas
Gregor (all such ethnographic reports should be taken with a grain of salt,
however, and Gregor's own account raises not a few suspicions).[12] Of
course, many if not all societies produce people who are, according to
the indigenous standards, sexual deviants. Such people, however, tend to
constitute themselves sexually in opposition to the prevailing local norms
rather than in terms approximating to the homosexual/heterosexual polarity
familiar to us. Even when these deviants qualify as deviants by virtue of
certain homosexual behaviors or practices, in other words, they do so in the
course of reversing the conventional definitions of who they "should" be in
their societies, and so they simply mirror, in inverted form, the norms of
their own culture (just as homosexuals today reverse the cultural definition
of heterosexuality). In the classical world, the *kinaidos* or *mollis*, the man
who desires to be used "as a woman" by other men, may have been one of
these "casualties" of sexual acculturation, expressing in his own person the
social potential for "error," the tendency of societies to create inadvertently,
as it were, life-forms exactly opposite to the ones they valorize. But, in any
case, I have argued that *kinaidoi*, even if they actually existed, represented a
type quite distinct from what is specified by the modern category of the
homosexual.

I personally do not find the possibility that the proportion of homosexuals
in the general population of a society may vary any more disturbing than
that the proportion of liberals and conservatives in American society may
vary. It may well be the case, as some anti-gay polemicists claim, that the
number of homosexuals in our society has increased during the past century,
but it does not follow that the number has increased simply as a result of
"permissiveness," nor does it follow that a moral crack-down would elimi-

nate the "problem." Changes in patterns of sexuality do not result from comparatively superficial fluctuations in the moral climate; they are signs of deep, seismic shifts in the structure of underlying social relations, and no society has come close to learning how to control the forces by which it is constituted. I suspect that the tendency to insist on a fixed percentage of homosexuals throughout societies worldwide is a defensive response on the part of gay people to the stigma of "unnaturalness," and I hope we are all now beyond that. I see nothing wrong with being truly singular in the annals of history: after all, if ever we achieve a society in which the relations between men and women cease to be structured hierarchically, that would be also be something of a singular achievement, and a good one.

Schneider. What would happen to your argument if, as seems possible, sexual orientation turns out to have a biological or genetic basis?

Halperin. If it turns out that there actually is a gene, say, for homosexuality, my notions about the cultural determination of sexual object-choice will— obviously enough—prove to have been wrong. Even in that hypothetical case, however, the scientists and their allies will still have a fair amount of fast talking to do. Take, for example, the instance of the New Guinea tribesman mentioned earlier. According to our hypothesis, science will now be able to reveal definitively whether he is or is not gay. Neither alternative, though, is going to be very satisfactory. For, according to one possibility, the tribesman isn't *really* gay—he just spends half his life having oral sex with other males (which makes him start to sound like a character out of Jean Genet); according to the only other possibility, the tribesman really *is* gay, but then how shall we explain why he shows no erotic interest in males outside of initiatory contexts or why he does not hesitate to marry and does not experience any sexual difficulty in his adult relations with women? Far from solving the interpretative problems raised by the ethnographic evidence, in other words, the hypothetical scientific (genetic) solution simply compounds them.

But I don't think it's likely in any case that a scientific "solution" will be forthcoming, and the trend now seems to be in the opposite direction (the hormonal hypothesis, for example, has recently been disposed of by Ron Langevin and his co-workers).[13] Any argument for the biological or genetic determination of sexual object-choice that I can envision seems destined to be reductionist, and thus to be vulnerable to the well-known "levels of description" objection—viz., that human meanings are not reducible to physical descriptions (hence, to specify the wave-length of green light is not to provide an exhaustive definition of the concept or the experience of green). Moreover, the search for a "scientific" aetiology of sexual orientation is itself a homophobic project, and it needs to be seen more clearly as such. Just as scientific attempts to describe in genetic terms the capacities of the various human races have now been generally abandoned—not because of their inherent scientific absurdity (*some* visible racial differentiae obviously have a genetic cause) but rather because of their long and odious history of complicity with racism—and just as scientific inquiries into biological and neurological differences between males and females are starting to fall into disrepute for similar reasons, so, too, will the effort to discover a genetic or hormonal basis for sexual preference eventually come to nothing, not so much for lack of scientific progress (which has never stopped research if other motives for it remained) as for lack of social credibility. All scientific inquiries into the aetiology of sexual orientation, after all, spring from a more or less implicit theory of sexual races, from the notion that there exist broad general divisions between types of human beings corresponding, respectively, to those who make a homosexual and those who make a heterosexual sexual object-choice. When the sexual racism underlying such inquiries is more plainly exposed, their rationale will suffer proportionately—or so one may hope.

In the meantime, it helps in evaluating current scientific work to have a good nose for smelling out a research plan that is designed to confirm current categories of analysis rather than to call those very categories into question. Let's take as an example the neurohormonal hypothesis, which may be the most fashionable aetiological theory of sexual orientation around at the moment.[14] This rearguard defense of the dominant sexual ideology proceeds by a particularly ingenious and cunning route. Since adult homosexuals have finally been shown, despite many earlier "scientific" predictions to the contrary and decades of supposedly conclusive research, to be hormonally indistinguishable from adult heterosexuals, the most recent biological attempts to reify contemporary sexual categories have had to alter traditional explanatory strategies, looking now to pre-natal neurohormonal influences on the embryonic development of those who, many years later, turn out to be homosexuals or heterosexuals. (According to one expert, increased stress on pregnant German women during the Second World War and its neurohormonal consequences account for why "a higher proportion of homosexual men were born [*sic*] in Germany during World War II than before or after the war.")[15] The hypothesized pre-natal neurohormonal influences are admittedly transient—they leave no clear trace, conveniently enough, in the bodies of the adult homosexuals who might be tested for them—whereas the fetuses or infants in whom they are supposed to operate have little occasion to make either homo- or heterosexual sexual object-choices (especially in the absence of another fetus), and so do not manifest their sexuality.

The first thing to notice about the theory, in other words, is that it is so hypothetical that it's difficult to falsify. Nor are there any experiments currently underway, so far as I know, that would test this hypothesis as it ought to be tested—namely, by monitoring the neurohormonal influences on a random sample of fetuses from the moment of conception until the completion of their psychosexual development (such an experiment would, of course, be fiendishly difficult to devise, and no scientist wants to have to wait thirty-five years before being able to publish the results of his or her research). The most that can be established on the basis of current scientific work is that individuals with certain rare genetic defects whose hormonal functioning is thereby impaired are on average more likely to become homosexuals—but such deductions are no more informative about the human population at large than were earlier inferences about the criminality of sexual deviants drawn from the observation of inmates in prisons or insane asylums. And experiments performed on laboratory animals in support of the neurohormonal hypothesis are often remarkable for the extent of their unexamined assumptions about the relation between sex, sex-role, gender, and sexual identity, as well as for their criteria for what counts as "homosexuality" in a rat.

These are exactly the sorts of experiments that might have been performed in Victorian Britain to prove the once-fashionable hypothesis that the so-called lower orders of society were throw-backs to an earlier stage of evolutionary development—inherently less civilized or morally advanced than the professional and ruling classes—if only nineteenth-century science had possessed a sophisticated genetics or endocrinology. Present-day scientific research into sexual orientation is technically refined, but the ideology informing it remains as crude and unreflective as its Victorian predecessor. Just as one might, even without undertaking a scientific study, be justifiably skeptical of an experiment designed to determine the genetic or hormonal "cause" of the underclass in American society—because one might not believe that sociological phenomena have biological causes or because one might be morally repelled by the idea of treating social inequities as reflections of natural, essential, and unalterable biological differences among groups of one's fellow-citizens—so one is entitled to remain skeptical, I think, about "scientific" experiments which provide a biological warrant for sexual racism and which are so plainly inscribed, despite the good intentions of many individual scientists, in prevailing strategies of homophobia.

Schneider. The idea that homosexuality was as deeply rooted as one's gender or race has been a cornerstone of the hope for increased social tolerance and eventual "liberation." Your argument seems to constitute a challenge to that hope, doesn't it?

Halperin. No, I don't think so. Just because my sexuality is an artefact of cultural processes doesn't mean I'm not stuck with it. Particular cultures are contingent, but the personal identities and forms of erotic life that take shape within the horizons of those cultures are not. To say that sexuality is learned is not to say that it can be unlearned—any more than to say that culture changes is to say that it is malleable. I'm not personally responsible for my sexuality any more than I am personally responsible for certain basic values that were part and parcel of my middle-class upbringing: yet both are constitutive of my character. I don't mean that I can't inquire into, criticize, or try to understand how I came to be what I am, but no amount of conscious reflection will enable me simply to walk away from my socialization and acquire a new cultural (or sexual) identity.

But I'm not sure in any case how politically useful it is to claim that sexuality is as essential and unalterable as gender or race. After all, something like that was tried by nineteenth-century German advocates for homosexual rights in an effort to persuade their contemporaries that homosexuality was not a sin or moral failing or acquired perversity for which homosexuals themselves were to blame but was rather a natural condition; indeed, these militants succeeded so well in convincing the early sexologists of their view that standard nineteenth-century accounts of "sexual inversion" often relied for their data on the self-representations of gay polemicists—with the result that instead of being sent to jail for a fixed term homosexuals were now shut up for life in insane asylums. Fighting entrenched social agencies and practices with nothing but ideology is not a game you can win (as feminists have discovered), because culturally dominant forces can always reconfigure whatever interpretation of yourself you may put forward to suit their own interests: no account is so positive as to be proof against hostile appropriation and transformation (thus, every positive image of women that feminists attempt to promote gets turned into an offensive stereotype).[16] I don't think the possibilities for social tolerance depend upon, much less ought to dictate, our own self-representations.

There is, however, one kind of hope for liberation that my argument does in effect deny. I offer no comfort to those who aspire to liberate us from our current pleasures in favor of some more free-wheeling, polymorphous sexuality. The assumption underlying that liberationist position has to do with the possibility of recovering a "natural sexuality" which an artificial and repressive civilization has denatured. But there is no such thing as a natural sexuality, if that refers to a sexuality unformed by a cultural discourse that defines the boundaries of the sexual and the non-sexual, of the attractive and the unattractive. Any system in which our desires were entirely unstructured by such a discourse, in which we would be somehow free to choose at every step what we found sexually attractive or gratifying, would not be a system of *sexuality* at all—and I readily confess that I find the idea of living under such a system as unthinkable as I find the idea of being an ancient Greek or a disembodied spirit. Moreover, the project of freeing us to embrace a "natural sexuality" seems to be a coercive one, and in our immediate situation it can only serve the cause of repression by fortifying the ideological division between "good" and "bad" sexuality. If sexuality, by definition, is codified and scripted in certain respects, that does not mean it should in every case be liberated. We must remember that sexual boundaries do not merely *constrict* possibilities; they also *create* possibilities: they describe zones of freedom, pleasure, and erotic excitement.

Schneider. But isn't there a contradiction here? If homosexuality is a cultural construct, and if such constructs operate at the level of individual subjectivities to determine personal identity, how can any of us—indeed, how can you—accept in any genuine sense the position that you are arguing for, a position that would seem to place whoever occupies it outside the cultural and sexual systems into which we were all born?

Halperin. That's a very canny question, but I'm not ashamed of the awkward spot it puts me in. I would be very untrue to the position I've been arguing for if I didn't acknowledge squarely and forthrightly the cognitive dissonance it involves. I don't think there's any way that I, or anyone else who grew up in bourgeois America when I did, could ever believe in what I've been saying with the same degree of conviction with which I believe, despite everything I've said, in the categories of heterosexuality and homosexuality. Those categories aren't merely categories of thought, at least in my case; they're also categories of erotic response, and they therefore have a claim on my belief that's stronger than intellectual allegiance. That, after all, is what it means to be acculturated into a sexual system: the conventions of the system acquire the self-confirming inner truth of "nature." If one could simply think oneself out of one's acculturation, it wouldn't be acculturation in the first place. And I can't imagine de-acculturating myself any more than I can imagine de-sexualizing myself, as I said earlier. Nor, once again, does it seem necessarily desirable to do so: every intellectual perspective on the world is a perspective from a particular vantage point, after all. So I freely admit that, in a sense, I don't, and couldn't possibly, *believe* in what I've been saying—not, at least, at the same deep level of conviction as the level at which my own desires are structured. But—predisposed, perhaps, by a long-held sense that my own experience of the world, such as it is, is not representative—I can affirm what I've been saying with a solid intellectual conviction. There's just no other equally sensible way to interpret the evidence I'm familiar with or to understand the gap between the recorded experiences of persons living in ancient and in modern societies.

3

Two Views of Greek Love:
Harald Patzer and Michel Foucault

I

The earliest scholarly studies of "Greek love" proceeded from the assumption that classical Greek society and sentiment were virtually unique in their acceptance—indeed, in their occasional celebration—of paederasty and that it was therefore the job of the ancient historian to provide a cogent causal explanation for this (allegedly bizarre) phenomenon.[1] Recent work, by contrast, has tended to interpret Greek sexual conventions in a wider (comparative, anthropological, or ethological) context[2] and to emphasize instead the uniqueness of modern European and American middle-class attitudes: we are the ones, it seems, whose sexual norms and institutions require historical explanation.[3] Not only does exclusive and "compulsory heterosexuality," as Adrienne Rich calls it,[4] now appear to be a distinctively modern, Western, even bourgeois production: the clinical concept of homosexuality, to which "Greek love" has often been unthinkingly assimilated, is turning out to be less transparently descriptive, and more culturally specific (hence, more ideologically loaded), than earlier interpreters had assumed. The first major work of classical scholarship to address itself centrally to the conceptual difficulties created for the study of Greek sexual codes and practices by new developments in the history of sexuality is Harald Patzer's *Die griechische Knabenliebe* (1982). The solution it presents—both scholarly and ideological—is perhaps revelatory of future trends in classical scholarship, and in any case it is worth scrutinizing in some detail.

"In recent years," writes Barry D. Adam, a Canadian sociologist, "there has been a growing realization that the contemporary social organization of homosexuality into lesbian and gay worlds is a socially and historically unique development and that the traditional academic construction of 'the homosexual' has participated in this reifying process."[5] It is the chief virtue of Patzer's monograph that it refuses to collaborate in the reification of modern sexual categories. Patzer's project is to distinguish, once and for all,

54

Greek *Knabenliebe* (i.e., paederasty) from homosexuality as we currently understand it; Patzer argues that Greek paederasty was, at the very least, such a peculiar (if not entirely idiosyncratic) variety of homosexual expression that the application of the modern concept of homosexuality to it can only lead to misunderstanding.[6] Patzer seeks instead to give an account of Greek paederasty that will effectively remove it from the context of modern sexual typologies and insert it into an entirely different conceptual universe.

Classical Greek paederasty differs from "homosexuality," according to Patzer, in the following respects: (1) Paederasty, as the word implies, refers only to sexual relations between adult males, on the one hand, and boys or youths between the ages of twelve and eighteen, on the other. (2) Paederastic relationships, once begun, never extend beyond the youth of the junior partner. (3) Paederastic love-affairs are not motivated by a peculiar, individual sexual inclination on the part of either person for a partner of the male sex—an inclination of the sort that would displace or exclude sexual relations with women: on the contrary, the senior lover is usually married or, at least, is accustomed to regular, heterosexual contacts with adult women. (4) In order for a paederastic relationship to be wholly honorable and dignified in the eyes of contemporary Athenian society, its sexual expression is restricted to one, quite specific, mode of copulation—namely, the intercrural (i.e., "between the legs")—which spares the junior partner (and future citizen) the effeminizing humiliation of bodily penetration and thereby ensures that his eventual authority as an adult male will not be compromised before the fact. (5) In a proper paederastic relationship, the younger partner does not share in his older lover's sexual desire but, like a good Victorian wife, surrenders out of a mingled feeling of gratitude, esteem, and affection; he is supposed to suffer and be still.[7]

It is possible, of course, to quibble with some details in Patzer's analysis. Against (1), it may be recalled that there is extensive debate among the ancient authors over the proper upper limit on the age of the junior partner (though most agree that the arrival of the beard marks the terminus of his legitimate desirability)[8] and that the ready availability of male prostitutes[9] and slaves provided Athenian men who were so inclined with an alternate mode of homosexual expression unconstrained by the moral conventions governing their relations with citizen youths. Against (3), it may be objected that the older lover was often a young man between the ages of twenty and thirty who was therefore quite probably *unmarried*[10] (or married to someone considerably younger than himself) and that Aristophanes's speech in Plato's *Symposium* (189c–193d), together with a number of other ancient texts, testifies quite explicitly to the strength of individual preferences (even to the point of exclusivity) for a sexual partner of one sex rather than another.[11] And against (4), we should bear in mind that avoidance of anal intercourse in paederastic relations is the normative ideal, not the reality.[12] Nonetheless,

Patzer's criteria for distinguishing between paederasty and homosexuality are generally sound enough to sustain his central thesis that what the Greeks exhibit is not homosexuality at all but rather paederastic behavior without (categorical and unqualified) homosexual desire. How is such a paradox to be explained?

Enter the ritual hypothesis of ancient Greek paederasty. Eighty years ago E. Bethe published a pathbreaking article on "Dorian paederasty" in which he maintained, by comparing the customs of archaic Crete and Sparta (both Dorian states) with those of various "primitive" peoples, that the classical Greeks inherited from their Dorian invaders and conquerors—and ultimately perverted to their own unnatural purposes—a ritual practice of initiation in which older males passed on numinous powers (chiefly military and moral vitality) to the generation of younger males by injecting them, through homosexual copulation, with the magical potency thought to reside in their semen.[13] Bethe's thesis was indignantly repudiated by contemporary classicists[14]—often, as Patzer rightly observes, on the shabbiest of grounds—but it has resurfaced from time to time in subsequent scholarship,[15] and it seems currently to be enjoying something of a renascence,[16] partly because Bethe's scant comparative data have since been supplemented by a wealth of new ethnographic evidence for the wide distribution of ritualized homosexual behaviors among tribal peoples[17] and partly because recent, anthropologically oriented research in classical studies has brought to light traces of what look like initiation rituals in ancient Greece.[18] It is Patzer's aim to resuscitate, correct, modify, and ultimately to vindicate a version of Bethe's thesis, for therein lies the key, he believes, to understanding the paradox of paederastic behavior without homosexual desire: in the context of an institutionalized ritual of initiation, on his view, copulation ceases to be an expression of individual sexual inclination, of personal habitus, and becomes instead the fulfillment of a universally binding social obligation. (Nice work if you can get it.)

Because the classical Greek practice of paederasty is entirely "alien to our modern Western culture," according to Patzer, it is necessary to look beyond the horizons of our culture, and beyond the borders of philological scholarship, for parallels that illuminate the Greek experience. To refuse to do so is to succumb to "ethnocentrism." An examination of initiation rites in New Guinea and Melanesia helps Patzer to bring into better focus the Cretan institution described by the fourth-century B.C. historian Ephorus, whose report is transmitted to us by Strabo (10.4.21). When a boy comes of age in Crete, according to this account, an older male who desires him informs his family and friends a few days in advance and then carries him off, overcoming their perfunctory show of resistance (if the lover is unworthy, however, the boy's relations intervene in earnest); pursued by them, the lover brings the boy to his *andreion* (a men's clubhouse), gives him various gifts, and then spends two months hunting and feasting with him in the countryside. The episode concludes with a mutual exchange of gifts and with the admission of the boy to the highest social status. Patzer has a fairly easy time demonstrating, by reference to the comparative ethnographic material, that the Cretan institution is indeed an initiation rite—one in which, moreover, sexual intercourse between man and boy seems to play a role.[19] The more difficult task Patzer now faces is to relate such rites (for which he finds traces in various parts of Greece, distributed equally among Dorian and non-Dorian races) to the classical Athenian institution of paederasty.

Classical paederasty, Patzer maintains, is a logical (though not in every case a temporal) development from the kind of initiation ritual attested for the Cretans. It differs from its ancestor in that (1) it aims at inculcating not military but civic virtue; (2) as a social obligation it is less universal and less binding and is not overseen by the state; (3) the relationship between lover and beloved is more private and unconstrained, though still socially regulated; (4) it flourishes most conspicuously among non-Dorians. (Moreover, although Patzer neglects to emphasize this, the classical version of paederasty he appeals to does away, supposedly, with phallic penetration of the junior partner and thereby implicitly abandons any pretense of bestowing benefits through *sexual*, as opposed to *social*, contact; on Patzer's own account, therefore, the continuing sexual element in classical paederasty remains unexplained.) Interpreting classical paederasty as a modified initiation ritual helps to make sense, according to Patzer, of its highly codified and (to his mind) peculiarly institutional features: it explains (1) why homosexual expression is restricted to temporally circumscribed relations between an adult male and a youth in the formative period of his development; (2) why hierarchical relations obtain only between persons of the same sex; (3) why paederasty does not exclude heterosexuality; (4) why paederasty is not sexually or erotically reciprocal; and (5) why paederasty is supposed to involve care for the junior partner's physical and moral welfare. Whereas in the earlier type of paederasty the quality that marked out a youth as worthy of a lover was bravery, in the later type the quality that makes a youth desirable (*erôs* now intrudes upon the psychological scene for the first time) is beauty— though, Patzer hastens to add, by "beauty" (*to kalon*) the Athenians understood not mere physical comeliness but rather a constellation of prized physical and moral endowments; in the absence of the latter, corporeal beauty effectively lost its power to attract an honorable Athenian paederast (a species of erotic let-down that is not unknown, I believe, even in "our modern Western culture"). In this transition from a socially enforced and rigidly institutionalized ritual of paederasty to a much more informal one, the experience of immanent magical or numinous power gives way to an experience of erotic and aesthetic ecstasy (on the lover's part, at least), but such eroticism remains, in Patzer's view, essentially non-sexual in character.[20]

A number of objections to this thesis immediately spring to mind. While Patzer is undoubtedly right to suppose that the rustic holiday prescribed for the happy couple by Cretan custom included sexual intercourse, nothing in Strabo's version of Ephorus leads us to attach any particular importance to the sexual element or to regard it in particular—rather than, say, the two months' worth of hunting[21]—as the focal point of the initiatory experience. Patzer's emphasis on the centrality in this ritual of a magical transfer of potency and military valor from man to boy through sexual contact receives no support from the text and seems to have been imported directly from New Guinea.[22] The great significance which Patzer, like Bethe before him, attaches to Strabo's remark that in Crete lovers desire boys who are exceptionally brave and well-behaved, instead of those who are exceptionally good-looking,[23] is misplaced: the remark is plainly apologetic in intent and is framed as a tacit rebuke to the writer's own society; a different picture emerges a few sentences later when Strabo says that it is regarded as a judgment on the characters of those who are handsome and well-born if they fail to obtain lovers in their youth—thereby implying that good looks and nobility in a lad were considered, other things being equal, erotic stimuli in archaic Crete no less than in classical Athens.[24] Finally, Patzer acknowledges that the Cretan institution is unusual in that it operates through elective affinities and pair-bonding rather than through rituals that involve entire age-classes: but isn't such an admission tantamount to conceding an important function to "personal inclination" in this paederastic system? Strabo speaks of the senior partner as an *erastês*, or lover, after all: this would seem to be a textbook example of the interdependence in culture of social practices and subjective experiences.

It is when we come to Patzer's discussion of classical Athens that his contrast between paederasty as personal inclination and paederasty as social obligation forfeits all plausibility. That paederasty was indeed a social institution in classical Athens—an institution often thought, moreover, to serve a variety of beneficial purposes—no one, I think, who studies classical antiquity will seriously doubt; that it was not also an expression of deeply felt sexual desire no one, I hope, will believe. In approaching this topic we have inevitably to deal with what Henry James once called "a traditional difference between that which people know and that which they agree to admit that they know, that which they see and that which they speak of, that which they feel to be a part of life and that which they allow to enter literature."[25] It is a great virtue of K. J. Dover's study of the moral and social conventions governing paederastic relations in classical Athens that in distinguishing a public ideal of "right *erôs*" from its reprehensible opposite he never loses sight of "the gulf between reality and . . . convention."[26] The ideal of legitimate *erôs* does indeed require that a lover neither do to a boy nor demand from him anything shameful, that he not attempt to bribe or constrain him, and that he sincerely wish to promote his beloved's well-being.[27] Patzer is right to take this ideal seriously but he is wrong to think that it regulates all decent behavior—wrong, that is, to interpret Dover's sketch of the public ideal as a description of the social norm.[28]

Are we then to interpret as scandalous the affectionate and charming story told about Sophocles by Ion of Chios—how the fifty-five year old tragic poet, while dining at the home of a friend during his tour of duty as general in the Samian War, managed to snatch a kiss from the handsome lad who was pouring the wine and thereupon remarked to the assembled company that he didn't turn out to be nearly so bad a strategist as Pericles had feared?[29] Or are we to suppose that Sophocles's ulterior aim was to groom the slave[30] for a civic role that the latter was destined never to assume? Sophocles's behavior on this occasion, decent though it seems to have been, does not look like that of someone who is motivated principally by social duty. Just as it would be wrong for a future historian of twentieth-century America to deduce from the pervasive ideal of marital fidelity among the American middle classes that the marriages of respectable people were unfailingly monogamous in practice or were universally thought to be so (and equally wrong to infer from a reading of the novels of John Updike that the ideal of monogamy did not significantly constrain the sexual choices of actual married people), so it is wrong for Patzer virtually to imply that Greek men made love to their boys with a copy of Plato's *Phaedrus* firmly tucked under one arm for easy consultation.

Patzer has, to be sure, a certain claim on our sympathy. He finds himself in the unenviable position of having to account for certain socially validated homosexual behaviors in the absence of a contemporary social construction of homosexual desire. He has already been criticized by classical scholars for his laudable attempt to repudiate "homosexuality" as an instrument of historical analysis;[31] now I, in turn, am about to criticize him for appealing to some equally unsound conceptions of "ritual" and "social duty" as substitutes for modern sexual categories. My aim in all this is to highlight the connection between Patzer's interpretative lapses and some aspects of traditional scholarly method in the human sciences. For, despite his insistence on the need to look beyond the boundaries of Western high culture for parallels with which to illuminate classical Greek institutions, Patzer's own intellectual horizons remain thoroughly circumscribed by assumptions implicit in the traditional practice of his discipline. In particular, Patzer remains very much in thrall to the principles of nineteenth-century hermeneutics which require, as a necessary (if not a sufficient) condition for the success of any interpretative venture, that the researcher confront and carefully set aside all his or her own prejudices and preconceptions.[32] Those principles were memorably articulated, with reference to the topic presently under discussion, by Ulrich von Wilamowitz-Moellendorff (the greatest of the traditional philologists): Plato's erotic theory, he wrote, "is rooted in paederastic feelings that remain alien to us because they are contrary to nature; nonetheless, we must not only grasp them historically but must enter into them sympathetically, for otherwise Socrates will remain simply incomprehensible to us, and of Plato we shall retain only a faded and distorted image."[33] But, despite these noble words, Wilamowitz's inquiries into the subject, as Patzer himself acknowledges, produced negligible results. Patzer's own strategy resembles Wilamowitz's, however, insofar as it involves insisting on the utter foreignness of Greek paederasty and therefore on the necessity of purifying our conception of it of anything that seems to be bound up with our own cultural experience—including the modern conceptualization of homosexuality.

But it is not enough simply to refuse to predicate "homosexuality" of ancient attitudes and behaviors. The larger discontinuities between the discursive formations responsible, respectively, for classical paederasty and for modern homosexuality remain to be specified. Patzer continues to assume that Athenian paederasty is primarily a matter for philological investigation, that it can be isolated from other aspects of ancient social relations (such as the position of women, which he omits to discuss), and that its conflation with homosexuality can be undone by an enlightened practice of *Kulturgeschichte*; he is unwilling to undertake, in short, the kind of investigation into the very conditions of sexual meaning that might enable the historian to situate Athenian paederasty in its wider cultural, sociological, or discursive context. Hence, his hermeneutic procedure, far from escaping "ethnocentrism," as it is intended to do, merely leads to a kind of ethnocentrism in reverse, an insistence on the absolute otherness of the Greeks, and thus to an ethnographic narcissism as old as Herodotus[34]—a tendency to dwell only on those features of alien cultures that impress us as diverging in interesting ways from "our own." In Patzer's case, the well-founded conviction that homosexuality-as-sexual-inclination is a distinctively modern phenomenon leads him to impose on the Greeks, by way of hermeneutic rigor, a paederasty-without-homoeroticism for which there is equally no trace in either the historical or the ethnographic record.

For even the most thoroughly ritualized instances of paederasty known to us—including those to which Patzer appeals for parallels—are hardly so duty-bound, so grimly Kantian in their outlook, as he makes them out to be (here Patzer seems to have been misled by one of his sources who described a community in which males tend to lose their enthusiasm for ceremonial homosexual copulation after they get married, and who therefore have to be shamed into it); far from excluding any element of sexual desire, such rites afford their participants a considerable degree of erotic pleasure and excitement, as more than one anthropologist has noted.[35] "It is as ethnocentric to deny eroticism among tribal peoples," writes Gilbert Herdt, perhaps the world's leading authority on ritualized paederasty, "[by] reduc-

ing their eroticism to customs and rites, as it is ethnocentric to 'read' eroticism into situations where none exists."[36]

In the light of Herdt's warning we can begin to discern in Patzer's misap-
propriated ethnographies and misapplied methodologies the lineaments of
a more sinister interpretative strategy. The ritual hypothesis of Greek paederasty conceals, I think, a potential (though unacknowledged) political
agenda—and that, I am afraid, may be part of its contemporary appeal. It
enables the ancient historian to exonerate the Greeks from the charge of
actually experiencing any homoerotic longings; it allows classicists to normalize Greek desire and to recuperate it for the cause of exclusive heterosexuality. For by purifying paederasty of sexual desire and interpreting it not as
an expression of personal preference but rather as a form of social ritual (thus
relegating it to the category of activities set apart from normal daily life and
only performed under specially sanctioned circumstances), Patzer in effect
maintains heterosexual activity as the *ordinary* locus of eroticism—even for
the Greeks, despite their various sexual peculiarities—and thereby preserves
it as the privileged and normative mode of human sexuality.[37]

It should not in any case have been necessary for Patzer to go so far afield
in search of cultural analogues to the ancient Greeks. Sexual conventions
alien to "our modern Western culture," and more closely approximating to
those of the classical Athenians, can still be found in abundance in sectors of
our own societies[38] as well as in the sex-segregated societies of the Mediterranean basin. More than fifty years ago A.E. Housman observed that what
seemed to baffle his learned colleagues in Germany about the paederastic
ethos inscribed in the obscene wit of certain Roman epigrams would be
immediately perspicuous to any modern inhabitant of Sicily or Naples.[39]
Contemporary Mediterranean sexual practices continue to afford us a promising avenue of inquiry into the conventions of classical Athenian paederasty;
let us explore it, at least, before we go whoring after strange cultures in the
futile hope of transcending our historical situation and so escaping from the
supposedly crippling constraints of our ethnocentrism. My contention is
not that the larger ethnographic record offers us no insights into the pre-
modern cultures of the West (quite the reverse),[40] merely that such insights
as it does offer us should not be pressed into the service of some sort of
collective disavowal or used to interpose a false clinical distance between the
interpreter and the objects of cultural interpretation. If there is indeed a way
to free ourselves from the conceptual tyranny of current sexual categories,
it lies not in an attempt simply to do away with those categories by means
of a methodological sleight of hand but in an effort to understand them
better as historically conditioned cultural representations—or, to be exact,
as instances of an ideology[41] which we not only fashion but also inhabit.
Michel Foucault, whose work Patzer wholly neglects, had already begun to
point us in the right direction six years before Patzer's monograph appeared.

II

> The study of history makes one "happy, unlike the metaphysicians,
> to possess in oneself not an immortal soul but many mortal ones."
> —Foucault, quoting Nietzsche[42]

Michel Foucault's *History of Sexuality*, originally projected as a six-volume work, now consists of a theoretical introduction, a volume on classical Greece, a volume on Greece and Rome during the Roman empire, and assorted published fragments. A fourth volume on early Christianity and monasticism has long been promised but has yet to appear. This unfinished masterpiece, which is not so much about the history of sexual theories and practices as it is about the shifting conditions that determine the nature of one's relation to oneself as a sexual being, may turn out to be, even in its currently truncated form, the most important contribution to the history of Western morality since the publication, a hundred years ago, of Nietzsche's *On the Genealogy of Morals*.

Foucault himself invites the comparison to Nietzsche when he describes, in the preface to the second volume (on classical Greece),[43] the motive for his unforeseen and, as it happened, costly decision to interrupt work on the original six-volume project announced in Volume One and to extend its scope backwards in time to include Graeco-Roman antiquity: in order to analyze the formation and development of the modern experience called "sexuality," he explains, it was necessary first of all to discover the provenance of the one theme common to the otherwise discontinuous experiences of "sexuality" and "carnality" (its Christian predecessor)—it was necessary, that is, to trace the " 'genealogy' " of desire and of man as a desiring subject (p. 11). Desire, as it figures in contemporary experience, is not a natural given, Foucault realized, but a prominent element—though featured in different ways—of both traditional Christian and modern "scientific" discourse; research into the origins of "sexuality" therefore requires the historian to do for desire what Nietzsche had done for "good" and "evil." If Nietzsche's genealogical inquiry often comes to mind in the course of reading Volume Two (with which I shall be concerned in the remainder of this essay), it does so not because Foucault is directly indebted to it for individual interpretations—unlike Arthur W. H. Adkins, for example, whose discussion of Homeric values in *Merit and Responsibility*[44] draws heavily, if silently, on Nietzsche's distinction between the kinds of valuation implicit in the vocabularies of good/bad and good/evil—but because Foucault is consciously and deliberately elaborating the "critical" tradition in modern philosophy that Nietzsche helped to found.[45] Characteristic of that tradition, among other things, is the practice of treating morality as an object of hermeneutic "suspicion" (to borrow Paul Ricoeur's term): both Nietzsche and Foucault, in other words, conceive morality not as a set of formal and explicit prescriptions whose content can be more or less accurately summarized but as a cultural discourse whose modes of signification reveal the conditions under which values are constituted as such.

Foucault's analysis, like Nietzsche's, is historical rather than functional, intuitive rather than systematic, selective rather than exhaustive. It is not designed to displace conventional scholarship. Despite the impression that one might receive from the show of territorial hostility with which his work has been greeted by members of the interested professions,[46] Foucault is not trying to beat classical philologists or ancient philosophers at their own games, nor does he propose to make historical exegesis irrelevant; rather, he is trying to do something that traditional scholars do not do—something that helps to arrange and place the insights culled from philology in a new and different light. His success, like Nietzsche's, reminds us that an interpreter's scholarship need not be above reproach in order to be adequate to the brilliant portrayal of a historical phenomenon. Dante, after all, managed to seize upon a set of meanings essential to the *Odyssey* without ever having read it. And Nietzsche's *The Birth of Tragedy* continues, deservedly, to reach a wide and varied audience, most of whose members have never heard of Ulrich von Wilamowitz-Moellendorff—or, if they have heard of him, know him not as Europe's supreme authority in the field of classical philology but only as that curious fellow who hounded Nietzsche out of the academic profession for having published his famous book.[47]

Foucault's classical scholarship, to be sure, is nothing like so good as Nietzsche's, but his account of the sexual morality of fifth- and fourth-century B.C. Greece turns out to be in substantial accord with the results of the best recent work on the topic. Specialists have complained, not unreasonably, about Foucault's slapdash use of ancient sources and about his seemingly uncritical willingness to assemble a portrait of Greek morals from the scattered testimony of highly unrepresentative authors. Foucault's reliance on philosophical and medical texts, in preference to the testimony of the Attic orators, comic poets, and vase-painters who furnished K. J. Dover with virtually all his sources of information in *Greek Popular Morality*[48] (which, however, Foucault does not omit to cite), his relative neglect of his authors' social context or purpose in writing, and his greater attentiveness to what people say than to what they do are all causes for justifiable alarm: Foucault himself seems unsure at times *whose* morality, precisely, he is describing.* The genius of his unprofessional approach, however, lies in its receptiveness to the general features of moral discourse in classical Greece;

---

* Foucault's concentration on "scientific" texts can be explained in part by his interest in "the history of truth" (p. 12) and by his corresponding concern to show how sexual experience is constituted as a morally problematic domain by the ethical discourse of the various relevant "experts." All the same, such a neglect of *praxis* is a strange failing, especially in Foucault, and it leads Flynn, 532, to suspect him of reverting from Nietzschean genealogy to mere Hegelian phenomenology.

it enables Foucault to articulate a sort of moral grammar common to popular sentiment and élitist prescription alike and thereby to attack familiar problems from a genuinely fresh perspective. To his credit, Foucault is alive to the dangers of homogenizing the irreducible particularities of his various sources into a deceptively coherent system: he freely concedes that his portrait is "cavalier and very schematic," a mere "sketch" of "certain general traits" (pp. 105, 277).

But despite all these weaknesses, it is a most impressive achievement, and one that professional classicists might well envy (or begrudge, as the case may be). The eight years which elapsed between the publication of Volumes One and Two were evidently put to good use. Handicapped from the outset by what he acknowledges to be an irremediable lack of requisite familiarity with classical Greek texts—though not, apparently, by an insufficient (for his purposes, at least) grasp of the classical languages[49]—Foucault submitted himself to the rigors of basic research in the field of ancient social relations, under the tutelage of Paul Veyne, and he seems to have emerged from this scholarly apprenticeship chastened by the experience. Even his respect for historical and philological method appears to have grown over the interval. The difference in the intellectual climate of Volumes One and Two is correspondingly palpable. Volume One, for all its admittedly bright ideas, is dogmatic, tediously repetitious, full of hollow assertions, disdainful of historical documentation, and careless in its generalizations: it distributes over a period spanning from the seventeenth to the twentieth centuries a gradual process of change well known to Foucault only in its later, mid-nineteenth-century manifestations. Volume Two, by contrast, is becomingly modest in its tone, cautious in its interpretations, conservative in its adherence to ancient literary sources, and tentative in its conclusions. Foucault hews closely to the lines of interpretation laid down by some of the soundest and most traditional British and American classicists, such as K. J. Dover and Helen North, and something of their scrupulousness appears to have rubbed off on him. Most touchingly of all, perhaps, he seems to have learned a good deal, in his turn, from those scholars on this side of the Atlantic (chiefly in California, where Foucault spent considerable time between Volumes One and Two) who had once learned so much from him, and who went on to contaminate his distinctive blend of phenomenology and structuralism[50] with their native brand of cultural anthropology.

Still, it would be a mistake to suppose that Foucault simply abandoned his now-familiar "archaeological" and "genealogical" methods in favor of "thick description" (which is not, after all, a historical procedure).[51] In Volume One he wrote, "Sexuality must not be thought of as a kind of natural given which power tries to hold in check, or as an obscure domain which knowledge tries gradually to uncover. It is the name that can be given to a historical construct [*dispositif*]: not a furtive reality that is difficult to grasp, but a great surface network in which the stimulation of bodies, the intensification of pleasures, the incitement to discourse, the formation of special knowledges, the strengthening of controls and resistances, are linked to one another, in accordance with a few major strategies of knowledge and power."[52] Volume Two still finds him unrepentantly concerned with the history of discursive formations, though no longer with "sexuality," which he has persuasively shown to be a modern "production": his purpose remains that of investigating the constitution of sexual experience—or, as he puts it, "the correlation, in a culture, between domains of knowledge, types of normativity, and forms of subjectivity" (p. 10). What Foucault calls "experience" is circumscribed by these three "axes";[53] it is the last of them that pertains most particularly to sex, in his opinion.

Why is it, Foucault asks, that sexual behavior and the various activities and pleasures associated with it comprise an object of moral preoccupation in our culture? How and in what terms did sex come to be constituted as a specifically *moral* domain? The stance of radical innocence implied by those questions is far removed from the merely naïve "objectivity" of the traditional historian (such as Patzer), with his studious avoidance of "preconceptions" and "prejudices,"[54] and it enables Foucault to reconceptualize morality in such a way as to bring it within the purview of an *histoire de la pensée*, a history of thought *as thought inhabits experiences and systems of action*[55] (not to be confused with the history of psychic and cultural representations, or "ideas"),[56] a project whose proper task is to describe "the conditions under which human beings problematize what they are, what they do, and the world they live in" (p. 16).[57] The conventional approach, which Foucault considers valid enough but uninformative for his purposes, treats morality as a set of values and rules of conduct that are prescribed for individuals and groups by various agencies of authority in the society, such as the Church or the family, and are either articulated explicitly in formal doctrines and codes of behavior or are handed down and enforced by a variety of informal strategies; it also takes into account the actual behavior of individuals, their relation to the dominant values, and the degree to which they resist or obey a moral code of whose content they are more or less aware (pp. 32–33). Virtually all students of ancient morality, I think it is fair to say, have been guided hitherto by a conception of morality that approximates to the one Foucault outlines. What is wrong with it is that it places too much interpretative weight on the *content* of a moral system and ignores the discursive structures that determine that system's characteristic orientation.

Foucault illustrates the defect of studying morality solely in terms of its content by identifying four themes attested in both pagan and Christian sources that would seem, in and of themselves, to argue for a continuing ethic of sexual austerity in Western culture: fear of sex; praise of monogamy; condemnation of effeminate men; and glorification of resistance to appetite.

These four themes, when examined as to their content, may well reveal striking differences in emphasis or tonality in their pagan and Christian manifestations, and there remain a number of valid historical criteria for distinguishing the unique flavor of otherwise identical pagan and Christian interdictions, but traditional methods do not provide a clear and simple means of describing the conceptual or discursive gap separating, say, Greek from Victorian prohibitions against masturbation.[58] Even worse, such thematic continuities might seem to suggest that sexuality is a cultural invariant and that historical variations in its expression merely reflect the differential impact on sexuality of the various mechanisms employed in different societies to repress it;[59] but that, as Foucault remarks, would be in effect to place desire and the desiring subject outside the field of human history (p. 10).

Foucault devotes a separate chapter of Volume Two to the classical Greek expression of each of these four themes: "diaetetics," or the regimen by which one controls the economy of one's own body and physical style of life; "economics," or the husband's relation to his wife and household; "erotics," or a man's relation to boys and other objects of longing; and the will to truth, or the philosophical renunciation of sexual pleasure. Foucault readily admits that the persistence of these themes raises complex questions about continuity and discontinuity in the evolution of Western morality, but he aspires to penetrate beyond such thematic correspondences by means of an emphasis on "ethics" rather than "morals." Following, apparently, Hegel's distinction between *Moralität* and *Sittlichkeit*, Foucault regards "ethics," in pointed contrast to "morals," *not* as a system of prescriptive codes and a pattern of behavioral response but as a relation that one establishes with oneself in the act of constituting oneself as a moral subject (this relation, of course, is not necessarily a self-conscious one, nor does it imply the moral independence of an individual from his or her society). In order to refute the "repressive hypothesis" and to uncover the discontinuities between different historical forms of sexual experience, Foucault sets out to construct a genealogy of "ethics": this comprises, as it pertains to sex, the genealogy of the subject as a subject of ethical actions and the genealogy of desire as an ethical problem.[60] Foucault acknowledges that morality includes both systems of rules, on the one hand, and forms of "subjectivation" and self-fashioning (*pratiques de soi*), on the other, but he finds that the morality of classical Greece features the latter more than the former; his history of ancient sexual morality (continued in Volume Three), then, concentrates neither on moral codes and systems of rules nor on human behavior that violates or conforms to them but analyzes the prevalent mode or modes in which human beings constitute themselves as ethical subjects, as the subjects of their own actions, and it catalogues the techniques by means of which they do so. What Foucault has tried to write, in short, is a history of "technologies of the self."[61]

Such a genealogy of man as an ethical subject must comprehend, according to Foucault, at least four aspects of ethical self-constitution: (1) "ontology," or determination of the ethical substance, the material that is going to be worked over by ethics—i.e., what part or aspect of myself is concerned with ethical conduct, what about me is taken as an object of moral observation and control? (2) "deontology," or mode of subjection—how do I establish my relation to moral imperatives, in what terms do I recognize my moral obligations or define my adherence to moral values? (3) "ascetics," or ethical work—what do I have to do to become moral, what are the means by which I change myself in order to become an ethical subject? (4) "teleology," or ethical goal—how do I conceive the end to which being moral will contribute, what is the kind of being to which I aspire when I behave in a moral way? (pp. 33–35).[62] This way of setting the question allows Foucault to address the problem of understanding the transition from pagan to Christian varieties of sexual experience not by asking how Christians took over, assimilated, or modified classical codes of morality (as historians of ideas have done) but by asking how one's relation to oneself as an ethical subject changed with the coming of Christianity (pp. 38–39).[63] Foucault's methodological apparatus has also proved useful to scholars in historical disciplines outside of classics[64] as well as to classicists who wish to extend Foucault's analysis to Greek texts omitted, either deliberately or inadvertently (depending on one's estimate of Foucault's competence), from his survey.[65]

Because Foucault's exposition is deliberately schematic, his thesis is easy to summarize. The ethical material on which the sexual morality of the classical Greeks was supposed to operate is what they called *aphrodisia*; their mode of submission is *chrêsis* (whence the title of Volume Two: *L'usage des plaisirs* translates *chrêsis aphrodisiôn*, "the management of venereal acts, pleasures, and desires": an Aristotelian tag);[66] the ethical work to be performed is *enkrateia*, "self-mastery"; and the goal is *sophrosynê*, a loaded and untranslatable term, meaning something like "prudent moderation," or "capacity for self-restraint." The first two of these elements require some amplification.

Aphrodisia refers to those actions, contacts, and forms of self-expression that procure the individual a certain type of pleasure. The word implies something very different from the modern understanding of "sexuality," according to Foucault, in that it does not refer to a mute force within us that makes itself felt in all sorts of indirect and devious ways other than the performance of sexual acts; rather, it designates the more concrete processes of sexual enjoyment: *aphrodisia* includes within its sphere three aspects of sexuality that we tend to distinguish—sexual acts, sexual pleasure, and sexual desire—and it thereby reflects the continuous circuit of responsiveness connecting the desire that leads to the act, the act that produces pleasure, and the pleasure that evokes (anticipatory) desire. Furthermore, *aphrodisia*, literally "the things of Aphrodite," are measured by their intensity and frequency (whence the corresponding and typical Greek concern about an agent's moderation or incontinence) as well as by the direction of their current, so to speak, which defines in every instance a subject and an object, an active and a passive participant. Finally, *aphrodisia* are never bad in themselves but are morally problematic for two reasons: first, they represent a lower pleasure, common to both men and beasts; second, the impulse associated with them is by nature "hyperbolic"—it tends greedily, if indulged, to seek more intense and frequent satisfaction, refusing to limit its demands to the bare requirements of need (pp. 49–61).

These observations contribute to Foucault's first major conceptual breakthrough, as I see it: namely, his ability to specify so clearly the ground of the Greeks' consistent assimilation of sexual desire to the other human appetites—these being, canonically, desires for food, drink, and sleep—and their tendency to view them all as qualitatively interchangeable "necessities," or compulsions, of human nature[67] (Plato, of course, is the bizarre exception to this tendency,[68] though Foucault apparently has failed to notice this). Foucault succeeds in recapturing something of the Greeks' original outlook when he places the Greek debate about how much sex it is good to have into the larger context of "diaetetics," the technique for achieving a properly balanced physical regimen. It would be interesting to determine, Foucault remarks, exactly when in the development of Western culture sex became more morally problematic than eating (pp. 61–62); he seems to think that sex won out only at the turn of the eighteenth century, after a long period of relative equilibrium during the Middle Ages.[69] The evidence newly assembled by Caroline Bynum in *Holy Feast and Holy Fast* (1987), however, suggests that cultural evolution may not have been such a continuously linear affair as Foucault imagines.

It is a feature of moral life in classical Greece, Foucault observes, that universal interdictions are few and far between. They tend also to be rather unspecific. The Greeks had no Decalogue, just some basic rules of thumb, of which the most prominent were: respect the laws and customs of the country; try not to offend the gods; and don't violate the dictates of your own nature (pp. 63–64). Foucault draws from these observations another startling and acute conclusion. The general requirements of Greek morality radically underdetermine the definition of proper conduct for an individual in any particular situation; they leave room for a self-imposed (though no doubt communally enforced) ethic of sexual restraint within the larger field of a Greek male's moral freedom. Greek morality, in other words, doesn't concern itself so much with the forbidden as with the voluntary (in principle, at least): morality is therefore not a matter of obedience to specific prescriptions but a regulated usage, or *chrêsis*, of morally unrestricted pleasures. No moral value, either positive or negative, attaches to certain kinds of caresses, sexual postures, or modes of copulation. Instead, the ethic governing the usage of pleasures takes the form of a kind of calculated economy of sexual spending: limit yourself to what you really need; wait until the most opportune moment to consume; and take into account your own social, political, and economic status. Sexual morality is thus subsumed by the more general practice of self-regulation with regard to enjoyment that constituted for free upper-class Greek males an art of living, a technique for maintaining personal equilibrium, "an aesthetics of being." Sexual morality is not part of an attempt to normalize populations but an element in a procedure adopted by a few people with the aim of living a beautiful and praiseworthy life—not a pattern of behavior for everybody but a personal choice for a small élite. Greek morality, Foucault concludes, does not justify and internalize interdictions: it stylizes freedom (pp. 103–111).

Here is the point at which Nietzsche naturally comes to mind. In the Third Essay of *On the Genealogy of Morals*, Nietzsche sought to distinguish the origins and significance of what he called the ascetic ideal from its multitude of subsequent adaptive uses, its later incorporation into a system of purposes. Nietzsche ultimately saw in asceticism not a symptom of weakness, not an example of the typically Christian tendency to make a moral virtue out of material necessity, but the expression of a powerful will. Currently manifested in the secular priesthood of philological scholarship as a will to truth (what Foucault, in the title of Volume One, calls a *volonté de savoir*), the will expressed by asceticism was, according to Nietzsche, originally an instrument of the power-hungry; it derived not from moral scruple or hatred of pleasure but from an instinct of mastery over self and others. Foucault similarly sees the Greek moralists in terms of a will to power, a strategy for achieving domination of self and others; that is the key, in his view, to an ethic that paradoxically combines categorical permission and voluntary suppression. Like Nietzsche, Foucault measures the change in outlook that accompanied the triumph of Christianity by gauging the extent of a shift in the valuation of activity and passivity: the paradigm of moral virtue is no longer represented by a man in a position of power who nonetheless takes no advantage of it but by a woman (usually) who is outwardly helpless but able to defend her moral integrity (specifically her chastity) against the onslaught of the wicked and powerful; the classical ideal of self-restraint has yielded to an ideal of purity, based on a model of physical integrity rather than on one of self-regulation.[70] Finally, one may even see in Foucault's own analysis an instance of a discursive tendency whose beginnings Nietzsche first glimpsed and heralded: the tendency of the will to truth to take *itself* as an object of genealogical scrutiny and, by means of a consequent heightening of self-consciousness, to put ethics—or moral science (as it used to be called)—out of existence. As Foucault has written elsewhere, with reference to Nietzsche, truth is an error with a history from which we are barely emerging.[71]

Unlike Patzer, then, Foucault treats sexual morality in classical Greece not as a problem to be solved, utterly remote from us and requiring unflinching methodological intrepidity on the part of those who would tackle it. Rather, Foucault's study of the construction of sexual experience in ancient Greece is designed to be what he calls a "history of the present,"[72] a genealogical inquiry into the provenance of present-day "sexuality."[73] As such, Foucault's project is framed by contemporary concerns and questions; it reflects his own relation (both conscious and unconscious) to current institutions and practices. Written from the perspective of particular modern interests—rather than from a "neutral" or "objective" position which, by situating itself "outside" of those interests (supposedly), conceals the extent of its own complicity in them—Foucault's genealogical explorations are undertaken with the avowed purpose of making a difference in the here-and-now; they are intended to affect the way we think of ourselves and to heighten our awareness of the various ways in which we are implicated in those régimes of power and knowledge within and against which we constitute ourselves.[74] Genealogy enables us to glimpse contingency where before we had seen only necessity; it thereby allows us to suspend, however briefly, the categories of thought and action within which we habitually conduct our lives. Foucault's classical scholarship, then, is designed to liberate us in the very limited but important sense of providing us with a kind of mental leverage against aspects of our world which we might wish to experience differently—or, at least, which we might enjoy being able to imagine *otherwise*.

Despite Patzer, the Greeks are hardly alien or lost to us. They are, on the contrary, all about us—not because we are (allegedly) their inheritors, not because we may expect to find vestiges of them buried within ourselves, faintly discernible beneath layers of historical encrustation, transformation, and displacement. Rather, the Greeks are all about us insofar as they represent one of the codes in which we transact our own cultural business: we use our "truths" about the Greeks to explain ourselves to ourselves and to construct our own experiences, including our sexual experiences. Far from being a repressed presence inside us, or a utopian alternative to us, the Greeks occupy an unexplicit margin framing our own self-understanding; as such, they are closely bound up with our self-definitions, with our senses of ourselves as situated in history and culture, as "descended from Greek civilization." To redefine our relation to the Greeks is therefore to inject a new element into our cultural, political, and personal consciousness; it is to discover a new way of seeing ourselves and, possibly, to create new ways of inhabiting our own skins.

The reasons for reading Patzer are, ostensibly, the traditional scholarly ones (including the search for "truth"), which tend to misconstrue the nature of our relation to the ancient sources and to disavow the "interested" quality of our engagement with them. The reasons for reading Foucault, by contrast, are much the same as the reasons for reading Nietzsche: not only does he enable us to understand considerably better what we already know, but he makes us more aware of the enigma we present to ourselves—and he helps us figure out how to pursue the elusive project of discovering, and changing, who we are.

PART II

4

Heroes and their Pals

"I wish we were labelled," remarks Rickie Elliot, the hero of E. M. Forster's *The Longest Journey* (1907), to his best friend at Cambridge; the novelist adds,

> He wished that all the confidence and mutual knowledge that is born in such a place as Cambridge could be organized. . . . [F]or man is so made that he cannot remember long without a symbol; he wished there was a society, a kind of friendship office, where the marriage of true minds could be registered.[1]

Readers today—who are, if anything, rather too well informed about the dreary details of Forster's personal life[2]—may look with a certain knowingness on Rickie's endearingly naïve and somewhat pathetic pipe-dream of a registry office for friendships. Rickie's longing to formalize and institutionalize his relations with his male friends, we lightly assume, simply expresses a displaced longing on the part of his creator for public recognition and validation of male homosexual pair-bonding.[3] But there is another dimension to Rickie's fantasy that might be easier to grasp if we could manage to resist both the complacent joys of biographical criticism and the more insidious temptation to sexualize the erotics of male friendship. I submit that Forster has accurately understood what he calls, in the same passage, "the irony of friendship"—its paradoxical combination of social importance and social marginality, its indeterminate status among the various forms of social relations. Friendship is the *anomalous* relation: it exists outside the more thoroughly codified social networks formed by kinship and sexual ties; it is "interstitial in the social structure" of most Western cultures.[4] It is therefore more free-floating, more in need of "labeling" (as Forster puts it)—more in need, that is, of social and ideological definition.

Homer's *Iliad* represents an instance of precisely this sort of ideological or definitional activity; it enables us to glimpse a certain species of social relation in the very act of being labeled, of undergoing literary construction. When I put it that way, however, my description may sound somewhat peculiar or tendentious: why do I not say, for example, that the *Iliad* beautifully portrays the friendship between Achilles and Patroclus or, perhaps, that it reflects something of what friendship was like among members of the warrior class during the Dark Age of Greece? My reason for avoiding each of those two more conventional interpretative strategies—the appreciative and the documentary, respectively—is not that I consider them invalid (although I confess to having doubts about both of them) but, rather, that I am interested in a dimension of the *Iliad* that lies beyond their reach: namely, the *Iliad*'s "symbolic" dimension (in Forster's sense), its role in producing and purveying the means of collective self-understanding that constitute social "labels." I believe this dimension of the *Iliad* emerges most clearly when Achilles and Patroclus are compared to similar pairs of heroic warriors in two other texts from roughly the same period: the Assyrian Gilgamesh Epic and the Books of Samuel in the Old Testament.★

The Gilgamesh Epic and the Books of Samuel offer one special advantage for comparative purposes: they both contain clear and, at least in the former case, historically determinate (i.e., not merely hypothetical) strata.[5] Stories about Gilgamesh and Enkidu are told in a number of early, Sumerian myths;[6] the Epic itself exists in a fragmentary Old Babylonian version, composed perhaps not long after 2000 B.C. and written down around 1600 B.C., in various intermediate versions, and in a fuller, more elaborate, though still incomplete, Standard Babylonian version (alternately called the Assyrian or the Late version), that seems to have been composed towards the end of the second millennium, was current in the first, and survives largely on seventh-century tablets from Nineveh.[7] The Books of Samuel (originally one book in Hebrew) are generally thought to represent an amalgamation of two sources, an Early and a Late Source (as they are aptly called), the former dated to the reign of Solomon in the mid-tenth century and the latter to the period spanning the years 750–650 B.C. (the age of Homer).[8] Moreover, analysis of the different versions of the Gilgamesh legend and of the Davidic histories reveals that in each case friendship did not always play a central role in the narrative, that it did not always possess the importance, the meaning, or the values attached to it in the final version. The comparative material suggests the possibility, then, that we may regard the friendship between Achilles and Patroclus depicted in our text of the *Iliad* not as some fixed, unchanging, and immovable feature of the epic but as a historical artefact, the product of a particular turn of thought at a particular juncture

---

★ It will be immediately apparent that the point of my comparison is not, in the first instance, the specific historical and cultural configuration known to the Greeks as *philia* ("love" or "friendship") but a somewhat more loosely defined modern concept called "friendship" which I am treating, for heuristic purposes only, as if it were a valid and universally applicable sociological category (which, of course, it isn't).

in the artistic elaboration of the traditional material. We are accordingly entitled to inquire into the valence of the specific terms in which that friendship is constructed.

Comparison of the three narratives reveals a common set of structures which serve to organize the basic elements that constitute each friendship while allowing plenty of scope for thematic variation among the individual works. First, all three narrative traditions feature a close friendship between two, and no more than two, persons. These two persons are always male; they form not only a pair, but a relatively isolated pair: the two of them are never joined by a third; there are no rivals, no other couples,[9] and no relations with women that might prove to be of a "distracting" nature.[10] The relationship, moreover, whatever its sentimental qualities, always has an outward focus, a purpose beyond itself in action, in the accomplishment of glorious deeds or the achievement of political ends. Each of the six friends, accordingly, is an exceptionally valiant warrior: we are dealing not with an instance of some neutral or universal sociological category called "friendship," then, but with a specific cultural formation, a type of heroic friendship which is better captured by terms like comrades-in-arms, boon companions, and the like.[11]

The ideology implicit in this peculiar and distinctive mode of constructing and representing friendship can be briefly described. Friendship, it seems, is something that only males can have,[12] and they can have it only in couples (the texts under discussion are, for the most part, uninterested in exploring the more general features of "men in groups").[13] The male couple constitutes a world apart from society at large, and yet it does not merely embody a "private" relation, of the sort that might be transacted appropriately in a "home." On the contrary, friendship helps to structure—and, possibly, to privatize*—the social space; it takes shape in the world that lies beyond the horizon of the domestic sphere, and it requires for its expression a military or political staging-ground. This type of friendship cannot generate its own *raison d'être*, evidently: it depends for its meaning on the meaningfulness of social action.†

The three heroic friendships before us also exhibit a common "micropolitics." They are based alike on a structural asymmetry, consisting in an unequal distribution of precedence among the members of the relationship and a differential treatment of them in the narrative: one of the friends has

---

* This is clearest in the case of the *Iliad*: as the ghost of Patroclus reminds Achilles, "we shall not sit apart from our dear companions, as we did when we were alive, hatching plans" (23.77–78). Cf. Sinos, 56, 60–61.

† This is clearest in the case of the Gilgamesh Epic: according to Jacobsen (1976), 199, Gilgamesh conceives the idea of going on an expedition against the monster Huwawa when he finds Enkidu weeping from boredom and from a sense of uselessness.

greater importance than the other; the latter is subordinated—personally, socially, and narratologically—to the former. This element can be variably materialized: in the Sumerian sources of the Gilgamesh Epic, for example, Enkidu had originally figured as Gilgamesh's servant (though even there he is occasionally termed a friend);[14] the final Tablet of the Epic, which consists of a fragmentary translation of a Sumerian legend, similarly refers to Enkidu as Gilgamesh's servant (XII, 54). The Old Babylonian redactor transformed that tradition in the interests of his own thematic preoccupations by ostensibly equalizing the relationship: now, Enkidu is created as a match for Gilgamesh (II, v, 27; cf. I, ii, 31–32 [Assyrian version]),[15] is called an equal (mašil, kīma),[16] and has complementary features (he is shorter than Gilgamesh but "stronger of bone"[17]: II, v, 15–17). But for all that, the traditional design of the material is hardly lost from view: it continues to be reflected, even in the late version of the Epic, by the relative apportionment of precedence, power, and narrative prominence among the two friends. Gilgamesh still has greater strength than Enkidu (I, v, 18),[18] is older (VIII, ii, 8–9; X, i, 53–54), and is the one whom the goddess Ishtar desires as a lover (Tablet VI); he remains the protagonist of the story, whereas Enkidu becomes his trusty companion, guide, and protector—almost a mascot, an expensive pet (III, i, 2–12; III, vi, 8–11; III, vi, 21–28 [Old Babylonian version]; cf. VIII, ii, 4–6). The Late Source of Samuel achieves an interesting variation on this theme by differentially distributing secular and sacred preëminence: in the secular order, Jonathan is David's superior, being the king's son and successor, whereas David is an entirely obscure person (an outsider, like Enkidu); in the sacred order, however, David is Jonathan's superior, being God's anointed, whereas Jonathan is the scion of a doomed royal house. Homer achieves a similar effect by making Patroclus, who—being the subordinate member of the relationship—is physically weaker than Achilles (e.g., 11.787, 16.709; cf. 16.140–42, 242–45) and socially subservient to him (11.786; cf. 1.337–47, 9.190–211, 620–21, 11.648–54), the older and wiser of the two and, hence, the one whose job it is to watch over and instruct his unruly comrade (11.787–89). In all three traditions, then, there is some effort to vary the structure, to make it more complex, or to redress the balance of power in the relationship between the friends; nonetheless, a fundamental asymmetry persists. Heroic friendships, then, are not merely dyadic but hierarchical. They exhibit a pattern (familiar to American radio and television audiences of an earlier era from the example of the Lone Ranger and Tonto) of the hero with his side-kick, his faithful retainer, his pal.[19]

Finally, in all three stories the weaker or less favored friend dies. (A Hittite version of Tablet VII, i–ii, makes it plain that Enkidu is singled out—arbitrarily, it would appear—for punishment as a consequence of deeds he performed *jointly* with Gilgamesh.) The subordinate friend is thus the expendable friend, the one whose death paves the way for the principal friend's further adventures. Death is the climax of the friendship, the occasion of the most extreme expressions of tenderness on the part of the two friends, and it weds them forever (in the memory of the survivor, at least). Indeed, it is not too much to say that death is to friendship what marriage is to romance.[20]

So much for structural affinities among the three friendships: they are sufficiently striking to provide a thematic and narratological context (not just a historical one) for further interpretation.[21] Two questions remain. First, what is the meaning attached to friendship in each of these three traditions? Second, what are the terms in which friendship is constructed? I shall attempt to answer both of those questions through a reading of each of the three narratives, taking them up in turn. Because my interpretation of the *Iliad* is intended to be contextual—to be shaped, that is, by reference to the comparative material—I shall treat the two non-Hellenic traditions first.

The Gilgamesh Epic is ultimately an argument for the adequacy of mortal life—and, especially, of civilized life—as the only sort of life truly livable for man.[22] Gilgamesh, a figure larger than life, two thirds god and only one third man (I, ii, 1), chafes against the limits of mortality.[23] He excels in every human accomplishment, having built the inimitable walls of Uruk (I, i, 9–15) and bested all of its inhabitants.[24] Even so, he is not satisfied: explaining to Enkidu his reasons for wishing to slay the monster Huwawa and cut down the Cedar Forest, he says:

> "Who, my friend, can scale he[aven]?
> Only the gods [live] forever under the sun.
> As for mankind, numbered are their days;
> Whatever they achieve is but the wind![25]
> . . . .
> Should I fall, I shall have made me a name:
> 'Gilgamesh'—they will say—'against fierce Huwawa
> Has fallen!' . . .
> A [name] that endures I will make for me!"
> (III, iv, 5–8, 13–15, 25 [Old Babylonian version])

Like Homer's Sarpedon who urged his comrade either to win glory for himself or yield it to others (12.326–28),[26] and like Achilles who had been willing to stake his life on "imperishable fame" (*kleos aphthiton*: 9.413; cf. 1.352–54), Gilgamesh initially is willing to console himself for mortality with the prospect of an immortal name.[27] In this mood of heroic exaltation, he and Enkidu conquer Huwawa and fell the Cedar Forest, challenge Ishtar and kill the Bull of Heaven which she sends to punish them, and finally ride in triumph through the market of Uruk. But then Enkidu dies, and

Gilgamesh's glory apparently ceases to console him; unable to assuage his grief through seven days and seven nights of mourning, Gilgamesh decides to seek immortality instead and, after further adventures, he fails (just barely) to obtain it. He encounters various figures along the way who attempt to dissuade him from his search, among them an ale-wife whose speech (reminiscent of the advice that Thetis offers to Achilles and Achilles later offers to Priam [24.128–31, 524–26, 601–20]) appears to reflect a *topos* in ancient Near Eastern wisdom literature.[28]

> "Gilgamesh, whither rovest thou?
> The life thou pursuest thou shalt not find.
> When the gods created mankind,
> Death for mankind they set aside,
> Life in their own hands retaining.
> Thou, Gilgamesh, let full be thy belly,
> Make thou merry by day and by night.
> Of each day make thou a feast of rejoicing,
> Day and night dance thou and play!
> Let thy garments be sparkling fresh,
> Thy head be washed; bathe thou in water.
> Pay heed to the little one that holds on to thy hand,
> Let a spouse delight in thy bosom!
> For this is the task of [woman]!"
> (X, iii, 1–14 [Old Babylonian version])[29]

The poem closes (in lines that echo its opening lines) with Gilgamesh exhibiting to the boatman who has brought him back from his quest for immortality the majestic ramparts of Uruk (XI, 305–09; cf. I, i, 16–21), thereby expressing a certain pride and contentment in the achievements of civilized life.[30] Our immortal longings are not to be satisfied but deflected onto attainable objects; the life of the human community furnishes us with a substitute for what we desire, not the thing itself but something that will help to console us for its absence.[31]

Enkidu's friendship plays several complementary roles in the larger thematic design of the epic.[32] His promotion from servant to friend[33] accounts for Gilgamesh's unquenchable grief at his loss and motivates the latter to turn "from the pursuit of lasting fame to a literal quest for immortality."[34] The story of Enkidu's origins and acculturation suggests that his alliance with Gilgamesh represents a kind of fusion of nature and culture, uniting the mysterious potency of the wilderness with the hierarchical power of urban civilization;[35] Enkidu's transition from country to city also contributes to the epic's celebration of the advantages of civilized life.[36] Finally, by providing a match for Gilgamesh, Enkidu distracts his friend from oppressing the inhabitants of Uruk and directs his superabundant energies outwards, towards the world, rather than inwards, towards his own community. The pleasure Gilgamesh takes in Enkidu's company anticipates and underwrites the ale-wife's later advice to find meaning through absorption in the minutiae of existence rather than through attempts to transcend it; the human relations that the ale-wife singles out as promising to Gilgamesh the consolatory pleasures of human companionship are relations with a child and a spouse.

It is this last point that helps to account for the particular way that friendship is constructed in the Gilgamesh Epic. Gilgamesh's affection for his friend is described in terms appropriate for relations both with kin and with objects of sexual desire. Enkidu is often called Gilgamesh's "brother" (aḫu).[37] Moreover, Gilgamesh's feeling for Enkidu is explicitly modeled on sexual attraction: in the two dreams that presage the arrival of Enkidu, Gilgamesh takes pleasure in his vision of Enkidu as in a woman (though he does not take such pleasure in Enkidu himself when the latter finally arrives).[38] The crucial phrase occurs only once (in the second dream) in the extant fragments of the Old Babylonian version (i, 33–34),[39] but the Assyrian version picks it up and repeats it relentlessly (I, v, 36, 47; I, vi, 4, 14, 19; cf. VIII, ii, 4–6).[40] The phrase itself has been variously rendered: E. A. Speiser translates, "[I loved it] and was drawn to it as though to a woman,"[41] whereas Jeffrey Tigay prefers, "[I loved it, and lik]e a wife I caressed it."[42] Whatever the exact meaning of the problematic term ḫabābu,[43] its implication is not in doubt: the word that describes Gilgamesh's anticipated attraction to Enkidu is also used to describe Enkidu's anticipated attraction to the prostitute from Uruk, with whom he mates for six days and seven nights (I, iv, 15). When Enkidu dies, moreover, Gilgamesh mourns for him like a widow (literally, "a wailing woman": VIII, ii, 3) and veils his corpse as if it were a bride (VIII, ii, 17).[44] The point of these analogies to kin and objects of sexual desire seems to be that Enkidu's friendship affords Gilgamesh a proleptic taste of the pleasures of human sociality, including marriage and paternity, with which he will be invited to console himself by the ale-wife after Enkidu's death.[45]

The meaning of the friendship between David and Jonathan is entirely dependent on the function that has been attached to it by the Late Source of the Books of Samuel, which is almost solely responsible for recounting it. The Early and Late Sources differ in their attitudes to the kingship and in their estimates of the importance of the priesthood which Samuel represents: the Early Source is distinctly favorable to the kingship, the Late Source hostile to it, regarding it merely as a concession by God to the unwise demands of the people; similarly, the Early Source respects Samuel as a seer and prophet, whereas the Late Source glorifies him as the arbiter of royal power, the conduit of God's favor, and thus the judge or ruler of all Israel. The two Sources differ, therefore, in their portrayal of the passing of the kingship from the house of Saul to the house of David. According to the

Early Source, David first enters Saul's court as a skilled lyre-player who can soothe Saul's periodic bouts of dementia; from that position he rises to become Saul's armor-bearer (1 Samuel 16:14–23). Alternately, David comes to Saul's attention by killing Goliath (17:1–58). In either case, David rises to a position of prominence in Saul's court largely on his own merits, and nothing is said about his eventually becoming king until after Saul and Jonathan die in battle. According to the Late Source, by contrast, God becomes dissatisfied with Saul because Saul fails to carry out to the letter the instructions from God that Samuel had given him; rejecting Saul while Saul is still reigning as king, God sends Samuel to anoint another king from among the sons of Jesse in Bethle-hem (15:1–16:13), and Samuel's act effectively transfers the true kingship to David from Saul during the latter's lifetime. The dramatic tension in the narra-tive ascribed to the Late Source derives from the acute and painful contrast between the secular order of authority, outwardly manifested by the court of Saul, and the sacred order of authority, inwardly expressed by the charismatic appeal of David, the anointed but as yet uncrowned king. That tension be-tween outward appearances (or social power) and inward authority (or per-sonal attractiveness) shapes the story of David's election[46] and is dramatized by Jonathan's love for him.

The friendship between David and Jonathan, as it is depicted by the Late Source, is a sign of the invisible transfer of royal authority from Saul to David. It is crucial to the telling of the story in the Late Source that after David has been anointed by Samuel, everything conspires to advance his fortunes; no more manifest and visible sign of the invisible transformation that has taken place through Samuel's secret intervention could be imagined than that the king's own son should desert the royal court in favor of the very man who is to usurp his place. The dynamics of the friendship express this scenario: it is Jonathan who falls in love with David (18:1–5), who goes out of his way to protect him from Saul (19:1–7), and who voluntarily relinquishes to him the succession to the throne (23:15–18). By contrast, the text is entirely silent on the subject of David's feelings towards Jonathan—whatever sentiments *he* may harbor,* after all, are clearly irrelevant to the story that the Late Source wishes to tell, which is the shifting of God's favor from Saul to David and the role played by Samuel in mediating it. Jonathan's love for David is one marker of this world–historical event, whereas David's response—whatever it may be—is merely an expression of his personal temperament and has little place in the design of the narrative. It is notewor-thy in this context that Jonathan's role had been taken up in the Early Source by Saul's daughter Michal[47]: she is the one who falls in love with David

---

* A source apparently independent of both the Early and the Late Sources testifies to the emotional closeness between the two friends (20:41); David's elegy for Saul and Jonathan also expresses his devotion to them (2 Samuel 1:17–27).

(18:20), marries him in the place of her elder sister Merab who had originally been promised to him (18:17–27), and later protects him from Saul (19:11–17). It seems that the Late Source found that tradition of conjugal love to be insufficiently remarkable, less telling as a symptom of the invisible workings of God's grace, and therefore transferred the role previously played by Saul's daughter to Saul's son, shifting the emphasis from conjugal love to friendship—as if friendship were something less expected, more startling and unusual, and therefore more mysteriously revealing.

Perhaps this strategy of substituting friendship for conjugal love as a motivating force in the narrative was suggested to the Late Source by the invidious comparison that climaxes David's famous lament for Jonathan and Saul, after their deaths in battle: apostrophizing Jonathan, David says, "Your love to me was wonderful, passing the love of women" (2 Samuel 1:26). In context, this much-interpreted remark would seem to mean *not* that David had sexual motives for preferring Jonathan's love to women's but rather that Jonathan's love for David was astonishing because—even *without* a sexual component—it was stronger and more militant than sexual love. Jonathan's love is uncanny, reflecting as it does David's divinely conferred charisma; it makes Jonathan a collaborator in his own effacement. Instead of being David's enemy, his rival for the royal succession, Jonathan becomes, as David calls him in the words of the elegy, "my brother Jonathan" (2 Samuel 1:26). As in the Gilgamesh Epic, so in the Books of Samuel the relationship between the friends is constructed as both fraternal and conjugal.

The friendship between Achilles and Patroclus is constructed out of a number of traditional elements which reflect, no doubt, early stages in the evolution of the legend, just as the asymmetry in the relations between Gilgamesh and Enkidu reflect the Sumerian versions of the story in which Enkidu was Gilgamesh's servant. Thus, the asymmetry in the relations between Achilles and Patroclus has been taken, plausibly enough, by Gregory Nagy to point to the traditional social configuration on which their friendship is modeled—namely, the relation between a hero and his retainer or *therapôn* (which Nagy derives from an earlier Anatolian term for "ritual substitute" and defines as *"alter ego"*);[48] W. Thomas MacCary has noted conventional elements in the relations between Homeric heroes and their charioteers which also seem to parallel the friendship between Achilles and Patroclus.[49] Other traditional elements have been studied by Dale Sinos and by W. M. Clarke, who sees a doublet of the relationship between Achilles and Patroclus in the friendship between Sthenelus and Deïpylus (his "dear companion, whom he honored beyond all others his age, because their hearts were close": 5.325–26).[50] What I take to be new in the version of the *Iliad* that has come down to us is not only the human depth and detail with which the relationship between Achilles and Patroclus is portrayed,[51] but the ways in which their friendship is made to image, as friendship does in both the

Gilgamesh Epic and in the Books of Samuel, the larger bonds of human sociality. For Homer dramatizes the social consequences of Achilles's wrath most poignantly by showing us not only how it disrupts his relations with the other Greek heroes[52] but also how it destroys his community of understanding with Patroclus, who does not share that wrath and cannot fathom Achilles's behavior: Patroclus tells his friend that he has become *amêkhanos* (16.29), while Achilles, in turn, treats Patroclus as someone to whom things must be explained (e.g., 16.80–86, 23.94–96, 24.592–95). Achilles's wrath, in fact, reduces his dearest friend to the emotional predicament of his most hated enemy: that is the point of Homer's use of the same simile at the beginning of Book 9 and Book 16 to convey the states of identical desperation to which Achilles drives Agamemnon and Patroclus alike: both men pour out their tears, Homer tells us (in Lattimore's brilliant rendering of these lines), "like a spring dark-running/that down the face of a rock impassable drips its dim water" (9.14–15, 16.3–4).[53]

Once again, we find that the friendship is parasitic in its conceptualization on kinship relations and on sexual relations. That is, it must borrow terminology and imagery from these other spheres of human relations in order to identify and define itself. Patroclus performs many of the functions for Achilles that a wife or female dependent normally performs in the Homeric world[54]: for example, he places food before Achilles when the two of them are dining alone (19.315–17) and, when they are entertaining guests, it is Patroclus who distributes the bread (9.216–17; cf. 11.624–41)—a function later assumed by Automedon, Achilles's charioteer (24.625–26), who had earlier performed other duties at mealtime (9.209)—whereas Achilles carves and serves the meat; Patroclus also makes up a spare bed for Phoenix when Achilles gives him the nod (9.620–21, 658–59; cf. *Odyssey* 4.296–301, 7.335–40). Similarly, in Phoenix's cautionary tale of Meleager, it is the hero's wife who induces him, after the appeals of his friends have failed, to reënter the fighting and save his community from destruction (9.585–99)—and, thus, she prefigures the role that Patroclus will eventually play in Achilles's tragedy.[55] Moreover, her name, Cleopatra (9.556), is constructed from the same linguistic elements (*kleos, pateres*) as that of Patroclus, only with the order reversed.[56] The conjugal associations, however, work reciprocally: at Patroclus's funeral, Achilles, as chief mourner, cradles the head of his dead comrade (23.136–37), the same gesture that is performed by Andromache at Hector's funeral (24.724). So each, in a sense, is wife to each.

The analogy from kinship performs a role in the *Iliad* similar to that performed by the analogy from sexual love in the Books of Samuel: Apollo is astonished by Achilles's love for Patroclus because it surpasses in its intensity, he says (24.44–52),[57] not the love of women but the love that most men bear towards a brother or a son (and Achilles himself acknowledges this: 19.321–27). Moreover, Homer's use of kinship associations—like his use of conjugal associations—emphasizes the reciprocal character of *philia*: Patroclus's dependency on Achilles is child-like, as Achilles has the dubious taste to point out to him in the famous simile at the beginning of Book 16 (7–11); the poet also compares Achilles at the funeral of Patroclus to a lion mourning for the loss of his cubs (18.316–23)[58] as well as to a father bewailing the death of his son (23.222–25). At the same time, however, Patroclus is older and wiser than Achilles and he has been appointed by his own father to act as Achilles's mentor. Finally, the two men will be buried together (23.82–92, 126, 245–48), as if they were members of the same family (23.84), equal in death.[59]

The strategies employed by Homer in constructing the friendship of Achilles and Patroclus thus recall similar strategies employed to similar ends in two roughly contemporary sources from non-Hellenic cultures to the East. In all three cases, the creators of the legends appeal to conjugal relations and to kinship relations in order to define, to make familiar, and to situate (both socially and emotionally) the central friendship they wish to explore; more specifically, they appeal to these other, better established and codified sorts of human relations in order to make the friendship between the main characters into an image of sociality, of human solidarity. Sociality has, to be sure, quite different and distinctive associations in each of the three traditions, as we have seen, but we find it constructed in each literary composition out of the same, rather limited, repertory of indigenous signifiers*—namely, kinship and conjugality.

In each of these narrative traditions, the friendship between the heroes appears to be an element that is crystallized relatively late in the process of formation of the transmitted texts.[60] Perhaps the impulse to explore and to fix more precisely the social meaning of friendship reflects a common desire, on the part of the interconnected cultures of the eastern Mediterranean around the turn of the first millennium, to claim and to colonize a larger share of public discourse, of cultural space, for the play of male subjectivity. At any rate, the erotics of male comradeship come to occupy a more prominent place in the collective imagination of these various cultures, and representations of heroic friendship come to circulate more freely throughout them. Those representations, moreover, all seem to exhibit a similar paradox: although their textual strategies make kinship and conjugality into privileged loci of signification for representing friendship, they also make friendship into a paradigm case of human sociality. They invoke kinship and conjugality, in other words, only to displace them, to reduce them to mere *images* of friendship.[61] This dialectic will ultimately prove to have had pregnant implications for the later history of the representation of the

---

* Our means of representing friendship remain limited: E. M. Forster's novel, *The Longest Journey*, with which I began, bears the dedication *Fratribus*.

relations between family and community, between *oikos* and *polis*, in Greek culture: in Plato's *Republic*, for example, the utopian effort to unite all the citizens of the just city in the bonds of fraternal love[62] effectively does away with the social significance of real brothers and sisters, of both kinship and conjugality, altogether. Having begun by borrowing its social significance and representational elements from kinship and conjugality, in other words, male *philia* ends up (in Plato's fantasy, at least) displacing them entirely. This development completes, though in a startling and unexpected fashion, a trend already visible in earlier literary constructions of friendship.

The final point I wish to make has to do with the cultural specificity of the erotic experience represented in these early texts. The high pitch of feeling evident in the relation between Achilles and Patroclus has led scholars to argue interminably about whether their romance was a sexual as well as a comradely one[63]—despite Homer's failure to describe any sexual contact between them. The question has been further complicated by the testimony of the classical Greeks, who, looking at the love of Achilles and Patroclus from the perspective of their own social and emotional institutions, tended naturally to assume that the relation between the heroes was a paederastic one.[64] According to the Attic orator Aeschines, for example, Homer did not bother to describe the love-affair more explicitly because "he considered that the extraordinary degree of their good will towards one another would be self-explanatory to those among the audience who were cultivated people" (1.142; generally, 1.132–33, 141–50).

But if later Greeks could agree (and they could not all agree)[65] that Achilles and Patroclus were a paederastic couple, they had more difficulty deciding who played which role in the relationship.[66] In his lost trilogy, the *Achilleis*—notorious even in antiquity for the erotic explicitness with which, in two of its surviving fragments, Achilles eulogizes the thighs and kisses of Patroclus (frr. 135, 136 [Radt])—the tragic poet Aeschylus made Achilles the lover and Patroclus the beloved. That was no more than what was consistent with the differential distribution of power in the relationship for, as we have seen, Achilles had both personal and narratological precedence over his comrade: to Aeschylus's mind, it was obvious that Achilles must have been on top in other respects as well (classical Greek paederasty, after all, tended to assimilate social and sexual roles). But Aeschylus's interpretation did not square with other details in Homer's narrative, as Phaedrus takes care to point out in Plato's *Symposium*: "Aeschylus talks nonsense when he claims that Achilles was in love with Patroclus, for Achilles was more beautiful not only than Patroclus but than all the other heroes, and he was still beardless, and furthermore he was much younger than Patroclus, as Homer says" (180a4–7).

Modern readers may reasonably feel amused at the difficulties the classical Greeks confronted when trying to map their own sexual categories onto the Homeric texts and onto the erotic and emotional patterns contained in them.

But those difficulties remain instructive for us as well. They demonstrate, in the first place, the extent to which shifts in the articulation of social and sexual catgories (even within the "same" culture) can cause literary classics to escape the critical grasp of the very interpretative communities responsible for canonizing them. So long as we, too, continue to read the *Iliad* in the light of later Greek culture—to say nothing of modern sexual categories— we shall continue to have trouble bringing the friendship between Achilles and Patroclus into sharper focus. The thrust of my analysis has been to remove that relationship from the classical Greek context, to which it does not properly belong, and to insert it instead into the context of an earlier narrative pattern, known largely from surviving Near Eastern texts, concerning heroes and their pals. Rather than viewing heroic comradeship as the origin of "Greek love," that is, I view it as the final playing-out, in the Greek epic, of an earlier narrative tradition. Once we situate Achilles and Patroclus in their rightful context, the lineaments of their relationship will come into clearer view, and we shall be able to interpret the erotics of their friendship in terms that do not have to be borrowed from the sexual categories of later ages (including our own). And then modern inquiries into "homosexuality" in Homer, like classical Greek inquiries into the respective erotic roles of Achilles and Patroclus, may prove at last to be genuinely enlightening—not for what they reveal about the ancient heroes, but for what they tell us about those shadowy folk whom the heroes themselves simply describe as "those who are yet to be."[67]

5

The Democratic Body: Prostitution and Citizenship in Classical Athens

> "You see these people here, the ones who occupy the brothels and admittedly practise that activity—well, even they, whenever it happens that they are driven to it by need, nevertheless make some attempt to shield themselves from disgrace and shut their doors. Now if someone were to ask you, as you were walking along the street, what such a person was doing at that moment, you would immediately name the deed, without seeing what was going on and without knowing who it was who had gone inside, but since you know for a fact what the person's chosen trade is, you know perfectly well what that person is doing" (Aeschines, 1.74).

This passage from a speech ("Against Timarchus") delivered by the Attic orator Aeschines in 346/5 B.C. holds a number of surprises in store for the modern student of ancient Greek prostitution.[1] First of all, both the prostitute and the hypothetical client postulated by Aeschines are male. That the *client* is male may occasion relatively little astonishment: prostitution then, as now, catered almost exclusively to men.[2] The sex of the *prostitute*, however, is perhaps more unexpected; in fact, prostitution in classical Athens routinely engaged young men and "boys" (i.e., adolescent males) as well as women of various ages.[3]

Youth seems to have been a more stringent requirement for male than for female prostitutes. A late antique text, unusual only in its explicitness about the fine points of male sexual taste in the ancient Greek world, may help to explain why. It portrays a debate between two men over the respective merits of women and boys as objects of love, and in the course of that debate the partisan of women advances an argument whose specific claims go unopposed by the advocate of paederasty: "from maidenhood to middle age, before the time when the last wrinkles of old age finally spread over her face, a woman is a pleasant armful to embrace," whereas by the age of twenty a boy is already ceasing to be desirable, "for then the limbs, being large and manly, are hard, the chins that once were soft are rough and covered with bristles, and the well-developed thighs are as it were sullied with hairs."[4] Each detail in this description of over-ripe boyhood is intended to produce revulsion and disgust. In particular, Greek men seem to have regarded the presence of hair upon the cheeks, thighs, and hindquarters of maturing youths with intense sexual distaste[5] (the Stoics, who are supposed to have deemed it permissible for men to maintain erotic relationships with boys until the latter reached the scandalously advanced age of twenty-eight, managed to stomach such liaisons—in the imagination of one late antique writer—only by requiring their boyfriends to shave both chin and rump).[6] Because in antiquity the sexual tastes of adult males determined the dimen-

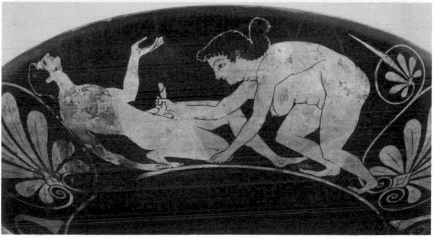

Women of a mature age shown functioning as prostitutes. The vase-painter seems to have taken pains, in his depiction of the women's faces, flesh, and musculature, to indicate that they are no longer in their first youth. (The J. Paul Getty Museum, Phintias, Attic Red-Figure Kylix, ca. 510 B.C., terracotta, height: 12.6 cm.; width: 39.1 cm.; diameter: 30.8 cm. 80.AE.31)

sions of the sexual market, youth (or youthful appearance, at any rate) was an essential attribute for male prostitutes.

Youthfulness in women, to be sure, was also prized for its sexual appeal to adult men. Ancient authors preserve no lack of malicious gossip about the miserable and impoverished old age of once-glamorous courtesans who, half-starved and unable to command high prices, can no longer afford to be choosy about their dwindling customers,[7] and many ancient texts describe the elaborate artifices—ranging from wigs[8] to hair-dye[9] to elevator heels[10] to a facial powder made from white lead[11]—by which female prostitutes as well as other women typically attempt to conceal their age and to disguise assorted physical shortcomings.[12] But mature age did not necessarily prohibit a woman from earning a living as a prostitute: male tastes varied[13] (two Hellenistic epigrams portray female prostitutes dedicating, severally, a purple horsewhip, reins, and a golden spur to Aphrodite),[14] and they seem to have included a liking for older women.[15] As one might expect, then, a sexual market for mature women is indeed attested in ancient sources (or, at least, it is treated by them as a plausible possibility).[16] Males, by contrast, were desirable to other males only between the onset of puberty and the arrival of the beard.[17] In particular, the *hôra* (or youthful "prime") of males— a slender zone between boyhood and manhood comprising what we now call late adolescence and corresponding roughly to the life-stage of American undergraduates—represented the peak of a male's sexual attractiveness and exercised, while it lasted, an apparently irresistible charm on older residents of classical Athens, both male and female,[18] free and slave. Once the frontier between youth and manhood had been crossed, however, a male became visibly *exôros* ("past his prime")[19]—as many an ancient lover remarks with alternating bitterness and relief[20]—and, in Aeschines's words, "no one will give him anything for it any more" (1.95). An older male who wished, for whatever reason, to attract either men or women had to do his best to look young,[21] and any adult male who actually did (or, what was worse, tried to) look younger than his years was liable to be suspected of pathic desires[22] or adulterous intentions.[23] Male prostitution in classical Athens was largely the province of those below the age of majority.[24]

Aeschines reveals, further, that male prostitution in Athens was not an especially clandestine or disreputable affair. To *be* a prostitute was hardly a noble vocation for a male, but to *hire* one did not cover you with shame. The very nonchalance with which the orator invites his audience to picture a male brothel implies that such an establishment was a fairly familiar and recognizable feature of the urban landscape. And it apparently conducted its business openly, unprotected from the knowing gaze of passers-by. (Both male and female prostitution must have been legal, for the city of Athens collected a special tax from the earnings of male and female prostitutes alike.)[25] Aeschines cannot risk offending the moral sensibilities of his audience, for fear of losing his suit, so he must be convinced that his listeners will not consider themselves insulted by the sort of conversancy with the world of male brothels that he imputes to them—as they well might if any stigma attached to patronizing such establishments or if male prostitution flourished only in the margins of Athenian society, away from the eyes of respectable people, and were confined to a hidden world of vice whose access was restricted to initiates by means of secret signs and code-words. But that does not appear to have been the case. The elderly Plato might dream of a society in which all non-marital sex would be attended with such infamy (and, hence, with such a fear of discovery) that it would be driven wholly underground, but even he acknowledges that the society of his imagination would be so different from the one he currently inhabits as to be virtually unrealizable in practice (*Laws* 838–841).[26]

Particular districts of Athens may have been especially favored by male prostitutes: in his play *The Mede*, produced c. 369–8 B.C., the comic poet Theopompus singles out the Lycabettus hill, a desolate region (still in use today for erotic assignations), as a locale where "lads gratify their age-mates" (fr. 29). Indeed, parks and other unfrequented places generally afforded those too young, too poor, or too independent to work out of a house a secluded spot in which to sell themselves or simply to meet their lovers[27] (sex, for the Greeks, required a degree of privacy).[28] The Peiraeus (the port of Athens) and the Ceramicus (the Potters' Quarter) also teemed with brothels of every sort.[29] But prostitutes do not seem to have lodged only in special ghettoes where citizens with no interest in patronizing them would never stumble upon them. On the contrary, prostitution (both male and female) seems rather to have been an ordinary feature of daily life in classical Athens.[30]

The apparent extent, visibility, and ordinariness of male prostitution in classical Athenian society combine to argue—and here, perhaps, is the final surprise afforded by our passage from Aeschines—for the ubiquity of paederasty.[31] The male desire for sexual contact with handsome youths was evidently not confined, as is sometimes alleged,[32] to a tiny, eccentric, and supposedly pro-Spartan aristocracy at Athens, nor was it the exclusive property of a handful of articulate and prolific intellectuals (although in later antiquity it did come to be closely identified with Socraticism).[33] Male prostitution apparently supported, and was in turn supported by, a broadly based paederastic constituency (the precise contours of which, however, are now impossible to determine); the explicitly sexual ends and mercenary means favored by the members of that constituency distinguished them in tone, but not in substance, from the romantic, conspicuously high-minded, and tirelessly self-promoting admirers of the Athenian *jeunesse dorée* who are celebrated in the writings of Plato and other Socratics[34] and who are defended—with some embarrassment, to be sure—as would-be educators of Athenian youth by the more chauvinistic classical handbooks. But paedagogy was not, even among the honorable members of that *beau monde*, the essence of paederasty. Despite modern appearance-saving claims to the contrary, the erotic excitement and bittersweet longing aroused in Athenian men (whether low- or high-minded) by attractive boys do not seem to have been primarily of a philosophic nature[35] and, when frustrated, obviously required something other than a purely Platonic means of expression.

Frustration must indeed have been a frequent experience. It was extremely difficult and hazardous for a male resident of Athens in the classical period to gain sexual access to any person of citizen status. The female relations of Athenian citizens, as well as their male and female slaves, were protected from sexual assault by the laws against *bia* ("violence")[36] and *hybris* ("outrage" or "infliction of shame");[37] free Athenian women were also shielded from the advances of a would-be seducer by the laws against *moikheia*, which was a more serious crime than rape.[38] *Moikheia*, a concept similar to that of "adultery" (by which the word is often translated) but considerably broader in scope, signified consenting but unauthorized sex with any female under the legal guardianship of a citizen—which is to say any woman of citizen status who was not herself a prostitute[39] (Athenian women were life-long statutory minors and were therefore *always* in the legal custody of a male relation).[40] Citizen women were also protected by the social custom of secluding them, to the greatest extent possible, in the interior, domestic space of the Greek household and of keeping a close watch on their activities and movements (the seclusion of women was more likely to have been an upper-class ideal than a social reality, however). A man caught by a citizen in the act of having sex with the latter's wife, mother, sister, daughter, or concubine kept "with a view to free children" (*ep' eleutherois paisin*) might be put to death on the spot with impunity,[41] according to the old (Draconian?) law that defined the grounds of justifiable homicide.[42] An apprehended seducer also faced a number of other heavy penalties, some of them exquisitely humiliating and unpleasant.[43] *Moikheia* was thus a high-risk venture—glamorous, to be sure, if one could get away with it, but imprudent in the best of circumstances. Contemporary moralists, both philosophers and comic poets, agreed that (female) prostitution offered the potential seducer a preferable alternative. In his comedy *The Pentathlete*, produced sometime in the middle or latter part of the fourth century B.C., Xenarchus made this point memorably (fr. 4):

> Terrible, terrible, and utterly intolerable, are the practices of the young men in our city—here, where there are, after all, very good-looking young things in the whore-houses, whom one can readily see basking in the sun, their breasts uncovered, stripped for action and drawn up in battle-formation by columns,[44] from among whom one can select whatever sort one likes—thin, fat, squat, tall, shrivelled, young, old, middle-aged, fully-ripened—without setting up a ladder

and stealthily entering [another man's house to seduce his women], or slipping through the smoke-hole in the roof, or getting oneself carried inside by trickery in a heap of chaff. For the girls themselves grab people and drag them in, naming those who are old men "little father," those who are younger, "little bro." And each of them can be had without fear, affordably, by day, towards evening, in every way you like. But as for those women [i.e., respectable women] whom one either can't see or can't see clearly when one looks at them, because one is always in a state of trembling and fear, frightened and carrying one's life in one's hands—how on earth can men fuck them, Lady Mistress Aphrodite, whenever, in the midst of humping, men remember the laws of Draco?

Thus spoke the voice of common sense.[45]*

Citizen youths were likewise protected from sexual assault by the laws against *bia* and *hybris*,[46] but the preservation of their sexual integrity had to proceed by a different set of legal and social strategies. That was partly because they could not be sexually impregnated, and so what happened to them had fewer immediate consequences for the integrity of their families as well as for the eventual transmission of property and ancestral identity within the family; it was also because they moved freely in the exterior realm of public space, inhabited by men, to which different rules had to be applied.[47] An elaborate system of laws and social customs accordingly restricted sexual access to the young males of citizen families, preventing slaves from courting free boys,[48] insulating citizen youths from the sexual overtures of their fathers' friends,[49] protecting students and athletes from abuse by their teachers and trainers, regulating access to schoolrooms and gymnasia, and thwarting encounters between youths and their male elders before dawn, after dark, and in the absence of third parties.[50]

Whereas unauthorized sexual contact with a woman of citizen status was always potentially a serious crime, sexual contact with a citizen youth did not necessarily require the consent of his guardian and was, at least in principle, obtainable.[51] But numerous obstacles remained. The paederastic ethos of classical Athens denied the junior member of a male couple a share in the *erôs* (or "sexual passion") assumed to animate his older lover: the youth was expected to submit—if, that is, he chose to submit at all—to the enflamed desire of his suitor solely out of a feeling of mingled esteem, gratitude, and affection (or *philia*).[52] A youth therefore did not have (or so it was thought) the sexual motive that women supposedly had to yield to

---

* To the Athenian way of thinking, of course, it would be much better for young men to master their desires rather than to expend the ancestral wealth of their households on prostitutes—and anyone so enslaved to his own desires as to need to frequent the brothels was clearly a man of no account in the eyes of other members of the propertied classes (see Dover [1973], 63–65)—but by the same calculus it was more prudent to betake oneself to prostitutes than to engage in adultery.

the entreaties of a male lover; furthermore, it was disgraceful for him to appear to be too easily seduced.[53] Thus, he had to be won by an elaborate ritual of courtship, which could be lengthy, arduous, highly competitive (good-looking young men were celebrated for their beauty),[54] and possibly quite expensive. Those who could not or would not lavish the requisite time and effort on such demanding affairs but who sought sexual contact with boys and young men could find in male prostitutes a more ready, if less edifying, outlet for their sexual *prohairesis* (or "preference," as Aeschines, 1.195, calls it).

The most telling evidence for the complete integration of male prostitution into the very structures of classical Athenian life also comes from the speech of Aeschines quoted at the outset. But it does not come from anything Aeschines says. Rather, it derives from the occasion of his speech, from the fact that it was written to be delivered at a *trial*: the evidence is furnished, in other words, by the speech's unarticulated social/political/juridical/sexual context. Aeschines's purpose in going to court is to parry the prior attack of Timarchus, a political enemy, who had indicted Aeschines on a charge of betraying the interests of Athens to a foreign power; Aeschines's method is to accuse Timarchus of having prostituted himself in his youth. In order to understand Aeschines's strategy, to grasp how his accusation could function as a defensive tactic against an essentially *political* charge, it will be necessary to elucidate the legal status of male prostitution as well as its social and symbolic significance in the world of classical Athens.

Any Athenian male of citizen status whose body had at any time been hired out to anyone for sexual use forfeited, by virtue of that very transaction, his entitlement as a citizen to take part in the civic and religious life of Athens.[55] If, therefore, Aeschines's prosecution of Timarchus proves to be successful (which in fact it did), Timarchus will suffer, at the very least, formal *atimía*—loss of status, or "disenfranchisement": that is, exclusion from the privileges of Athenian public life—including, not coincidentally, the privilege of being able to bring a charge of treason against Aeschines.[56] The crime of which Timarchus stands accused is not, however, prostitution. It was not illegal (in the sense of being an actionable offense) for an Athenian citizen or for a youth of citizen status to prostitute himself. To be sure, insofar as prostitution disqualified an Athenian male from sharing in the democratic rule of the city and brought with it automatically (in theory, at least) the penalty of *atimía*,[57] it was not exactly legal either: by disenfranchising citizens who engaged in prostitution Athenian law provided a substantial deterrent against it, especially for wealthier citizens or for those who might intend to be politically active and who could therefore expect their personal credentials to be under constant attack (legal and paralegal) by their enemies. Moreover, any guardian who prostituted a boy in his charge, any person who enticed a youth of citizen status into prostitution by offering him money for sexual favors, and anyone who acted as a procurer for an Athenian youth was thought to have ruined the boy and to have "defrauded [*aposterein*] him of the city"—to have deprived him, that is, of his share in the community and his right to participate in its affairs;[58] the person who caused an Athenian to prostitute himself therefore incurred grave penalties (including death, in the case of procurers).[59] But once an Athenian had established himself as a prostitute, neither he nor his patrons faced any legal charges.[60] What Timarchus is accused of, then, is exercising his citizen privileges of speaking before the people in the public assembly and proposing laws and foreign policy there *after* having been, in his youth, a prostitute; the purpose of the trial is to establish Timarchus's identity as a prostitute, to strip him of his civil rights, and to bar him from prosecuting his suit against Aeschines. Once an Athenian had forfeited his citizen rights on grounds of having been a prostitute, it was a capital crime to exercise those rights,[61] and the same law applied to anyone who had forfeited his rights by failing to pay what he owed to the state,[62] by having beaten or omitted to support his parents, shirked his military duties or thrown away his shield (i.e., fled ignominiously from the field of battle), or wasted his patrimony through extravagant living or neglect of his estate—all acts that implied a shameful failure to fulfill one's obligation to the community under the pressure of economic or physical hardship.[63]

How exactly does prostitution fit into this scheme? A recent commentator, after surveying the entire range of offenses punishable by *atimía* (or loss of status) in classical Athens, a range of offenses that was even broader than I have indicated here, concludes that "*atimía* was the penalty *par excellence* which an Athenian might incur in his capacity of a citizen [*sic*], but not for offenses he had committed as a private individual."[64] But that understanding of *atimía* renders obscure the peculiar appropriateness of *atimía* as a penalty for prostitution. For if *atimía* actually was—as it seems indeed to have been— a punishment for civic rather than for private offenses, then according to what conception of prostitution would prostitution qualify for that penalty? The very inclusion of (male) prostitution in the category of offenses punishable by *atimía*, in other words, would seem to define prostitution implicitly as a betrayal of communal solidarity, and thus to blur the distinction between civic and private offenses on which the foregoing interpretation of the meaning of *atimía* depends. For what could be more "private" and less "civic" than sex?

The logic behind the conceptualization of prostitution as a dereliction of *civic* duty and behind the consequent disenfranchisement of citizen prostitutes emerges most clearly from an analysis of the democratic ideology of the Athenian state and of the cultural poetics of manhood which that ideology at once took for granted and actively mobilized in its support. One of the first tasks of the radical democrats at Athens, who brought into being a form of government based (in theory at least) on universal male suffrage, was to enable every citizen to participate *on equal terms* in the corporate body of the community and to share in its rule. The transition to a radical democracy therefore required a series of measures designed to uphold the dignity and autonomy—the social viability, in short—of every (male) citizen, whatever his economic circumstances. Economic disparities could not, of course, be eliminated, nor were serious efforts made to eliminate them. But a limit could be set to the political and social consequences of such inequities, a zone marked out where their influence might not extend. The body of the male citizen constituted that zone.

At the boundaries of a citizen's body the operation of almost all social and economic power halted.[65] One of the earliest constitutional regulations of the emerging democracy stipulated that a citizen could not be enslaved for debt (although he still might be temporarily disenfranchised),[66] which is to say that his body could not become the target of economic, physical, or sexual violence.[67] Nor could a citizen be tortured to produce evidence in a court of law, as slaves and foreigners might be: his body was thus exempt as well from judicial violence.[68] The very body of a citizen was sacrosanct; foreigners and slaves, once again, might be manhandled in various ways, but a citizen might not (except under certain exceptional circumstances, such as that of being apprehended in the act of committing *moikheia*). Freedom from servility, exemption from torture, and corporeal inviolability were markers that distinguished citizens from slaves and from foreign residents in Athens. To violate the bodily sanctity of a citizen by treating him as one would a slave, by manhandling him, or even by placing a hand on his body without his consent was not only to insult him personally but to assault the corporate integrity of the citizen body as a whole and to offend its fiercely egalitarian spirit.[69] It was an act of *hybris*, or "outrage," which signified the violation of a status distinction, the attempted reduction of a person to a status below the one he actually occupied ("using free men as slaves," Demosthenes loosely but vividly defined it [21.180–81]).[70] *Hybris* was thus the anti-democratic crime *par excellence*, and it called down upon the offender the full wrath of the democratic judicial system.

Prostitution can be spoken of, especially in the case of males, as hiring oneself out "for *hybris*" (*eph' hybrei*)—meaning, "for other people to treat as they please," to use one's body for the purposes of their own pleasure.[71] It was understood, for example, that a man went to prostitutes partly in order to enjoy sexual pleasures that were thought degrading to the person who provided them and that he could not therefore easily obtain from his wife or boyfriend[72] (insertive oral sex, for instance).[73] The liability to be subjected to degrading sexual acts made prostitutes impure in the Athenian imagination—hence, unfit to perform sacred duties on behalf of the city[74]—and, similarly, the length of time required for a man to purify himself ritually after sexual contact with a prostitute was, at least in some places throughout the ancient Greek world, longer than the period required for purification after intercourse with a wife.[75] For a free male, then, to be a prostitute was equivalent to choosing to be the victim of what would have been, had one's surrender not been voluntary, *hybris*. As K. J. Dover puts it,

> There seems little doubt that in Greek eyes the male who breaks the 'rules' of legitimate eros detaches himself from the ranks of male citizenry and classifies himself with women and foreigners; the prostitute is assumed to have broken the rules simply because his economic dependence on clients forces him to do what they want him to do; and conversely, any male believed to have done whatever his senior homosexual partner(s) wanted him to do is assumed to have prostituted himself. . . . It is not only by assimilating himself to a woman in the sexual act that the submissive male rejects his role as a male citizen, but also by deliberately choosing to be the victim of what would be, if the victim were unwilling, hubris [= *hybris*]. The point of the fierce sanctions imposed by Attic law on hubris was that the perpetrator 'dishonoured' (*atîmazein*) his victim, depriving him of his standing as a citizen under the law, and standing could be recovered only by indictment which in effect called upon the community to reverse the situation and put down the perpetrator. To choose to be treated as an object at the disposal of another citizen was to resign one's own standing as a citizen [i.e., to embrace *atimía* of one's own accord].[76]

Because the classical Athenians, in other words, tended *both* to construct social and sexual roles hierarchically *and* to collapse the distinctions between them, associating sexual penetration and phallic pleasure alike with social domination,[77] any citizen male who became a prostitute positioned himself in a socially subordinate relation to his fellow citizens: he lost his equal footing with them and joined instead the ranks of women, foreigners, and slaves—those whose very bodies, receptive by definition to the administrative or pleasure-seeking projects of the masculine and the powerful, acknowledged the citizens of Athens as their rightful masters. For a male of citizen status, then, prostitution signified a refusal of the constitutional safeguards of his bodily integrity provided by the Athenian democracy; it represented a forfeiture of his birthright as an Athenian to share on an equal basis with his fellow-citizens in the government of the city. To be a prostitute meant, in effect, to surrender one's phallus—to discard the marker of one's socio-sexual precedence—and so it was, next to enslavement, the worst degradation a citizen could suffer, equivalent to voluntary effeminization.

Anyone who prostituted himself, whether out of economic necessity or greed (sexual desire is never mentioned as a possible motive),[78] indicated by that gesture that his autonomy was for sale to whoever wished to buy it.[79] The city as a collective entity was supposedly vulnerable in the person of such a citizen—vulnerable to penetration by foreign influence or to corruption by private enterprise. No person who prostituted himself could be allowed to speak before the people in the public assembly because his words might not be his own; he might have been hired to say them by someone else, someone whose interests did not coincide with those of Athens, or he might simply want to bring about a political change that would advance his private interests at the expense of the public good[80]—servility and greed evidently being the dominant features of his personality.* The acceptance of money for sexual favors violated the ideal of self-sufficiency which, paradoxically enough, constituted the basis of mutual trust among members of the citizen collective, who had to assume that their common interests as full and equal sharers in the privileges of democracy guaranteed their common purpose in advancing the welfare of the city, even when they disagreed with one another. But a prostitute gave up those interests. He showed a willingness to serve (in the worst way) the pleasure, the interests of his client; he proved himself the instrument of another person's pleasure, or the slave of his own straitened circumstances[81] or luxurious tastes, and he thereby demonstrated that he had ceased to be an autonomous actor in his own right. Such a person threatened the coherence of democracy from within and had to be disenfranchised.

The institution of the democracy at Athens brought with it, then, the social production and distribution to the citizens of a new kind of body—a free, autonomous, and inviolable body undifferentiated by distinctions[82] of wealth, class, or status: a democratic body, the site and guarantee of personal and political independence. That, of course, was the ideal; the reality of economic hardship and social dependency was quite different,[83] and the poor often found themselves performing the sorts of menial duties routinely assigned to slaves—and therefore being assimilated to slaves in the estimate of their more fortunate neighbors.[84] But the *reality* of economic and social life was not in every case the point of the democratic reforms: the democracy was not expected to function perfectly or to extend its benefits indifferently to everyone in practice. In the fourth century B.C. the Attic orator Demosthenes specifically denied that Solon (an early-sixth-century law-giver who by the time of Demosthenes had turned into a kind of "author function" attached to the democratic constitution of Athens as a whole)[85] had intended his legislation to prevent citizens from engaging in prostitution altogether. According to Demosthenes, Solon did not wish to "check" or "punish" (*kolazein*) male prostitutes—had he wished to do so, he could have imposed a variety of harsher penalties—but to prevent them from going into politics, where they might do some real damage; Solon did not, allegedly, consider the law he enacted a "heavy" law (by which Demosthenes seems to mean a

---

* Hence the habit of attacking the honesty of politicians by comparing them to or connecting them with prostitutes: see Henry, 13–16, 19–24, 29, on the evidence from Old Comedy.

law that would impose an economic burden on the vast majority of the citizens, including those already so poor as to have scant means of earning a livelihood), because it hardly affected anyone: "for Solon saw that most of you, though you have the right to speak [in the public assembly], do not speak" (22.30).* Apart from safeguarding the political arena from potential oligarchs, then, the goal of the democratic legislation was not practical or moral but symbolic: it was designed not to alter the facts of Athenian social life or to reform individual Athenians but to disseminate among the citizens of Athens a new collective self-understanding, an image of themselves as free and autonomous and equal participants in the shared rule of the city precisely insofar as they were all (rich and poor alike)—*in principle*, at least—equally lords over their own bodies.

That ideological face-saving strategy was a vitally important one. Because distinctions of status in classical Athens, as we have seen, tended to be congruent with sexual roles, the poorer citizens were liable to find themselves degraded by economic dependency, by the social fact of being at the beck and call of their wealthier compatriots; thus deprived of their autonomy, assertiveness, and freedom of action—of their masculine dignity, in short—they were in danger of being assimilated not only to slaves but to prostitutes,[86] and so ultimately to women: they were at risk of being effeminized by poverty. The merest suggestion to that effect, of course, would have been shockingly hybristic, and we do not find it expressed outright in our sources, but a sensitivity to this issue can be discerned in the extreme care with which the Athenians differentiated honorable and dishonorable forms of sexual relations between citizen males (so as to uphold the masculine dignity of the subordinate partner);[87] it can also be discerned in the public image of aggressive masculinity represented by the citizen-soldier (or "hoplite"), an image cultivated by the upper strata of classical Athenian society ostensibly on behalf of everyone.[88] A submerged association between poverty and effeminacy must have remained a significant element in the collective political unconscious of Athenian culture, and it was precisely such an association that the democratic legislation was designed to repress. By constructing corporeal sovereignty as the principal, if not the sole, political means of recuperating whatever other losses to his dignity a citizen of Athens might unavoidably suffer through enforced social or economic dependency, the democratic constitution made it the ultimate line of defense of every citizen's social and political integrity.

In another sense, however, prostitution at Athens—far from being democ-

---

* In this sense, the disenfranchisement of prostitutes might be read as a covert property qualification for active citizenship: those Athenians so desperately impoverished as to be easily taken for prostitutes were debarred, in effect, from exercising the more coveted privileges of citizenship.

racy's invisible and guilty secret—was its visible and proud creation. But now it is a question not of male but of female prostitution; now we confront a different sort of democratic body. Among the reforms credited in the classical period to Solon, the titular architect of Athenian democracy, is the institution of (state?) brothels, staffed by slave women at a price that put them within the reach of all the citizens. Solon, we are told, purchased slave women and established them in houses for public enjoyment.[89] The assumption underlying this "Solonian" reform would seem to have been that a society is not democratic so long as sexual pleasure remains the exclusive perquisite of the well-to-do.[90] At any rate, it was on this score that Solon earned the gratitude of a nameless character in *The Brothers* by the late-fourth/early-third century B.C. comic poet Philemon (fr. 4): the speaker is evidently one of the young men rescued from "erotic necessity"[91] by Solon's leveling of sexual inequities.

> But you found a law for the use of everyone; for you were the first, Solon, they say, to discover this practice—a democratic one, by Zeus, and a saving one (I should know, Solon!): seeing the city full of young men and seeing them under the compulsion of nature misbehaving in ways they should not, you bought and stationed women in various public locations, equipped and fitted out as common possessions for all. They stand there naked, so you won't be fooled: what you see is what you get. You don't happen to feel quite yourself; you have something bothering you: how so? The door is wide open. One obol, and in you hop. There isn't a bit of prudishness or nonsense, and she doesn't shy away from you, but goes straight to it, just as you like and in whatever way you like. You come out: tell her to go to hell, she's nothing to do with you.[92]

In this way, by insuring that there would always be a category of persons for every citizen to dominate, both socially and sexually, Solon underwrote the manhood of the Athenian citizen body. And, to commemorate his achievement, Solon went on to found, with the proceeds from the brothels he had established, the temple of Aphrodite Pandemos, "Aphrodite of the entire people,"[93] a cult whose very name seems designed to drive home Solon's democratic message: sexual pleasure belongs to all the citizens.

There are, of course, good reasons for doubting the literal truth of this whole story. The earliest extant documents in which it appears date to about three hundred years after the reforms of Solon; those documents are the products of highly imaginative (not to say untrustworthy) authors, and competing explanations for the establishment of the cult of Aphrodite Pandemos are available elsewhere (see Appendix 1). It would be highly imprudent to conclude on the basis of the ancient evidence that Solon himself actually introduced state prostitution to Athens in the early part of the sixth century B.C. as part of his package of constitutional reforms. For our purposes, however, what is important is not the literal truth or falsity of the story but the fact that it could be publicly told in classical Athens; even more important is the understanding of the relation between prostitution and democracy which it expresses. Although it may offer no reliable testimony about the historical achievement of Solon, in other words, the story told by Philemon does offer possible insight into the codes of social and sexual life in classical Athens: it shows that at least *some* people in classical Athens could look on prostitution as an intrinsic element of the democracy (for that is what the ascription of this sexual reform to Solon signifies). And, similarly, if the account of Solon's financing of the cult of Aphrodite Pandemos ultimately proves to be improbable, we should not dismiss it before observing that the interpretation of *pandêmos* implicit in it reflects at least one of the demonstrable meanings associated with Aphrodite's cult epithet in fourth-century Athens.[94] Whether or not classical Athens actually maintained prostitutes, housed in state brothels at artificially depressed prices in order to make them available to even the poorest citizens (as the fragment of Philemon suggests), classical Athenians were evidently willing to ascribe an important social function to the wide social distribution of male sexual pleasure. And whether this was due to Solon or not, prostitution at Athens—unlike at Corinth[95]—was proverbially cheap[96] (see Appendix 2 for details).

The production at Athens of a democratic body was, obviously enough, a matter of no small consequence for women as well as for men. For it entailed not only the distribution to all the male citizens of an irrefutably "masculine" body but the appropriation of the actual bodies of individual women for the purposes of male sexual pleasure. Moreover, to define the body of the male citizen as socially and sexually assertive was also to reinscribe the traditional definition of the female body as socially and sexually submissive in the very structures of Athenian democracy; it was to tie the status of Athenian women even more closely to the social significance of their bodies. Together with the democratic provision of cheap brothels went initiatives to protect the integrity of the *oikos*,[97] the family and household, making membership in an *oikos* the basis of participation in the life of the community and redrawing the lines of inheritance so as to privilege lineal over lateral kinship.[98] These reforms had the effect both of strengthening the position of the wife-and-mother within the household and of restricting the activities of women even more narrowly to that sphere; they placed each woman securely in the custody of a male *kyrios*, a "master" or guardian, and granted her access to the legal, political, and cultural life of Athens—to the world beyond the *oikos*—only through the mediation of her guardian. These social reforms represent the dark underside of Solon's boasted "liberation" of the female principle in the person of "the great mother of the Olympian gods, dark Earth"[99]: if Solon could claim that his removal from the land of the *horoi*, the boundary stones marking economic divisions, freed Mother

Earth from "slavery" to the social institutions of male society,[100] other democratic legislation had the countervailing effect of deepening the dependency of real Athenian women on their male relations.[101]

Two distinctive features of Athenian life in the classical period might be viewed in the context of these developments. The first is the extraordinary phallicism that typically (though not invariably) characterized sexual expression in classical Athens. Sex was phallic action, at least in the eyes of Athenian men[102]: it revolved around who had the phallus, was defined by what was done with the phallus, and was polarized by the distribution of phallic pleasure. Sexual pleasures other than phallic pleasures did not count in articulating sexual roles or sexual categories: caresses and other gestures that did not fit the penetration model also did not figure in evaluating or classifying sexual behavior. This emphasis on the phallus among the classical Athenians becomes easier to understand when the social dimensions of the phallus as a cultural signifier become more visible.

The second feature of Athenian life that might profitably be placed in this context is the increasingly strict demarcation of the public realm as a male preserve[103] and, thus, as a place of potential exposure and violation for women. Those women who do inhabit the public space are either prostitutes or are assumed to be sexually accessible to men,[104] and respectable women who enter that space are thought to open themselves thereby to the risk of sexual assault.[105] In order to maintain her honor, a woman required the shelter of a household and the protection of a male guardian. Hence, we find a sharp conceptual and social division in Athens between respectable and non-respectable women, between the wife and the whore. Such a division is, to be sure, not unique to classical Athens: the social vulnerability of adult males through the sexual behavior of their women is a generalized and well-known feature of Mediterranean societies; the "split" between wife and whore, as it structures the male psyche, has long been a staple of psychoanalytic literature.[106] But in the Athenian evidence we see this "split" socially elaborated, enacted, and capitalized upon; it is enlisted for a specific social purpose—that of consolidating the corporate body of male citizenry. The Greek historical record, then, allows us to catch, as it were, a cultural item that is often claimed to lead some sort of ideal existence (whether as a universal category of the human psyche or a universal structure of patriarchal society) in the act of being formally institutionalized and inserted into a concrete system of social practices in order to serve a variety of concrete social ends.

The disenfranchisement of male prostitutes and the cheap provision of female prostitutes beg to be seen together, then, as complementary aspects of a single democratizing initiative in classical Athens intended to shore up the masculine dignity of the poorer citizens—to prevent them from being effeminized by poverty—and to promote a new collective image of the citizen body as masculine and assertive, as master of its pleasures, and as perpetually on the superordinate side of a series of hierarchical and roughly congruent distinctions in status: master vs. slave, free vs. unfree, dominant vs. submissive, active vs. passive, insertive vs. receptive, customer vs. prostitute, citizen vs. non-citizen, man vs. woman. If, among the Kabyle, an adult male can express his sense of inalienable and irreducible masculinity (that is, his basic social and sexual identity), by saying, "I, too, have a moustache,"[107] in classical Athens, it seems, the symbolic language of democracy proclaimed on behalf of each citizen, "I, too, have a phallus." Rather than outlaw prostitution on the part of Athenian citizens, the democratic constitution of Athens sought to establish the political and ideological *incompatibility* of citizenship and prostitution, thereby incorporating prostitution (if only as a disqualified activity) into the symbolic codes of classical Athenian political and personal life.

As such, the disenfranchisement of male prostitutes and the cheap provision of female prostitutes belong to a series of developments in the cultural poetics of Athenian manhood that took place during the era of the emerging democracy. Notable among them is the invention of the ithyphallic herm as the tutelary door-keeper and guardian of the household. It is of course impossible to know exactly when these structures—quadrangular posts of a type distinctive to Attica,[108] with a head of Hermes carved at the top and an erect penis carved at the bottom —became common in classical Athens: stone herms (of which numbers have survived) were doubtless preceded by wooden herms, and none of those stood a chance of being preserved.[109] It may be significant, however, that herms do not appear on vase-paintings until 520–500 B.C., which is also the period to which are dated the earliest stone herms that have come down to us.[110] That very moment, moreover, is the same one in which a scattering of literary texts (the earliest being the pseudo-Platonic *Hipparchus* [228b–229e]) place Hipparchus's introduction of herms to Attica. A ruling son of the tyrant Peisistratus, Hipparchus apparently set up herms at halfway points on the roads leading to Athens from the rural townships. Robin Osborne accordingly interprets the Hipparchan herms as promoting a "split between town and country by which the Peisistratids divorced politics from daily life and hence made easier the acceptance of their domination of the former."[111] But for our purposes the more pertinent aspect of the herms is their immediate popularity and wide distribution, their absorption by the Cleisthenic democracy and their adoption by individual households as residential door-keepers. The import of Osborne's work for the topics addressed here has been clearly seen by John J. Winkler, who argues that the herm is "a leveling sign"—or, at least, that it eventually came to be such when it was widely deployed during the Cleisthenic period and after: "In a political community whose atomic units are representatives of family groups, the herm expresses the notional equality of each household, represented in the person of its patriarch and symbolized by a simplified image of the man—a bearded face and an upright phallos."[112] The erection of herms may be another symptom, in other words, of the growing sense of masculine self-assertion and the new pride in masculine egalitarianism that accompanied the consolidation of the democracy at Athens,[113] and that also expressed themselves in the social construction of a symbolic opposition between citizenship and prostitution.

Democracy at Athens, then, was not what we might call a purely "political" system; it was a system of sex and gender as well. The social legislation which gave all free adult males of Athenian parentage a potential say in the government of the city brought with it a clearer articulation of gender categories and a stricter enforcement of sexual roles (at least for the key players in the political game),[114] thereby creating an ideal of masculinity with both sexual and political applications. In order to grasp the distinctive political, juridical, social, and sexual codes that combined to adumbrate the identity of the ideal citizen at Athens in the classical period, and in order to bring that ideal citizen into sharper focus, we need to view him against the background of at least three other social types in relation to which his identity was defined: (1) the enslaved foreign women who (for the most part) staffed the brothels which the citizen might easily visit; (2) the respectable wives, mothers, and daughters shut out of all but the religious dimension of Athenian communal life; and (3) the invisible others, the (young) men and boys who sat, out of sight of the political arena, in the male brothels and bathhouses, those who from the official point of view were social non-persons and did not exist except to serve the pleasure of their more respectable neighbors—and also to embody all the social liabilities from which the citizen himself, by virtue of being a citizen, had been freed. It is only within these cross-cutting fields of gender, sex, and status that the meaning of citizenship in classical Athens appears in all its ideological complexity.

Appendix 1: Aphrodite Pandemos and Temple Prostitution

In the second century A.D. Pausanias, a travel-writer, described a place of worship, below the Athenian Acropolis, dedicated to Aphrodite Pandemos (1.22.3). Recent excavations have securely placed that shrine below and to the southeast of the bastion of Athena Nike at the entrance to the Acropolis.[115] The cult was evidently active throughout the fifth century B.C., although the cult title Pandemos is not attested in literary sources until the middle of the fourth[116] and is not definitively matched up with the archaeological remains until the third. But Aphrodite Pandemos must have been established as a local deity at Athens much earlier than that. The question therefore is: what did her cult epithet mean?

Plato, *Symposium* 180d–82a, and Xenophon, *Symposium* 8.9–10, interpret

Pandemos in a fashion consistent with the story of its Solonian foundation: the word signifies to them the "popular" or "vulgar" (i.e., physical) dimension of erotic desire. But they also define *pandêmos* in opposition to *ourania*, "heavenly" (or "descended from Uranus"), a term which they invest with a highly tendentious ethical signification. Because the *pandêmos/ourania* contrast seems to be exploited here for wholly idiosyncratic philosophical purposes, the meaning which these authors ascribe to *pandêmos* does not seem likely on the face of it to represent the original import of the cult epithet. A more respectable interpretation of the cult title is offered by Pausanias (1.22.3), who explains that Theseus (a mythical founder of Athens) established the shrine when he brought the Athenians into one city *apo tôn dêmôn*, "from the demes" (or surrounding townships). A related, though not identical, explanation is provided by Apollodorus of Athens in the second century B.C., who refers the goddess's title to her proximity to the *agora*, the market-place and political center of Athens, where the *dêmos* (or "people") gathered of old in its assemblies.[117] Both of these explanations offer support for a civic interpretation of Aphrodite Pandemos as a guarantor of social harmony among the citizens.[118]

Now Pausanias and Apollodorus might have been relying on accounts by the Atthidographers (early chroniclers of Athens); alternately, they might be merely guessing at the meaning of *pandêmos*: perhaps they do not wish to accept what they consider to be the disreputable interpretation of *pandêmos* proffered by Plato and Xenophon. Rather than dismiss the testimony of Plato, Xenophon, Philemon, and Nicander in favor of two later and mutually conflicting accounts, both of which refer to events so far in the legendary past that their authors cannot have had accurate knowledge of them (although they might well be preserving an earlier tradition), we should try to reconcile the two traditions which they represent. Now that we have a clearer understanding of the social context and significance of prostitution in classical Athens, we can rehabilitate the association of *pandêmos* with common or bodily sexual pleasure, while recognizing the Platonic-Xenophontic contrast of *pandêmos* with *ourania* as a tendentious, philosophical exploitation of that term; similarly, while retaining the identification of *pandêmos* with common sexual pleasure, we can still construe it in a positive, public-spirited sense—as a proclamation of the democratic leveling of sexual inequities and the imparting to the male citizen body of a new phallic pride. To interpret *pandêmos* in terms of the democratization of sexual pleasure does not exclude a civic function for the cult in promoting and maintaining social harmony among the citizens. Such a civic dimension, in fact, is precisely what we might expect from the temple's location near the entrance to the Acropolis. Perhaps it is what Plutarch had in mind when he numbered Solon among those who crowned *Erôs* "king and archon and him who makes things fit together" (*basileus kai archôn kai harmonstês: Moralia* 763e).

A sexier cult of Aphrodite was located outside of Athens on the Sacred Way, near modern Daphni: dedications with representations of vulvae have been found there[119] (no such dedications to Aphrodite Pandemos happen to have turned up). We also hear of a temple to Aphrodite Pornê, "Aphrodite the Whore," at Abydos in the Dardanelles: the cult epithet commemorated, according to Neanthes (a third-century B.C. historian),[120] the patriotism of a local prostitute. Temple-prostitution on a grand scale reminiscent of the ancient Near East appears to have occurred only on the periphery of the Greek world[121]—with the possible exception of Corinth, where in Roman times (according to Strabo, 8.6.20) the famous and wealthy shrine of Aphrodite owned more than a thousand temple-slaves who worked as prostitutes, making Corinth the Amsterdam of the ancient world.[122] (In the classical period the city of Heraclea in Pontus evidently had so many male prostitutes that Stratonicus, a famous wit, is said to have called it "Androcorinth.")[123] In 464 B.C. a native son of Corinth by the name of Xenophon promised to dedicate a hundred girls to Aphrodite if she helped him on to victory in the Olympic games. She did—he won both the foot-race and the pentathlon—and he not only fulfilled his vow to her but commissioned Pindar, who had also composed a victory ode in honor of his athletic achievement (*Olympian* 13), to celebrate his lavish gift to the goddess. Fragments of Pindar's somewhat embarrassed encomium survive (fr. 122 Snell):

> Young girls who welcome many strangers
>   with your hospitality,
> handmaidens of seductive Persuasion in wealthy
>   Corinth,
> you who kindle blond tears of smoke from fresh
>   green frankincense, flitting often
> in your thoughts to heavenly Aphrodite, the mother
>   of desires,
>
> to you, my children, free from accusation, she
>   has granted to cull the soft, sweet fruit
> of youthful beauty in your lovely beds of desire.
>
> Everything done under compulsion is fine.
> ....
> But I wonder what the lords of the Isthmus
>   will say to me, now that I have devised
> this sort of beginning for the charming festive
>   song, joining my lot with common women. . . .
>
> We have taught the nature of gold on a pure
>   touchstone. . . .
>
> Mistress of Cyprus [Aphrodite], here to your grove
>   Xenophon has brought a hundred-limbed herd

of maidens to graze, and he takes joy
in the fulfillment of his vows.

Appendix 2: Prices

I am about to dwell at what some readers may find great and perhaps
unnecessary length on the question of the prices reportedly charged by Greek
prostitutes. My chief motive for so doing is to counteract a prevailing
tendency on the part of classical scholars to overlook such "sordid" matters,
even when the evidence is available. The *Oxford Classical Dictionary*, revised
in 1970, contains no entry for "Labour," "Work," "Wages," "Fees," "Pay,"
"Salaries" (there is an entry for *salarium*, however), "Economics," "Employ-
ment," "Taxation"—or "Prostitution" (except for "Prostitution, Sacred").
It is time we dealt more fully with these topics.*

The prices charged by prostitutes seem to have remained relatively stable
throughout antiquity, despite occasionally severe fluctuations in the value
of metal currency. To be sure, prices could vary enormously within a single
community at any point in time: the Peripatetic philosopher Lycon, while
a philosophy student at Athens, reportedly managed to acquire an exact
knowledge of the fees charged by all the prostitutes there (the Peripatetics
tended to be snappers-up of unconsidered trifles).[124] Prices might also vary
with the sexual position requested.[125] The lowest price on record is the one
mentioned by Philemon, fr. 4, quoted above: one obol (a sixth of a drachma);
the same price figures in a story about Antisthenes the Socratic, who is
supposed to have remarked, upon seeing an adulterer beating a hasty retreat,
"Miserable fellow, what a lot of danger you might have escaped for an
obol!"[126] It would be hazardous to infer from these sources that a cut-
rate prostitute in fourth-century B.C. Athens cost no more than an obol,
however, because "one obol" may simply be a metonym for "dirt cheap"
(like "two bits" in old-fashioned American slang).

One obol would have been a minimal fee indeed. In 408/7 B.C. day-
laborers working on the Erechtheum on the Athenian Acropolis were earning a drachma per day;[127] by 329/8 hired laborers (*misthôtoi*) working on the
temples at Eleusis were still getting only a drachma and a half per day, but
skilled artisans—such as bricklayers and plasterers—collected two or two
and a half drachmae, and workers employed in carving inscriptions in connection with the same project received seven obols a day for rations (*sitia*)
alone.[128] The daily keep (*trophê*) of public slaves (*dêmosioi*) attached to the

---

* The evidence for prices has in fact been fully collected by German scholars: see, especially,
Schneider, cols. 1343–47, and Herter, 80–85, from whom I have derived most of the information
contained in this Appendix and who provide additional details omitted here. My purpose is to
make this material accessible to English readers.

same works was half a drachma—three obols—per day.[129] If there were sexual fees as low as one obol when Philemon's comedy was performed, they surely represented the cheapest price available for the sexual use of slaves owned by a brothel-keeper, which doubtless procured the customer only the most rudimentary satisfaction.

In the fourth century B.C. the Athenian comic poet Theopompus speaks (whether longingly or indignantly, we cannot say) of a place where second-rate courtesans charge a stater—that is, at Athens, two drachmae (fr. 21). In the first century B.C. Philodemus of Gadara claims in an epigram to frequent a girl who offers a bulk-purchase plan—five drachmae for twelve visits[130]—while in the following century a rather obscure epigrammatist by the name of Bassus (evidently a Roman writing in Greek) boasts of the two-obol fee demanded by one Corinna[131]: how far these price-quotations reflect any actual experience of the market is hard to say, but there are grounds for skepticism. One drachma seems to have become the proverbial fee for commercial sex in the Greek literary tradition: it is the amount demanded for the sexual use of a dancing-girl in the *Thesmophoriazusae* (1195), a comedy by Aristophanes staged in 411 B.C.;[132] it is the sum willingly paid by the Augustan epigrammatist Antipater of Thessalonica,[133] and it is treated as the standard cost of sexual gratification by Plutarch (*Moralia* 759e) towards the turn of the second century A.D.

At the upper end of the scale, by contrast, there does not seem to have been any limit on what could be charged: fancy boys, respectable women, and glamorous courtesans could ask for any amount the market in luxuries would bear. In the classical period, Aeschines (1.158) mentions the case of one Diophantus, an Athenian citizen who appealed to a magistrate for help in collecting the four drachmae owed to him for his sexual favors by a foreigner: whether that sum represented his entire fee or only the outstanding balance of it cannot now be determined, although the context suggests the former; perhaps, as a youth of citizen status, Diophantus was a bit more expensive than an ordinary boy[134] (a certain Eucrates is said to have sold himself for an obol).[135] Strato, a Greek epigrammatist writing under the high Roman empire in the early second century A.D., pictures a boy who asks for five drachmae (the delighted poet offers him ten).[136] By contrast, the kept women in Lucian's *Dialogues of the Courtesans*, written a generation or two later, consider five drachmae a cheap price (8, 14.2 [shoes cost two drachmae in 7.2]): an eighteen-year-old girl (7.3), or a virgin (6.1),[137] can normally bring in a mina (one hundred drachmae)—or can even demand twice that if the customer is personally unappetizing (7.3). A gift of three hundred drachmae is sufficient to purchase a nameless slave-girl[138] or to procure the regular companionship of Theodotus, a free Plataean boy, in the late fifth century B.C., at least according to hostile litigants in two different law-suits; in the latter case, however, the other litigant claims that his opponent has vastly magnified the amount he actually gave the lad.[139] Such exaggeration reaches a new height in a letter imputed to the authorship of the Attic orator Aeschines, in which Melanopus is said to have prostituted his youthful prime for three thousand drachmae (the total yield, presumably, from a brief if lucrative career).[140] In fourth century B.C. New Comedy at Athens the company of an accomplished *hetaira* (see below) costs from twenty to sixty minae,[141] and one girl who earns "more than ten whores combined" brings in the fantastic sum of three minae a day from a wealthy foreigner.[142] The height of such hyperbole is reached in the tales concerning the famous courtesans of the classical period—Lamia, Laïs, Phryne—who are said to have charged up to ten thousand drachmae for a single rendezvous[143] (though in her old age Laïs is reported to have settled for a stater or even three obols).[144]

As this disparity between the amounts charged by different prostitutes suggests, there were a variety of sexual markets operating in antiquity, each with its own clientele and social function. At the bottom of the heap were the *pornai*, or female "whores," who staffed the brothels. These were presumably slaves owned by a *pornoboskos*, a "whore-shepherd" or brothel-keeper, who also had to pay a tax on the income generated by them to a state official with the title of *pornotelônês*, or "whore-tax-farmer."[145] When a wealthy man in the *Epitrepontes*, a comedy by the fourth-century B.C. Athenian comic poet Menander, complains that his son-in-law spends twelve drachmae a day at the brothel (136–37), he may either be understandably shocked at his son-in-law's extravagance, since twelve drachmae might normally have gone a long way in such establishments, or he may be revealing his own tight-fistedness, since twelve drachmae is a trivial sum to the fantastically rich and romantic young men depicted in Attic New Comedy.

On the next rung up were the streetwalkers,[146] who might be free but impoverished women, either foreign residents or citizens, as well as slaves, and who plied their trade in the open. Archaeologists have recovered a sandal designed to leave imprinted in the dust of the street the Greek word *AKOLOUTHI* ("follow me"), and similar messages appear on a variety of surviving ancient objects;[147] among the Church Fathers, Clement of Alexandria was thoroughly conversant with this method of soliciting.[148] The sort of response that might be evoked by such techniques has been imagined for us by an anonymous epigrammatist: "Greetings, miss." "Same to you." "Who's that walking ahead of you?" "What's it to you?" "I have a reason for asking." "She's the lady of our house." "May one hope?" "What are you looking for?" "A night." "Got anything with you?" "Gold." "Take heart." "This much." "You can't."[149] Both whores and streetwalkers were hired for transitory sexual use, though presumably a client might return periodically to a brothel where he had found a woman or boy to his liking.

More expensive than whores or streetwalkers were the various female dancers and flute-players who provided the indispensable entertainment at *symposia*, wealthy men's drinking-parties, and were hired for the space of an evening by the host to perform musical and sexual services for him and his guests.[150] These entertainers were likely to have been slaves, but free women with slender means and the requisite training might also have earned their living in this fashion. They could be spoken of interchangeably with prostitutes.[151] According to Aristotle's *Constitution of Athens* (50.2), it was the responsibility of the *astynomoi*, the officials in charge of good order in the city, to see to it that flute-girls and other hired female musical entertainers charged no more than two drachmae (for an evening's work, one assumes).[152] This regulation was part of the city's sumptuary laws, whose purpose was to conserve the wealth of the citizens by preventing members of the propertied classes from competing with one another at lavish entertainment and thereby needlessly squandering their resources. Skillful musicians and beautiful dancers were evidently in great demand and, if not for the law (or, perhaps, even despite it), they could cause a spiraling escalation in entertainment costs. Just how valuable such girls might be, and how routine were the sexual demands placed upon them by their profession, can be glimpsed from the following entry in a treatise belonging to the Hippocratic medical corpus:

> A kinswoman of mine owned a very valuable singer, who used to go [i.e., had regular intercourse] with men. It was important that this girl should not become pregnant and thereby lose her value. Now this girl had heard the sort of thing women say to each other—that when a woman is going to conceive, the seed remains inside her and does not fall out. She digested this information, and kept a watch. One day she noticed that the seed had not come out again. She told her mistress, and the story came to me. When I heard it, I told her to jump up and down, touching her buttocks with her heels at each leap. After she had done this no more than seven times, there was a noise, the seed fell out on the ground, and the girl looked at it in great surprise.[153]

Although concubines do not truly qualify as prostitutes, it is important to say a few words about them nonetheless. In classical Athens a man could purchase a female slave as a concubine (*pallakē*) or he could arrange with another man, either with or without a contract, to enjoy the use of a woman in the latter's custody.[154] Concubinage was not a transitory relation, although the man could terminate it abruptly and capriciously.[155] It differed from marriage, among other respects, in that the woman did not bring a dowry with her and the children produced by the union were not legitimate.[156] A concubine could expect, however, to be maintained by the man with whom she lived for the term of their cohabitation. Concubinage thus might represent an alternative domestic arrangement to marriage among those sectors of the resident Athenian population too poor, or too marginal in status, to aspire to marry into Athenian citizen families but who nonetheless wished to secure a minimally precarious economic position for their marriageable women. An Athenian citizen, for his part, might decide to acquire a concubine if he already had a family and wanted a regular sexual outlet that did not create new financial obligations or multiply new burdens on his estate; he might find himself in such a situation, for example, if his wife died after having borne him several healthy male children.[157] But there were no doubt many other possible motives for maintaining a concubine. By designating the concubinage a sexually exclusive one, a man helped to define his concubine as someone with whom he lived "with a view to free children" (which afforded her greater legal safeguards and, if the concubine were a slave, perhaps raised the offspring of the union to the status of the father).[158] Alternately, two or more men might acquire joint shares in a female slave for the sake of their own sexual enjoyment (as Timanoridas and Eucrates reportedly bought Neaera for a sum of thirty minae: [Demosthenes,] 59.29); or, the owners of such concubines could hire them out for sex or lend them to friends as a favor or for a special occasion. Hence, the institution of concubinage fulfilled some of the same functions as prostitution.

At the highest end of the scale of commercially available sexual partners were the *hetairai*, the "companions" or mistresses,[159] who have also been referred to throughout this discussion as *courtesans*. These might include women from respectable families who made a living from their beauty and sexual availability, foreigners who maintained houses of pleasure, kept women, and *demimondaines* of various sorts.[160] Some of these women offered their favors to anyone for a (high) price, others attempted to win the constant support of one man or another—or, in some cases, of several men at a time, keeping each in ignorance of the others. Still others became the life-long mistresses of wealthy citizens: the most notorious of these last was Aspasia, a Milesian woman, who lived with Pericles and had children by him, including a son of the same name whom he managed to have made an Athenian citizen in contravention of his own citizenship law. The contemporary comic poet Cratinus, however, referred to Aspasia as Pericles's *pallakê*, or "concubine"—which might have been a more courteous designation for the consort of Athens' leading statesman, had it not been prefixed by the Homeric epithet "dog-faced";[161] no doubt the dividing line between the two categories of kept women was indistinct.[162] Another comic poet, Anaxilas, defined a *hetaira* as a woman who submits to her lover *pros kharin* ("as an expression of gratitude or good-will": fr. 21), but in another passage Anaxilas uses *hetaira* interchangeably with *pornê* ("whore"), as Dover points out.[163] The costs of maintaining a *hetaira* depended on the scope of her patron's ambition—on whether, that is, he wanted to spend a night with her, to retain her as a companion, or to enjoy the exclusive use of her—just as the cost of a common prostitute increased as the client's demands became more restrictive: most expensive of all was to purchase a prostitute outright from his or her owner. In the high-priced world of Athenian New Comedy, a hetaira who is down on her luck can expect no better than to pick up an occasional ten drachmae by consenting to be a man's dinner companion for an evening,[164] but in Lucian (four or five centuries later) we hear of *hetairai* earning one talent (six thousand drachmae) in eight months (*Dialogues of the Courtesans*, 8) and charging a customer two talents for exclusive rights to her affection (15.2). The standard fee for one night with the legendary *hetairai* of classical Athens, such as Phryne and Gnathaena, would seem to have been a mina,[165] if we can trust (which we surely can't) the reports of later, star-struck gossip-mongers who seem to have had the ear of Christian apologists: the latter liked to boast that God demanded fewer sacrifices from the faithful than did whores.[166] At any rate, prostitution was evidently lucrative for some women: in the fourth century B.C. Neaera is said to have raised on occasion twenty minae from her wealthy lovers and her own assets ([Demosthenes,] 59.30–32), and in Coptos, in Egypt, in 90 A.D. prostitutes had to pay a special passport fee of 108 Egyptian drachmae, whereas other women got by with paying only twenty.[167]

6

Why is Diotima a Woman?

> "Now for the discourse about *erôs* which I once heard from a
> Mantineian woman, Diotima, who was learned in that subject and
> in many other things—she once got the Athenians to perform
> sacrifices against the plague and thereby procured them a ten-year
> delay of the disease—and it was she, as well, who taught me
> erotics: I shall try to run through for you, entirely on my own
> (insofar as I can), on the basis of what Agathon and I have agreed
> to, the discourse she pronounced."
>
> —Plato, *Symposium* 201d

1. The Problem

Socrates is the speaker of these words. The occasion of his uttering them
is a symposium, an all-male drinking party, held at the home of the newly-
victorious tragic poet Agathon. The topic of conversation at Agathon's
symposium is *erôs*, or passionate sexual desire, and in keeping with the
paederastic ethos of classical Athens, to which Agathon and most of his
guests subscribe, the evening's discussion of *erôs* is couched almost exclusively in male, homoerotic terms. Socrates has just cross-examined Agathon
about the latter's stated views of *erôs* and, in so doing, has refuted them (at
least, to his own and Agathon's apparent satisfaction).[1] He is about to tell
the story of how his own views of *erôs*, once similar to Agathon's, were
refuted in turn by Diotima, a prophetess, who imparted to him an account
of *erôs* which he now believes and which he commends to others (212b).

Diotima is better informed about the desires of men than are men themselves. Without her expert intervention in their affairs men would never be
able to uncover the true sources, objects, and aims of their own desires. It
takes a woman to reveal men to themselves. Diotima's instruction, moreover, does not consist in enlightening men about women, revealing to men
only what they could not themselves be expected to discover about a realm
of experience forever closed off to them by virtue of being, supposedly, the
exclusive preserve of another sex. On the contrary, what Diotima propounds
to Socrates is an ethic of "correct paederasty" (*to orthôs paiderastein*: *Symposium*
211b5–6; cf. 210a4–5, 211b7–c1)[2] aimed at regulating and enhancing relations
between "men" and "boys."* She thereby founds, or re-founds, an impor-

---

* The terms "men" (*andres* in Greek) and "boys" (*paides*) refer by convention to the senior
and junior partners in a paederastic relationship (respectively), or to those who play the
appropriate roles, regardless of their actual ages: see "One Hundred Years of Homosexuality,"
note 26.

tant institution of male society in classical Athens, providing at the same time an ideological (philosophical) justification for it.

Why is Diotima a woman? Why did Plato select a woman to initiate Socrates into the mysteries of a male, homoerotic desire? It might seem that any adequate answer to this question would have to emerge from an understanding of "sexual difference" in Hellenic antiquity and from the unique, or distinctive, or (at the very least) characteristic attributes of women as they were defined in classical Greek culture. It is only by identifying those gender-specific features belonging essentially to women in the Greek imagination that we can discover, or so one might suppose, the sources of Diotima's superior erotic expertise—and, thus, determine exactly what it is that qualifies her, in Plato's eyes, to be a professor of (male) desire.

But the project, so described, turns out in practice to be highly paradoxical. For it focuses—necessarily—not on women but on men; it proves to be less about "sexual difference" than about male identity. Or, to be more precise, it traces the inscription of male identity in ancient representations of female "difference" and thereby recovers not the presence but the absence of "the feminine" from male constructions of it. Rather than attempt to escape these paradoxes, I have tried in what follows to make their operation visible at three levels of the analysis: (1) at the level of Plato's text, which will be shown both to construct and to deny female "difference"; (2) at the level of scholarly commentary on that text, which in its efforts to explicate Diotima's gender has replicated Plato's own tactic, either denying her difference or resolving it into male identity; and (3) at the level of my own interpretative practice, which by erasing female presence from the terms of its discourse, even as it adheres to an ostensibly feminist program, reproduces and exemplifies the very strategies of appropriation—characteristic of male culture—that it purports both to illuminate and to criticize.

2. The Question and Two Commonsense Answers

Let us return, then, to the original question, and begin by asking, once again, in all innocence, "Why is Diotima a woman?" The two most plausible answers to this question that have been put forward hitherto have tended alike to take a negative form: Diotima is a woman, apparently, because she is not a man. Each of the arguments for this solution is worth reviewing briefly.

According to the first argument, Plato could not afford to portray the youthful Socrates as having been initiated into the mysteries of erotic desire by an older and wiser *male* because such a portrait would inevitably have suggested to Plato's contemporaries that Socrates owed his much-vaunted insight into the nature of erotics[3] to the passionate ministrations of a former paederastic lover.[4] Now that is an insinuation Plato strenuously wanted to

Male revelers at a symposium disporting themselves in feminine attire. Female entertainers provide musical accompaniment. (The J. Paul Getty Museum, The Briseis Painter, Brygos (signed as the potter), Attic Red-Figure Cup, Type B, ca. 480–470 B.C., terracotta, height: 11.7 cm.; diameter: 30.7 cm. 86.AE.293)

avoid, not only because it would have lent the stamp of Socratic approval to a social practice for which Plato himself entertained the liveliest mistrust but, more importantly, because it would have had the effect of valorizing the Athenian institution of paederasty on the very grounds on which Plato's Pausanias, earlier in the *Symposium*, had celebrated it under the high-sounding cultic title of *Aphroditê Ourania* (or "heavenly love").[5] For Pausanias had argued that a youth who is eager for moral self-improvement may legitimately, even laudably, choose to gratify the sexual passion of an older and wiser male in exchange for obtaining from his lover the edifying instruction he desires (182d–185c, esp. 184b–e).[6] But Plato, for a variety of philosophical reasons, wishes to repudiate the paederastic ethos articulated by Pausanias[7] along with the economic model used to justify it (cf. *Symposium* 175d; *Republic* 518b–d): that is the point of the famous episode in which Alcibiades proposes to Socrates precisely the sort of transaction endorsed by Pausanias and receives from his admired preceptor a sharp and uncompromising rebuff (*Symposium* 218c–219d). If Plato, then, had represented the youthful Socrates as having benefited—however passionlessly—from the erotic expertise of a mature male, the principle underlying Socrates's subsequent rejection of Alcibiades would have been obscured, and Plato would have risked conveying to his audience an impression diametrically opposite to the one he is determined to convey. Or so the first of these two arguments goes.

The second argument harmonizes nicely with the previous one. It so happens that Diotima's discussion of erotic desire issues, significantly, in the specification of a set of procedures to be followed by any truly serious student of "correct paederasty," as she calls it. If the author of those prescriptions had been a male, he might well have been suspected of being influenced in his framing of them by a variety of personal factors, inasmuch as his own sexual activity would be materially affected by whatever erotic curriculum he proposed. Diotima, by contrast, is not personally implicated in the content of the erotic discipline she recommends to the aspiring paederast. Plato, then, by omitting to make a male the mouthpiece of his erotic doctrine, manages to clothe that doctrine in the guise of pure disinterestedness; he also invests his chosen spokesman with an easy transcendence over potentially troubling sources of personal involvement in the subject under discussion.[8] Diotima's serene mastery of her material gives her the requisite authority to perform her appointed task of wisdom-bearer within the larger scheme of Plato's dialogue.[9]

I have no wish to quarrel with those who argue that Diotima must be a woman because she may not be a man. Indeed, I consider the two arguments I have just run through to be plausible enough on their own terms. But to leave matters there would be, in effect, to collaborate with those age-old traditions in Western culture that define every "subject" as male and that tend to construe woman as a mere absence of male presence. Once we admit the possibility that there may be more to being a woman than not being a man, we are obliged to seek for *positive* reasons behind Plato's startling decision to introduce a woman into the clannish, masculine society of Agathon's household in order to enlighten a group of articulate paederasts about the mysteries of erotic desire.[10] Any sensitive reader of the *Symposium* will surely acknowledge, after all, that Diotima's gender loudly calls attention to itself within the dramatic setting of the dialogue.

Plato provides his modern readers with some additional encouragement to search for a positive philosophical dimension to Diotima's being a woman. He hints unmistakably that Diotima's gender is not without its significance for the erotic doctrine she articulates. Diotima underscores the specifically "feminine"* character of her purchase on the subject of erotic desire by means of the emphatically gender-polarized vocabulary and conceptual apparatus that she employs in discussing it. She speaks of *erôs* as no male does, striking a previously unsounded "feminine" note and drawing on a previously untapped source of "feminine" erotic and reproductive experience. In particular, Diotima introduces and develops the unprecedented imagery of male pregnancy,[11] insisting on it despite what might seem to be the wild incongruousness of procreative metaphors in a paederastic context.[12] In Diotima's formulation, men become pregnant (*kyein*),[13] suffer birth pangs (*ôdis*),[14] bear (*gennan*)[15] and bring forth (*tiktein*)[16] offspring,[17] and nourish their young (*trephein*).[18] Indeed, the authentic aim of erotic desire, according to Diotima, is procreation (206e).[19] Diotima's gender, then, is not a merely peripheral fact or an accidental circumstance, unconnected to her teaching; it is, apparently, a condition of her discourse, and it is inscribed in what she says. Just as all the other speakers in Plato's *Symposium* project onto *Erôs* the features of their own personalities,[20] so Diotima, too, seems to be existentially implicated in the content of her erotic doctrines;† by virtue of the very language she uses to enunciate them, she lets her audience know that a "woman" is speaking—or, to be more precise, that Socrates is speaking in what he expects his audience to recognize as a woman's voice. At any rate, Plato clearly means us to notice that Diotima's conceptualization of *erôs* derives from a specifically "feminine" perspective.‡

---

* I enclose such terms as *feminine* and *masculine* in quotation marks because I do not wish to commit myself as the author of this essay to any of the various essentialist definitions of gender which I shall be discussing. By "feminine," then, the reader should understand *feminine as constructed by the writer, social group, or historical culture in question.*

† The Greeks seem to have been somewhat less obsessed with the talismanic power of disinterestedness to underwrite the authority of their experts, and more skeptical about the possibility of achieving it, than were certain nineteenth-century German methodologists—as the story of the Judgment of Paris indicates.

‡ I say "feminine," rather than "heterosexual," because what is foregrounded by Plato is Diotima's identity as a woman, not her relation to men, let alone her "sexuality."

What is it about such a perspective that Plato especially prizes? No immediate answer presents itself. Plato's attitude to women is notoriously ambivalent.[21] The low social and economic status of women in classical Athens,[22] the disparaging pronouncements by male authors in general, and the thoroughgoing depreciation of females by Aristotle in particular[23] have made it difficult for students of the classical period to identify those positive values conventionally associated with women by Plato's contemporaries which Plato might have sought to actualize through his sponsorship of Diotima. In what follows I propose, first, to review some (but by no means all) of the explanations that scholars have offered for Diotima's presence in the *Symposium* and, then, to add to them two novel ones of my own which are designed to highlight Plato's philosophical exploitation of femininity (as the ancients tended to construct it). * My general aim is to sharpen our awareness of the strategies by which the Greeks mapped socially and ideologically significant distinctions onto biological differences between the sexes;[24] more specifically, I should like to contribute a chapter to the still largely unwritten history of the function of "the feminine" in the social reproduction of male culture—whose latest chapter, no doubt, is represented by the appropriation of feminist scholarship by male academics (the present author not excepted).[25]

3. Diotima and Platonic Psychopathology

The various explanatory hypotheses advanced in the scholarly literature can be conveniently divided into three basic groups according to whether they refer Plato's portrait of Diotima to personal, historical, or doctrinal factors. Let me begin with those explanations that connect Plato's artistic decision to his personal temperament. Scholars are occasionally heard to remark (though none, so far as I know, has yet confided this argument to print) that Diotima's presence in the *Symposium* shows Plato to have been a closet heterosexual; Plato, on this account, sought to endow relations between the sexes with greater dignity by sketching for the edification of his contemporaries an attractive picture of a fruitful intellectual exchange between a man and a woman.[26] Other commentators relate Diotima and her doctrines to Plato's alleged homosexuality—a diagnosis fast becoming entrenched in Platonic scholarship.[27] Indeed, one of the unexpected consequences of the spirit of candor about sexual matters that has animated classical studies in recent years has been the sudden outpouring into the scholarly literature of a flood of newly revealed academic hallucinations about the psychology of homosexuals, ancient and modern. Paul Plass, for

---

* Readers who do not expect to be entertained by the vagaries of classical scholarship are invited to skip ahead to section 6, entitled "Erotic Hierarchies and Platonic Reciprocities," which introduces my own interpretation.

example, has assembled a collection of twentieth-century clinical evidence[28] that purports to document just how thickly fantasies of male pregnancy cluster about the inner lives of homosexual men; he suggests, further, that Diotima's talk of "pregnancy, birth pangs and delivery" may represent a kind of gay "argot," a set of " 'in' phrases" whose emotional value teeters precariously on the edge between self-affirmation and self-mockery.[29] Bennett Simon, by contrast, interprets Diotima's procreative imagery to be "typical of pregenital sexual fantasy" and goes on to relate the central themes of Plato's philosophy to a trauma experienced by the philosopher as a child upon witnessing the primal scene.[30] In a much more light-handed and witty essay, Dorothea Wender claims that Plato's willingness to grant a certain measure of authority to women stemmed from his sexual disposition: he didn't like women, but since he was a "paedophile" and therefore indifferent to the sexuality of women he did not feel threatened by them, and so he had little motive to deny them social equality when they merited it—unlike Xenophon, for example, a heterosexual man who liked women, and liked them in their place.[31] The chief accomplishment of this school of Platonic interpretation, in my view, has been to demonstrate that if Michel Foucault had never existed it would have been necessary to invent him.

4. Diotima and Athenian (Literary) History

Common, at least implicitly, to the views of all the authorities cited so far is the assumption that Diotima was not a real person but a fictional creation of Plato's. Many recent students of the *Symposium* share that assumption, but they were not always so numerous as they are today. With occasional exceptions, such as Wilamowitz (who declared himself a thoroughgoing agnostic about Diotima's historical existence)[32] and Bury (who denied it altogether),[33] classical philologists of the nineteenth and early twentieth centuries tended to grant Diotima a measure of historical authenticity,[34] and their arguments still merit consideration. Foremost among those arguments is the claim that Plato does not normally introduce fictitious persons into his dialogues.[35] Even off-hand allusions in Plato to people and places are on occasion confirmed in their historical accuracy by Greek inscriptions, or so it is alleged,[36] and those Platonic characters, such as Callicles, who have yet to turn up in our sources may well be casualties of gaps in the documentary record.[37] Thucydides (2.47.3) testifies to the early and scattered incidence of the plague in the years preceding its disastrous outbreak at Athens in 430, and it is not inconceivable that a foreign prophetess might have been called in for consultation during that period; Diotima may reflect Plato's recollection of what he had been told as a boy about the intervention of a Peloponnesian witch-doctor on behalf of the Athenians a decade and a half before his birth.[38] Some scholars have argued that Plato includes details about Diotima's identity that seem irrelevant to the dramatic context in which they occur[39]—Socrates tells us how, by ordering the Athenians to perform sacrifices, she managed to avert the plague from Athens for ten years (201d)—and such details would therefore seem to acquire the ring of historical authenticity.[40] But the parallel case of Epimenides, who staved off the Persian invasion of Attica for ten years by similar means (*Laws* 642de), does not inspire confidence;[41] Epimenides is all too obviously a stock folktale figure (whatever his historical origin),[42] and the willingness of some historians[43] to uphold his authenticity on the basis of the analogy to Diotima should be a warning to the rest of us. Other historians have claimed to unearth an ancient Mantineian tradition of female philosopher-sages,[44] but that tradition represents, in all likelihood, a folktale of the modern academic variety.

More compelling is the argument that in no extant source does Socrates name as his teacher a person who cannot be shown to have existed historically;[45] Diotima, who did indeed "teach" (*didaskein*) Socrates erotics, according to his own testimony (*Symposium* 201d5, 204d2, 207a5; cf. 206b5–6, 207c6),[46] would be the sole exception. But this argument begs the fundamental question of how we are to assess Diotima's function in Plato's dramaturgy: does her role more closely resemble that of Callicles or Er?[47] Should we, that is, regard her as a real person or as a pure device, a Jamesian *ficelle*? Such questions, unfortunately, are not easy to answer in principle; they lie at the core of interpretation. Moreover, the pertinent issue for the interpreter is not whether Diotima actually existed but what it is that Plato accomplishes by introducing her into the *Symposium*, and that is not an issue whose resolution depends on Diotima's historical authenticity. This point will become clearer, perhaps, once all the alternatives have been explored.

The search for Diotima has turned up a considerable number of ancient verbal and pictorial documents, including most notably a large sculpted relief, found in the *agora* at Mantineia and now housed in the National Museum at Athens, which dates to approximately 410–400 B.C. and depicts a woman holding in her hand what appears to be a liver: she was evidently an important local prophetess.[48] This and the other documents do indeed constitute a remarkable and significant body of material; unfortunately, none of them furnishes testimony that is either conclusive (in the case of the relief) or sufficiently early to escape suspicion of having been contaminated by Platonic influence. In weighing the fact that no mention of Diotima demonstrably independent of Plato survives we should remember that we possess vastly fewer names of classical Greek women than we do names of Greek men and that a number of cultural factors have systematically militated against their preservation.[49] Diotima, of course, is a perfectly good Greek name for a woman (it is securely attested in the early classical period).[50] Scholars have suspected Platonic wordplay in its etymology, to be sure, as well as in the etymology of the name of Diotima's birthplace: Diotima of

Mantineia means, literally, something like "Zeus-honor from Prophet-ville,"[51] and Plato may have wished to underscore by means of such a pun the religious sources of Diotima's well-nigh oracular authority. But inasmuch as some priesthoods in classical Greece were in effect the property of certain families,[52] and girls belonging to those families who were expected to be priestesses were often given appropriately august names—a fact re-flected in the actual names attested for Greek priestesses[53]—the aptness of Diotima's name need not count against her historical existence, nor need it be ascribed to linguistic gamesmanship on Plato's part.[54] Moreover, the name of Socrates's mother, the midwife, is reported to have been Phaenarete (*Theaetetus* 149a; *Alcibiades Major* 131e)—literally, "she who brings virtue to light"—and if that name, which is almost too good to be true, is not taken to be an outright joke[55] (it is attested as a woman's name in Aristophanes's *Acharnians* [49] and is, more suspiciously, recorded as the name of Hippocra-tes's mother, who was also a midwife according to later legend), hardly any motive remains for doubting the authenticity of Diotima's. Let us suppose for the moment, then, that she was an actual person. What should follow from that supposition for our interpretation of her function in Plato's *Symposium*?

There are two alternatives.[56] First, it may be the case that Plato's account in the *Symposium* is an accurate, or roughly accurate, report of an actual conversation that really did take place between Socrates and Diotima many years before the dramatic date of Agathon's drinking-party: such was the view of A. E. Taylor, for example.[57] The very notion, however, that the historical Socrates was actually initiated into the mysteries of Platonic love— to say nothing of the Theory of Forms, on which Plato's erotic doctrine depends—around the middle of the fifth century B.C. by a Peloponnesian prophetess is so wildly improbable as to deprive its adherents of any further claim to a serious hearing.[58] The second and more likely alternative is that Diotima, though a real person, functions in the *Symposium* as a dramatic fiction, somewhat in the manner of Parmenides in the Platonic dialogue that bears his name.[59] The literary character corresponds to an actual individual, in other words, but the situation depicted in the dialogue is the invention of its author. Parmenides, of course, is an appropriate figure for Plato to bring forward to criticize the Theory of Forms, since that theory had its origins in a specifically Parmenidean problematic.[60] But even in the event that all the fragments of and references to Parmenides which we now possess had been lost and that his name meant as little to us as Diotima's does now, Plato still furnishes us with enough relevant information about him (he is, for example, a formidable logician)[61] to make his presence in the *Parmenides* at least minimally perspicuous. In Diotima's case, by contrast, Plato gives us very little pertinent information: Socrates says only that he will relate a discourse about *erôs* which he once heard from a woman of Mantineia,

Diotima, who was learned in that subject and in many other things, and who gave the Athenians ten years' reprieve from the Great Plague by advising them to sacrifice—presumably in 440 B.C. (201d). Although we can never rule out the possibility that the most prominent authority on *erôs* in fifth-century Greece was a certain Diotima, whose name and doctrines have wholly vanished from the historical record, nothing in Plato encourages us to entertain it. Nor does Plato, superb portraitist though he is, attempt to give us much of a portrait of Diotima, as he might well have done had he decided to breathe life into a well-known historical personage (though, admittedly, his portrait of Aspasia in the *Menexenus* is hardly more lifelike, despite its historical basis, but then Plato seems to be less interested in her than in her relations with Pericles). Far from being vividly individualized,[62] Diotima keeps a cool distance from us: she remains aloof—suavely impersonal and provocatively business-like.[63] We still have to figure out what she's doing in the *Symposium*.

There is yet a third possibility, however. The impetus to make Diotima a woman may have had its origin in history but not in actuality: that is, Plato may have been responding to a previous, and now largely lost, literary tradition. The topic of Socrates's relations with women seems to have furnished a staple, in fact, of Socratic literature in Plato's time.[64] In the *Memorabilia*, or "Recollections" of Socrates, for example, Xenophon tells the story of a visit paid by Socrates and his friends to Theodote, a famous *hetaira* or courtesan, whom Socrates proceeds to question and instruct in his usual manner about the art of seduction (3.11; cf. 2.6.28–39). Theodote, scantily clad, happens to be posing for a painter at the moment the company arrives, and Socrates inquires of his friends whether they ought to be obliged to her for allowing them to see her beauty or she to them for the privilege of being admired. After a brief, if breathtaking, display of discursive reasoning, Socrates triumphantly concludes, "We already desire to touch what we have seen; we shall go away excited, and when we have gone we shall feel an unsatisfied longing. The natural inference is that we are performing a service [i.e., by spreading her reputation] and she is receiving it" (3.11.2–3). Theodote is eventually persuaded of Socrates's expertise in these and other matters and invites him to visit her often, to which Socrates responds by declining to join her parties but encouraging her to attend his discussions; he promises to receive her—"unless," he adds rather ungallantly, "I have someone with me I like better" (3.11.15–18). The episode evidently became notorious in antiquity and was taken up by subsequent writers on Socrates.[65]

The figure who seems to have dominated such stories about Socrates is Aspasia, a Milesian woman who was the mistress of Pericles and was, like Theodote, a *hetaira*. In the extant Socratic literature Aspasia's relation to Socrates is most fully adumbrated in Plato's *Menexenus*, where Socrates claims Aspasia as his instructor in rhetoric (*didaskalos . . . peri rhêtorikês*: 235e; cf. 236c3) and says that she has made many other men good orators, especially Pericles (235e). He goes on to recite a funeral oration which, he maintains (236ab), Aspasia composed partly from what she happened to invent on the spur of the moment and partly from fragments of a previous funeral oration delivered by Pericles which, however, Socrates also ascribes to her authorship. Socrates adds that he learned the speech from her and was nearly beaten by her for failing to get it right (236bc); he is in the habit of visiting her, evidently (249d), and he knows some of her political speeches as well (249e). Menexenus, nonetheless, remains politely skeptical about Aspasia's responsibility for the discourses which Socrates persists in ascribing to her (236c, 249de).

Most of the other literary passages bearing on Socrates and Aspasia pertain to erotic matters, somewhat more in keeping with the tone of the Theodote-episode in Xenophon's *Memorabilia*.[66] Elsewhere in that work, for example, Xenophon's Socrates claims to have gotten good advice from Aspasia about match-making (2.6.36); in Xenophon's *Oeconomicus* Socrates offers to introduce Critobulus to Aspasia who, he says, can speak about the relations between husbands and wives more knowledgeably than he can (3.14; cf. 2.16). Antisthenes, perhaps the most philosophically flamboyant of Socrates's disciples, wrote a Socratic dialogue entitled *Aspasia*,[67] now lost, in which he described Pericles's passionate attachment to that lady;[68] how Antisthenes portrayed Aspasia and how he treated her relations with Socrates cannot now be securely reconstructed.[69] Another Socratic, Aeschines of Sphettus, also composed an *Aspasia*[70] which seems to have treated erotic themes;[71] he portrayed Pericles as breaking down in tears while defending Aspasia against a charge of impiety,[72] described Aspasia's cross-examination of Xenophon and his wife on the subject of marriage,[73] and claimed that Aspasia made the hitherto undistinguished Lysicles (with whom she lived briefly after the death of Pericles) the first man in Athens.[74] The Alexandrian poet Hermesianax included the (so far as we know) previously unattested tale of Socrates's passion for Aspasia in a rather heterogeneous catalogue of the loves of famous poets and philosophers in the third book of his lost elegiac poem, the *Leontion*.[75] Herodicus of Babylon, a pupil of Crates who flourished around 125 B.C. and wrote an anti-Platonic tract entitled *Pros ton philosôkratên* ("A Reply to the admirer of Socrates"), named Aspasia as Socrates's *erôtodidaskalos*, his instructor in love, and quoted a poem addressed to Socrates and supposedly composed by Aspasia, in which she alternately advises and chaffs Socrates about his passion for Alcibiades.[76] Plutarch, Lucian, Maximus of Tyre, and Athenaeus all refer to Aspasia as Socrates's teacher;[77] Maximus of Tyre and Synesius of Cyrene maintain specifically that she taught Socrates erotics.[78] Aspasia's name continues to be associated with that of Socrates's throughout antiquity[79] and eventually seems to become interchangeable with Diotima's.[80] All of these passages as well as many others have been assembled and exhaustively analyzed by a recent *Quellenforscherin*, Barbara Ehlers, who derives virtually the entire tradition from Aeschines's lost dialogue, the *Aspasia*. In that dialogue, as she laboriously reconstructs it—on very slender but not unreasonable evidence— Aspasia did not appear in person; rather, Socrates cited her words and her example alike in order to demonstrate that *erôs* can be an instrument of moral improvement, a positive moral force in its own right (whether Socrates portrayed Aspasia as his instructor in erotics, as Ehlers claims, is, on my reading of the evidence she presents, much more doubtful).[81] If Ehlers is correct, Plato's Diotima may be a stand-in for Aeschines's Aspasia[82]: Plato did not wish to bring forward the same personage to fill the role of erotic expert because he wanted to distinguish his own views from those of Aeschines's; in the course of taking over and transforming Aeschines's erotic doctrine, he also displaced and replaced Aspasia with Diotima.[83]

I find this line of reasoning both attractive and helpful. It explains, first of all, Plato's choice of an otherwise obscure woman to play what is after all a crucial role in his dialogue and it accounts for his rather perfunctory characterization of her: Plato can afford not to particularize her personality because she is filling a function previously performed by a much more notorious personage. Whereas Aspasia fits comfortably into the design of the *Menexenus* (since the topic of that dialogue is political rhetoric and Aspasia had a reputation for making her lovers into successful politicians), she would be quite out of place in the *Symposium*, where Plato clearly wants to put some distance between his own outlook on *erôs* and the customary approach to that topic characteristic of the Athenian demimonde.[84] Secondly, this way of answering our question puts Diotima's gender in the forefront of the explanatory strategy: rather than making her gender the consequence of some other, putatively more important, consideration, it implies that Plato had a primary reason for preferring a woman, any woman, to be the mouthpiece of his erotic theory. But in order to replace Aspasia with another woman who was *not* a *hetaira*, Plato had to find an alternate source of erotic authority, another means of sustaining his candidate's claim to be able to pronounce on the subject of erotics. In the *Phaedrus* he appeals to "the fair Sappho" as a fount of erotic wisdom (235c); in the *Symposium*, however, he looks to religious sources of authority, to which some Greek women were believed by the Greeks to have access.[85] This solution suggests, then, that Diotima's vocation is to be explained at least in part by reference to her gender, not *vice versa*. Plato makes Diotima a prophetess (or appeals to the historical figure of a prophetess), on this view, because he has already decided to make her a woman: he was not obliged to make her a woman because he had resolved to articulate his doctrine through the medium of a seer.

5. Diotima, Divination, and Platonic Metaphysics

For if Plato had wanted to invoke a religious authority, he need not have chosen a woman: he had manifold devices ready to hand for putting the prestige of traditional wisdom at the service of his own philosophy. In fact, Plato's usual strategy for introducing positive doctrines into his dramatic dialogues is to ascribe them to the authority of some more august personage than Socrates. The briefest survey of Plato's writings reveals the extraordinary flexibility and adaptability of this transparent subterfuge. In the *Meno*, for example, Socrates ascribes the doctrine of recollection to certain unnamed "men and women who are learned in divine matters [*sophoi peri ta theia pragmata*]"—specifically, "those priests and priestesses who have made it their business to be able to give an account [*logos*] of the functions they perform" (81ab).[86] In the *Charmides*, similarly, Socrates, pretending on the advice of Critias to know a cure for the ailment afflicting their handsome interlocutor, claims to have acquired medical expertise, while on military duty in Thrace, from one of the doctors who attend the god-king Zalmoxis (156d–157c, 158b, 175e).[87] Elsewhere, Socrates appeals for authority to Er (*Republic* 614b ff.), to "one of the sages" (*Gorgias* 493a1–2), to "some clever fellow, perhaps a Sicilian or an Italian" (*Gorgias* 493a5–6), and—in the case of the myth in the *Phaedo*—simply to "someone" (108c8; cf. *Theaetetus* 201c8, e1). In short, Socrates is quite eclectic about the authorities he cites and is hardly averse to revealing the sources of his wisdom. "Once I learn something," he declares in the *Hippias Minor*, "I never turn around and deny it or pretend that what I've learned is my own discovery. Rather, I praise my teacher for being a wise man and I make clear what I learned from him" (372c; cf. *Republic* 338b). Diotima's function in the *Symposium*, then, is but one variation on the recurring theme of Socratic modesty and Platonic anonymity.[88] As Paul Friedländer remarks, Diotima is "the highest embodiment, as it were, of the more or less vague 'somebody' whom [the Platonic Socrates] frequently posits playfully in conversation as another person in order to conceal himself ironically"; but in the case of Diotima, Friedländer adds, "there is much disagreement on the meaning and purpose of this creation."[89]

But it might be objected that "the meaning and purpose" behind Diotima's vocation and gender are not as obscure as Friedländer pretends. Diotima's identity as a prophetess is directly connected, on one view, to the precepts she articulates: like the doctrine of recollection in the *Meno*, the doctrine of erotic aspiration in the *Symposium* properly demands to be entrusted to the authorship of a man or a woman who is learned in divine matters and able to give an account of his or her sacred function.[90] Diotima certainly fits that description neatly enough: not only does her record of successful intervention[91] on behalf of the Athenians vouch for her expertise in divine matters, but she also provides, in the form of her doctrine of daemonic mediation, a lucid account of the commerce between men and gods which is designed to explain the operation of Greek religious practice in general and of her own specialty, *mantikê*, in particular (202e–203a). To the extent that Plato characterizes Diotima at all, he characterizes her as a prophetess and he makes much of her identity as someone skilled in the mantic arts: at one point, in response to her declaration that the aim of erotic desire is "procreation in the beautiful, both in body and in soul," Socrates remarks that it would take the art of prophecy (*manteia*) to figure out what Diotima means (206b9). Socrates, in fact, has good reason to be baffled, as Diotima subsequently acknowledges when she employs vocabulary proper to the mystery religions in order to represent her own teaching, implicitly at least, as a revelation: she speaks of the possibility of Socrates's being "initiated into erotics" and she divides her own disquisition into two parts which she associates, respectively, with the Lesser and Greater Mysteries (209e5–210a4)—the former having to do with the erotic aim (207a5–209e4), the latter with the erotic object (210a4–212a7; cf. *Gorgias* 497c). To all these hints in the *Symposium*, moreover, one might add Socrates's teaching in the *Phaedrus* that *mantikê* and *erôs* are akin to one another insofar as they are both forms of beneficial madness (244a–245c).[92]

Plato's mantic imagery is replete with philosophical significance. For despite what Plato's Eryximachus alleges (to his disgrace),[93] Platonic erotics is not a science but a mystery—at least, for those who have yet to complete the mystical ascent to the Forms.[94] To study erotics is not merely to explore the phenomenon of sexual attraction but to inquire into the structure of reality; only a correct understanding of the nature of being will unlock the secret of our immortal longings.[95] As Plato's Aristophanes establishes by means of his famous myth in the *Symposium*, the ultimate aim of sexual desire is not what most ancients and moderns alike believe it to be (namely, sexual intercourse) but something else, something that may well remain an impenetrable mystery even to the most experienced lovers. Those who spend their entire lives together "could not say what they wish to gain from one another," according to Aristophanes. "No one would think it was sexual intercourse, or that for the sake of sex each partner so earnestly enjoys his union with the other. But it is clear that the soul of each lover wants something else, which it is not able to say, but it divines (*manteuesthai*) what it wants and hints at it" (192cd). Aristophanes's lovers, in other words, stand just as much in need of prophecy to reveal to them what they really desire as Socrates stands in need of it when he is questioned by Diotima about the erotic aim. And just as Socrates greets Diotima's definition of the erotic aim, once she unveils it, with wonder and amazement (208b7), even so, Aristophanes hypothesizes, if Hephaestus were to approach two lovers while they were in bed having sex and offer to fuse them into a single being, they would instantly recognize the true goal of their desire (192de). Without the benefit of such a privileged glimpse into the deep structures of their motivation,[96] both the most experienced lovers and Socrates himself might remain ignorant of the reason and purpose behind their own *erôs*—what Aristophanes and Diotima alike call its *aition* (192e9; 207e7; cf. 207b7, c7).

In the *Republic*, Socrates uses language similar to that employed by Aristophanes in the *Symposium* in order to describe our difficulty in apprehending the nature of the Good: it is "what every soul pursues, that for the sake of which it does everything, something whose existence it divines (*apomanteues-thai*)," but cannot seize upon; rather, the soul remains "at a loss and unable to grasp adequately what it is" (505de). The ultimate erotic object, which Diotima reveals to be the Beautiful and which is quite possibly just another aspect of the Good, poses analogous problems for the human understanding: the project of identifying the precise idea or value instantiated in all the objects of one's longing may take one, unaided, a lifetime to complete—as Proust later discovered. Plato is not, of course, the first Greek to use Eleusinian imagery in speaking of *erôs*—that honor goes, perhaps, to Euripides, who referred in a lost play to those "uninitiated [*atelestoi*] in the labors of *erôs*"[97]—but his emphasis on the mysterious quality of erotic experience and on the difficulty of penetrating to an accurate understanding of it reflects a systematic element in his thinking. If philosophy is a form of revelation, then the mystery religions can provide a metaphor for philosophical enlightenment. But in order to prevent Socrates from appearing in the *Symposium* to be some sort of fake mystagogue—which is how Aristophanes had portrayed him in the *Clouds* (e.g., 143)—Plato needed to transfer the initiatory function proper to a professor of desire from Socrates to his alter ego, Diotima. And if Diotima is to qualify as an official representative of the Eleusinian mysteries,[98] according to this argument, she will need to be a woman.

But that, unfortunately, is where this line of reasoning breaks down: it serves very well to explain why Plato clothes his metaphysical theories in imagery borrowed from the Eleusinian mysteries—indeed, much more might be said about the correspondences between the mysteries and Plato's erotic doctrines, both of which share an interest in the processes of birth, death, and renewal, in the miracles of sex and immortality—but it doesn't explain why Diotima is a woman. For unlike the general run of classical Greek cults devoted to various female deities, and unlike other rites of Demeter in particular, the Eleusinian mysteries were dominated by male officials.[99] That, in fact, is why Alcibiades and his friends could be accused of parodying the mysteries, each of them taking a separate priestly role, at an (all-male) symposium (Plutarch, *Alcibiades* 19.1).[100] To be sure, there were also women associated with the cult—one priestess of Demeter and Kore, two hierophantids, and possibly a priestess of Pluto, to be exact, plus the regular priestesses of the sanctuary[101]—but the chief officers were drawn exclusively from the (male) members of two prominent Attic *genê*, or clans, and some, if not all, of the *mystagôgoi*, the priests who actually performed the rites of initiation and inducted people into the cult, were also men. Diotima's gender, then, is not properly construed as making a specific reference to the Eleusinian mysteries,[102] and Plato can hardly have borrowed a woman from earlier Socratic tradition simply in order to justify his practice of crowding Eleusinian images around his metaphysical "re-structuring of what there is on the scaffolding of what is more and less real."[103]

Now that we are, at last, at the end of this digression, it may be useful to take stock of our progress. I am arguing (1) that the mysterious nature of Platonic *erôs* is not sufficient in itself to explain Plato's choice of a female spokesman for his erotic theory and (2) that Plato need not have emulated Aeschines and Antisthenes in making Socrates's conversation with a woman the occasion of an erotic discourse if it hadn't suited his own purposes: Plato is so resourceful in creating specious authorities for Socrates to cite that, if he had wished, he could well have imputed Diotima's doctrine to some male sage or other whom Socrates need never have met (thus sanitizing the paedogogic relation of any possible paederastic overtones) but whose account of *erôs* he had somehow managed to learn—that is, by the same devious and indirect means, whatever they were, that he managed to absorb the myth of the *Gorgias*, the myth of the *Phaedo*, or the myth of Er in the *Republic*.

One might even argue, for that matter, that it very nearly *doesn't* suit Plato's purposes to introduce a woman into the *Symposium* to play the role of a philosophical authority: Plato has gone out of his way, after all, from the very outset of the narrative, to make Agathon's drinking-party an unusually masculine affair. Greek symposia, of course, were by definition men's parties[104] but, as Xenophon's own *Symposium* (to say nothing of Attic vase-paintings) illustrates, there was plenty of occasion for women to be present at them, though in no very dignified capacity, to put it delicately.[105] At Agathon's, by contrast, the customary orgy of intoxication and copulation has been ruled out from the start and the flute-girl has been sent off to pipe to herself or to the women inside (176a–e); the female sex makes its reappearance at Agathon's only when Alcibiades staggers in with another flute-girl in tow (212cd). Furthermore, the first two speakers at the symposium take special care to disqualify both *erôs* for women and women's *erôs* from figuring among the topics of the proposed encomia: Phaedrus goes to ingenious lengths to devalue Alcestis's *erôs* for her husband in comparison to Achilles's *philia* for his comrade Patroclus (whom Phaedrus considers Achilles's *erastês*, or active lover), just as he disparages Orpheus's *erôs* for his wife (179b–180b),[106] while Pausanias restricts women as objects of *erôs* to the devotees of "vulgar Aphrodite" (181b2);[107] paederastic *erôs* is also singled out for (ironic) praise by Aristophanes (191e6–192a7). Alcestis is rehabilitated only by Diotima (208d) who, like Plato's Aristophanes, detaches the value of *erôs* from the gender of both its subject and its object (she has no more use than does Pausanias for the physical love of men for women: 208e–209e).[108] Far from picturing Socrates as amusing his friends by describing his private relations with a famous woman, as Aeschines apparently did and as Plato himself did in the *Menexenus*, the author of the *Symposium* has taken care to banish women from the dramatic setting as well as from the topics of conversation in that dialogue.[109] The ultimate effect is to achieve the maximum possible contrast when Socrates conjures up his encounter with Diotima, rendering her erotic authority so intrusive and making what she says so inappropriate to the terms of the foregoing discussion that it is hard to account for Plato's decision to include her *simply* by supposing that he was somehow wedded to an earlier tradition in Socratic literature or that for some reason he had to employ a prophetess at all costs in order to articulate his erotic doctrine. Those considerations may help to explain Diotima's presence, but they are not sufficient in and of themselves to account for it. I think it is time to confront the programmatic importance for Platonic doctrine of Diotima's being . . . not a surrogate for Aspasia, not a prophetess, not an Eleusinian priestess, but a woman.

6. Erotic Hierarchies and Platonic Reciprocities

I venture to suggest that Diotima's gender serves to thematize two of the most distinctive and original elements of Plato's erotic theory. By the very fact of being a woman, that is, Diotima signals Plato's departure from certain aspects of the sexual ethos of his male contemporaries and thereby enables him to highlight some of the salient features of his own philosophy. For Plato's philosophical explorations of erotic desire issue in a model of erotic dynamics that, in at least two respects, corresponds to the model, or models, of desire constructed as "feminine" according to the terms of the sex/gender system of classical Athens.

It would be wrong to ascribe to the Athenians a unitary, let alone a consistent, notion of women—a single discourse of "the feminine." As in many societies, the ideology of gender in classical Athens was subject to the shifting requirements of masculine interest; it therefore had room in it for all sorts of contradictory notions. Plato's philosophical exploitation of that ideology capitalizes on two, mutually conflicting, aspects of it. According to one Greek stereotype, women are less able than men to resist pleasures of all sorts; they enjoy sex too much, and once initiated into the delights of sex they become insatiable and potentially treacherous, ready to injure their own children—if necessary—or to introduce a suppositious child into their husband's household. According to a second stereotype, women do not possess (as men do) a free-floating desire that ranges from one object to another, stimulated in each case by beauty, nobility, or other cultural values advertised by the object; rather, their desire is conditioned by their physical nature, which aims at procreation and needs to fulfill itself by drawing off substance from men.[110]

In Plato's conception (male) *erôs*, properly understood and expressed, is not hierarchical but reciprocal; it is not acquisitive but creative. Plato's model of successful erotic desire effectively incorporates, and allocates to men, the positive dimension of each of these two Greek stereotypes of women, producing a new and distinctive paradigm that combines erotic responsiveness with (pro)creative aspiration.[111] I shall take up each of these two points in turn, treating the first in this section of my essay, the second in the following section. In order to appreciate the nature and extent of Plato's originality in each department, we must begin by measuring how far the sort of desire defined and prescribed by his erotic theory departs from the conventional understanding and experience of male desire in classical Athens.

I have already argued in the title essay of this collection that sex, as it is represented in classical Athenian documents, is a deeply polarizing experience: constructed according to a model of penetration that interprets "penetration" as an intrinsically unidirectional act, sex divides its participants into asymmetrical and, ultimately, into hierarchical positions, defining one partner as "active" and "dominant," the other partner as "passive" and "submissive." Sexual roles, moreover, are isomorphic with status and gender roles; "masculinity" is an aggregate combining the congruent functions of penetration, activity, dominance, and social precedence, whereas "femininity" signifies penetrability, passivity, submission, and social subordination. In this socio-sexual system, the position of the junior partner in a paederastic relationship was, as Foucault has persuasively argued,[112] a necessarily problematic one. The Athenian ethos governing the proper sexual enjoyment of citizen youths attempted to negotiate the resulting difficulties by denying the youths a significant share in the experience of *erôs* in their relations with adult men. It was clearly unacceptable, after all, for the future rulers of Athens to exhibit any eagerness or desire to submit themselves to anyone, especially to their (eventual) peers.[113]

Xenophon is explicit: in his *Symposium*, Socrates emphasizes that "the boy does not share in the man's pleasure in intercourse, as a woman does; cold sober, he looks upon the other drunk with sexual desire" (8.21).[114] The accuracy of Xenophon's characterization of the conventional Athenian *attitude*—if not of the social and sexual *actuality* concealed by it—is overwhelmingly confirmed by the pictorial representations of male homosexual behavior on Attic vases as well as by a variety of ancient literary sources. In Aristophanes's *Clouds*, for example, Just Argument, the defender of traditional morality, declares that a well-bred youth would never do anything to encourage the interest of a lover, such as immodestly meeting his gaze: "he would not go about speaking in a forced, effeminate voice to his lover, acting as his own procurer with his eyes" (979–80).[115] Since the Greeks located the source of *erôs* in the eyes (of the beloved, usually), and since they considered eye-contact between lover and beloved the erotic stimulus *par excellence*,[116] the respectable youth's downcast eyes signify his refusal to engage in the opening phases of an erotic relationship. Aristotle, for whom reciprocity is a necessary ingredient of friendship (*Nicomachean Ethics* 8.1155b27–1156a5), refuses to consider the erotic relationship between man and boy a species of friendship on precisely these grounds[117]:

[In the case of friendships based on pleasure and utility,] the friendships are most enduring when they [the two friends] get the same thing—e.g. pleasure— from each other, and, moreover, get it from the same source, as witty people do. They must not be like the erotic lover and the boy he loves. For these do not take pleasure in the same things; the lover takes pleasure in seeing [gazing at] his beloved, while the beloved takes pleasure in being courted [or served] by his lover. When the beloved's bloom is fading, sometimes the friendship fades too; for the lover no longer finds pleasure in seeing his beloved, while the beloved is no longer courted by the lover. Many, however, remain friends if they have similar characters and come to be fond of each other's characters from being accustomed to them. . . . [In the category of friendships between contraries] we might also include the erotic lover and his beloved, and the beautiful and the ugly. Hence an erotic lover also sometimes appears ridiculous, when he expects to be loved in the same way as he loves; that would presumably be a proper expectation if he were lovable in the same way, but it is ridiculous when he is not (*Nicomachean Ethics* 8.1157a3–14, 1159b11–19, trans. Irwin, with my amplifications).

Perhaps the first hint of Plato's departure from the hierarchical norm governing sexual relations between males can be glimpsed in Aristophanes's speech in the *Symposium*: as Foucault has observed, Aristophanes's notion that each lover is half of a former whole individual makes the desire of each human being formally identical to that of every other, and so militates against the asymmetry of conventional paederastic relations.[118] Note, however, that Aristophanes avoids drawing such a conclusion from his own myth: in classical Athenian society, as he portrays it, male homoerotic individuals are philerasts and paederasts *by turns* (191e6–192b5). Plato makes a clean break with the conventional ethos of Athenian paederasty only in the *Phaedrus*, when Socrates describes the dynamic of attraction obtaining in a proper relationship between lover and beloved:

[When lover and beloved are together, a flood of passion] pours in upon the lover; and part of it is absorbed within him, but when he can contain no more the rest flows away outside him; and as a breath of wind or an echo, rebounding from a smooth hard surface, goes back to its place of origin, even so the stream of beauty turns back and re-enters the eyes of the fair beloved; and so by the natural channel it reaches his soul and gives it fresh vigour, watering the roots of the wings and quickening them to growth: whereby the soul of the beloved, in its turn, is filled with love. So he loves, yet knows not what he loves: he does not understand, he cannot tell what has come upon him; like one that has caught a disease of the eye from another, he cannot account for it, not realising that his lover is as it were a mirror in which he beholds himself. And when the other is beside him, he shares his respite from anguish; when he is absent, he likewise shares his longing and being longed for; since he possesses that counter-love which is the image of love, though he supposes it to be friendship rather than love, and calls it by that name. He feels a desire, like the lover's yet not so strong, to behold, to touch, to kiss him, to share his couch: and now ere long the desire, as one might guess, leads to the act (255c–e, trans. Hackforth).

What the beloved experiences or ought to experience, according to Plato, is not *philia* but *erôs*, specifically an *anterôs* ("counter-love" in Hackforth's translation)—that is, an *erôs* in return for *erôs*, which is an image or replica (*eidôlon*) of his lover's *erôs*. Because *erôs*, on the Platonic view (as we shall see), aims at procreation, not at possession, and so cannot be sexually realized, Platonic *anterôs* does not lead either to a reversal of sexual roles or to the promotion of sexual passivity on the part of the beloved. Rather, Plato all but erases the distinction between the "active" and the "passive" partner—or, to put it better, the genius of Plato's analysis is that it eliminates passivity altogether: according to Socrates, both members of the relationship become active, desiring lovers; neither remains a merely passive object of desire. By granting the beloved access to a direct, if reflected, erotic stimulus and thereby including him in the community of lovers, Plato clears the erotic relation between men and boys from the charge of exploitativeness and allows the beloved to grow philosophically in the contemplation of the Forms.[119] Thus, the way is cleared for a greater degree of reciprocity in the expression of desire and in the exchange of affection. The younger man is now free to return his older lover's passion without shame or impropriety.

Plato dramatizes his theory of erotic reciprocity in the Socratic dialogues, where relations between Socrates and the members of his circle abundantly illustrate the reciprocal dynamic of Platonic *erôs*. Some of the dialogues culminate in the actual conversion of a beautiful youth to an active and aggressive erotic role: the *Charmides* ends with its title character threatening playfully to "force" (i.e., rape) Socrates if the latter resists his pursuit (176b ff.);[120] in the *Alcibiades Major*, Socrates's youthful interlocutor ruefully concedes that "we shall in all likelihood reverse the usual pattern, Socrates, I taking your role and you mine" (135d).[121] More is at stake in these turn-arounds than subtleties of erotic psychology: Plato's remodeling of the homoerotic ethos of classical Athens has direct consequences for his program of philosophical inquiry. Erotic reciprocity animates what Plato considers the best sort of conversations, those in which each interlocutor is motivated to search within himself and to say what he truly believes in the confidence that it will not be misunderstood; mutual desire makes possible the ungrudging exchange of questions and answers which constitutes the soul of philosophical practice. Reciprocity finds its ultimate expression in dialogue.[122]

Plato's (male) fellow-citizens, accustomed as they were to holding one another to an aggressively phallic norm of sexual conduct—and, consequently, to an ethic of sexual domination in their relations with males and females alike—preferred not to acknowledge or to understand mutuality in *erôs*. To be sure, they kept themselves in line by taunting one another with the scare-figure of the *kinaidos*, of the man who will do anything for pleasure and actively enjoys submitting himself to sexual domination by other men.[123] And a few widely scattered texts admit that some men actually enjoy "passive" sex.[124] But, for the most part, erotic reciprocity was relegated to the province of women, who were thought capable of both giving and receiving pleasure in the sexual act at the same time and in relation to the same individual, and whose enjoyment of sex is, at least according to Teiresias in Hesiod's famous myth,[125] far more intense than that of their male partners.[126] Like the interlocutors in a Socratic dialogue, women are both active and passive at once, both subjects and objects of desire: as Phaedrus and Diotima agree in Plato's *Symposium*, Alcestis's heroïsm proceeds from her active *erôs* (179b–180b, 208de).[127] Only women, according to the customary Greek idiom, normally experience *anterôs*[128]: Xenophon's Socrates, speaking of a newly and happily married man, says that he desires and is desired in return by his wife (*erôn tês gynaikos anteratai: Symposium* 8.3).[129] The "passive" role, defined in relation to a conception of "activity" modeled on the act of penetration, is an indignity for a man to assume and a symptom of moral incapacity for him to enjoy, but on the Greek view it is natural and naturally pleasurable to a woman. The positive pleasure women take in passivity contributed to justifying, in masculine eyes, their socially as well as sexually subordinate position in Athenian society, for their enjoyment of the passive role signified to Greek men that women are naturally constituted in such a way that they actually *desire* to lose the battle of the sexes.

In the seventh book of the *Nicomachean Ethics*, Aristotle accordingly classes the predilection in males for the "passive" role in intercourse among those dispositions which are disease-like or a result of habituation, since they are pleasurable without being naturally so, although he does not deny the possibility that in some cases nature may be the cause of such degeneracy. He then goes on to observe that "no one could describe as 'lacking in self-control' those for whom nature is the cause, any more than (*sc.* we so describe) women (*lit.*) because they do not mount sexually but are mounted" (1148b26–35).[130] What is a sign of moral failure or incontinence in a man is natural to a woman. Let us not put words into Aristotle's mouth: he says that no one *blames* women for liking to be penetrated because it is natural for them to like it. But in this very predisposition to passivity it is possible to measure, or so Aristotle seems to imply, the extent of the inferiority of women's nature to men's. Similar notions appear in Aristotle's biological writings and they continue to be echoed today by reputable sexologists, psychoanalysts, gynaecologists; and philosophers.[131]

Plato's contemporaries routinely contrasted male and female *erôs* in terms of hierarchy and reciprocity, respectively. Recall Xenophon's emphasis on the psychological distance between the man's inflamed desire and the boy's sober disinterest: "the boy does not share in the man's pleasure in intercourse, *as a woman does*. . . ." That remark is well illustrated by Attic vase-painting, according to Mark Golden, who has made an exhaustive study of this particular theme:

> Women on the vases often appear to enjoy sex. But passive homosexual partners show no sign of pleasure; they have no erection and usually stare straight ahead during intercourse. . . . Women in vase paintings are depicted in a wide variety of sexual postures and are often shown being penetrated from behind. Women are sometimes shown leaning on or supported by their male lovers, physically dependent on them. . . . Passive males, however, regularly face their partners. They are upright; it is the active partner who bends his knees and (often) his head.[132]

A corresponding emphasis on women's sexual and psychological responsiveness to men emerges from James Redfield's discussion of the place and function of *kharis* in the Greek ideology of marriage (e.g., Semonides, fr. 7.86–89 [West]).[133]

After the classical period, the contrast between women and boys as sexual objects in terms of the relative degrees of their responsiveness to adult males becomes more explicit.[134] "I don't have a heart that's wild for boys," writes the Hellenistic epigrammatist Meleager, who goes on to ask, "What delight is there in mounting men if it involves taking [*sc.* pleasure] without giving [any]? After all, one hand washes another . . ." (*Palatine Anthology* 5.208 = Meleager, 9 [Gow-Page]). The remainder of the text is corrupt, but enough is decipherable to indicate that Meleager made the love of women an explicit point of contrast. Similarly Ovid, in the second book of his *Art of Love*, issued the following proclamation: "Let the man and woman derive an equal part of pleasure from the act; I hate couplings that do not gratify each of the two partners: that is why I am less inclined to the love of boys" (682–84).[135] Plutarch, championing the cause of *erôs* in marriage and emphasizing the benefits of sexual love, notes that impregnation cannot take place unless both parties have been moved or affected by one another; he goes on to contrast the union of husband and wife with unerotic partnerships that are merely mixtures of separate elements, like Epicurus's atoms which collide but do not fuse (*Moralia* 769ef; also, 140ef; 142e–143a).[136] In the *Erôtes*, a work included in the Lucianic corpus that belongs to the same genre as Plutarch's work just cited, the contrast between the love of women and the love of boys is even more explicit; the advocate of the former argues as follows:

> Why do we not pursue those pleasures that are mutual and bring delight to the passive and to the active partners? . . . Now men's intercourse with women involves giving like enjoyment in return. For the two sexes part with pleasure only if they have had an equal effect on each other—unless we ought rather to heed the verdict of Teiresias that the woman's enjoyment is twice as great as the man's. And I think it is honourable for men not to wish for a selfish pleasure or to seek to gain some private benefit by receiving from anyone the sum total of enjoyment but to share what they obtain and to requite like with like. But no one could be so mad as to say this in the case of boys. No, the active lover, according to his view of the matter, departs after having obtained an exquisite pleasure, but the outraged one suffers pain and tears at first, though the pain relents somewhat with time and you will, men say, cause him no further discomfort, but of pleasure he has none at all (27; trans. Macleod).

The most entertaining and sophisticated version of this debate occurs in the second book of *Leucippe and Cleitophon*, a Greek romance by Achilles Tatius. I quote, at obscene length, the remarks of the advocate of women from the forthcoming unexpurgated translation of Achilles Tatius by John J. Winkler:

> A woman's body is well-lubricated in the clinch, and her lips are tender and soft for kissing. Therefore she holds a man's body wholly and congenially wedged into her embraces, into her very flesh, and her partner is totally encompassed with pleasure. She plants kisses on your lips like a seal touching warm wax; and if she knows what she is doing she can sweeten her kisses, employing not only the lips but the teeth, grazing all around the mouth with gentle nips. . . .
>
> When the sensations named for Aphrodite are mounting to their peak, a woman goes frantic with pleasure, she kisses with mouth wide open and thrashes about like a mad woman. Tongues all the while overlap and caress, their touch like passionate kisses within kisses. Your part in heightening the pleasure is simply to open your mouth.
>
> When a woman reaches the very goal of Aphrodite's action, she instinctively gasps with that burning delight and her gasp rises quickly to the lips with a love-breath, and there it meets a lost kiss, wandering about and looking for a way down: this kiss mingles with the love-breath and returns with it to strike the heart. The heart then is kissed, confused, throbbing. If it were not firmly fastened in the chest it would follow along, drawing itself upwards to the place of kisses.

> Schoolboys are hardly so well-educated in kissing, their embraces are awkward, their love-making is lazy and devoid of pleasure (2.37).

While the speaker emphasizes the pleasures accruing to the lover from intercourse with a female partner, he makes it clear that her responsiveness contributes a great deal to her lover's enjoyment. Nor does the advocate of paederasty have much to say against that specific argument:

> His kisses, to be sure, are not sophisticated like a woman's, they are no devastating spell of lips' deceit. But he kisses as he knows how—acting by instinct, not technique. Here is a metaphor for a boy's kiss: take nectar, crystallize it, form it into a pair of lips— these would yield a boy's kisses. You could not have enough of these: however many you took, you would still be thirsty for more, and you could not pull your mouth away from his until the very excess of pleasure frightened you into escaping (2.38).

Here all the emphasis is on the subjective sensations of the lover: he does not tell us what, if anything, his partner experiences or what it is like to be the recipient of a male lover's amorous attentions. The description is utterly self-referential and narcissistic: the boy registers on the lover's consciousness only insofar as he is the vehicle for a certain sort of private pleasure and the occasion of insatiable desire on the lover's part.[137]

Sexual relations *between* women may reveal with particular clarity the mutuality of erotic responsiveness that is supposed to characterize women's eroticism—if, that is, we are to believe the somewhat idealized promotional advertisement devised by Simone de Beauvoir: "Between women love is contemplative; caresses are intended less to gain possession of the other than gradually to re-create the self through her; separateness is abolished, there is no struggle, no victory, no defeat; in exact reciprocity each is at once subject and object, sovereign and slave; duality becomes mutuality."[138] Some such construction of female eroticism seems to have commended itself to Plato, the only writer of the classical period to speak about sexual desire between women (*Symposium* 191e2–5);[139] at least, Plato valued it insofar as he could find in it an image of the reciprocal erotic bond that unites philosophical lovers who are jointly engaged in conversation and the quest for truth (cf. Plato, *Letter* 7.341cd). The ideal interlocutor, exemplified by Socrates, experiences desire and arouses it in others, and the members of his circle are equally encouraged to take an active, aggressive part in the pursuit of knowledge even as they continue to serve as objects of desire and sources of inspiration to others (cf. Plotinus, *Enneads* 5.8.11). Since any beautiful soul can serve as a mirror for any other, reciprocal desire need not be confined to the context of physical relations between the sexes (which Plato, at least according to one reading of *Phaedrus* 250e, appears to have despised).[140] The kind of mutuality in *erôs* traditionally imputed to women in Greek culture could therefore find a new home in the erotic dynamics of Platonic love.*

7. Erotic Acquisition and Platonic Procreation

I now turn to the second feature of Plato's erotic doctrine that sets it apart from the conventions governing male eroticism in classical Athens and assimilates it instead to a "feminine" paradigm—and, hence, is appropriately figured by a female authority on erotics. In a separate study,[141] I have argued that it was characteristic of the ancient Athenians to regard sexual desire as an appetite and, hence, to construe it (by analogy with hunger and thirst) as an acquisitive passion, a longing for the possession and consumption of a desirable object. Now Lesley Ann Jones, in an important forthcoming paper, has shown that such a conception of *erôs*—with its emphasis on the object-directed, acquisitive nature of desire—represented to the Athenians a specifically "masculine" model of erotic dynamics. Female desire, as the Greeks constructed it, tended by contrast to be related to the physiological economy of the female body—to the body's needs, rather than the mind's desires; hence, it is not aroused by individual objects but is governed instead by the requirements of woman's physical constitution with its generative functions.[142] The unreconstructed Socrates proves to be typically "masculine" in his outlook, and that is exactly where he goes wrong when Diotima initially interrogates him: in response to her question about what the lover of the beautiful desires, Socrates answers, predictably enough, "To have it" (204d). Diotima is not satisfied with that answer and eventually reveals to Socrates that "*erôs* is not for [*sc.* the possession of] the beautiful, as you think." "What is it for, then?" he asks. "It is for birth and procreation in the beautiful," she replies (206e).[143]

This is not the place to explicate Diotima's doctrine of erotic procreation. It will be sufficient merely to note that Diotima's heterodox definition of the

---

* It is, I suppose, an embarrassment for the interpretation proposed here that Diotima's conversation with Socrates culminates in a mini-lecture by Diotima (208c1–212a7), though her lecture does conclude with a question and her discourse does occur in the context of a living conversation. Perhaps it is not necessary for Diotima to enact as well as to figure reciprocity; perhaps, too, the encounter is more reciprocal than it appears to us: that is, we know what the sexual version of erotic reciprocity looks like, so we are able to recognize it easily enough, but how do we detect the intellectual version? What does reciprocal intellectual eroticism look like to someone standing outside its incandescent circuit? Is it not possible that the very fact that Diotima's encounter with Socrates gave rise to a discourse that continues to be passed by word of mouth from one person to another over the generations and that awakens a desire to hear it in those who only have heard about it (*Symposium* 172a–173e, 215cd)—might this not testify to the intellectual eroticism animating, in a reciprocal dynamic, the two original interlocutors whose passionate conversation we are still prolonging? (So Kranz [1926/b], 323.)

erotic aim has momentous consequences for Plato's view of erotic intention-ality: "For the picture of man as pleasure-chaser," Gregory Vlastos has observed, Diotima "substitutes an image of man as creator, producer, new-maker."[144] The notion that sexual desire aims not at physical gratification but at moral and intellectual self-expression, at the release of the lover's own creative energies, is one to which Plato remains deeply committed. It reappears in the *Phaedrus*, where spoken discourses that are written in the souls of the listeners become the speaker's sons (*hyeis*: 278a6),[145] and it figures most notably in a famous passage of the *Republic*, where the philosopher's *erôs* enables him to achieve intellectual intercourse with "what really is," to beget (*gennan*) intelligence and truth, and thereby to cease at long last from travail (*ôdis*: 490b).[146] In the *Theaetetus*, moreover, Socrates describes himself as a midwife and represents his dialectical method as a technique for deliver-ing other people's ideas (148e–151d, 157cd, 160e–161b, 184ab, 210b–d).[147]

Such an understanding of the function and purpose of erotic desire not only diverges from the conventional Athenian outlook in general: it also departs specifically from the traditional masculine paradigm of erotic pursuit and capture (most familiar to us from the lyric poetry of the archaic period)[148] and structures itself instead according to a model of erotic responsiveness whose central terms are fecundity, conception, gestation, and giving birth. Plato's theory of erotic procreativity, in short, is oriented around what his contemporaries would have taken to be a distinctively feminine order of experience.[149]

To be sure, the metaphor of intellectual and masculine conception is—if not exactly conventional—at least not entirely original with Plato, although it does not seem to be attested earlier than Aristophanes's *Clouds*: in that play, Strepsiades is reproached by one of Socrates's disciples for kicking the door of the Thinkery and thereby causing the miscarriage of a newly con-ceived plan (135–37).[150] In the *Frogs* a great poet is characterized as one who is "fecund" (*gonimos*), although the term is not immediately perspicuous and requires some elucidation (96–98); later in the same play, Aeschylus claims that a poet must beget (*tiktein*) expressions that are equal in magnitude to the sentiments and thoughts they express (1058–59). Similarly, Cratinus, defending himself in *The Wineflask* from the charge of drunken decrepitude, maintains that no man who drinks water can produce (*tiktein*) anything decent.[151] And in Xenophon's *Cyropaedia* a character speaks of mental reflec-tion as gestating (*kyein*: 5.4.35). But nothing in the previous literary tradition approaches Plato's imagery in the *Symposium*. Plato turned what was a mere figure of speech—or even, perhaps, a dead metaphor[152]—into an extended allegory and an explicit programme, elaborating it deliberately and systemat-ically as no one had done before.[153] Or, to be more precise, what Plato did was to take an embedded habit of speech (and thought) that seems to have become detached from a specific referent in the female body and, first, to *re-*

embody it as "feminine" by associating it with the female person of Diotima through her extended use of gender-specific language, then to *disembody* it once again, to turn "pregnancy" into a mere *image* of (male) spiritual labor, just as Socrates's male voice at once embodies and disembodies Diotima's female presence.[154]

Some scholars, however, have doubted that Plato's language images what the Greeks took to be a characteristically feminine experience;[155] they point to the widespread Greek tendency to regard the male parent as the only generative agent and to treat the female parent as a human incubator—a notion supported by the god of medicine himself in Aeschylus's *Oresteia*,[156] though implicitly repudiated by Plato in the *Timaeus*.[157] Recent studies of Greek embryology, however, have shown that a major, if not the dominant, theme in ancient thinking on this topic emphasized the contribution which the female makes to conception;[158] not only are Alcmaeon, Parmenides, Democritus, Empedocles, and Epicurus, among others, reported by some sources (of widely varying quality) to have held that women emit seed,[159] but the Hippocratic writers and the anonymous author of a gynaecological treatise transmitted to us as the tenth book of Aristotle's *History of Animals* went so far as to insist that woman's sexual pleasure is necessary for conception because unless she achieves an orgasm she will not ejaculate her seed.[160] Aristotle's contrary view, articulated in *On the Generation of Animals*,[161] proved to be short-lived in antiquity: it was abandoned by Strato of Lampsacus, Herophilus, Erasistratus, and was ridiculed by Galen,[162] although it subsequently regained its credibility.[163] More decisive than the academic disputes of the Greek physicians, however, is the kinship structure of classical Athens: the law permitted half-brother and -sister to marry only if they were descended from different mothers, thereby in effect denying the claim of the Aeschylean Apollo that the father is the only true parent.[164] The thesis that Plato's contemporaries generally disbelieved that women played any contributory role in conception cannot plausibly be maintained.

But there are even more telling indications that what is imaged by Diotima's figurative language in the *Symposium* is indeed what the Greeks considered a feminine, gender-specific experience. The clue is provided not merely by the recurrent, if banal, reference to procreation but by Diotima's delineation of a peculiar type of eroticism in which the distinction between sexual and reproductive functions has been totally abolished. Diotima's argument that *procreation* is the *aim* of erotic *desire* depends, after all, on a firmly unconscious assimilation of sexual to reproductive activity. Hence the difficulty of translating the central terms in her vocabulary: does *kyein* mean "to be pregnant," "to conceive," or merely "to be fertile or fecund"?[165] Does *tokos* mean "conception," "procreation," or "giving birth"? In certain passages Plato's emphasis seems to fall on the sexual dimension: thus, we need beauty in order to procreate, for no erotic impulse is evoked in us by ugliness

(206cd, 209b); in the presence of the ugly we "contract" and "shrivel up," Diotima declares, employing an almost embarrassingly anatomical meta-phor to describe the soul's revulsion from the formless (206d).[166] But in other passages the emphasis is on the procreative dimension, the connection between the two being furnished by the Greek verb *tiktein*, "to generate," and its derivatives, which cover both sexual and reproductive functions.[167] Thus, when we attain puberty, our nature desires *tiktein*, which it is not able to do in an ugly medium but only in a beautiful one; moreover, the inter-course of man and woman is a *tokos* (206c3–6;[168] cf. 209b1–2). The climax to which beauty summons us, however, is manifestly not of a sexual kind, as every student of "Platonic love" knows: beauty arouses only those who are *already* pregnant, and intercourse culminates not in orgasm but in giving birth (206cd, 208e–209e). The two strands of sex and reproduction are so thoroughly interwoven in Diotima's discourse that they are virtually impossible to disentangle, as the following passages illustrate: "When what is pregnant draws near to the beautiful," Diotima tells us, it rejoices, "engen-ders [*tiktei*], and gives birth [*gennai*]," and thereby is "released from great travail [*ôdis*]" (206de); the young man who is spiritually pregnant with moral virtue "cherishes beautiful bodies rather than ugly ones *because he is pregnant*" (209b4–5). In short, Diotima speaks as if erotic desire consisted in an excita-tion brought on by pregnancy and climaxing in the ejaculation of a baby.[169]

Even the figure of Diotima seems to span and unite in itself these two dimensions of human experience: she reveals, in addition to her powerful grasp of erotic phenomenology, something of a maternal dimension. When Socrates asks her what philosophers are, if neither ignorant nor wise, she replies chidingly, "Why such a thing is obvious even to a child!"(204b1), and throughout their conversation she gently incites her interlocutor with the goad of indulgent raillery, in the customary fashion of Greek mothers ancient and modern.[170]

Diotima's systematic conflation of sexual and reproductive functions indi-cates that Plato has shifted, intellectually and mythopoetically, to a realm of desire conventionally marked as female. For women's *erôs*, as the Greeks constructed it, did not aim now at (non-procreative) pleasure, now at repro-duction, as men's did, but was intimately bound up with procreation.[171] As Plato puts it in the *Timaeus*,[172]

> there is in women a living animal passionately desirous of making children [i.e., the womb, which,] when it remains fruitless for a long time past its season, bears its irritation harshly, wandering all about the body, blocking the channels of the breath and not allowing them to breathe, thereby driving the body to extremes of desperation and producing all sorts of illnesses, until the desire and passion [*erôs*] of man and woman drive them together, plucking down the fruit from the branching trees [of their reproductive systems] and sowing in the furrow of the womb living creatures unformed and invisible because of their smallness (91cd).

Woman's sexual nature desires to give birth;[173] the womb is an *animal avidum generandi*.[174] That the womb is "eager for procreation" is also a view enshrined in the gynaecological writings of the Hippocratic corpus, which treat women's sexuality only as it bears on the dynamics of reproduction[175] and which persistently conflate sexual and reproductive functions—prescribing sexual intercourse for diseases of the womb and curing gynaecological complaints with aphrodisiac drugs.[176]

The amalgamation of women's sexual and reproductive functions is not simply an article of faith among certain authorities, however, but is implicitly rooted in ancient habits of thought—specifically, as the passage from the *Timaeus* illustrates, in the age-old homology between woman and earth. That the earth is female and that women are earthy, especially in comparison with men, seems to be a feature of Greek cosmology;[177] as Aristotle says, "Male is what we call an animal that generates into another, female that which generates into itself. That is why in the universe as a whole the earth's nature is thought of as female and mother, while the sky and sun or such others are called begetters and fathers" (*Generation of Animals* 716a14–17).[178] The same outlook is written into the *engyê*, the Athenian betrothal ceremony, in which the father of the bride says to her future husband, "I give you this woman for the plowing of legitimate children."[179] It reappears in the symbolic language of the ritual practices associated with such common Greek cults as the Thesmophoria, which represents the relation of husband to wife as a domestic form of cultivation homologous to agriculture whereby women are tamed, mastered, and made fruitful.[180] The notion also surfaces in the tendency of the natural philosophers and medical writers to insist that women are physically colder and wetter than men[181] and require constant irrigation by men to keep their bodies healthy;[182] in the absence of men, women's sexual functioning is aimless and unproductive, merely a form of rottenness and decay, but by the application of male pharmacy it becomes at once orderly and fruitful.

It may be typical of patriarchal cultures to view women's sexual capacity *functionally*—as a means of producing children for men—rather than as an autonomous domain of desire, a subjectivity of one's own. At any rate, the reluctance of modern readers to discern in Diotima's collapsing of the distinction between sexual and reproductive functions an appeal to what the Greeks took to be a specifically feminine order of experience may signify something of the extent to which contemporary male attitudes to female eroticism coincide—in this one respect, at least—with their ancient ideological forebears. For recent expressions of an outlook similar to that exhibited by classical Greek masculinist discourse one need look no further than the enlightened discipline of modern gynaecology, one of whose exponents has written, "The fundamental biologic factor in women is the urge of motherhood balanced by the fact that sexual pleasure is entirely secondary or even absent."[183] Now that, to be sure, was set down during the dark days before the Kinsey Reports (when, *no doubt*, it was true); but even after twenty years of scientific progress the author of an article on "Psychology and Gynaecology," published in the third edition of a standard collection of essays on clinical obstetrics, could still write, "Childbirth should be the crowning fulfilment of a woman's *sexual* development; her physical and psychological destiny have been achieved."[184] In fact, *at least half* of the gynaecological textbooks published in the United States between 1963 and 1972 (when my information runs out) maintain that the sex drive in women aims primarily at reproduction, not at sexual pleasure.[185] The refusal to separate sexual pleasure and reproduction in women seems also to underlie the traditional insistence of modern gynaecologists on the reality and importance of the vaginal orgasm, an insistence that continued for decades after Kinsey claimed to observe that portions of the vagina contain no nerve endings and therefore lack all sensation; thus, one expert writing in 1962 sternly warns women to leave the clitoris alone: "If there has been much manual stimulation of the clitoris it may be reluctant to abandon control, or the vagina may be unwilling to accept *the combined role* of arbiter of sensation and vehicle of reproduction."[186] This emphasis on the merging in female eroticism of the otherwise isolated impulses to sexual pleasure and to reproduction casts into a modern medical idiom what our evidence indicates to have been at least a prominent theme in Greek constructions of female *erôs*.[187]

8. Plato's Erotic Theory and the Politics of Gender

Plato's exploitation of this theme raises a complicated and interesting question about the cultural politics of gender. For the interdependence of sexual and reproductive capacities is in fact a feature of male, not female, physiology. To be sure, neither in men nor in women does sexual desire necessarily *aim* at procreation. But it is only in men, not in women, that reproduction depends on sexual desire and that reproductive function cannot be isolated from sexual pleasure (to the chagrin of Augustine and others),[188] whereas in women orgasm and reproduction are entirely independent, as even Aristotle and Galen maintained.[189] Plato, then, would seem to be constructing female desire according to a male paradigm—as his ejaculatory model of female procreativity suggests; he would seem, in fact, to be interpreting as "feminine" and allocating to men a form of sexual experience which is masculine to begin with and which men had previously alienated from themselves by defining as feminine. In other words, it looks as if what lies behind Plato's erotic doctrine is a double movement whereby men project their own sexual experience onto women only to reabsorb it themselves in the guise of a "feminine" character. This is particularly intriguing because it suggests that in order to facilitate their own appropriation of what they take to be the feminine men have initially constructed "femininity" according to a male paradigm while creating a social and political ideal of "masculinity" defined by their own putative ability to isolate what only women can *actually* isolate—namely, sexual pleasure and reproduction, recreative and procreative sex.

The determination of men to acquire the powers they ascribe (whether correctly or incorrectly) to women is a remarkably persistent and widespread feature of male culture. For many years now a number of anthropologists and their psychoanalytic collaborators have been detailing the various strategies by which males, in many different cultures, arrogate to themselves the power and prestige of female (pro)creativity: these strategies range from rites of ceremonial mutilation, in which adolescent boys, in the course of separating themselves from their mothers, inscribe female characters into their own flesh,[190] to the couvade—the stylized enactment by males of false pregnancy, labor, and giving birth coincident with the actual pregnancy and labor of a female family member (a practice that seems to have survived in Western societies in the form of certain psychosomatic illnesses that typically afflict the husbands of pregnant women)[191]—to, it has been claimed, the modern, male-dominated professions of obstetrics and gynaecology, in which men superintend and make themselves responsible for the successful realization of women's fertility.[192]

The most elaborate deployments of male pseudo-procreative imagery often occur (appositely enough, for the purposes of Platonic comparisons) in a paederastic context—specifically, in secret male initiation rituals (best studied in New Guinea) that feature sexual contact between men and boys.[193] The explicit ideological basis for such rituals is the notion that men are not born but made, that boys will not become men through a natural process of unassisted growth but must be transformed into men by means of intricate machinations (including sexual contact with grown men) designed to transfer physical prowess and social identity from one generation of males to the next. Thus, ritual paederasty represents the procreation of males by males: after boys have been born, physically, and reared by women, they must be born a second time, culturally, and introduced into the symbolic order of "masculinity" by men. The processes by which one generation of males gives birth to the succeeding one are explicitly thematized as female reproductive functions: ritual nose-bleeding, ear-piercing, scarification of the tongue, or penile incision signifies male menstruation,[194] for example, and the oral insemination of youths by older males is represented as breast-feeding.[195] It seems that when men go about reproducing themselves socially, socializing and acculturating the new generation of youthful males, they tend to claim for themselves a reproductive capacity analogous to that of women. Behind their claim, it is often alleged, lies a sense of male inadequacy in the face of women's awesome power to generate new life. Men strive to compensate for their perceived lack, for the absence of a womb, on this view, by means of a kind of cultural sublimation —by appropriating procreative functions from women and reconstituting them ritually in the form of cultural practices.[196] Such procedures have been interpreted, however, with at least equal plausibility, not as an expression of "male envy" but as a male strategy for controlling reproductive politics.[197]

In the light of all this ethnographic evidence, Diotima's metaphors of male pregnancy and parturition would appear to be not only not incongruous but, indeed, to be virtually inevitable, given the paederastic setting of Plato's *Symposium.* Diotima's figurative language has in fact been situated in just such a cross-cultural context by Barry D. Adam, a Canadian sociologist. Noting that in Melanesia sex between men and boys is represented as "one among many ways in which men reproduce themselves in opposition to women," Adam interprets Greek paederasty as a crucial element in "the social reproduction of male culture" which functions as "a second stage of parenting that succeeds the mother-child relationship."[198] Nothing so elaborate and explicit as the New Guinea initiation rituals has been documented in the case of classical Greece, to be sure, but some evidence for the existence of roughly similar rites in the archaic period has come down to us.[199] Bachofen found examples of the couvade attested in ancient sources;[200] moreover, Greek males often voice a longing for the possibility of male asexual generation[201]—seeming to fear, correspondingly, the prospect of female parthenogenesis (and, hence, male uselessness).[202] And Greek men's fantasies about being able to give birth to themselves and their own institutions without the complicity of women usually involve the coöptation of "the feminine" in some suppressed capacity or other—think of Athena and the Erinyes in Aeschylus's *Oresteia.*[203]

Diotima's function in the *Symposium* invites a similar interpretation. Diotima's feminine presence at the originary scene of philosophy, at one of its founding moments, contributes an essential ingredient to the legitimation of the philosophical enterprise; her presence endows the paedagogic processes by which men reproduce themselves culturally—by which they communicate the secrets of their wisdom and social identity, the "mysteries" of male authority, to one another across the generations—with the prestige of female procreativity. Diotima's erotic expertise, on this view, constitutes an acknowledgment by men of the peculiar powers and capacities of women; thus, Diotima is a woman because Socratic philosophy must borrow her femininity in order to seem to leave nothing out and thereby to ensure the success of its own procreative enterprises, the continual reproduction of its universalizing discourse in the male culture of classical Athens.[204]

But Plato's figuration of the feminine gender by means of the combined sexual and reproductive imagery which Diotima uses to convey the central tenets of her erotic theory—and which, in turn, uses Diotima to guarantee the allegedly feminine character of the experience it images—does not simply represent an instance of male cultural imperialism, a typical attempt by men to colonize female "difference" in order to claim it for a universalizing male discourse. For at the same time as Plato invests Diotima with an erotic and prophetic authority, his construal of her "difference" takes back what it gives, denying in effect the autonomy of women's experience. We can distinguish two strategies that combine to cancel Diotima's "difference." First, as we have seen, Plato's figuration of Diotima's supposed "femininity" reinscribes male identity in the representation of female "difference": it is a projection by men of their own experience onto women, a male fantasy intended for internal consumption—a version of pastoral. Second, to construct woman as the presence of a quite specific male lack is to deny her difference just as surely as it is to construct her as a lack of male presence: such a procedure does not truly acknowledge otherness, does not admit the possibility of an autonomous experience different from that of men, but treats woman only as "the inversed *alter ego* of the 'masculine' subject or *its* complement, or *its* supplement."[205] Hence, when Diotima speaks, she does not speak for women: she silences them.[206]

The radical *absence* of women's experience—and, thus, of the actual feminine—from the ostensibly feminocentric terms of Plato's erotic doctrine should warn us not to interpret Plato's strategy simplistically as a straightforward attempt to appropriate the feminine or as a symbolic theft of women's procreative authority. For Plato's appropriation of the Other works not only by misrecognizing the Other but by constructing "the other" as a masked version of the same—or, to borrow the language of Julia Kristeva, it works by constructing a "pseudo-Other."[207] To study the various strategies by which men simultaneously construct and coöpt female "difference," in other words, is not at all to study men's attitudes towards (real) women; rather, it is to study the male imaginary, the specular poetics of male identity and self-definition.[208] The pseudo-feminocentrism implicit in Plato's staging of Diotima's discourse is, as Nancy Miller (writing about a modern variety of pseudo-feminocentrism) puts it, "a strategy elaborated to translate . . . masculine self-affirmation"; " 'woman,'" she adds, "is the legal fiction, the present absence that allows the male bond of privilege and authority to constitute itself within the laws of proper circulation" in "the phallocentric . . . economies of representation."[209]

The use of "women" to license male speech is a striking feature of classical Greek high culture. As Helene Foley has recently emphasized, "Although women in fact play virtually no public role other than a religious one in the political and social life of ancient Greece, they dominate the imaginative life of Greek men to a degree almost unparalleled in the Western tradition. . . . Greek writers used the female—in a fashion that bore little relation to the lives of actual women—to understand, express, criticize, and experiment with the problems and contradictions of their culture."[210] What I have tried to suggest is that the silence of actual women in Greek public life and the volubility of fictional "women" (invented by male authors) in Greek cultural expression do not represent opposed, contradictory, or paradoxical features of classical Greek society but, on the contrary, are connected to one another by a strict logical necessity. Greek men effectively silenced women by speaking for them on those occasions when men chose to address significant words to one another in public, and they required the silence of women in public in order to make themselves heard—and to impersonate women— without impediment.[211] As Agathon (not Plato's Agathon, this time, but Aristophanes's) says, explaining the relation between his composition of tragedies about women and his habit of dressing in women's clothes, "Whatever we don't have, we capture by *mimêsis*"—that is, by imitation or representation (*Thesmophoriazusae* 155–56).[212]

The essential element in Plato's staging of "femininity," similarly, is a mimetic transvestitism.[213] What is crucial for Plato's strategy is not that Diotima present a woman's perspective but that she *represent* it in a form that is recognizable to men. This insight casts a new light on the ethnographic evidence cited above and offers a way of rereading it that more closely fits the features of Plato's text. According to this new interpretation, the viability of the procedures by which men reproduce themselves culturally depends on a paradoxical combination of success and failure in their assumption of "feminine" attributes. Even in the midst of mimicking menstruation, pregnancy, giving birth, and breast-feeding, the male actors must share with their audience the understanding that their procreative performances are symbolic, not real—that nose-bleeding is *not* menstruating, that oral insemination is *not* breast-feeding. The point of all those rites, after all, is to turn boys into men, not into women: for the cultural construction of masculinity to succeed it is necessary that the process intended to turn boys into men be genuinely efficacious, no less "generative" than female procreativity itself, but it is also necessary that the men who do the initiating retain their identity as men—something they can only do if their assumption of "feminine" capacities and powers is understood to be an impersonation, a cultural fiction, or (at the very least) a mere analogy. The cultural traffic in "masculine" and "feminine" characters, in other words, is predicated on the basic non-confoundability of the genders.[214] The "feminine" identity acquired by men in the course of performing rites of initiation therefore must be an incomplete identity, and its status as a fiction—as an impersonation rather than a total appropriation of "the feminine"—must be exposed by a selective puncturing of the illusion, either by a dropping of the mask or by a thematizing of its status as mask. In this context, however, exposure is not demystification: it is not a strategy designed simply to make visible the contradictions in the cultural discourse of gender so as to explode the various meanings (such as "masculinity," "femininity") constituted by it. On the contrary: the very act of self-exposure contributes an essential element to the successful operation of the symbolic procedures whereby "masculine" and "feminine" identities circulate within a continuous system of male self-representation.

9. Sexual Politics and Textual Strategies

That Diotima's "femininity" is illusory—a projection of male fantasy, a symbolic language employed by men in order to explain themselves and their desires to one another across the generations—is similarly acknowledged by Plato. The textual strategies of the *Symposium* reveal Diotima's fictionality as much as they conceal it. Plato hints that Socrates has—if not simply invented Diotima out of whole cloth—at least shaped the doctrine he ascribes to her to suit the needs of the present occasion. Socrates avails himself of Diotima's authority, first of all, to depict *Erôs* as a barefoot philosopher, thereby portraying the god as a mythic embodiment of himself: in effect, Diotima teaches that *Erôs* by its very nature is intrinsically Socratic (203d). Alcibiades later confirms this identification of Socrates and *Erôs* by describing Socrates in terms that recall the ones Socrates himself had used to describe *Erôs* (219e–221b).[215]

Next, Socrates has Diotima rebut the view of *erôs* that Aristophanes had articulated a few moments earlier, on the same evening as his own speech (205d–206a). To be sure, Socrates is not so artless as to have Diotima allude by name to his "future" interlocutor: she merely claims to have heard a version of what turns out to be Aristophanes's account of *erôs* from other unspecified sources (she introduces her refutation with the vague but none-theless pointed phrase, *kai legetai men ge tis logos*: "some people say. . . ."). But Aristophanes is not fooled: Plato's narrator tells us that when Socrates had finished speaking Aristophanes tried to say something *inasmuch as Socrates [not* Diotima] *had mentioned him by referring to his speech in his own speech* (212c). The sudden eruption of Alcibiades into the scene saves Socrates from having to confront Aristophanes's implicit challenge to Diotima's authenticity, but the suspicion has already been planted in the reader's mind. Similarly, Socrates claims that his earlier conversation with Diotima dove-tails so perfectly with the present discussion that Diotima's arguments can be used to complete his reply to Agathon; conversely, the premises agreed upon by Socrates and Agathon can be imported intact into the logical foundation on which Diotima builds her own lesson in erotics.[216] Unless the author of the *Symposium* has been so beguiled by his own artistry that he doesn't notice these strains on the reader's willing suspension of disbelief in Diotima's autonomous existence, he must actually want to let Socrates's mask slip and to expose "Diotima" as an effect of Socratic ventriloquism.[217]

Another hint that Diotima may be not a person but a mask, a "feminine" costume designed from the start to be worn by men, can be found in the implied contradictions of the *Poros* and *Penia* myth. In the story of the birth, or origin, of *Erôs*, which Diotima narrates, *Penia* ("Poverty" or "Want") seduces *Poros* ("Means") and thereby conceives *Erôs*, who derives his ugliness and poverty from his mother, his enthusiasm for investigation and his resourcefulness in setting traps for his love-objects from his father (203b2–d8). Cleverness (*sophia*) is an attribute of *Poros* (204b6)—who is, in any case, the son of *Mêtis*, "cunning intelligence" (203b3)—and yet it is *Poros* who is tricked by *Penia*. An analogous reversal of roles appears to be played out in the narrative of the *Symposium*. Diotima, a source of wisdom, represents something of the plenitude of *Poros*, which is what Socrates represents to his fellow symposiasts, although compared to Diotima both he and they are figures of *Penia*.[218] Agathon, like Alcibiades, is aware of his lack and, like Alcibiades, believes he can draw off some of Socrates's wisdom by seducing and possessing him: "Come here, Socrates," Agathon urges his guest, "and recline next to me, so that I can lay hold of you and thereby enjoy the benefit of that piece of wisdom which occurred to you while you were on the porch; for it's clear that you found it and have it." Socrates, of course, rebukes Agathon, declaring his own wisdom to be as tenuous as a dream and explaining that, in any case, it is not in the nature of wisdom to flow from one person to another like liquid flowing from a fuller vessel to an emptier one (175c–e).[219] And yet, despite Socrates's denials, some such hydraulic transaction seems to have taken place between himself and Diotima. Socrates appears to have drawn off some of Diotima's wisdom, to have been filled sufficiently full of it to make him, by his own admission, an expert in erotics (177d7–8, 198d1–2) and to make his soul a repository of at least some of the golden adornments which Alcibiades discovers in it.[220] Diotima, however, has been effectively emptied in the process; she is entirely used up in the course of her brief appearance in the dialogue. Depleted by Socrates, she vanishes, but Socrates's erotic wisdom and his entrancing speeches endure (as the elaborate narrative frame of the dialogue attests), remaining in perpetual circulation in Athenian society.[221]

10. Conclusion

"Have you any notion how many books are written about women in the course of one year?" Virginia Woolf asked the audience at a women's college in 1928. "Have you any notion how many are written by men? Are you aware that you are, perhaps, the most discussed animal in the universe?"[222] Four years later, as if in response to these queries from his English publisher, Sigmund Freud began his hypothetical lecture on "Femininity" (a work recently made notorious by the brilliant commentary of Luce Irigaray), as follows.

"Ladies and Gentlemen,— . . . . Throughout history people have knocked their heads against the riddle of the nature of femininity— . . . . Nor will *you* have escaped worrying over this problem—those of you who are men; to those of you who are women this will not apply—you are yourselves the problem."[223]

In the light of Woolf's questions and Freud's formulation, I shall appear to have been engaged throughout this essay in wrestling with a man's problem about a man's text: my own ostensible involvement with women's issues will be seen to have concealed—and, thereby, in a sense, to have disclosed—a more fundamental preoccupation with issues of great traditional importance to men. I had begun this paper by promising to identify those positive values conventionally associated with women by Plato's contemporaries that Plato might have sought to actualize through his sponsorship of Diotima. In the end, however, I have had relatively little to say about women but quite a lot to say about men. I have uncovered Diotima's absence rather than her presence: that very absence, moreover, has proven to be the empty center around which my entire discussion has revolved. Diotima has turned out to be not so much a woman as a "woman," a necessary female absence—occupied by a male signifier—against which Plato defines his new erotic philosophy. And my own interpretation of Plato has exemplified the same strategy, insofar as it has appropriated a feminist perspective for the purpose of legitimating its own discourse about the erotics of male culture.

But if I have reproduced, in effect, the traditional male strategy of speaking *about* women by speaking *for* women (the very strategy that served to erase Diotima's feminine presence from Plato's *Symposium* in the first place), if I have recovered not Diotima's presence but her absence and thereby obscured the real political significance of Plato's decision to represent a woman surpassing men in the practice of philosophy (a decision doubtlessly not unconnected to Plato's admission of women to his own Academy),[224] I can claim to have done so as part of an effort to expose, to illustrate, and to reverse the assumptions articulated with such deliberately devastating candor by Freud in the opening gambit of his lecture. To be explicit, what I have tried to do is to suggest that whenever there is a question of understanding women, it is usually *men*, not women, who (in Freud's wry formulation) are themselves the problem—who constitute, that is, the very enigma they think they are trying to penetrate. For "femininity" must continue to remain a mystery so long as it is defined wholly by reference to "masculinity"—whether as a lack of male presence or as the presence of a male lack.

Thus, Plato's textual practice, along with the tradition of scholarly commentary generated by it (including my own commentary), dramatizes the originary and inescapable contradiction within any discourse about "sexual difference"[225] that constructs such "difference" asymmetrically—making one gender (guess which?) the peculiar locus or site of "difference"—and that thereby ultimately denies "sexual difference" altogether, reconstituting it instead as what Teresa de Lauretis calls sexual *(in)difference*.[226] Even a would-be feminist analysis, such as my own, which aims to establish and to distinguish, or to salvage and preserve, what is authentically "feminine" from inauthentic male constructions of "the feminine," must succumb to the same tendency so long as it clings to an essentialist notion of female "difference": each progressive attempt to transcend traditional male-oriented discourses about "sexual difference" (in the hope of being able to specify what is *genuinely* "feminine"), or to invent a "politically correct" space outside such discourses, supposedly free from structures of domination (whether social or epistemological), simply reproduces at a higher level of abstraction the very asymmetry from which it had sought to escape. Instead of repeating vain attempts to transcend this originary contradiction, then, I have tried to elaborate and enlarge it, identifying and analyzing some of the various strategies by which men continually reinscribe male identity in their representations of female "difference" (as illustrated by Plato's representation of Diotima as well as by scholarly representations of that representation). For it is precisely by working within such contradictions, I believe, that feminist criticism can create its most effective opportunities.

To conclude that Plato has in effect reinscribed male identity in his representation of female difference is not to answer the question I have been asking throughout this essay but to move well beyond it. I have argued that Plato found in "woman" a figure for representing two properly philosophical (i.e., *male*) values: reciprocity and creativity. Gender enters the text of Plato's *Symposium*, then, not as it enters the text of Aristotle's *Generation of Animals*—not, that is, as a subject of inquiry in its own right—but as part of a larger figurative project whose aim is to represent the institutional and psychological conditions for the proper practice of (male) philosophy. Women's *erôs*, as Plato understands it, is evidently *like* the attitudes and dispositions exhibited by the ideal (male) philosopher who is engaged in the search for truth. "Diotima," in short, is a trope for "Socrates": "she" is a figure by means of which Plato images the reciprocal and (pro)creative erotics of (male) philosophical intercourse. That strategy of figuration, however, is distinctive to the *Symposium*; in the *Phaedrus*, by contrast, where Socrates is permitted to assert *explicitly* that the most philosophical sort of male lovers are animated by a reciprocal erotic desire (255c–e, quoted and discussed above), Plato can afford largely to ignore women: he is able to talk about erotic reciprocity directly and does not need to represent it figuratively.

But if Diotima is not a woman but a "woman," it no longer makes any sense to inquire into her gender. For "woman," too, turns out to be a trope: in the representational economy of Plato's text (as elsewhere), "woman" is always a sign of something else—of a spurious sexual "difference" that men (as they see themselves) at once lack and possess. Nothing in herself, "woman" is that pseudo-Other who both makes good what men want and exempts men from wanting anything at all; she is an alternate male identity whose constant accessibility to men lends men a fullness and totality that enables them to dispense (supposedly) with otherness altogether. "Femininity" is not referential, then, but figural: it is structured like a trope in the sense of being constructed as the opposite of "masculinity" according to the logic of "same-but-different" which, in classical rhetoric, defines the operations of simile and metaphor.[227] To mistake this construct for "the authentically feminine" would therefore amount to the most elementary of rhetorical errors, which is to confuse a figural with a literal denomination. But it is hard to see how any represention of "the feminine" that defines it, in essentialist terms, as the opposite of "the masculine" will not be vulnerable to a similar critique. If we follow this logic, we find that from the perspective of the male world, at least, there is no such thing as authentic femininity. "Woman," and "man," are figures of male speech.[228] Gender—no less than sexuality—is an irreducible fiction.[229] And so to ask why Diotima is a woman is to pose a question that ultimately has no answer.

Notes

(Full references to works cited here only by the author's last name—or, in the case of multiple works by the same author, by the author's last name and the year of publication—can be found in the Bibliography.)

Introduction

1 E. M. Forster, *Goldsworthy Lowes Dickinson* (1934; repr. New York, n.d.), 46.

2 See Herzer, 15–17.

3 See Michael Heseltine, trans., *Petronius*, Loeb Classical Library (Cambridge, MA, 1956), xviii. A revised version of Heseltine's translation, restoring the passages omitted by him, was published by the Loeb Classical Library in 1969.

4 See Walter C. A. Ker, trans., *Martial: Epigrams*, Loeb Classical Library (London, 1925–27), two volumes.

5 For this information I am indebted to Jocelyn, 44, n. 2. The essay of Housman's in question is cited in my Bibliography.

6 See, for example, Jeffrey Henderson, *The Maculate Muse: Obscene Language in Attic Comedy* (New Haven, 1975); Amy Richlin, "The Meaning of *Irrumare* in Catullus and Martial," *Classical Philology*, 76 (1981), 40–46, and *The Gardens of Priapus: Sexuality and Aggression in Roman Humor* (New Haven, 1983); J. N. Adams, *The Latin Sexual Vocabulary* (London, 1982); and the numerous studies by H. D. Jocelyn in the *Liverpool Classical Monthly* and elsewhere.

7 Dover (1978), 182; in his supplementary notes to the British paperback edition of *Greek Homosexuality*, Dover corrected the error.

8 Müller, *Die Dorier*, 4.4.6–9 = *Geschichte hellenischer Stämme und Städte*, 2d ed. (Breslau, 1844), III, 285–93. (I have seen only the second edition of this work.) For an account of the various resonances which the adjective "Dorian" acquired among British intellectuals, as a direct if unintended result of Müller's study, see Linda Dowling, "Ruskin's Pied Beauty and the Constitution of a 'Homosexual' Code," *Victorian Newsletter*, No. 75 (Spring 1989), 1–8, esp. 2ff.

9 I have seen only a copy of the second edition, which is undated: H. Hössli, *Eros. Die Männerliebe der Griechen, ihre Beziehungen zur Geschichte, Literatur und Gesetzgebung aller Zeiten, oder Forschungen über platonische Liebe, ihre Würdigung und Entwürdigung für Sitten-, Natur- und Völkerkunde* (Münster, Switzerland: author, n.d.).

10   I have not seen the original article by Meier, entitled "Paederastia," in the *Allgemeine Encyclopädie der Wissenschaft und Kunsten*, ed. J. S. Ersch and J. J. Gruber (Leipzig, 1837), 3.9.149–88. Meier's work is almost exclusively accessible in the amplified version: M.-H.-E. Meier, *Histoire de l'amour grec dans l'antiquité*, rev.ed.by L.-R. de Pogey-Castries (Paris, 1930).

11   See Kennedy, 43–53.

12   J. A. Symonds, *A Problem in Greek Ethics, being an inquiry into the phenomenon of sexual inversion, addressed especially to medical psychologists and jurists* (London, 1901): the essay was originally composed in 1873, privately circulated in an edition of ten copies in 1883, later revised, and posthumously appended to the first printing of Havelock Ellis's *Sexual Inversion* in April, 1897. Ellis's work had to be withdrawn from sale, however, when its publisher was convicted on a charge of obscenity, and it has not been published in England since.

13   For further information, see the partial bibliographies supplied by Boswell (1980), 17n.; the Editors' general introduction to Halperin, Winkler, and Zeitlin; and the notes to "Two Views of Greek Love," in this volume.

14   Boswell (1980), 28–30; (1982–83), 109, n. 42; (1989), 75.

15   "Law, Society and Homosexuality in Classical Athens," *Past & Present*, 117 (November 1987), 3–21. This has already proved to be an influential essay, but its arguments and conclusions should be treated with considerable caution.

16   Foucault's theoretical approach to sexuality has been turned back and applied to gender by Teresa de Lauretis, *Technologies of Gender: Essays on Theory, Film, and Fiction* (Bloomington, 1987), esp. 1–30.

17   Foucault (1978), 127.

18   Dover (1988).

1 One Hundred Years of Homosexuality

Earlier versions of this paper have appeared, under the present title, in *Diacritics*, 16, no. 2 (Summer 1986), 34–45, esp. 34–40; under the title, "Sex before Sexuality: Pederasty, Politics, and Power in Classical Athens," in *Hidden from History: Reclaiming the Gay and Lesbian Past*, ed. George Chauncey, Jr., Martin Bauml Duberman, and Martha Vicinus (New York: New American Library, 1989), 37–53, 482–92; and under the title, "Is There a History of Sexuality?" in *History and Theory*, 28.3 (October 1989), 257–74. The present essay is closely based on those earlier works; it was first recast for delivery at a conference on "Homosexuality in History and Culture, and the University Curriculum," held at Brown University on February 20–21, 1987, and was later given as a public lecture at Duke University on April 20, 1987. Subsequent versions have been presented at a conference on "The Body and Literature" at the State University of New York at Buffalo; at the University of California at Santa Cruz, the University of New Mexico, the University of California in San Francisco, Ohio State University, Babson College, Rice University, Harvard University, Wesleyan University, Brown University, and Northwestern State University of Louisiana. I am grateful to the organizers of these conferences and events for having invited me to speak as well as to my audiences for their sympathetic but rigorous scrutiny. I owe a considerable debt of gratitude to George Chauncey, Jr., who urged me to revise and expand this paper and suggested how I might go about it. I also wish to thank Barry D. Adam, Judith M. Bennett, Mary T. Boatwright, John Bodel, Elizabeth A. Clark, Ann Cumming, Kostas Demelis, Judith Ferster, Ernestine Friedl, Maud W. Gleason, Madelyn Gutwirth, Jean H.Hagstrum, John Kleiner, Richard D. Mohr, Glenn W. Most, Cynthia B. Patterson, Daniel A. Pollock, H. Alan Shapiro, Marilyn B. Skinner, Emery J. Snyder, Gregory

Vlastos, John J. Winkler, and Sylvia Yanagisako for much friendly help and advice and for numerous valuable suggestions.

1   See R. W. Burchfield, ed., *A Supplement to the Oxford English Dictionary* (Oxford, 1976), II, 136, s.v. homosexuality. Inasmuch as the same entry in the *OED* records the use of the word by J. A. Symonds in a letter of the same year, it is in fact most unlikely that Chaddock alone is responsible for its English coinage. The first use of the term "homosexual" in an American medical journal also dates to 1892, according to Jonathan Katz, *Gay/Lesbian Almanac* (New York, 1983), 232n.; the passage in which the word occurs, however, turns out to have been lifted in its entirety from Chaddock's translation of Krafft-Ebing (see note 17, below, for a full citation of the relevant article).

2   The terms "homosexual" and "homosexuality" appeared in print for the first time in 1869 in two anonymous pamphlets published in Leipzig and composed, apparently, by Karl Maria Kertbeny. Kertbeny (*né* Benkert) was an Austro-Hungarian translator and *littérateur* of Bavarian extraction, not a physician (as Magnus Hirschfeld and Havelock Ellis—misled by false clues planted in those pamphlets by Kertbeny himself—maintained); he wrote in German under his acquired Hungarian surname and claimed (rather unconvincingly), in the second of the two tracts under discussion, not to share the sexual tastes denominated by his own ingenious neologism. For the most reliable accounts of Kertbeny and his invention, see Herzer; Kennedy, 149–56; also, Féray. The earlier of Kertbeny's two pamphlets is reprinted in the *Jahrbuch für sexuelle Zwischenstufen*, 7 (1905), 1–66.

Dynes, 67, notes that Kertbeny's term "might have gone unnoticed had not [Kertbeny's friend] Gustav Jaeger popularized it in the second edition of his *Entdeckung der Seele* (1880)." In fact, "homosexuality" owes its currency to Krafft-Ebing, who employed an adjectival form of it in the second edition of his *Psychopathia sexualis* (Stuttgart, 1887), 88, explicitly acknowledging Jäger as his source for the word; he came to use the new terminology with increasing freedom and frequency in subsequent editions. See Herzer, 6–9, esp. 6: "For Jäger . . . the same thing holds as for all later users of Kertbeny's terms, including Kertbeny himself: nowhere is a reason given for using these new words. The new nomenclature is introduced without discussion; information on the origin of the words is omitted, as are definitions."

The year 1869 also witnessed the introduction of a terminological competitor (subsequently favored over "homosexuality" by both Krafft-Ebing and Moll), *die conträre Sexualempfindung* ("contrary sexual feeling"), by Carl Friedrich Otto Westphal in an article which Féray, 16, and Michel Foucault take to be the inaugural event of the new era (see note 52, below): C. Westphal, "Die conträre Sexualempfindung, Symptom eines neuropathischen (psychopathischen) Zustandes," *Archiv für Psychiatrie und Nervenkrankheiten*, 2 (1870), 73–108 (the first fascicle of this volume, in which Westphal's article appears, was actually published in the latter part of 1869, according to Féray, 256; also, Herzer, 17–18). See Foucault (1978), 43, who goes on to provide an entertaining list of the lexical novelties fashioned in this period to catalogue the newly discovered varieties of sexual behavior. On nomenclature generally, see Claude Courouve, *Vocabulaire de l'homosexualité masculine* (Paris, 1985).

3   Chauncey (1982–83), 116. See Foucault (1978), 37–38; Féray, esp. 16–17, 246–56; Weeks (1981/a), 82ff.; Marshall; Davidson (forthcoming). To be sure, the formal introduction of "inversion" as a clinical term (by Arrigo Tamassia, "Sull' inversione dell' istinto sessuale," *Rivista sperimentale di freniatria e di medicina legale*, 4 [1878], 97–117: the earliest published use of "inversion" that Ellis, 3, was able to discover) occurred a decade *after* Kertbeny's coinage of "homosexuality," but Ellis suspected the word of being considerably older: it seems to have been well established by the 1870's, at any rate, and it was certainly a common designation throughout the 1880's. "Homosexuality," by contrast,

did not really begin to achieve currency in Europe until the Eulenburg affair of 1907–1908 (see Féray, 116–22), and even thereafter it was slow in gaining ascendancy. The main point, in any case, is that "inversion," defined as it is by reference to gender-deviance, represents an age-old outlook on sexual non-conformity, whereas "homosexuality" marks a sharp break with traditional ways of thinking.

4   Chauncey (1982–83), 117–22, citing W. C. Rivers, "A New Male Homosexual Trait (?)," *Alienist and Neurologist*, 41 (1920), 22–27; the persistence of this outlook in the United States, along with some of its practical (military, legal, and ecclesiastical) applications, has now been documented by Chauncey (1985/86) in a study of the role-specific morality that once governed sexual attitudes and practices among members of the United States Navy (for even more recent expressions of the traditional outlook in Great Britain, see the citations discussed by Marshall, 149–52). See, also, Albert J. Reiss, Jr., "The Social Integration of Queers and Peers," *Social Problems*, 9 (1961/62), 102–20, with references to earlier work; Gagnon and Simon, 240–51. The classic statement of the "inversion" thesis is the opening chapter of Proust's *Sodom and Gomorrah*: see Marcel Proust, *A la recherche du temps perdu*, ed. Pierre Clarac and André Ferré (Paris, 1954), II, 601–32, esp. 614–15, 620–22; *Remembrance of Things Past*, trans. C. K. Scott Moncrieff and Terence Kilmartin (New York, 1981), II, 623–56, esp. 637–38, 643–45.

5   See Hubert C. Kennedy, "The 'Third Sex' Theory of Karl Heinrich Ulrichs," in *Historical Perspectives on Homosexuality*, ed. Salvatore J. Licata and Robert P. Petersen = *Journal of Homosexuality*, 6.1–2 (1980/81), 103–111; now, Kennedy, 43–53. In the light of the current self-representations of so-called transsexuals, I should point out that Ulrichs was attempting to account for his own pattern of sexual object-choice, not merely for his personal sense of sexual identity (some of the various issues that have figured in the history of efforts to distinguish sexual identity from object-choice are treated by Dave King, "Gender Confusions: Psychological and Psychiatric Conceptions of Transvestism and Transsexualism," in Plummer, 155–83).

6   See Chauncey (1982–83), 122–25; Marshall, 137–53; Davidson (1986/87), 258–71; Neu, 153ff. For the modern distinction between "inversion" (i.e., sex-role reversal) and "homosexuality," see Tripp, 22–35.

7   For the lack of congruence between traditional and modern sexual categories, see the suggestive comparative material discussed by Herdt (1984), viii–x; De Martino and Schmitt, 3–10. The new scientific conceptualization of homosexuality reflects, to be sure, a much older habit of mind, distinctive to northern and northwestern Europe since the Renaissance, whereby sexual acts are categorized not according to the modality of sexual or social roles assumed by the sexual partners but rather according to the anatomical sex of the persons engaged in them: see Trumbach, 2–9, with notes. This habit of mind seems to have been shaped, in its turn, by the same aggregate of cultural factors responsible for the much older division, accentuated during the Renaissance, between European and Mediterranean marriage-patterns; northern and northwestern Europe typically exhibits a pattern of marriage between mature coevals, a bilateral kinship system, neolocal marriage, and a mobile labor force, whereas Mediterranean societies are characterized by late male and early female marriage, patrilineal kinship organization, patrivirilocal marriage, and inhibited circulation of labor: see R. M. Smith, "'The People of Tuscany and their Families in the Fifteenth Century: Medieval or Mediterranean?'" *Journal of Family History*, 6 (1981), 107–28; recent work has produced evidence for the antiquity of the Mediterranean marriage-pattern: see M. K. Hopkins, "The Age of Roman Girls at Marriage," *Population Studies*, 18 (1964/65), 309–27; Richard P. Saller, "Men's Age at Marriage and its Consequences in the Roman Family," *Classical Philology*, 82 (1987), 21–34, esp. 30; Martha T. Roth, "Age at Marriage and the Household: A Study of Neo-Babylonian and Neo-

Assyrian Forms," *Comparative Studies in Society and History*, 29 (1987), 715–47 (but, for opposing arguments, see Brent D. Shaw, "The Age of Roman Girls at Marriage: Some Reconsiderations," *Journal of Roman Studies*, 77 [1987], 30–46; Donald G. Herring, "The Age of Egyptian Women at Marriage in the Ptolemaic Period," paper delivered on January 7, 1989, at the 120th annual meeting of the American Philological Association, in Baltimore).

8   E.g., K. Freund, "A Laboratory Method for Diagnosing Predominance of Homo- or Hetero-Erotic Interest in the Male," *Behavior Research and Therapy*, 1 (1963–64), 85–93; N. McConaghy, "Penile Volume Change to Moving Pictures of Male and Female Nudes in Heterosexual and Homosexual Males," *Behavior Research and Therapy*, 5 (1967), 43–48. For a partial, and critical, review of the literature on testing procedures, see Bernard F. Riess, "Psychological Tests in Homosexuality," in Marmor, 296–311. Compare the parallel tendency in the same period to determine the "true sex" of hermaphrodites: see Foucault (1980/a), vii–xi. Vanggaard, 17 and *passim*, differentiates further between normal (or "pseudo-") and abnormal (or "inverse"—i.e., inverted) homosexuality; in this he follows a taxonomic tradition that originated with Iwan Bloch (see Ellis, 4) and that derived, in its turn, from the mid-nineteenth-century physiological distinction between (acquired) "perversity" and (congenital) "perversion." Similarly, Lionel Ovesey, *Homosexuality and Pseudohomosexuality* (New York, 1969), attempts to move beyond the constitutional model of sexual preference towards an adaptive one by arguing that sexual fantasies may be rooted in "dependency needs" or "power needs" rather than in a determinate sexual orientation. On this point, see Takeo Doi, *The Anatomy of Dependence*, trans. John Bester (Tokyo: Kodansha, 1973), 113–21.

9   See Foucault (1972), 190, for the introduction of this concept; for its application to the history of sexual categories, see Davidson (1987/88), 48.

10   On the emergence of the concept of homosexuality, see Jeffrey Weeks, " 'Sins and Diseases': Some Notes on Homosexuality in the Nineteenth Century," *History Workshop*, 1 (1976), 211–19, and Weeks (1981/b), 96–121; also, Marshall; George L. Mosse, *Nationalism and Sexuality: Respectability and Abnormal Sexuality in Modern Europe* (New York: Howard Fertig, 1985), 23–47; now, Ed Cohen, "Legislating the Norm: From Sodomy to Gross Indecency," *South Atlantic Quarterly*, 88.1 (Winter 1989), 181–217. For a lucid discussion of the sociological implications, see McIntosh, who also examines some of the quasi-theological refinements ("bisexuality," "latent homosexuality," "pseudo-homosexuality") that have been added to this intellectual structure in order to buttress its central concept.

     Other sociological critiques, derived from "symbolic interactionism" or "labeling theory," can be found in Gagnon and Simon, 132–37, 176–81; Kenneth Plummer, *Sexual Stigma: An Interactionist Account* (London, 1975), 93–101, and Plummer (1981); Barbara Ponse, *Identities in the Lesbian World: The Social Construction of Self*, Contributions to Sociology, 28 (Westport, CT: Greenwood Press, 1978); Thomas S. Weinberg, "On 'Doing' and 'Being' Gay: Sexual Behavior and Homosexual Male Self-Identity," *Journal of Homosexuality*, 4 (1978/79), 143–56, and *Gay Men, Gay Selves: The Social Construction of Homosexual Identities* (New York: Irvington, 1983); John Hart and Diane Richardson, eds., *The Theory and Practice of Homosexuality* (London, 1981), esp. 5–124; Lon G. Nungesser, *Homosexual Acts, Actors, and Identities* (New York, 1983); Vivienne C. Cass, "Homosexual Identity: A Concept in Need of Definition," in *Bisexual and Homosexual Identities: Critical Theoretical Issues = Journal of Homosexuality*, 9.2–3 (1983/84), 105–26 (elaborated by Richard R. Troiden, "Self, Self-Concept, Identity, and Homosexual Identity: Constructs in Need of Definition and Differentiation," *Journal of Homosexuality*, 10.3–4 [1984], 97–109); Michael W. Ross, "Beyond the Biological Model: New Directions in Bisexual and Homosexual Research," *Journal of Homosexuality*, 10.3–4 (1984), 63–70; J. P. Paul, "Bisexuality: Reassessing Our Paradigms of Sexuality," in Klein and Wolf, 21–34. Further difficulties (moral, clinical, conceptual) are treated by E. Mansell Pattison (a hostile witness), "Confusing Concepts about the Concept of Homosexuality," *Psychiatry*, 37 (1974), 340–49; Lee Birk, "The Myth of Classical Homosexuality: Views from a Behavioral Psychotherapist," in Marmor, 376–90; Salzman; Robert J. Stoller, "Problems with the Term 'Homosexuality,' " *The Hillside Journal of Clinical Psychiatry*, 2 (1980), 3–25; René Girard, *Things Hidden since the Foundation of the World*, trans. Stephen Bann and Michael Metteer (Stanford, 1987), 335–38; Alan Soble, "Preface: Changing Conceptions of Human Sexuality," in Shelp, I, xi–xxiv, esp. xvii–xix.

11 *A Problem in Modern Ethics*, quoted by Weeks (1977), 1.

12 While condemning "homosexuality" as "a bastard term compounded of Greek and Latin elements" (p. 2), Ellis acknowledged that its classical etymology facilitated its diffusion throughout the European languages; moreover, by consenting to employ it himself, Ellis helped further to popularize it. On the philological advantages and disadvantages of "homosexuality," see Féray, 174–76.

13 This passage, along with others in a similar vein, has been well discussed by Marshall.

14 Marshall, 148, who goes on to quote the following passage from the preface to a recent survey by D. J. West, *Homosexuality Reassessed* (London, 1977), vii: "A generation ago the word homosexuality was best avoided in polite conversation, or referred to in muted terms appropriate to a dreaded and scarcely mentionable disease. Even some well-educated people were hazy about exactly what it meant." Note, however, that Edward Westermarck, writing for a scholarly audience in *The Origin and Development of the Moral Ideas*, could allude to "what is nowadays commonly called homosexual love" (vol. II, p. 456) as early as 1908. Westermarck's testimony has escaped the *OED* Supplement, which simply records that in 1914 George Bernard Shaw felt free to use the word "homosexual" adjectivally in the *New Statesman* without further explanations and that the adjective reappears in *Blackwood's Magazine* in 1921 as well as in Robert Graves's *Good-bye to All That* in 1929. The French version of "homosexuality," by contrast, showed up in the *Larousse mensuel illustré* as early as December, 1907 (according to Féray, 172).

15 The only meaning attested for "Lesbian" in the first edition of the *OED* pertains to carpentry, not to sexuality. This suggests that the *OED*'s omission of "homosexuality" from its original edition is not a mere oversight that can be entirely accounted for by the word's recent coinage.

16 The earliest literary occurrence of the German loan-word "homosexualist," of which the *OED* is similarly ignorant, took place only in 1925, to the best of my knowledge, and it illustrates the novelty that evidently still attached to the term: in Aldous Huxley's *Those Barren Leaves* we find the following exchange between a thoroughly modern aunt and her up-to-date niece, who are discussing a mutual acquaintance.

> "I sometimes doubt," [Aunt Lilian] said, "whether he takes any interest in women at all. Fundamentally, unconsciously, I believe he's a homosexualist."
> "Perhaps," said Irene gravely. She knew her Havelock Ellis [Part III, Chapter 11].

(The earliest occurrence of "homosexualist" cited in the *OED* Supplement dates from 1931.)

17 According, once again, to the dubious testimony of the *OED*'s 1976 Supplement, II, 85, s.v. heterosexuality. The *OED* does establish, to be sure, that the adjective "heterosexual," like the adjective "homosexual," appeared in print for the first time in English in 1892. But what did the word actually mean at that date? Those who employed it seem to have

been far from unanimous in their understanding of it. A distinguished American alienist, for example, summarizing in 1892 Krafft-Ebing's taxonomy of sexual disorders, uses "heterosexuals" as an alternate designation for "psychical hermaphroditism" and defines "heterosexuals" in a note by explaining, "In these inclinations to both sexes occur as well as to abnormal methods of gratification" (here, in other words, "heterosexual" signifies approximately what we now mean by "bisexual"): Jas. G. Kiernan, "Responsibility in Sexual Perversion," *The Chicago Medical Recorder*, 3 (1892), 185–210 (quotation on pp. 198–99n.; I am indebted to Vernon A. Rosario II for calling my attention to this usage). Note that Kertbeny, the coiner of the term "homosexual," opposed it not to "heterosexual" but to *normalsexual* in his published writings; the earliest printed occurrence of "heterosexual" (in German, of course) therefore had to wait until the second edition of Jäger's *Entdeckung der Seele* in 1880. Nonetheless, Kertbeny did employ both *heterosexual* and *homosexual* as early as May 6, 1868, in the draft of a letter addressed to Karl Heinrich Ulrichs: see Kennedy, 152–53; Herzer, 6–9; Féray, 171; and note 2, above. On the dependence of "heterosexuality" on "homosexuality," see Féray, 171–72; Beaver, 115–16; Eve Kosofsky Sedgwick, "Epistemology of the Closet (I)," *Raritan*, 7.4 (Spring 1988), 39–69, esp. 53–56.

18　For a parallel argument, see Greenblatt, 32: "Though the term 'individualism' is relatively recent, a nineteenth-century coinage, the existence of individuals has long seemed to be a constitutive, universal element in the natural structure of human experience and hence more the basis than the object of historical investigation. But the belatedness of the general term for the phenomenon of individuals should make us wary of assuming the stable existence of individualism as a category of human life. . . ." See Davidson (1987/88), 44–47, on the "link between sexuality and individuality"; also, 17: "the history of sexuality is . . . an area in which one's historiography or implicit epistemology will stamp, virtually irrevocably, one's first-order historical writing."

19　Some doubts about the applicability of the modern concept of homosexuality to ancient varieties of sexual experience have been voiced by Devereux, 71–76; MacCary, 178–85; Patzer; Richardson, 106–07; Sergent, 46–47; and by Fernando Gonzalez-Reigosa and Howard Kaminsky, "Greek Homosexuality, Greek Narcissism, Greek Culture: The Invention of Apollo," *The Psychohistory Review*, 17.2 (Winter 1989), 149–81, esp. 168.

20　On the eighteenth century as a transitional era in the West, see McIntosh; Trumbach; on varieties of sexual non-conformity in the early modern era, see the essays in Robert Purks Maccubin, ed., *'Tis Nature's Fault: Unauthorized Sexuality during the Enlightenment* (Cambridge, 1987), and in Kent Gerard and Gert Hekma, eds., *The Pursuit of Sodomy: Male Homosexuality in Renaissance and Enlightenment Europe* (New York, 1989) = *Journal of Homosexuality*, 16.1/2 (1988).

21　Boswell (1982–83), 93. Proponents of this view (which Boswell himself rejects; even more baldly categorical is Bullough, 2, 62: "homosexuality has always been with us; it has been a constant in history, and its presence is clear") include Hocquenghem, 36–37; Veyne (1978), 52; Padgug; Weeks (1981/b), 96–121; Bray, 8–9, 13–32; Patzer; Rubin (1984), 285–86; De Martino and Schmitt; Rousselle (1986), 259–61; Davidson (1987/88); most pertinently, the contributors to Plummer (1981); and, now, Greenberg. Additional fuel for the fires of historicism can be found in the writings of those who relate the rise of homosexuality to the rise of capitalism: see Hocquenghem; Weeks (1980); Dennis Altman, *The Homosexualization of America* (New York, 1982), esp. 79–107; John D'Emilio, "Capitalism and Gay Identity," in Snitow, Stansell, and Thompson, 100–13; Adam (1985/b). For a different emphasis on the connection between capitalism and the oppression of homosexuals, see Pearce and Roberts; David Fernbach, "Toward a Marxist Theory of Gay Liberation," *Socialist Revolution*, no. 28 = 6.2 (April–June 1976), 29–41; Irigaray (1985/b), 192–97; David F. Greenberg and Marcia H. Bystryn, "Capitalism, Bureaucracy and Male Homosexuality," *Contemporary Crises: Crime, Law and Social Policy*,

8 (1984), 33–56; Eve Kosofsky Sedgwick, *Between Men: English Literature and Male Homo-social Desire* (New York, 1985); Michael Moon, " 'The Gentle Boy from the Dangerous Classes': Pederasty, Domesticity, and Capitalism in Horatio Alger," *Representations*, 19 (Summer 1987), 87–100; and cf. the exemplary discussion of a specific instance by Stuart Hall, "Reformism and the Legislation of Consent," in *Permissiveness and Control: The Fate of the Sixties Legislation*, ed. National Deviancy Conference (London, 1980), 1–43, 176–81.

22   So Dynes, vii–viii.

23   Boswell (1982–83), 94–101, ingenuously noting that "The problem is rendered more difficult in the present case by the fact that the equivalent of gravity [in sexual matters] has not yet been discovered: there is still no essential agreement in the scientific community about the nature of human sexuality." Bullough, 3, similarly appeals to Aristophanes's myth as "one of the earliest explanations" of homosexuality.

24   Boswell (1982–83), 99; compare Auguste Valensin, "Platon et la théorie de l'amour," *Études*, 281 (1954), 32–45, esp. 37.

25   Something like this point is implicit in Brisson, 42–43; see, also, Neu, 177, n. 1. My own (somewhat different) reading of Aristophanes's speech is set forth in greater detail in Halperin (1985), 167–70; I have reproduced some of my earlier formulations here.

26   The term "boy" (*pais* in Greek) refers by convention to the junior partner in a paederastic relationship, or to one who plays that role, regardless of his actual age; youths are customarily supposed to be desirable between the onset of puberty and the arrival of the beard: see Dover (1978), 16, 85–87; Buffière, 605–14; Kay, 120–21.

27   On the meaning of the term "philerast," see Elaine Fantham, "*Zêlotypia*: A Brief Excursion into Sex, Violence, and Literary History," *Phoenix*, 40 (1986), 45–57, esp. 48, n. 10.

28   For an explication of what is meant by "a certain (non-sexual) pleasure in physical contact with men," see note 31, below.

29   See Dover (1978), 73–109; a general survey of this issue together with the scholarship on it can be found in Halperin (1986).

30   Public lecture delivered at Brown University (21 February 1987).

31   In Halperin (1986) I argued that the picture drawn by Plato's Aristophanes is a historically accurate representation of *the moral conventions* governing sexual behavior in classical Athens, if not of the reality of sexual behavior itself. To be sure, the paederastic ethos of classical Athens did not prohibit a willing boy from responding enthusiastically to his lover's physical attentions: Aristophanes himself maintains that a philerast both "enjoys" and "welcomes" (*khairein, aspazesthai*: 191e–192b) his lover's embraces. But that ethos did stipulate that whatever enthusiasm a boy exhibited for sexual contact with his lover sprang from sources other than sexual desire. The distinction between "welcoming" and "desiring" a lover's caresses, as it applies to the motives for a boy's willingness, spelled the difference between wanting to coöperate and wanting to submit—hence, between decency and degeneracy (so, also, Rousselle [1986], 260); that distinction is worth empha-sizing here because the failure of modern interpreters to observe it has led to considerable misunderstanding (as when historians of sexuality, for example, misreading the frequent depictions on Attic pottery of a boy leaping into his lover's arms [see Dover (1978), 96], take those paintings to be evidence for the strength of the junior partner's *sexual* desire). A very few Greek documents seem truly ambiguous on this point, and I have reviewed their testimony in some detail: see Halperin (1986), 64, nn. 10 and 11, and 66, n. 14; also ambiguous, but very interesting, is a fragmentary painting on a tripod-pyxis from a sanctuary on Aegina, reproduced in Dietrich von Bothmer, *The Amasis Painter and His*

World: Vase-Painting in Sixth-Century B.C. Athens (Malibu, 1985), 237. For an example of how the vase-painters could play with the conventions, see the tondo of a kylix by the Carpenter Painter (Getty Museum 85.AE.25), recently published by Bothmer, in which an amorous boy grabs his sedate—and evidently astonished—adult suitor: the image is reproduced as the frontispiece to this book. (See Addendum.)

32 Boswell's general thesis is supported by a series of impressive arguments as well as by a vast array of textual and historical citation; I have confined my critique to that very small portion of his evidence about which I am competent to form an independent judgment, but I observe that scholars in other fields often have similar complaints about Boswell's use of his sources: see, for example, the Scholarship Committee (Gay Academic Union), ed., *Homosexuality, Intolerance, and Christianity: A Critical Examination of John Boswell's Work*, Gai Saber Monograph No. 1 (New York: Gay Academic Union, 1981); MacMullen; Payer, 135–39; Wright (with the qualification by Petersen); Arno Schmitt, "Alles nur Schein: Bemerkungen zu John Boswell," in De Martino and Schmitt, 37–45; Richard B. Hays, "Relations Natural and Unnatural: A Response to John Boswell's Exegesis of Romans 1," *Journal of Religious Ethics*, 14 (1986), 184–215; Kari Ellen Gade, "Homosexuality and Rape of Males in Old Norse Law and Literature," *Scandinavian Studies*, 58 (1986), 124–41, esp. 124–25; Glenn W. Olsen, "St. Anselm and Homosexuality," in *St. Anselm and St. Augustine: Episcopi ad saecula*, ed. Joseph C. Schnaubelt and Frederick Van Fleteren (Millwood, NY: Krauss, 1988), 91–139.

33 The notable exceptions are Bullough, 3–5, who cites it as evidence for the supposed universality of homosexuality in human history, and Boswell (1980), 53n., 75n.

34 See Schrijvers, 11.

35 I have borrowed this entire argument from Schrijvers, 7–8; the same point had been made earlier—unbeknownst to Schrijvers, apparently—by Boswell (1980), 53, n. 33; 75, n. 67.

36 Translation, with emphasis added, by Drabkin, 413.

37 As his chapter title, "De mollibus *sive subactis*," implies. For an earlier substantive use of *mollis* in this almost technical sense, see Juvenal, 9.38. On the meaning of *mollis*, see the rather enigmatic discussions by Boswell (1980), 76, and Philippe Ariès, "St Paul and the Flesh," in Ariès and Béjin, 36–39; for the word's later technical use in the mediaeval penitentials, see the citations provided by Boswell (1980), 180, n. 38, and by Payer, 170, nn. 113, 114 (with discussion on pp. 40–41).

38 See, esp., the pseudo-Aristotelian *Problemata* 4.26, well discussed by Dover (1978), 168–70, and by Winkler (1989/b); generally, Boswell (1980), 53; Foucault (1985), 204–14.

39 Compare Aeschines, 1.185: Timarchus is "a man who is male in body but has committed a woman's transgressions" and has thereby "outraged himself contrary to nature" (discussed by Dover [1978], 60–68); for a similar formulation, see Hyperides, fr. 215 Kenyon = Rutilius Lupus, 2.6, and compare the *Greek Anthology*, 11.272. On the ancient figure of the *kinaidos*, or *cinaedus*, the man who actively desires to submit himself passively to the sexual uses of other men, see Winkler (1989/a) and Gleason. Davidson (1987/88), 22, is therefore quite wrong to claim that "Before the second half of the nineteenth century persons of a determinate anatomical sex could not be thought to be really, that is, psychologically, of the opposite sex."

40 The Latin phrase *quod ultramque Venerem exerceant* is so interpreted by Drabkin, 901n., and by Schrijvers, 32–33, who secures this reading by citing Ovid, *Metamorphoses* 3.323, where Teiresias, who had been both a man and a woman, is described as being learned in the field of *Venus utraque*. Compare Petronius, *Satyricon* 43.8: *omnis minervae homo*.

41 I follow, once again, the insightful commentary by Schrijvers, 15.

42 I quote from the translation by Drabkin, 905, which is based on his plausible, but nonetheless speculative, reconstruction (accepted by Schrijvers, 50) of a desperately corrupt text. For the notion expressed in it, compare Proust, III, 204, 212 (French text) = III, 203, 209 (English): discussion by Eve Kosofsky Sedgwick, "Epistemology of the Closet (II)," *Raritan*, 8.1 (Summer 1988), 102–30.

43 Anon., *De physiognomonia* 85 (vol. II, p. 114.5–14 Förster); Vettius Valens, 2.16 (p. 76.3–8 Kroll); Clement of Alexandria, *Paedagogus* 3.21.3; Firmicus Maternus, *Mathesis* 6.30.15–16 and 7.25.3–23 (esp. 7.25.5).

44 See Jeffrey Weeks, "Questions of Identity," in Caplan, 31–51.

45 Gleason trenchantly analyzes many other examples of this outlook, which even today remains largely unchanged in Mediterranean cultures: see Gilmore (1987/b), esp. 10–12.

46 For some definitions of sex and sexuality as biological concepts, see Lynn Margulis, Dorion Sagan, and Lorraine Olendzenski, "What is Sex?" in *The Origin and Evolution of Sex*, ed. H. O. Halvorson and Alberto Monroy (New York, 1985), 69–85.

47 For a similar insistence on the distinction between sex and sexuality, see Davidson (1987/88), 23–25; Henderson (1988), 1250. Because so much of my argument derives from Foucault, I should point out that Foucault himself decisively abandoned the distinction between sex and sexuality, as I have drawn it. Not only is Foucault's final conception of "sex" much less positivistic (he categorically denies that "sex" is a biological fact), but his own understanding of the distinction between "sex" and "sexuality" reverses the sequence postulated here: "sexuality," on his view, arises in the eighteenth century and eventually produces "sex," as an idea internal to its own apparatus, only in the nineteenth century. See Foucault (1978), 152–57; (1980/b), 190, 210–11.

48 Padgug, 16. Compare duBois (1984); Moodie, 228: "We tend to think of sexuality as a psychological unity. Different aspects of the self such as 'desire', 'moral ideals', 'proper conduct', 'gender attitudes', 'personal relationships', 'mental images', and 'physical sensations' tend to be tied together by us to form a particular sexual character. With the self thus sexually defined, homosexuality and heterosexuality . . . are seen as specific personality types."

49 Padgug, 8, analyzes the connection between the modern interpretation of sexuality as an autonomous domain and the modern construction of sexual identities thus: "the most commonly held twentieth-century assumptions about sexuality imply that it is a separate category of existence (like 'the economy,' or 'the state,' other supposedly independent spheres of reality), almost identical with the sphere of private life. Such a view necessitates the location of sexuality within the individual as a fixed essence, leading to a classic division of individual and society and to a variety of psychological determinisms, and, often enough, to a full-blown biological determinism as well. These in turn involve the enshrinement of contemporary sexual categories as universal, static, and permanent, suitable for the analysis of all human beings and all societies."

50 See Féray, 247–51; Laqueur; Davidson (1986/87), 258–62; also, Weeks (1980), 13 (paraphrasing Foucault): "our culture has developed a notion of sexuality linked to reproduction and genitality and to 'deviations' from these. . . ." The biological conceptualization of "sexuality" as an instinct is neatly disposed of by Tripp, 10–21.

51 See Foucault (1978), 68–69; (1980/a), vii–xi; (1985), 35–52.

52 See Foucault (1978), 43: "As defined by the ancient civil or canonical codes, sodomy was a category of forbidden acts; their perpetrator was nothing more than the juridical subject of them. The nineteenth-century homosexual became a personage, a past, a case history,

and a childhood, in addition to being a type of life, a life form, and a morphology, with an indiscreet anatomy and possibly a mysterious physiology. Nothing that went into his total composition was unaffected by his sexuality. It was everywhere present in him: at the root of all his actions because it was their insidious and indefinitely active principle; written immodestly on his face and body because it was a secret that always gave itself away. It was consubstantial with him, less as a habitual sin than as a singular nature." Cf. Trumbach, 9; Weeks (1977), 12; Richard Sennett, *The Fall of Public Man* (New York, 1977), 6–8; Padgug, 13–14; Féray, 246–47; Schnapp (1981), 116 (speaking of Attic vase-paintings): "One does not paint acts that characterize persons so much as behaviors that distinguish groups"; Payer, 40–44, esp. 40–41: "there is no word in general usage in the penitentials for homosexuality as a category. . . . Furthermore, the distinction between homosexual acts and people who might be called homosexuals does not seem to be operative in these manuals. . . ." (also, 14–15, 140–53); Bynum (1986), 406; Petersen.

In this light, the significance of Westphal's famous article (see note 2, above) is clear: the crucial and decisive break with tradition comes when Westphal defines "contrary sexual feeling" not in terms of its outward manifestations but in terms of its inward dynamics, its distinctive *orientation* of the inner life of the individual. Apologizing in a note for the necessity of coining a new formula, Westphal explains, "I have chosen the designation 'contrary sexual feeling' at the suggestion of an esteemed colleague, distinguished in the field of philology and classical studies, inasmuch as we were unable to succeed in constructing shorter and more apt correlatives. The phrase is intended to express the fact that 'contrary sexual feeling' does not always coincidentally concern the sexual drive as such but simply *the feeling of being alienated, with one's entire inner being, from one's own sex*—a less developed stage, as it were, of the pathological phenomenon" (p. 107n.; my emphasis: I wish to thank Linda Frisch and Ira Levine for assisting me with the translation of this passage; a nearly identical version has now been provided by Herzer, 18). See Davidson (1987/88), 21–22, who identifies a "psychiatric style of reasoning that begins, roughly speaking, in the second half of the nineteenth century, a period during which rules for the production of true discourses about sexuality change radically. Sexual identity . . . is now a matter of impulses, tastes, aptitudes, satisfactions, and psychic traits."

53   For attestations to the strength of individual preferences (even to the point of exclusivity) on the part of Greek males for a sexual partner of one sex rather than another, see, e.g., Theognis, 1367–68; Euripides, *Cyclops* 583–84; Xenophon, *Anabasis* 7.4.7–8; Aeschines, 1.41, 195; the *Life of Zeno* by Antigonus of Carystus, cited by Athenaeus, 13.563e; the fragment of Seleucus quoted by Athenaeus, 15.697de (= Powell, 176); an anonymous dramatic fragment cited by Plutarch, *Moralia* 766f–767a (= Nauck, 906, #355; Kock, III, 467, #360); Athenaeus, 12.540e, 13.601e and ff.; Achilles Tatius, 2.35.2–3; pseudo-Lucian, *Erôtes* 9–10; Firmicus Maternus, *Mathesis* 7.15.1–2; and a number of epigrams, by various hands, contained in the *Palatine Anthology*: 5.19, 65, 116, 208, 277, 278; 11.216; 12.7, 17, 41, 87, 145, 192, 198, and *passim*. See, generally, Dover (1978), 62–63; Boswell (1982–83), 98–101; Winkler (1989/a); and, for a list of passages, Claude Courouve, *Tableau synoptique de références à l'amour masculin: Auteurs grecs et latins* (Paris: author, 1986).

54   Foucault (1985), 10, 51–52, remarks that it would be interesting to determine exactly when in the evolving course of Western cultural history sex became more morally problematic than eating; see, also, Foucault (1983), 229; (1986), 143. For a criticism of Foucault's answer to that question, see "Two Views of Greek Love," in this volume.

55   Hilary Putnam, *Reason, Truth and History* (Cambridge, 1981), 150–55, in the course of analyzing the various criteria by which we judge matters of taste to be "subjective," implies that we are right to consider sexual preferences more thoroughly constitutive of

the human personality than dietary preferences, but his argument remains circumscribed, as Putnam himself emphasizes, by highly culture-specific assumptions about sex, food, and personhood.

56 Hence, some students of classical Greek medicine prefer to speak of the authors of the gynaecological treatises in the Hippocratic corpus as concerned exclusively with human "genitality" rather than "sexuality": see, for example, Manuli (1980), 394; (1983), 152; Rousselle (1980), 1092. For similar arguments about Renaissance painting, to the effect that it is concerned (*pace* Leo Steinberg, *The Sexuality of Christ in Renaissance Art and Modern Oblivion* [New York, 1983]) not with Jesus's sexuality but with his genitality, see Bynum (1986), 405–10; Davidson (1987/88), 25–32.

57 I accept, in this sense, the point insisted upon by K. J. Dover: "The fact t¹   e object of homosexual desire in the Greek world was almost always, like Ganymec   lescent does not justify . . . [the] denial that [paederasty] is homosexuality. Homos._uality is a genus definable by the sex of the person participating (in reality or in fantasy) in action leading towards genital orgasm, and the predilections of a given society at a given time constitute one or more species of the genus" (*Journal of Hellenic Studies*, 104 [1984], 240).

58 Thus, Boswell (1982–83), 99n., argues that the term "paederast," at least as it is applied to Gnathon by Longus in *Daphnis and Chloe* 4.11, is "obviously a conventional term for 'homosexual,' " and he would presumably place a similar construction on *paiderastês* and *philerastês* in the myth of Plato's Aristophanes, dismissing my interpretation as a terminological quibble or as a misguided attempt to reify lexical entities into categories of experience.

59 For a philosophical defense and qualification of this claim (and of other, similarly "constructionist," claims), see Ian Hacking, "Making Up People," in Heller, Sosna, and Wellbery, 222–36, 347–48.

60 See Joan Kelly, "The Social Relation of the Sexes: Methodological Implications of Women's History," in *Women, History, and Theory: The Essays of Joan Kelly* (Chicago, 1984), 1–18.

61 See, now, Winkler (1989/a). See, generally, Henderson (1988)—the single best, most comprehensive and reliable introduction to Greek sexual *mores* for non-specialists.

62 See, generally, Dover (1978), 16, 84–106; Foucault (1985), 46–47.

63 On the characteristic failure of "culturally dominant ideologies" actually to dominate all sectors of a society, and for a demonstration of their greater pertinence to the dominant than to the dominated classes, see Nicholas Abercrombie, Stephen Hill, and Bryan S. Turner, *The Dominant Ideology Thesis* (London, 1980), esp. 70–127. For the documentation of a particular instance, see R. M. Smith, "Marriage Processes in the English Past: Some Continuities," in *The World We Have Gained: Histories of Population and Social Structure*, ed. Lloyd Bonfield, Richard M. Smith, and Keith Wrightson (Oxford, 1986), 43–99, esp. 46–47.

64 See Winkler (1989/b).

65 Artemidorus, *Oneirocritica* 1.2 (pp. 8.21–9.4 Pack).

66 Winkler (1989/b).

67 I say "phallus" rather than "penis" because (1) what qualifies as a phallus in this discursive system does not always turn out to be a penis (see note 83, below) and (2) even when phallus and penis have the same extension, or reference, they still do not have the same intension, or meaning: "phallus" betokens not a specific item of the male anatomy *simpliciter* but that same item *taken under the description* of a cultural signifier; (3) hence, the meaning of "phallus" is ultimately determined by its function in the larger socio-sexual

discourse: i.e., it is that which penetrates, that which enables its possessor to play an "active" sexual role, and so forth: see Rubin (1975), 190–92.

68 Foucault (1985), 215, puts it very well: "sexual relations—always conceived in terms of the model act of penetration, assuming a polarity that opposed activity and passivity— were seen as being of the same type as the relationship between a superior and a subordinate, an individual who dominates and one who is dominated, one who commands and one who complies, one who vanquishes and one who is vanquished."

69 In order to avoid misunderstanding, I should emphasize that by calling all persons belonging to these four groups "statutory minors," I do not wish either to suggest that they enjoyed the *same* status as one another or to obscure the many differences in status that could obtain between members of a single group—e.g., between a wife and a courtesan—differences that may not have been perfectly isomorphic with the legitimate modes of their sexual use. Nonetheless, what is striking about Athenian social usage is the tendency to collapse such distinctions as did indeed obtain between different categories of social subordinates and to create a single opposition between them all, *en masse*, and the class of adult male citizens: on this point, see Golden (1985), 101 and 102, n. 38.

70 Veyne (1978), 55, and (1985). Cf. Alan Dundes, Jerry W. Leach, and Bora Özkök, "The Strategy of Turkish Boys' Verbal Dueling Rhymes," *Journal of American Folklore*, 83 (1970), 325–49, supplemented and qualified by Mark Glazer, "On Verbal Dueling Among Turkish Boys," *Journal of American Folklore*, 89 (1976), 87–89; J. M. Carrier, "Mexican Male Bisexuality," in Klein and Wolf, 75–85; De Martino and Schmitt, esp. 3–22; Michael Herzfeld, *The Poetics of Manhood: Contest and Identity in a Cretan Mountain Village* (Princeton, 1985); now, Gilmore (1987/a).

71 I have borrowed this analogy from Arno Schmitt, who uses it to convey what the modern sexual categories would look like from a traditional Islamic perspective: see De Martino and Schmitt, 19.

72 See Dover (1978), 84; Henderson (1988), 1251: "Social status defined one's sexual identity and determined the proper sexual behavior that one was allowed."

73 Godelier (1981), 17.

74 On this general theme, see Golden (1985). For some comparative material, see Adam (1985/a), 22; De Martino and Schmitt, 3–22; Gill Shepherd, "Rank, Gender, and Homosexuality: Mombasa as a Key to Understanding Sexual Options," in Caplan, 240–70.

75 The same point is made, in the course of an otherwise unenlightening (from the specialist's point of view) survey of Greek social relations, by Bernard I. Murstein, *Love, Sex, and Marriage through the Ages* (New York, 1974), 58.

76 So Padgug, 3–4; Sartre, 12–14.

77 See Padgug, 3, who mistakenly ascribes Athenaeus's comment to Alexis of Samos (see *FGrHist* 539, fr. 2).

78 See Dover (1978), 63–67, for an extensive, but admittedly partial, list. For some Roman examples, see Richardson, 111. For ritual regulations, see Parker, 94; Cole (1991).

79 *P. Tebtunis* I 104, translated by A. S. Hunt and C. C. Edgar, in *Women's Life in Greece and Rome*, ed. Mary Lefkowitz and Maureen B. Fant (Baltimore, 1982), 59–60; another translation is provided, along with a helpful discussion of the document and its typicality, by Pomeroy, 87–89.

80 "Une bisexualité de sabrage": Veyne (1978), 50–55; cf. the critique by MacMullen, 491–97. Other scholars who describe the ancient behavioral phenomenon as "bisexuality" include Brisson; Schnapp (1981), 116–17; Kelsen, 40–41; Lawrence Stone, "Sex in the

West," *The New Republic* (July 8, 1985), 25–37, esp. 30–32 (with doubts). *Contra*, Padgug, 13: "to speak, as is common, of the Greeks, as 'bisexual' is illegitimate as well, since that merely adds a new, intermediate category, whereas it was precisely the categories themselves which had no meaning in antiquity."

81   Cf. Robinson, 162: "the reason why a heterosexual majority might have looked with a tolerant eye on 'active' homosexual practice among the minority, and even in some measure within their own group [!], . . . is predictably a sexist one: to the heterosexual majority, to whom (in a man's universe) the 'good' woman is *kata physin* [i.e., naturally] passive, obedient, and submissive, the 'role' of the 'active' homosexual will be tolerable precisely because his goings-on can, without too much difficulty, be equated with the 'role' of the male *hetero*sexual, i.e., to dominate and subdue; what the two have in common is greater than what divides them." But this seems to me to beg the very question that the distinction between heterosexuality and homosexuality is supposedly designed to solve.

82   An excellent analysis of the contemporary Mediterranean version of this ethos has been provided by Gilmore (1987/b), 8–16.

83   By "phallus" I mean a culturally constructed signifier of social power: for the terminology, see note 67, above. I call Greek sexual discourse phallic because (1) sexual contacts are polarized around phallic action—i.e., they are defined by who has the phallus and by what is done with it; (2) sexual pleasures other than phallic pleasures do not count in categorizing sexual contacts; (3) in order for a contact to qualify as sexual, one—and no more than one—of the two partners is required to have a phallus (boys are treated in paederastic contexts as essentially un-phallused [see Martial, 11.22; but cf. *Palatine Anthology* 12.3, 7, 197, 207, 216, 222, 242] and tend to be assimilated to women; in the case of sex between women, one partner—the "tribad"—is assumed to possess a phallus-equivalent [an over-developed clitoris] and to penetrate the other: sources for the ancient conceptualization of the tribad—no complete modern study of this fascinating and long-lived fictional type, which survived into the early decades of the twentieth century, is known to me—have been assembled by Friedrich Karl Forberg, *Manual of Classical Erotology*, trans. Julian Smithson [Manchester, 1884; repr. New York, 1966], II, 108–67; Brandt, 316–28; Gaston Vorberg, *Glossarium eroticum* [Hanau, 1965], 654–55; Werner A. Krenkel, "Masturbation in der Antike," *Wissenschaftliche Zeitschrift der Wilhelm-Pieck-Universität Rostock*, 28 [1979], 159–78, esp. 171; see, now, Judith P. Hallett, "Female Homoeroticism and the Denial of Roman Reality in Latin Literature," *Yale Journal of Criticism*, 3.1 [1989], forthcoming).

84   I owe this insight to the acute criticisms of an earlier version of the present essay by Sylvia Yanagisako, "Sex and Gender: You Can't Have One Without the Other," Paper presented at the first annual meeting of the Society for Cultural Anthropology, Washington, D.C. (20 May 1988).

85   Halperin (1986), 63–66; also, note 31, above, and section 6 of "Why is Diotima a Woman?" in this volume.

86   See Lucian, *Dialogues of the Courtesans* 5. On "tribads," see my discussion of Caelius Aurelianus as well as note 83, above.

87   See Dover (1974), 101–02.

88   See Halperin (1985), 164–66, and section 7 of "Why is Diotima a Woman?" in this volume; Jones (1991/b).

89   I am indebted for this observation to Professor Peter M. Smith of the University of North Carolina at Chapel Hill, who notes that Sappho and Plato are the chief exceptions to this

general rule. See, further, Paul A. Rahe, "The Primacy of Politics in Classical Greece," *American Historical Review*, 89 (1984), 265–93, who makes a similar point in the course of an otherwise schematic and idealized portrayal of the political culture of classical Greece.

90 Compare, e.g., Herodotus, 6.107.

91 S. R. F. Price, "The Future of Dreams: From Freud to Artemidorus," *Past and Present*, 113 (November 1986), 3–37, abridged in Halperin, Winkler, and Zeitlin; see, also, Foucault (1986), 3–36, esp. 26–34.

92 See Waud H. Kracke, "Dreaming in Kagwahiv: Dream Beliefs and Their Psychic Uses in an Amazonian Indian Culture," *The Psychoanalytic Study of Society*, 8 (1979), 119–71, esp. 130–32, 163 (on the predictive value of dreams) and 130–31, 142–45, 163–64, 168 (on the reversal of the Freudian direction of signification—which Kracke takes to be a culturally constituted defense mechanism and which he accordingly undervalues); Thomas Gregor, " 'Far, Far Away My Shadow Wandered . . .': The Dream Symbolism and Dream Theories of the Mehinaku Indians of Brazil," *American Ethnologist*, 8 (1981), 709–20, esp. 712–13 (on predictive value) and 714 (on the reversal of signification), largely recapitulated in Gregor, 152–61, esp. 153. Cf. Foucault (1986), 35–36: "The movement of analysis and the procedures of valuation do not go from the act to a domain such as sexuality or the flesh, a domain whose divine, civil, or natural laws would delineate the permitted forms; they go from the subject as a sexual actor to the other areas of life in which he pursues his [familial, social, and economic] activity. And it is in the relationship between these different forms of activity that the principles of evaluation of a sexual behavior are essentially, but not exclusively, situated."

93 duBois (1984), 47–48; Edmunds, 81–84.

94 Jack H. Abbott, "On 'Women,' " *New York Review of Books*, 28.10 (June 11, 1981), 17. It should perhaps be pointed out that this lyrical confession is somewhat at odds with the more gritty account contained in the edited excerpts from Abbott's letters that were published a year earlier in the *New York Review of Books*, 27.11 (June 26, 1980), 34–37. (One might compare Abbott's statement with some remarks uttered by Bernard Boursicot in a similarly apologetic context and quoted by Richard Bernstein, "France Jails Two in a Bizarre Case of Espionage," *New York Times* [May 11, 1986]: "I was shattered to learn that he [Boursicot's lover of twenty years] is a man, but my conviction remains unshakable that for me at that time he was really a woman and was the first love of my life.")

95 See Davidson (1987/88), 16.

96 See Padgug, 5: "In any approach that takes as predetermined and universal the categories of sexuality, real history disappears."

97 See, now, Henriques, Hollway, Urwin, Couze, and Walkerdine. Also, Rubin (1975), 178–83; Godelier (1976), 295–96: "The process of reproducing life—sexuality, that is, in its broadest sense—can only exist if it is *subordinated* to the reproduction of other social relations; that subordination takes the form, first of all, of the subordination of sexuality to the reproduction of kinship relations. The subordination of sexuality of which I speak here is not yet the subordination of one sex to the other in their personal relations, it's rather the subordination of a domain of social practices to the conditions of the functioning of other social relations—it's the position that that domain occupies by virtue of its role in reproducing the deep structure of the society, not the position it occupies, at the surface of social reality, in the visible hierarchy of institutions. But that subordination of sexuality, of the process of reproducing life to the process of reproducing the deep structure of social relations, has concrete effects *on the person* of individuals and on the *personal relations* that they establish with one another according to their sex. The sexuality of individuals must *submit* to the constraints posed by the functioning of kinship relations or, to put it

differently, the desire of each individual is not authorized unless it is directed to those 'others' who *fit in with* the functioning of kinship relations and, through them, the reproduction of the ensemble of social relations." For a similar argument, see Donald L. Donham, *History, Power, Ideology: Themes in Marxism and Anthropology* (Cambridge, forthcoming). Further empirical support for this approach is provided by Moodie as well as by the anthropological studies of Herdt (1981) and (1984), whose import is well summarized by Adam (1985/a), 29: "Most remarkable in the Melanesian examples is the way in which the kinship code functions successfully to create categories of the attractive and the erotic. These structures do work, such that sexual arousal occurs and is consummated repeatedly for most participants. . . . Sexual interest does arise at the prescribed structural locations and prescribed categories of people, regardless of gender, are eroticized."

98 Cf. William Simon and John H. Gagnon, "Sexual Scripts," *Society*, no. 153 = 22.1 (1984), 53–60, esp. 53, and "Sexual Scripts: Permanence and Change," *Archives of Sexual Behavior*, 15.2 (1986), 97–120, esp. 100: "Desire is not reducible to an appetite, a drive, an instinct; it does not create the self, rather it is part of the process of the creation of the self."

99 "Translations" (1972), lines 32–33, in Adrienne Rich, *Diving into the Wreck: Poems 1971–1972* (New York, 1973), 40–41 (quotation on p. 41).

100 "Canzone" (1942), lines 1–2, in W. H. Auden, *Collected Poems*, ed. Edward Mendelson (New York, 1976), 256–57 (quotation on p. 256).

101 Weeks (1981/a), 111.

2 "Homosexuality": A Cultural Construct (An Exchange with Richard Schneider)

An earlier version of this interview was published in the *Harvard Gay and Lesbian Newsletter*, 5.2 [= 3] (Fall 1987), 3–7. I wish to thank its editor, Richard Schneider, for the stimulating discussion that led up to this exchange. I also wish to thank Edward Stein for a thoroughgoing and searching critique of the revised text.

1 Epstein, 11. See, also, Rubin (1984), 275–76, who defines "sexual essentialism" as "the idea that sex is a natural force that exists prior to social life and shapes its institutions. Sexual essentialism is embedded in the folk wisdoms of Western societies, which consider sex to be eternally unchanging, asocial, and transhistorical. Dominated for over a century by medicine, psychiatry, and psychology, the academic study of sex has reproduced essentialism. These fields classify sex as a property of individuals. It may reside in their hormones or their psyches. It may be construed as physiological or psychological. But within these ethnoscientific categories, sexuality has no history and no significant social determinants." Boswell (1989), 74, rightly observes that "essentialism" is a retroactive and pejorative label applied by constructionists to the outlook they oppose: "no modern specialists in any field call themselves essentialists," he points out.

For a general consideration of sexual essentialism and its critics, see Jack Katz, "Essences as Moral Identities: Verifiability and Responsibility in Imputations of Deviance and Charisma," *American Journal of Sociology*, 80 (1974/75), 1369–90; Weeks (1981/a), 86ff.; Diane Richardson, "The Dilemma of Essentiality in Homosexual Theory," in *Bisexual and Homosexual Identities: Critical Theoretical Issues = Journal of Homosexuality*, 9.2–3 (1983/84), 79–90; Gregory A. Sprague, "Male Homosexuality in Western Culture: The Dilemma of Identity and Subculture in Historical Research," *Journal of Homosexuality*, 10.3–4 (1984), 29–43. For the fullest treatment of the question as it pertains to homosexuality, see

Epstein, whose own modified, dialectical version of constructionism approximates to the position taken here.

2 See Pearce and Roberts, 51: "although we assume that all men and women are potentially bisexual the likely patterning of their activities is determined from their earliest moments of sociality when gender identities are assigned to them with the attendant expectations concerning appropriate conduct for someone with their particular genital equipment. The dominant definitions effecting the social organisation of sexual contact, will constantly define likely options for them and will reinforce or undermine their changing self-concepts throughout their lives." Compare Weeks (1980), 19: "A homosexual identity is not given in nature, nor is it simply imposed as a social control on a deviant minority: it is the product of a long social process involving both definition and self-definition. . . . And all these definitions, categorisations, regulations are social impositions upon the flux of sexual possibilities there in the human animal at the time of birth." These formulations nicely balance the contributions made to the formation of a personal identity by social organization and cultural codes, on the one hand, and by individual interpretation or response, on the other.

3 See Boswell (1982–83). Now, however, Edward Stein, in an unpublished lecture on "The Philosophy of Sexual Preference" delivered at the State University of New York at Purchase on April 17, 1989, demonstrates that, *pace* Epstein, essentialists and constructionists do not necessarily line up on opposite sides of the nature/nurture or determinism/voluntarism debates.

4 Epstein, 45.

5 Freud made something like this point seventy-five years ago in a footnote to the third edition of his *Three Essays on the Theory of Sexuality*: "Thus from the point of view of psycho-analysis the exclusive sexual interest felt by men for women is also a problem that needs elucidating and is not a self-evident fact based upon an attraction that is ultimately of a chemical nature" (Strachey, VII, 146).

6 I owe this analogy to Henry Abelove.

7 See Rubin (1984), 285–86, for a similar argument.

8 See, e.g., Aeschines, 1.132–35.

9 See Dover (1978), 86–87; Golden (1984), 321–22; Ungaretti, 13. An interesting text, not mentioned by Dover (no doubt because it is so late), is Xenophon of Ephesus, 3.2.2–4, which describes a love-affair between two boys who were both so young, or so close in age, that no one suspected them of being lovers and so no one attempted to prevent their being alone together (or having sex); the text makes clear, however, that only one of them experienced *erôs*, or "sexual passion," for the other, who was prevailed upon to "pity" and "have mercy" on the former: it would seem, then, that their affair conformed, at least in its outward manifestations, to the conventional pattern.

10 Dover (1978), 87, citing the case of the beautiful Critobulus in Xenophon, *Symposium* 8.2, who is newly married (2.3), the beloved of many older men, and the lover of the younger Cleinias (4.10–18)—all at the same time.

11 Winkler (1989/a).

12 Gregor, 8, notes that homosexuality is "excluded" and "ruled out" among the Mehinaku Indians of Central Brazil; he then goes to document, on pp. 59–60, the ease with which a foreigner was able to induce some members of the tribe to engage in sexual relations with him ("as young men began to sport such high-status gifts as radios and bicycles . . . the visitor had no shortage of consorts"). Any systematic account of a society's "sexuality" ought to explore further the conditions that make possible such sexual versatility.

13 Ron Langevin, ed., *Erotic Preference, Gender Identity, and Aggression in Men: New Research Studies* (Hillsdale, NJ: Lawrence Erlbaum, 1985), 227–59, 279–80. Earlier work is summarized by Michael Ruse, *Homosexuality: A Philosophical Inquiry* (Oxford, 1988), 84–129, who defends the value of hormonal studies but who does not mention (although he may know) Langevin's research.

14 The new *summa*, at least on one view (see note 15, below), is represented by Lee Ellis and M. Ashley Ames, "Neurohormonal Functioning and Sexual Orientation: A Theory of Homosexuality-Heterosexuality," *Psychological Bulletin*, 101.2 (1987), 233–58.

15 Jerry Woolpy, "The Biology of Homosexuality," *Earlhamite* (Winter 1989), 9–11 (quotation on p. 9), reproducing the phraseology of Ellis and Ames (preceding note), 247. I wish to thank Adam Thorburn for calling my attention to this article. The original studies of pre-natal stress in Germany were conducted by the notorious Gunter Dörner with a variety of collaborators and published in *Endokrinologie*, 75 (1980), 365–68, and in *Experimental and Clinical Endocrinology*, 81 (1983), 83–87.

16 See, generally, Sander L. Gilman, *Difference and Pathology: Stereotypes of Sexuality, Race, and Madness* (Ithaca, NY, 1985).

3 Two Views of Greek Love: Harald Patzer and Michel Foucault

This essay represents an amalgam of two earlier papers. Versions of the first paper appeared under the title, "One Hundred Years of Homosexuality," in *Diacritics*, 16, no. 2 (Summer 1986), 34–45, esp. 40–45, and under the title, "Normalizing Greek Desire," in *Classics: A Discipline and Profession in Crisis?*, ed. Phyllis Culham and Lowell Edmunds (Lanham, MD: University Press of America, 1989), 257–73. An earlier version of the second paper was published under the title, "Sexual Ethics and Technologies of the Self in Classical Greece," in the *American Journal of Philology*, 107 (1986), 274–86.

1 E.g., M.-H.-E. Meier, *Histoire de l'amour grec dans l'antiquité*, rev. ed. by L.-R. de Pogey-Castries (Paris, 1930; orig. ed., 1837); also, Bethe.

2 The trend seems to have begun with a chapter on "The Perversions of Love" by Paolo Mantegazza in *Gli amori degli uomini* (1885), translated by Samuel Putnam as *The Sexual Relations of Mankind*, ed. Victor Robinson (New York: Eugenics Publishing Co., 1935), 78–96; also, Richard F. Burton, trans., *The Book of the Thousand Nights and a Night* (London, c. 1886), X, 205–54 (the famous "Terminal Essay D." on what Burton called "the Sotadic Zone"); and Edward Westermarck, *The Origin and Development of the Moral Ideas*, Volume II (London, 1908), 456–89. More recently, Vanggaard; Trumbach, 2–9; Bremmer; Rancour-Laferriere, 341–54; Adam (1985/a); Sergent, esp. 40–54; Moodie.

3 So Trumbach; Gisela Bleibtreu-Ehrenberg, *Tabu Homosexualität. Die Geschichte eines Vorurteils* (Frankfurt, 1978); Weeks (1980), 16–17; Veyne (1985), 28; and Halperin, "One Hundred Years of Homosexuality," in this volume.

4 Adrienne Rich, "Compulsory Heterosexuality and Lesbian Existence," in Snitow, Stansell, and Thompson, 177–205.

5 Adam (1985/b), 658.

6 A similar argument had been made earlier—much more sketchily, to be sure, and apparently unbeknownst to Patzer—by Wion.

7 In all this Patzer follows closely the arguments advanced a decade earlier by Vanggaard, esp. 43–45. The Victorian analogy is elaborated by Dover (1978), 90.

8 See Dover (1978), 16, 85–87; Buffière, 605–14; Kay, 120–21.

9 See Halperin, "The Democratic Body: Prostitution and Citizenship in Classical Athens," in this volume.

10 See Dover (1978), 171; Golden (1984), 312, n. 18; Sergent, 39.

11 See Halperin, "One Hundred Years of Homosexuality" in this volume, note 53, for a partial list of passages from ancient writers that record a preference by males for sexual contact with males.

12 K. J. Dover, whose ingenious and largely convincing reconstruction of this ideal provides the basis for Patzer's argument, actually presents evidence for the prevalence of anal intercourse in Greek paederasty: see (1978), 99, 100n.; now, Golden (1984), 314, n. 34.

13 Bethe's work was based on the first ethnographic reports from New Guinea and on the earlier philological study by Karl Otfried Müller, *Die Dorier*, 4.4.6–9 = *Geschichten hellenischer Stämme und Städte*, 2d ed. by F. W. Schneidewin (Breslau, 1844; repr. Graz, 1969; orig. ed. 1820–24), III, 285–93, who had argued for the antiquity of Dorian paederasty and had emphasized its educational function; the chapter on paederasty is somewhat elliptically translated in the English version: C. O. Müller, *The History and Antiquities of the Doric Race*, trans. Henry Tufnell and George Cornewall Lewis, 2d rev. ed. (London, 1839; orig. ed. 1830), 2 vols. Bethe's theory seems to reflect a fashion in the comparative religion of his day: cf. Theodore Schroeder, " 'Divinity' in Semen: A Study in the Erotogenetics of Religion," *Alienist and Neurologist*, 41 (1920), 93–101; Schroeder's earlier work had appeared contemporaneously with, and independently of, Bethe's.

14 Anatol Semenov, "Zur dorischen Knabenliebe," *Philologus*, 70 (1911), 146–50; Albert Ruppersberg, "*Eispnêlas*," *Philologus*, 70 (1911), 151–54. Compare the attitude articulated fifteen years later by T. Zielinski, *The Religion of Ancient Greece*, trans. G. R. Noyes (Chicago, 1975), 73: "some go further . . . [and] speak of 'fetishism' in the religion of ancient Greece. Excellent: now we have a common religious foundation for the Greeks and for the savages of Upper and Lower Guinea" (quoted by Bernard Frischer, *The Sculpted Word: Epicureanism and Philosophical Recruitment in Ancient Greece* [Berkeley, 1982], 105).

15 An instance is Rolf Lagerborg, *Die platonische Liebe* (Leipzig, 1926), esp. 42–44.

16 See Wion; Vanggaard, 12, 32–45, 61–70; Bremmer; Cartledge; Oswyn Murray, "Symposion and Männerbund," in *Concilium Eirene XVI* (Proceedings of the 16th International Eirene Conference), ed. Pavel Oliva and Alena Frolikova (Prague, 1982), I, 47–52; Calame (1984), xi–xvi; Durand and Schnapp, 57–66; Schnapp (1984); Keuls, 274–99, esp. 276–85; Sartre, 14–16; Sergent; Cantarella, 77–83; and, most recently, Jan N. Bremmer, "Adolescents, Symposium and Pederasty," in *Sympotica*, ed. Oswyn Murray (Oxford, forthcoming). Cf., however, Oswyn Murray, "The Symposion as Social Organisation," in Hägg, 195–99, esp. 199: "we do not have the evidence to talk about the organisations of young men in early Greece. At least I do not think that we should generalise the evidence from Sparta and Crete, or throw it back into the distant past, without careful thought."

17 The most important studies are by F. Karsch-Haack, *Das gleichgeschlechtliche Leben der Naturvölker* (Munich, 1911); Gunnar Landtmann, *The Kiwai Papuans of British New Guinea* (London, 1927); B. Malinowski, *The Sexual Life of Savages in Northwestern Melanesia* (New York, 1929); Williams; C. S. Ford and F. A. Beach, *Patterns of Sexual Behavior* (New York, 1951); J. Van Baal, *Dema* (The Hague, 1966); Alan Dundes, "A Psychoanalytic Study of the Bullroarer," *Man*, n.s. 11 (1976), 220–38; Gisela Bleibtreu-Ehrenberg, *Mannbarkeitsriten. Zur institutionellen Päderastie bei Papuas and Melanesiern* (Frankfurt, 1980); Herdt (1981) and (1984); Charles Callender and Lee M. Kochems, "The North American Berdache," *Current Anthropology*, 24.4 (1983), 443–70; Weston La Barre, *Muelos: A Stone Age Superstition about Sexuality* (New York, 1984); Walter L. Williams, *The Spirit and the*

Flesh: Sexual Diversity in American Indian Culture (Boston, 1986); see, generally, Blackwood. See, also, E. E. Evans-Pritchard, "Sexual Inversion among the Azande," *American Anthropologist*, 72 (1970), 1428–34, who contrasts the Azande with the Greeks.

18 Henri Jeanmaire, "La cryptie lacédémonienne," *Revue des études grecques*, 26 (1913), 121–50, and *Couroi et Courètes. Essai sur l'éducation spartiate et sur les rites d'adolescence dans l'antiquité hellénique* (Lille, 1939); George Thomson, *Aeschylus and Athens: A Study in the Social Origins of Drama*, 2d ed. (London, 1946); Walter Burkert, "Kekropidensage und Arrhephoria: Vom Initiationsritus zum Panathenäenfest," *Hermes*, 94 (1966), 1–25; Angelo Brelich, *Paides e parthenoi*, Istituto per gli studi micinei ed egeo-anatolici: Incunabula graeca, 36 (Rome, 1969); Walter Burkert, "Apellai und Apollon," *Rheinisches Museum für Philologie*, 118 (1975), 1–21; Calame (1977); Fritz Graf, "Apollon Delphinios," *Museum Helveticum*, 36 (1979), 2–22; Pierre Vidal-Naquet, "Recipes for Greek Adolescence," in Gordon, 163–85; Cartledge; Giacomo Costa, "Hermes dio delle iniziazioni," *Civiltà classica e cristiana*, 3 (1982), 277–95; Walter Burkert, *Homo Necans: The Anthropology of Ancient Greek Sacrificial Ritual and Myth*, trans. Peter Bing (Berkeley, 1983), 84–93, and (1985), 260–64; Koehl; Gregory Nagy, "Pindar's *Olympian* 1 and the Aetiology of the Olympic Games," *Transactions of the American Philological Association*, 116 (1986), 71–88; Sergent; and the forthcoming article by Bremmer (cited in note 16, above). For an opposing point of view, however, which emphasizes that "rituals of manhood" in Mediterranean cultures are relatively unformalized, life-long affairs, see Gilmore (1987/b), 15–16, and compare Dover (1988).

19 For a similar interpretation, see, most recently, Koehl, 105–08, who surveys some of the previous scholarly literature on the topic.

20 A more subtle discussion of the function of paederasty in "the social reproduction of male culture" is provided by Adam (1985/a); many of the works cited in notes 16 and 18, above, apply the ritual model to ancient Greek paederasty with greater interpretative nuance.

21 See Sergent, 11–15, 38. On the connection between *erôs* and the hunt in Greek culture, see Pierre Vidal-Naquet, "The Black Hunter and the Origin of the Athenian *Ephebeia*," in Gordon, 147–62; Borthwick; Marcel Detienne, *Dionysos Slain*, trans. Mireille Muellner and Leonard Muellner (Baltimore, 1979), 23–52; P. Schmitt and A. Schnapp, "Image et société en Grèce ancienne: Les représentations de la chasse et du banquet," *Revue archéologique* (1982.1), 57–74; Gundel Koch-Harnack, *Knabenliebe und Tiergeschenke: Ihre Bedeutung im päderastischen Erziehungssystem Athens* (Berlin, 1983); Nancy Felson Rubin and William Merritt Sale, "Meleager and Odysseus: A Structural and Cultural Study of the Greek Hunting-Maturation Myth," *Arethusa*, 16.1–2 (1983), 137–71; Durand and Schnapp; Schnapp (1984); and see now Froma Zeitlin, "Configurations of Rape in Greek Myth," in *Rape*, ed. Sylvana Tomaselli and Roy Porter (Oxford, 1986), 122–51, 261–64.

22 For some cautionary remarks, emphasizing that "the New Guinea male cults, and the ritual processes whereby boys are inducted into them, appear to combine species of a genus distinctive in important ways from those in other parts of Melanesia and other regions of the tribal world," see Keesing, 5.

23 Bethe, 447, 452–53; similarly, Sergent, 25; also, 29, 37, where Sergent notes and dismisses evidence for the possible significance of male beauty in Cretan paederasty.

24 On nobility as an erotic stimulus in classical Athens, see Plato, *Lysis* 205c–d. For a critique, along quite similar lines, of Patzer's reading of Strabo, see Dover (1988), 124.

25 Henry James, "The Art of Fiction," *Partial Portraits* (1888; repr. New York: Haskell House, 1968), 373–408 (quotation on p. 405).

26 Dover (1978), 125n., remarked by Jeffrey Henderson in his review of Dover (*Classical World*, 72 [1978–79], 434) and by Nussbaum (1979), 156.

27 Dover (1978), 39–49.

28 For a case study of the differences in classical Athens between the public ideal of sexual conduct and the social norm (as revealed by social practices), see Winkler (1989/a).

29 The story is quoted verbatim by Athenaeus, 13.603e–604d (*FGrHist* 362, fr. 6 = Sophocles, Testimonium 75 Radt); it is discussed in detail by Ungaretti, 9–10.

30 Further grounds for supposing that the boy in question must indeed have been a slave are supplied by Golden (1985), 98, n. 24.

31 E.g., by K. J. Dover in his review of Patzer in the *Journal of Hellenic Studies*, 104 (1984), 239–40, esp. 240 (I quote the passage in "One Hundred Years of Homosexuality," in this volume, note 57).

32 This outlook is well satirized by Nietzsche in *On the Genealogy of Morals*, 3.12. For a general consideration of the issue, see David E. Linge's editorial introduction to Hans-Georg Gadamer, *Philosophical Hermeneutics* (Berkeley, 1976), xi–lviii; most recently, Thomas Nagel, *The View from Nowhere* (New York, 1986).

33 Wilamowitz, I, 44.

34 See James Redfield, "Herodotus the Tourist," *Classical Philology*, 80 (1985), 97–118.

35 Williams, 158: "I am told that some boys are more attractive and consequently receive more attention of this kind [i.e., 'sodomy'] than do others. . . ." Herdt (1981), 3: "Although homosexual practices emerge from ritual trauma, abundant evidence indicates that most youths also experience them as pleasurable and erotically exciting"; 282; "although initiates . . . are initially impelled into this act [oral insemination], their later participation (e.g., choice of partners, frequency, interpersonal tone) is mostly a matter of personal interest. Bachelors tend to engage regularly in homosexual fellatio. They seem (impressionistically) excited by it, joking among themselves about especially attractive boys whom they prefer as fellators, but are often willing or wanting to have sex with any appropriate initiate"; 287–88: "most youths still 'desire' sex with boys. Not just any sex; for what excites the bachelor is a certain mode of structured . . . erotic encounter between *unequals*; first with boys, then with women. . . . [M]en are not simply biding time by fooling around with initiates. . . . [B]achelors are sometimes passionately fond of particular boys"; 319: "Homosexual practices, . . . in varying degrees, are coerced. And that enforced role component, in addition to boys' great need or desire to 'become men,' is enough to determine that [they] are not homosexuals, not in our Western sense. . . . Viewed this way, there is no reason to ignore the fact that ritualized homosexuality is also a personal, eventually erotic experience." Compare Moodie, 243.

36 Herdt (1984), 81, n. 50; see, generally, Herdt's introduction to this volume, pp. 1–81, esp. 63–64.

37 I wish to thank Marilyn B. Skinner for helping me with this formulation.

38 See Chauncey (1985/86); Marshall, 149–52; Albert J. Reiss, Jr., "The Social Integration of Queers and Peers," *Social Problems*, 9 (1961/62), 102–20, with references to earlier work; Gagnon and Simon, 240–51; Vanggaard, 50–58; Parker Rossman, "The Pederasts," *Society*, 10 (March/April 1973), 28–35, and *Sexual Experience between Men and Boys: Exploring the Pederast Underground* (New York, 1976); and Alan Dundes, "Into the Endzone for a Touchdown: A Psychoanalytic Consideration of American Football," *Western Folklore*, 37 (1978), 75–88, who interprets American football as an instance of ritualized homosexuality that has been symbolically displaced. See also my discussion of Jack H.

Abbott, "On 'Women,' " *New York Review of Books*, 28.10 (June 11, 1981), 17, in "One Hundred Years of Homosexuality," in this volume.

39 Housman, 408, n.1. Fuller indications can be found in the oral histories collected among the inhabitants of Sicily by Gavin Maxwell, *The Ten Pains of Death* (New York, 1960); compare J. M. Carrier, "Homosexual Behavior in Cross-Cultural Perspective," in Marmor, 100–22. For earlier periods, see Guido Ruggiero, *The Boundaries of Eros: Sex Crime and Sexuality in Renaissance Venice* (London, 1985), esp. 109–45, 159–61; James M. Saslow, *Ganymede in the Renaissance: Homosexuality in Art and Society* (New Haven, 1986).

40 See section 8 of "Why is Diotima a Woman?" in this volume, for an attempt to interpret Greek practices in the light of the New Guinea ethnographies.

41 See Stuart Hall, "Culture, the Media and the 'Ideological Effect,' " in *Mass Communication and Society*, ed. James Curran, Michael Gurevitch, Janet Woollacott, et al. (London, 1977), 315–48, esp. 330: "ideology as a *social practice* consists of the 'subject' positioning himself in the specific complex, the objectivated field of discourses and codes which are available to him in language and culture at a particular historical conjuncture" (quoted by Ken Tucker and Andrew Treno, "The Culture of Narcissism and the Critical Tradition: An Interpretive Essay," *Berkeley Journal of Sociology*, 25 [1980], 341–55 [quotation on p. 351]); see, generally, Hall's discussion of the constitutive role of ideology in "Deviance, Politics, and the Media," in *Deviance and Social Control*, ed. Paul Rock and Mary McIntosh, Explorations in Sociology, 3 (London, 1974), 261–305. On homosexuality as ideology, see Hocquenghem; on homosexuality as a demystification of ideology, see Beaver. But see Foucault (1980/b), 118, who finds fault with the concept of ideology for three reason· (1) it tends to define itself as the opposite to "truth"; (2) it posits the existence of a trans-historical "subject"; (3) it stands in a secondary relation to a material or economic determinant.

42 Foucault (1977), 161; the quotation is from *The Wanderer and His Shadow* (Opinions and Mixed Statements), no. 17.

43 *L'usage des plaisirs* (Paris: Gallimard, 1984), translated into English by Robert Hurley as *The Use of Pleasure* (New York, 1985). All pages references in this essay will be to the French edition, and all translations of Foucault contained in it—unless otherwise noted—are my own.

44 Arthur W. H. Adkins, *Merit and Responsibility: A Study in Greek Values* (Oxford, 1960).

45 See Foucault (1977), 139–64, for a discussion of the differences between conventional history and "genealogy"; also, Foucault (1983), 237–43. For a commentary, see the lucid account by Flynn, esp. 531–32: "Foucault's point, however, is not to uncover something more fundamental than truth as its precondition, such as Heidegger's *aletheia*, for example, but to reveal the sheer multiplicity of truths that 'truth' was intended to contain. The project is Nietzschean." See, generally, Dreyfus and Rabinow, 104–17; Michel Foucault, "Final Interview," *Raritan*, 5 (1985), 1–13, esp. 7–10; (1980/b), 133.

46 See the reviews by Nussbaum (1985) and by Lefkowitz.

47 *Pace* William M. Calder, III, ed., *Ulrich von Wilamowitz-Moellendorff: Selected Correspondence, 1869–1931* = *Antiqua*, 23 (Naples, 1983), 13: "Today *Die Geburt der Tragödie* is read only by those interested in the intellectual biography of Nietzsche or the relation of Wagnerian opera to Greek tragedy. Wilamowitz' *Einleitung in die griechische Tragödie* remains the fundamental book in the field."

48 Dover (1974).

49 Nussbaum (1985), 14, plainly implies—without, however, stating outright—that Foucault "lacks . . . knowledge of Greek and Latin"; she apparently bases that insinuation on

Foucault's often uncritical use of some faulty texts and translations in the bilingual Budé series: see her reply to David Konstan, *New York Times Book Review* (December 22, 1985) 4, 29.

50 Foucault, however, repeatedly claimed that his thought owed less to phenomenology, structuralism, and Marxism than it did to Nietzsche: see Foucault (1984), 336; also, Foucault and Sennett, 3–5; Foucault, "Final Interview" (note 45, above), 8–9.

51 The phrase "thick description" was appropriated from Gilbert Ryle by Clifford Geertz and applied to anthropological "readings" of social "texts": see Geertz, *The Interpretation of Cultures: Selected Essays* (New York, 1973), 5–20, 448–53.

52 Foucault (1978), 105–06.

53 See Flynn, 532–33.

54 See Foucault (1977), 146–47, 152–53, 158–59, 162–63, for further remarks on historical objectivity.

55 Foucault (1984), 334–35.

56 Reiner Schürmann, " 'What Can I Do?' in an Archaeological-Genealogical History," *Journal of Philosophy*, 82 (1985), 540–47, esp. 542.

57 Foucault defines "problematization" as "the ensemble of discursive and non-discursive practices that makes something enter into the play of the true and the false and constitutes it as an object of thought (whether in the form of moral reflection, scientific knowledge, political analysis or the like)": interview with François Ewald, "Le souci de la verité," *Magazine littéraire*, 207 (May 1984), 18, quoted by Flynn, 533.

58 See Foucault and Sennett, 6, on the shifting significance of masturbation in moral discourse about sex.

59 Cf. G. Rattray Taylor, *Sex in History* (New York, 1954), 13: "The history of civilization is the history of a long warfare between the dangerous and powerful forces of the id, and the various systems of taboos and inhibitions which man has erected to control them."

60 See Foucault (1983), 240; Foucault and Sennett, 3–5.

61 Foucault (1983), 230; Foucault and Sennett, 3–5.

62 See, also, Foucault (1983), 237–43, for an explanation of his analytical method.

63 See Foucault and Sennett, 5. To say, as Lefkowitz, 465, does, that "Foucault seems to have been interested in what Greek and Roman writers said about sex because of their influence on our ways of thinking" is therefore to get his whole enterprise exactly backwards.

64 E.g., Moodie.

65 E.g., Edmunds.

66 See Flynn, 535, and David Konstan, "Letter to the Editor," *New York Times Book Review* (December 22, 1985) 4, who observes that the word *plaisir* in Foucault's title and conceptual vocabulary does not signify "pleasure" in the ordinary sense but represents a vernacular equivalent—albeit an obviously inadequate one—of the Greek *aphrodisia* (in the singular). This point is important, because Nussbaum (1985), 14, has accused Foucault of employing, unwittingly, a nineteenth-century "empiricist-utilitarian" notion of plea-sure and of neglecting Greek controversies about its nature—i.e., whether pleasure is a sensation, an activity, or "something that supervenes on activity"—but that (peculiarly Aristotelian) problematic, evident even to a Greekless reader of the *Nicomachean Ethics*, bears entirely on the definition of *hêdonê*, not *aphrodisia*; far from being blinded to the subtleties of ancient philosophical discourse by philological incompetence ("Foucault is

not enough of a classical scholar even to perceive the issues," Nussbaum claims), Foucault reads his texts with rather more precision than Nussbaum who, in her haste to play Wilamowitz to Foucault's Nietzsche, has apparently confused *aphrodisia* with *hêdonê*.

67 Heinz Schreckenberg, *Ananke. Untersuchungen zur Geschichte des Wortgebrauchs = Zetemata*, 36 (Munich, 1964), esp. 50–61; Dover (1978), 60–62.

68 See Halperin (1985), 164–69.

69 Foucault (1983), 229; also, Foucault and Sennett, 5–6; Foucault (1986), 141.

70 In Foucault and Sennett, 5–6, Foucault illustrates this shift by attempting to document a change in the emphasis of sexual ethics from a concern with penetration to a concern with erection. See, also, the sole published excerpt from Foucault's Volume Four, "Le combat de la chasteté," in Philippe Ariès and André Béjin, eds., *Sexualités occidentales = Communications*, 35 (1982), 15–25; translated into English by Anthony Forster in Ariès and Béjin (1985), 14–25.

71 Foucault (1977), 144. See Charles Taylor, "Foucault on Freedom and Truth," *Philosophy and the Human Sciences: Philosophical Papers*, 2 (Cambridge, 1985), 152–84.

72 For the introduction of this term, see Michel Foucault, *Discipline and Punish: The Birth of the Prison*, trans. Alan Sheridan (New York, 1977), 31.

73 See Foucault (1977), for the Nietzschean distinction between *Herkunft* ("provenance"), *Entstehung* ("origination"), and *Ursprung* ("origin").

74 See Henriques, Hollway, Urwin, Couze, and Walkerdine, 104; also, Dreyfus and Rabinow, 118–25.

4 Heroes and their Pals

An earlier version of this paper, entitled "Homer and the Literary Construction of Friendship," was presented on December 30, 1987, at a Panel on *Philia*, organized by GailAnn Rickert, at the annual meeting of the American Philological Association in New York. I wish to thank the organizer of the Panel for inviting me to join it as well as my fellow panelists, Eva Stehle, Seth Schein, and Mary Whitlock Blundell, for much stimulating discussion. I also wish to thank Mark W. Edwards for a most helpful critique of the revised version.

1 E. M. Forster, *The Longest Journey* (New York, 1962), 69 (chapter 7). Cf. Hammond and Jablow, 242: "Lacking institutionalization, friendship is more private, less open to scrutiny than courtship and marriage. There are no rituals to describe and no statistics to report."

2 More than one wants to know can be found in the superb biography by P. N. Furbank, *E. M. Forster: A Life* (New York, 1977–1978).

3 Forster himself suggests such an interpretation in the coded passage immediately preceding: "Nature has no use for us: she has cut her stuff differently. Dutiful sons, loving husbands, responsible fathers—these are what she wants, and if we are friends it must be in our spare time. Abram and Sarai were sorrowful, yet their seed became as sand of the sea, and distracts the politics of Europe at this moment. But a few verses of poetry is all that survives of David and Jonathan." It is a typically Forsterian fusion of protest and acceptance.

4 Hammond and Jablow, 243, who point by way of contrast to the prominence of institutionalized friendships—blood brothers, trade friends, bond friends—in non-Western societies. Hence, social scientists tend to regard the comparatively informal sort of friendship characteristic of the West as a "vague institution," even an "institutionalized non-institu-

tion" or a "quasi-institution" (just as the role of "friend" is "a quasi-role"): for references, see Hammond and Jablow, 243, 257.

5 See Tigay, 2.

6 See Tigay, 23–38, summarizing earlier studies.

7 See, generally, Tigay.

8 See Herbert G. May and Bruce M. Metzger, eds., *The New Oxford Annotated Bible with the Apocrypha* (New York, 1977), 330.

9 But see text at note 50, below, on Sthenelus and Deïpylus in Homer. The friendship between Sthenelus and Diomedes also seems to mirror, if only distantly, that between Achilles and Patroclus (compare, for example, *Iliad* 16.97–100 with 9.45–49).

10 David is the only one of the six whose wife is mentioned, although Jonathan was undoubtedly married: his children figure in 2 Samuel. Achilles and Patroclus each have their own concubines—though Achilles has more than one, and Patroclus's concubine is a gift from Achilles (*Iliad* 9.663–68, 24.675–76). Gilgamesh's closest family member seems to be his mother Ninsun.

11 Hammond and Jablow, 245: "The tradition always dramatizes the devotion between male friends, usually a dyad, forged in an agonistic setting."

12 See Hammond and Jablow, 241–42, for an emphasis on the ideological significance of this postulate.

13 Cf. Lionel Tiger, *Men in Groups* (New York, 1969).

14 See the discussion by Tigay, 29–30.

15 All citations of the Gilgamesh Epic, unless otherwise noted, refer to the late ("Assyrian" or "Standard Babylonian") version and employ the customary method of citation by tablet, column, and line. I have specified the Assyrian version here because I am explicitly concerned in this context with the Old Babylonian version.

16 Tigay, 30; also, 46, n. 26, for references to Enkidu's being "like" Gilgamesh in the Old Babylonian version.

17 All English quotations from the Gilgamesh Epic, unless otherwise noted, are derived from the translation by E. A. Speiser, in *Ancient Near Eastern Texts relating to the Old Testament*, ed. J. B. Pritchard, 3d ed. with supplt. (Princeton, 1969: hereafter *ANET*), 72–99. Jacobsen (1976), 199, says Enkidu is "equally as strong" as Gilgamesh.

18 Unless the prostitute, who speaks this line, is merely attempting to rouse Enkidu by appealing to his competitive spirit.

19 So Gresseth, 15. On this pattern, see Hammond and Jablow, 251–53.

20 Cf. Gresseth, 15–16.

21 For other comparative treatments of the friendships in the Gilgamesh Epic and the *Iliad*, see Sinos, 58; MacCary, 103–04, 107. I have not seen a systematic comparison of all of the three relationships discussed here.

22 So Gresseth.

23 I oversimplify here for the sake of economy; for a more thorough and subtle analysis of Gilgamesh's motivation, as it is represented in the various extant versions of the Epic, see Forsyth, 25–27.

24 I follow the interpretation of Tigay, 178–91.

25 For parallels in ancient Near Eastern wisdom literature, especially in earlier Sumerian myths, see Tigay, 164–65.

26 The passage is brilliantly discussed by Redfield, 99–103.

27 See Jacobsen (1976), 215–17. So in the Sumerian myth, entitled "Gilgamesh and the Land of the Living" by its translator Samuel Noah Kramer, the sight of people dying had prompted Gilgamesh to journey to the Cedar Mountain in order to set up his name: Tigay, 29. For an alternate interpretation of the relevant passage, see Forsyth, 25–26.

28 See the discussion by Tigay, 167–69.

29 I have departed from Speiser's translation by reading, with Tigay, 168, "a spouse" instead of "thy spouse" in line 13 and by restoring "woman" instead of "mankind" in line 14: see Tigay, 168, note 17, for the evidence on which this restoration is based.

30 See Kilmer, 131.

31 Critics who complain about the Gilgamesh Epic's supposed "pessimism" (see the survey by Gresseth, 2–3) may be reacting to this theme; for an alternate view of the poem, see Held, 139–40.

32 See, generally, Giuseppe Furlani, "Das Gilgamesch-Epos als Hymnus auf die Freundschaft," trans. Rüdiger Schmitt, in *Das Gilgamesch-Epos*, ed. Karl Oberhuber, Wege der Forschung, 215 (Darmstadt, 1977), 219–36.

33 The Akkadian words are *ibru* and *tappu*: Tigay, 30. For line references in the early versions, see Tigay, 30, note 30, and 46, note 25.

34 Tigay, 29–30.

35 See William Berg, *Early Virgil* (London, 1974), 15–17; Halperin (1983), 91–94.

36 See Tigay, 198–213.

37 For references, see Tigay, 30, note 30.

38 For opposing views, arguing for the existence of a sexual component in the love between Gilgamesh and Enkidu, see Jacobsen (1929/30); Kilmer; Held, 137.

39 See Tigay, 88.

40 For a detailed discussion of the sexual imagery in this passage, see Kilmer; also, Held, 136–37.

41 *ANET*, 76.

42 Tigay, 85.

43 See Jacobsen (1929/30), 69, n. 2, and, now, Tigay, 30, note 31; 184, note 22; 274, *ad* Gilg. P. i, 34.

44 See Kilmer, 130.

45 Cf. Tigay, 184, note 22. Kilmer, 130, emphasizes Gilgamesh's rejection of the ale-wife's advice to marry: see the supplement to Tablet X, iii, printed in *ANET*, 507. So, also, Jacobsen (1976), 218–19, who remarks, "Throughout the epic the relationship with Enkidu competes with, and replaces, marriage" (p. 218n.).

46 Halperin (1983), 96–97.

47 The Early Source is, of course, aware of the tradition of the covenant between David and Jonathan: see 2 Samuel 9:1–13.

48 Nagy, 292–93; also, Sinos, 29–38; more recently, P. A. L. Greenhalgh, "The Homeric *Therapon* and *Opaon* and their Historical Implications," *Bulletin of the Institute of Classical Studies* (University of London), 29 (1982), 81–90.

49 MacCary, 127–36.

50 Clarke, 389. A fresh review of the various interpretations of the meaning of *philos* in Homer that scholars have put forward, together with a defense of the word's emotive dimension, has lately been provided by James Hooker, "Homeric *philos*," *Glotta*, 65.1–2 (1987), 44–65.

51 See, for example, *Iliad* 9.190–91, with the remarks by Clarke, 390–91.

52 See Redfield, 7.

53 See Beye, 8, who also notes that not every repetition of a simile in Homer is necessarily significant. Cf. Cedric H. Whitman, *Homer and the Heroic Tradition* (New York, 1958), 279–80.

54 So Clarke, 390.

55 Beye, 8.

56 See Nagy, 102–11; Sinos, 41, with references to earlier discussions.

57 See Nagy, 108–09, who compares this passage to 9.628–38.

58 Similarly, Gilgamesh storms over the corpse of Enkidu "like a lion, Like a lioness deprived of [her] whelps" (VIII, ii, 18–19): noted by M. L. West, [Review of Burkert (1984)], *Journal of Hellenic Studies*, 106 (1986), 233–34, esp. 234.

59 For a different interpretation of the meaning of the double burial, see Sinos, 58–62.

60 This is clearer in the case of the Gilgamesh Epic and the Books of Samuel, but see M. L. West, "The Rise of the Greek Epic," *Journal of Hellenic Studies*, 108 (1988), 151–72, esp. 170, on the late influx of Near Eastern ideas and themes into the Greek epic tradition—a cultural repertory to which belongs, in West's view, the literary elaboration of the friendship of Achilles and Patroclus in the *Iliad* as we have it; more generally, Walter Burkert, "Oriental Myth and Literature in the Iliad," in Hägg, 51–56, and Burkert (1984).

61 Cf. Hammond and Jablow, 246: "With hindsight, the narratives of friendship seem to be political propaganda for abrogating familial ties in favor of male solidarity."

62 See Vlastos (1981), 11–19; Richard Kraut, "Egoism, Love, and Political Office in Plato," *Philosophical Review*, 92 (1973), 330–44, esp. 336–37; and cf. Aristotle's critique in the *Politics* 2.1262b1–25.

63 Recently, Clarke has argued for the sexual interpretation; for counter-arguments, see D. S. Barrett, "The Friendship of Achilles and Patroclus," *Classical Bulletin*, 57.6 (April 1981), 87–93, and Patzer, 94–98. See, generally, Dover (1978), 196–99. A good compromise is offered by MacCary, 178–90.

64 The literary sources have been collected by Stefan Radt *ad* Aeschylus, fr. 134a. For a survey of the pictorial evidence, see Stella G. Miller, "Eros and the Arms of Achilles," *American Journal of Archaeology*, 90 (1986), 159–70, esp. 165–67, with references to the scholarship on Aeschylus's *Achilleis*.

65 See Xenophon, *Symposium* 8.31.

66 Clarke, 388.

67 *Iliad* 6.358, *Odyssey* 8.580: discussion by James Redfield, "The Making of the *Odyssey*," in *Parnassus Revisited: Modern Critical Essays on the Epic Tradition*, ed. A. C. Yu (Chicago, 1973), 141–54.

5 The Democratic Body: Prostitution and Citizenship in Classical Athens

Earlier versions of this essay have appeared under the title, "Atene, il corpo violato," in *La storia della prostituzione,* ed. Guido Ruggiero = *Storia e Dossier,* 4.25 (January 1989): *Dossier,* 4–23, and under the present title in the *South Atlantic Quarterly,* 88.1 (Winter 1989), 149–60, and in *Differences,* 4 (1989), forthcoming. I am grateful to Guido Ruggiero, for originally proposing that I write this essay, and to John J. Winkler, for encouraging me to do so and advising me every step of the way. Michael Jameson provided me with generous help and much stimulating discussion throughout the revision of the paper; Cynthia B. Patterson offered valuable and friendly criticism. David Cohen, Susan Guettel Cole, Thomas A. J. McGinn, and Josiah Ober read the penultimate draft and contributed further comments and corrections. An abbreviated version was delivered as a lecture at a panel on "Body Politics and Bodies Politic in the Classical World" at a conference on "Pedagogy & Politics" at The Lesbian and Gay Studies Center at Yale on October 30, 1988, where it benefited from a lively discussion. All remaining imperfections are my own.

1   The documents relating to prostitution in the ancient Greek world have been collected by Schneider; Brandt, 329–410, 436–40; Herter; Krenkel (1978) and (1979); and Keuls, 153–203. I have freely pilfered from these compilations.

2   We do not hear from any classical Greek source of women frequenting male prostitutes (but cf. Aristophanes, *Ecclesiazusae* 877–1111 and *Wealth* 959–1096; later, Parmenion, 13 [Gow-Page, who note the novelty of the theme]): the laws governing citizenship, marriage, and inheritance in the classical Greek city-state, and the social customs giving men control of women's sexual choices, made such a possibility unthinkable. But we do hear, though quite exceptionally, of women patronizing female prostitutes: our fullest description, in a second-century A.D. author (Lucian, *Dialogues of the Courtesans* 5), might explain the otherwise enigmatic allusion to *hetairistriai* by Plato's Aristophanes at *Symposium* 191e2–5, were it not that Lucian (5.2) seems to have set out deliberately to gloss the Platonic passage. Cf. also Anacreon, fr. 13 (*PMG* 358, p. 183); Asclepiades, 7 (Gow-Page). See, generally, Dover (1978), 172–73.

3   Male prostitution in classical Athens has not been much studied: Brandt, 436–40; Dover (1978), 19–42; and Krenkel (1978) and (1979), 183–85, provide general discussions. For documentation, see (in addition to Aeschines, 1, our best source) Lysias, 3; Aristophanes, *Wealth* 155; Xenophon, *Memorabilia* 1.6.13; [Demosthenes,] *Letter* 4.11; Wilamowitz's reconstruction of the lost *Philoi* of Eupolis (in Kock, I, 330); and cf. Anacreon, fr. 43.5 (*PMG* 388, p. 195); Cratinus, fr. 4 (unless otherwise noted, all citations of the fragments of the Athenian comic poets refer to Kock's edition). In the midst of prosecuting an Athenian citizen for exercising his civic rights after having lost his legal claim to them through being a prostitute (see below), Aeschines, 1.195, hastens to reassure the court that he is not attempting to undermine the practice of male prostitution: his professed aim, on the contrary, is to make sure that those who pursue "such young men as are easily caught turn to foreigners and resident aliens *so as not to be deprived of what they prefer*" without causing harm to Athenian citizens in the process. Male prostitution in classical Athens is treated as a routine matter by Athenaeus, the compiler of a late antique literary miscellany, who cites (in addition to Aeschines, 1.75–76), Alexis, fr. 242; Ephippus, fr. 20; cf. Aulus Gellius, 2.8.1–4; Diogenes Laertius, 2.9.105. That prostitution involves males as well as females is taken for granted in the classical period by Demosthenes, 22.61, in the second century B.C. by Polybius, 12.13.2, and around the turn of the second century A.D. by even such stern moralists as Dio Chrysostom, 7.133, and Epictetus, *Discourses* 4.1.35; cf. Plutarch, *Moralia* 759f–760c. For references to male prostitution in later authors, see Wright.

4 Pseudo-Lucian, *Erôtes* 25–26 (trans. Macleod); on the genre of this debate, to which Plutarch's *Eroticus* and Achilles Tatius, 2.33–38, also belong, see Friedrich Wilhelm, "Zu Achilles Tatius," *Rheinisches Museum für Philologie*, 57 (1902), 55–75 (passages from these works are cited in section 6 of "Why is Diotima a Woman?" in this volume). For other complaints about the physical attributes of maturing males, similar to the complaints voiced here, see the *Palatine Anthology*, 5.277 (Eratosthenes Scholasticus); 11.326 (Automedon, 10 [Gow-Page]); and 12.220 (Strato). It is typical of some late antique authors to articulate explicitly the sexual assumptions which classical authors either did not wish or did not need to spell out.

5 See, e.g., Xenophon, *Symposium* 4.28; Alcaeus of Messene, 8; Asclepiades, 46; Meleager, 90, 94; Phanias, 1; Philip, 59 (Gow-Page); Plutarch, *Moralia* 770bc; Philostratus, *Letters* 13, 14; *Palatine Anthology*, 5.277; 11.51, 326; 12.186, 191, 195, 220. Cf. Theognis, 1327–28; Plato, *Protagoras* 309a; Diocles 4 (Gow-Page); *Palatine Anthology*, 5.28 (Rufinus); 11.53; 12.13, 21, 39, 40, 174 (Fronto), 176, 204, 215, 249; Athenaeus, 12.518ab, 13.605d; ps.-Lucian, *Erôtes* 10. Many further sources are cited, in the course of a general discussion of this theme, by Tarán, who properly notes that the first appearance of down upon a boy's cheeks is often treated by Greek writers as an *enhancement* of his attractiveness: e.g., Homer, *Iliad* 24.347–48 and *Odyssey* 10.278–79; Plato, *Protagoras* 309ab; Xenophon, *Symposium* 4.23; Theocritus, 15.85; and a variety of later authors, including Philostratus, *Letters* 13 and 15, who expatiates upon this topic. See, also, Martial, 11.22, with the valuable commentary by Kay, 118–21, esp. 120. The evidence provided by Greek vase-paintings corroborates this testimony: see Dover (1978), 71; Golden (1984), 322.

6 Athenaeus, 13.564f, 565f; cf. Philostratus, *Letter* 58. (This appears to reflect a later misunderstanding of the Stoic doctrine of *erôs*, which defined *erôs* not as a desire to have sex but as "an impulse to form friendships," according to Diogenes Laertius, 7.130: see the entries 66C and 67D, with attached commentary, in A. A. Long and D. N. Sedley, eds., *The Hellenistic Philosophers* [Cambridge, 1987], I, 423, 430; II, 418–19, 424.) For an insistence on preserving an isomorphic relation between age–categories and sexual roles, see the *Palatine Anthology*, 12.228, 255.

7 Anaxilas, fr. 22; Antiphanes, fr. 26.12–15; Epicrates, fr. 2/3; Machon, 300–310 (Gow); also, Philetaerus, fr. 9; Timocles, fr. 25; Herodicus (quoted by Athenaeus, 13.586a); *Palatine Anthology*, 5.21; 6.1, 18–20, 283; 9.260; 11.67, 71–73, 256.

8 Lucian, *Dialogues of the Courtesans* 11.3, 12.5; *Palatine Anthology*, 11.68. Cf. Philostratus, *Letter* 22.

9 Lucian, *Dialogues of the Courtesans* 11.3; *Palatine Anthology*, 9.139, 11.67–69. Cf. Achilles Tatius, 2.38.2; ps.-Lucian, *Erôtes* 40; *Palatine Anthology*, 11.66, 408.

10 Alexis, fr. 98.7–8. Cf. Xenophon, *Oeconomicus* 10.2.

11 Alexis, fr. 98.17; Martial, 1.72.6; Alciphron, 4.12.2. Cf. Lysias, 1.14; Aristophanes, *Ecclesiazusae* 878, 929, 1072, and *Wealth* 1064; Eubulus, fr. 98.1; Xenophon, *Oeconomicus* 10.2; Dio Chrysostom, 7.117; *Palatine Anthology*, 11.408; and, for papyrological and epigraphical occurrences, LSJ, s.v. *psimythion*. See, further, Lloyd G. Stevenson, "On the Meaning of the Words *Cerussa* and *Psimithium* (*Psimythion*)," *Journal of the History of Medicine and Allied Sciences*, 10 (1955), 109–111; Bernard Grillet, *Les femmes et les fards dans l'antiquité grecque* (Lyon, 1975), 33–35.

12 See, generally, Grillet (previous note), esp. 97–111.

13 Aristophanes, fr. 148 (Kassel-Austin).

14 Asclepiades, 6 and 35 (Gow–Page, who ascribe the latter to the authorship of Poseidippus) = *Palatine Anthology*, 5.203 and 202. See Alan Cameron, "Asclepiades' Girl Friends," in Foley, 275–302, esp. 294–95.

15 Philodemus, 2 (Gow-Page); *Palatine Anthology*, 5.20, 26, 304; Philostratus, *Letter* 51; cf. Ovid, *Ars amatoria* 2.663–68. In the sixth century A.D. Paulus Silentiarius claimed to prefer the old age of one Philinna to the charms of a young girl (*Palatine Anthology*, 5.258).

16 Aristophanes, fr. 148 (Kassel-Austin); Xenarchus, fr. 4.9; Asclepiades, 41 (Gow-Page); Machon, 422–24 (Gow); Plutarch, *Moralia* 125ab; *Palatine Anthology*, 6.47, 11.73. Once again, the vase-paintings corroborate the evidence derived from literary sources: for older women shown as prostitutes, see Keuls, 176–86, who vividly conveys the harshness of their lot. For the depiction of female prostitutes on Greek vases, see, generally, Otto J. Brendel, "The Scope and Temperament of Erotic Art in the Greco-Roman World," in *Studies in Erotic Art*, ed. Theodore Bowie and Cornelia V. Christenson (New York, 1970), 3–69, esp. 19–42; Sutton, 46–56, 99–105, 290–304, 347–69.

17 For some expressions of resistance to this rule, see Euripides's celebrated remark about Agathon ("even the autumn of beauty is beautiful"), related by Plutarch, *Moralia* 770c, and by Aelian, *Varia Historia* 13.5; see, also, Strato in the *Palatine Anthology* 12.10, 178, 248; Philostratus, *Letter* 15: discussion by Tarán, 103–05.

18 See Dover (1978), 172.

19 Aeschines, 1.95; cf. Pherecrates, fr. 71.

20 See, in addition to the texts cited in notes 4 and 5 (above), Alcaeus of Messene, 7, and Thymocles, 1 (Gow-Page); *Palatine Anthology*, 12.229 (Strato).

21 For the sexual appeal of male youthfulness to women, see *Homeric Hymn to Aphrodite* 225–36; Dio Chrysostom, 7.117; Pausanias, 7.23.1–2; Lucian, *Dialogues of the Courtesans* 7.2–3; ps.-Lucian, *Erôtes* 9; *Palatine Anthology*, 6.76 (Agathias Scholasticus).

22 Alexis, fr. 264; Lucian, *The Ignorant Book-Collector* 23. See the discussion of the depiction of Agathon in Attic comedy by Dover (1978), 144.

23 See, for example, the discussion of "the smooth style" in masculine grooming habits throughout antiquity by Gleason, at notes 63 and 64.

24 See Aeschines, 1.94, 162 (identifying the "client" [*misthôsamenos*] with the "senior" [*presbyteros*] partner in the relationship); cf. Ephippus, fr. 20; Demosthenes, 19.233, 285; Aeschines, 1.194; Timaeus, *FGrHist* 566, fr. 124b.

25 Aeschines, 1.119–20; Pollux, 7.202: see Herter, 106; Dover (1978), 30. The ancient sources documenting this tax have been assembled by Th. Lenschau, "*Pornikon telos*," in *Paulys Real-Encyclopädie der classischen Altertumswissenschaft*, ed. Georg Wissowa, vol. 22, pt. 1 (Stuttgart, 1953), col. 265.

26 Winkler (1989/a); cf. Parker, 95.

27 See Herter, 86.

28 See Homer, *Iliad* 14.331–40; Hesiod, *Theogony* 56–57; Herodotus, 1.203.2; *Dissoi Logoi* 2.4; Xenophon, *Anabasis* 5.4.33–34; Apollonius of Rhodes, *Argonautica* 2.1015–25; Artemidorus, *Oneirocritica* 1.8; Athenaeus, 12.517ef: discussion by Dover (1974), 206; Arthur, 108; Walcot, 145–46. Cf. Aeschines, 1.74, 90; Demosthenes, 22.22. The degree of privacy required could be minimal, by our standards at least: Sophocles is said to have made love to a boy outside the city wall of Athens, lying upon the boy's *himation* (or "cloak") and wrapping the two of them in his own *chlamis* ("mantle"): Athenaeus, 13.604de; see, also, Asclepiades 1.3–4 (Gow-Page). Similar expedients are depicted on Attic vase-paintings: Dover (1978), 86, 98–99. An exception to all this would have been sex with hired entertainers, among friends, at an all-male symposium: see Appendix 2 for details.

29 For the Peiraeus, see Aristophanes, *Peace* 165, with scholia; Aeschines, 1.40; Theopompus of Chios, *FGrHist* 115, fr. 290; Alciphron, 1.6.2; Pollux, 9.5.34. For the Ceramicus, see Alexis, fr. 203; the scholia *ad* Aristophanes, *Knights* 772, and *ad* Plato, *Parmenides* 127c; Hesychius, s.v. *Kerameikos*. For further details, see Herter, 85–86, 88.

30 Xenophon, *Memorabilia* 2.2.4, who doubtless exaggerates the extent of prostitution at Athens for rhetorical effect.

31 I infer from the evidence I have presented thus far that male prostitution in classical Athens did indeed exhibit a specifically paederastic character (so, also, Krenkel [1978], 49). There is, of course, no way of knowing whether the paederastic model, which mapped onto the distinction of life-stages between man and youth a whole series of further hierarchical distinctions in sexual conduct between active and passive, insertive and receptive, dominant and submissive, and desiring and non-desiring roles, was maintained in the world of the male brothel, especially since a customer could presumably obtain whatever he was willing to pay for. In late antiquity Greek authors occasionally mention males hiring other males to penetrate them sexually (the eunuch priests of the Syrian goddess Atargatis in ps.-Lucian, *The Ass* 35–38, are a case in point), but our best evidence for this market derives from Roman sources: Juvenal's Ninth Satire, for example, portrays a male hustler by the name of Naevolus who considers a large penis to be a hustler's chief sexual asset (*longi mensura incognita nervi*: 34; *penem legitimum*: 43–44) and who, although he will sexually penetrate anyone— male or female—who pays him (cf. 25–26), depends for his livelihood on adult males; even Naevolus, however, customarily takes pains to look boyish (12–15). Cf. Petronius, 92.7–9, 105.9; Seneca, *Natural Questions* 1.16.1–3; Martial, 1.96.10–13, 9.33; 11.63, 88; Dio Cassius, 80.16.1–5. See, generally, Kay, 179, 208, *ad* Martial, 11.51 and 63. It is probable that in classical Athens, however, male brothels catered largely to adult men's taste for adolescents, which seems to have been for insertive anal intercourse: see, e.g., Timaeus, *FGrHist* 566, fr. 124b (discussed by Dover [1978], 103).

32 See, for example, the reviews of K. J. Dover's *Greek Homosexuality* by E. L. Bowie in *The Pelican* (1978–79), 39–42, and by Robinson, 161–62. *Contra*, Sartre, 12.

33 Plutarch, *Moralia* 751a, 752a; Lucian, *Dialogues of the Courtesans* 10; Alciphron, 4.7; Athenaeus, 13.572b; ps.-Lucian, *Erôtes* 23–24, 31, 35, 48–49, 51.

34 See, also, Aeschines, 1.132–35.

35 See Foucault (1985), 195–96.

36 Cf. Lysias, 1.32.

37 Aeschines, 1.15.

38 Lysias, 1.32–33; Plutarch, *Life of Solon* 23.1; cf. Xenophon, *Hiero* 3.3–4. See, generally, Harrison, 34–35; also, Dover (1973), 62. For a detailed study of the scanty evidence, see Cole (1984). Cf. Walcot; Cohen, 159, n. 20.

39 Harrison, 36–37; for an opposing argument, to the effect that *moikheia* applied *only* to the seduction of wives, see Cohen, who does at least establish that Athenian men were much more concerned about the chastity of their wives than about that of their mothers, sisters, or daughters.

40 Women who represented exceptions to this rule were such improbable creatures as to verge almost on the fantastic: see David Konstan, "Between Courtesan and Wife: Menander's *Perikeiromene*," *Phoenix*, 41.2 (1987), 122–39, esp. 129.

41 Demosthenes, 23.[53], 55; cf. Lysias 1.32.

42 For the ascription to Draco of the law permitting a citizen to kill the man he catches having sex with one of his free female dependents, see Demosthenes, 23.51; Pausanias,

9.36.8; cf. Lysias, 1.30; Aristotle, *Constitution of Athens* 7.1, 57.3: discussion by Harrison, 32–33; Cole (1984), 100.

43 Cf. Lysias, 1.24–26, 49 (a phrase used to define slaves by Dio Chrysostom, 15.24); Isaeus, 8.44; Xenophon, *Memorabilia* 2.1.5; [Demosthenes,] 59.65–66: for an ingenious interpretation of these passages, see Cohen, 158–59, who observes that the practice of killing those adulterers caught in the act may have fallen out of fashion in Athens by the classical period. Punishments for adultery—in the popular imagination, at least— comprised *aporhaphanidôsis*, or "radishment" (anal rape of the seducer by means of radishes [daikon?]), and (pubic?) hair-pulling: see (with scholia) Aristophanes, *Clouds* 1083; *Thesmophoriazusae* 537; *Wealth* 168, and, for a skeptical commentary, David Cohen, "A Note on Aristophanes and the Punishment of Adultery in Athenian Law," *Zeitschrift der Savigny–Stiftung für Rechtsgeschichte* (Romanistische Abteilung), 102 (1985), 385–87.

44 For the exhibition of prostitutes to customers, see (in addition to Philemon, fr. 4, quoted below), Eubulus, frr. 67, 84; Philostratus, *Letter* 19; and the vases discussed by Keuls, 158–59.

45 Compare Eubulus, fr. 67; Xenophon, *Memorabilia* 1.3.14–15 and *Symposium* 4.38; Cercidas, fr. 5 (Powell); Diogenes Laertius, 6.4; Lucretius, 4.1063–67; Horace, *Satires* 1.2.111–34; Martial, 9.32.

46 Lysias, 1.32; Aeschines, 1.15.

47 See Foucault (1985), 197–98.

48 Aeschines, 1.138–39; Plutarch, *Moralia* 152d, 751b, and *Life of Solon*, 1.3. Further sources in M.-H.-E. Meier, *Histoire de l'amour grec dans l'antiquité*, rev. ed. by L.-R. de Pogey-Castries (Paris, 1930), 284–90.

49 Cf. Aristophanes, *Birds* 137–42.

50 Aeschines, 1.9–12, 18.

51 Foucault (1985), 198.

52 See Halperin (1986), 63–66, and section 6 of "Why is Diotima a Woman?" in this volume.

53 Dover (1978), 81–91; Vlastos (1987), 95–96.

54 See Dover (1978), 111–24.

55 Aeschines, 1.1, 3, 14, 19, 21, 28–29, 40, 46, 51, 72–73, 87, 119, 134, 154, 160, 164, 188, 195; Demosthenes, 22.21–24, 30–32. Cf. Demosthenes, 24.181; 45.79. For the clearest discussion of the evidence, see Dover (1978), 23–34; also, the highly detailed and valuable account by Hansen, 54–98, esp. 74, which should, however, be read with a critical eye. For a discussion of how the law was applied in practice, see Winkler (1989/a).

56 For the political motive behind the trial of Timarchus, see Aeschines, 1.1–2, 19–20; Demosthenes, 19.283–87, esp. 286.

57 For the distinction between "automatic" and what I have been calling "formal" *atimía*, see Hansen, esp. 66–67. The very fact that one could go to court to secure another person's formal *atimía* ("by sentence," in Hansen's formulation) indicates that "automatic" *atimía* in classical Athens was, in practice, less than perfectly automatic.

58 Demosthenes, 45.79 and 21.92.

59 Aeschines, 1.13–14, 184, and cf. 43. See Dover (1978), 27–28, 34.

60 So, also, in the case of female prostitutes of citizen status (MacDowell, 126): Lysias, 10.19; [Demosthenes], 59.67; Plutarch, *Life of Solon* 23.1. All modern authorities seem to agree on this point: see Justus Hermann Lipsius, *Das attische Recht und Rechtsverfahren* (Leipzig, 1905–15), 436; Thalheim, "*Hetairêseôs graphê,*" *Paulys Real-Encyclopädie der classischen*

Altertumswissenschaft, ed. Georg Wissowa, 8.2. (Stuttgart, 1913), cols. 1372–73; Harrison, 37; MacDowell, 126; Dover (1978), 27–34, esp. 29: "if an Athenian citizen made no secret of his prostitution, did not present himself for the allocation of offices by lot, declared his unfitness if through someone's inadvertence he was elected to office, and abstained from embarking on any of the procedures forbidden to him by the law, he was safe from prosecution and punishment." Compare Parker, 96: "offenders are not exiled or put to death but deprived of 'honour' and forced to find a place amid the flotsam of foreignness and vice that laps around the citizen body."

61 Aeschines, 1.20, 72–73; cf. 32. Hansen, 54, emphasizes that the only sort of *atimía* that was actionable was a "second" offense—i.e., a failure to abide by the restrictions upon one's conduct imposed by an already existing condition (whether formal or informal) of *atimía*; so, also, Harrison, 37.

62 Demosthenes, 21.182.

63 Aeschines, 1.28–32, 154, 194–95. See Winkler (1989/a).

64 Hansen, 72–74 (quotation on p. 74).

65 In this paragraph I shall be summarizing the arguments advanced by Winkler (1989/a), whose interpretation I follow closely.

66 Aristotle, *Constitution of Athens* 6.1; Plutarch, *Life of Solon*, 15.4, 23.2. For some recent reinterpretations of the meaning of "debt" in archaic Athens, see Oswyn Murray, *Early Greece* (Glasgow, 1980), 181–84; Wood, 93–96. On temporary *atimía*, see Hansen, 67–70.

67 On the sexual use of slaves in antiquity, see Peter Brown, *The Body and Society: Men, Women and Sexual Renunciation in Early Christianity* (New York, 1988), 23.

68 Lysias, 13.27, 59. See MacDowell, 246–47; now, C. Carey, "A Note on Torture in Athenian Homicide Cases," *Historia*, 37 (1988), 241–45, who argues that although free non-citizens at Athens could be tortured in connection with cases affecting the safety of the city, they could not legally be tortured to produce evidence at trials for homicide or wounding.

69 See Demosthenes, 21.178–80; on *hybris* as a collective insult, see Demosthenes, 21.45; Aeschines, 1.17.

70 Aeschines, 1.15–17, emphasizes that Athenian law prohibited *hybris* against women and slaves (so, also, Demosthenes, 21.46–49), but what the statute in question prohibited (*pace* Rousselle [1986], 258–59) was in all likelihood indirect offenses against their Athenian guardians or owners—that is, it prohibited treating women and slaves without due regard for the fact that they belonged to Athenian citizens. Cf. Cole (1984), 109.

71 Aeschines, 1.29, 87; cf. Demosthenes, 19.309: Dover (1978), 34–39, esp. 35. For uses of *hybris* in the sense of "sexual degradation," see Aeschines, 1.55, 108, 116, 188; cf. [Demosthenes], *Letter* 4.10–11: "he does by preference the very things that one might call down upon him as a curse."

72 Plutarch, *Moralia* 142c; Martial, 11.104. Cf. Aeschines, 1.55, 70, 185, where the orator titillates his audience by suggesting without naming the unspeakable things that Timarchus's customers required of him.

73 For evidence that oral sex was considered degrading to the person who performed it, see, generally, V. Grassman, *Die erotischen Epoden des Horaz* (Munich, 1966), 3–4, 14–15, 18–19, 25–26, 28–29 (cited by Kay, 137); Dover (1978), 101–102, 182; Jocelyn; Werner A. Krenkel, "Fellatio and Irrumatio," *Wissenschaftliche Zeitschrift der Wilhelm-Pieck-Universität Rostock*, 29 (1980), 77–88, and "Tonguing," *Wissenschaftliche Zeitschrift der Wilhelm-Pieck-Universität Rostock*, 30 (1981), 37–54; Parker, 99–100; Winkler (1989/b). On the male liking for heterosexual anal intercourse with prostitutes and others, see Aristophanes,

Wealth 149–52; Machon, 226–30, 327–32, 422–32 (Gow); Dioscorides, 7 (Gow-Page); *Palatine Anthology*, 5.116 (Marcus Argentarius) and 11.73.7 (Nicarchus); pseudo-Lucian, *Erôtes* 27; other documents are listed by Kay, 163, *ad* Martial, 11.43; Jocelyn, 20 (with p. 50, n. 83); Krenkel, "Tonguing," 39.

74 Archedicus, fr. 4; Timaeus, *FGrHist* 566, fr. 35b; Polybius, 12.13: discussed by Dover (1978), 99. Also, Aeschines, 1.19, 188; Demosthenes, 22.73, 77; 24.181; [59].73–86, 107–13. See Parker, 94–97.

75 See Cole (1991).

76 Dover (1978), 103–104. Cf. Paul, *Romans* 1.26: *pathê atimias*.

77 See "One Hundred Years of Homosexuality" in this volume.

78 But see Anacreon, fr. 43.5 (*PMG* 388, p. 195), for the term *ethelopornos*, "willing (male) whore"—which, however, seems to be merely a term of abuse.

79 See Aeschines, 1.29, 188.

80 Cf. Demosthenes, 22.30–32.

81 See Dover (1974), 109–10, for the Athenian tendency to equate poverty with moral incapacity.

82 Consider in this context the statutory regulation of dress in classical Athens, where the wearing of sumptuous clothing was severely restricted: see Harrianne Mills, "Greek Clothing Regulations: Sacred and Profane?" *Zeitschrift für Papyrologie und Epigraphik*, 55 (1984), 255–65, esp. 262–65; A. G. Geddes, "Rags and Riches: The Costume of Athenian Men in the Fifth Century," *Classical Quarterly*, 37 (1987), 307–31.

83 See Ste. Croix, 179–203, esp. 181–86.

84 Golden (1984), 310, n. 9. For an expression of the outlook that identified even non-laboring employees with slaves, see Xenophon, *Memorabilia* 2.8.3–6, discussed by Ste. Croix, 181–82.

85 See, e.g., Demosthenes, 22.25; Aeschines, 1.17–18 (with commentary by Dover [1978], 33–34).

86 See, for example, Demosthenes, 19.200: "[Don't these jurors know, Aeschines,] that you worked as a clerk for the magistrates and could be corrupted for two or three drachmae? [. . . And to think that] such a man [as you had the nerve to] seek a judgment against another on a charge of prostitution!" Cf. Xenophon, *Hellenica* 2.3.48–49 on "men who, through destitution, would sell the city for a drachma": Dover (1974), 109. See, further, G. Ferrari Pinney, "For the Heroes are at Hand," *Journal of Hellenic Studies*, 104 (1984), 181–83 and plate 8c–d.

87 See Dover (1978), 73–109; Golden (1984), 313–16; Foucault (1985), 187–225.

88 See Winkler (1989/a). Seaford, 122, interprets the function of the *arkteia* at Brauron in an analogous fashion: those Athenian girls who do participate in that ritual represent, for all intents and purposes of the civic ideology, *everyone*—all the eligible girls in the Athenian population.

89 There are two sources for this story: Philemon, fr. 4 (quoted below), and Nicander's lost *Colophoniaca* (or "History of Colophon") = *FGrHist* 271–272, fr. 9, both cited by Athenaeus, 13.569d–f. It is quite possible, of course, as Gordon Williams has observed to me, that the two sources are not independent of one another: Nicander may be embroidering on Philemon, who may have invented the whole story. But, as I hope to make clear, I am in any case less concerned here with the truth of the story (which is, surprisingly, defended by Herter, 73, against more numerous skeptics, including now

Henry, 10), or with its value as a testimony to the actual reforms of Solon, than I am with the possibility of using it to show that some people in classical Athens evidently considered prostitution an intrinsic constituent of democracy.

90 This gives an unintended twist to Aristotle's statement in the *Politics* that Solon's reforms granted the poorest citizens only "the barest minimum" (*tēn anagkaiotatēn dynamin*: 2.9.4 = 1274a16)—of political rule, that is. I am grateful to Martha Nussbaum for pointing this out to me.

91 Athenaeus, 13.569d, with Kaibel's reading, *anagkēn*, for the transmitted *akmēn*.

92 I have been guided in my translation of this fragment by Charles Burton Gulick's Loeb version.

93 According to Nicander, *FGrHist* 271–272, fr. 9, preserved by Athenaeus, 13.569d, and by Harpocration, s.v. *Pandēmos Aphroditē* = *FGrHist* 244, fr. 113.

94 See Plato, *Symposium* 180d–182a; Xenophon, *Symposium* 8.9–10. These passages are discussed in Appendix 1.

95 See the proverb, "The journey to Corinth does not profit every man"—i.e., not everyone can afford a trip to Corinth: Strabo, 8.6.20; Horace, *Epistles* 1.17.36 (Brandt, 340–41). See, also, Aristophanes, *Wealth* 149–52.

96 Eubulus, frr. 67.7, 84.6–7; Xenarchus, fr. 4.16; Theopompus of Chios, *FGrHist* 115, fr. 253 (with Wilamowitz's emendation). Cf. Horace, *Satires* 1.2.119–22; Dio Chrysostom, 7.140; Athenaeus, 13.568d; *Palatine Anthology*, 9.416.5.

97 Herter, 73, inclines to believe in the historical truth of the Solonian brothels because he sees them as part of Solon's program for supporting the integrity of the Athenian family.

98 See Cynthia B. Patterson's forthcoming book on Athenian family, kinship, and inheritance.

99 Solon, fr. 36.3–7 (West).

100 See A. French, "Solon's Act of Mediation," *Antichthon*, 18 (1984), 1–12.

101 Cf. Wood, 115–20, who speculates on the relation between Solon's liberation of the "peasantry," as she calls it, and the restriction of women's property-rights.

102 For an attempt to recover a competing interpretation of sex on the part of Athenian women, see Winkler (1989/c).

103 See Vernant (1974).

104 Anacreon, fr. 43.4–5 (*PMG* 388, p. 195), associates bread-sellers with prostitutes; cf. Eubulus, fr. 98, on garland–sellers.

105 See Cole (1984), 97.

106 See, for example, Sigmund Freud, "On the Universal Tendency to Debasement in the Sphere of Love," *Contributions to the Psychology of Love*, 2, in Strachey, XI, 179–90.

107 See Pierre Bourdieu, *Outline of a Theory of Practice*, trans. Richard Nice, Cambridge Studies in Social Anthropology, 16 (Cambridge, 1977), 13, who goes on to note, "While the logic of honour presupposes the recognition of an ideal equality in honour, the popular consciousness is nonetheless aware of actual inequalities."

108 Herodotus, 2.51.1; Thucydides, 6.27.1; Pausanias, 1.24.3 and 4.33.3: cited by Osborne, 68, nn. 5–6, with discussion on pp. 47–48.

109 This point was emphasized to me by Michael Jameson.

110 Osborne, 48: the earliest depiction of a (wooden) herm is in the tondo of a kylix by Epictetus (Copenhagen NM 119); the legend reads "*Hiparkhos kalos*" ("Hipparchus is beautiful"). The painting is reproduced on the cover of Halperin, Winkler, and Zeitlin.

111 Osborne, 57.

112 John J. Winkler, "Representing the Body Politic," *Rehearsals of Manhood*, Martin Classical Lectures (Princeton: Princeton University Press, forthcoming).

113 Cf. Osborne, 53, 58–61, 65.

114 Winkler (1989/a).

115 *IG* I^2, 700 (= I^3, 832); II^2, 659 (*SIG*^{3} 375), 4596, 4862; for the most recent excavations, see G. Dontas, *Praktika* (1960), 4–9, and *To Ergon* (1960), 10–13; L. Beschi, "Contributi di topografia ateniese," *Annuario della Scuola archeologica di Atene*, 45/46 (1967/68), 520–26. I owe these references, along with the rest of the information in this Appendix, to a work in progress entitled "Aphrodite in Athens" by Michael Jameson, who has graciously allowed me to make use of it here.

116 Plato, *Symposium* 180d–82a; Xenophon, *Symposium* 8.9–10; Menander, *Kolax* fr. 1 (Sandbach = 292 Kock).

117 *FGrHist* 244, fr. 113: Harpocration, s.v. *Pandêmos Aphroditê*.

118 The dedication to Aphrodite by one [Pyth]odoros in the 470's B.C. (A. E. Raubitschek, *Dedications from the Athenian Acropolis* [Princeton, 1949], #296, pp. 318–20 = *IG* I^2, 700 = *IG* I^3, 832), including a request for *agathôn* . . . *aphthonian* and relief from slander, is suggestive but not decisive. See, also, James H. Oliver, *Demokratia, the Gods, and the Free World* (Baltimore, 1960), 91–117; F. Sokolowski, "Aphrodite as Guardian of Greek Magistrates," *Harvard Theological Review*, 57 (1964), 4; Francis Croissant and François Salviat, "Aphrodite gardienne des magistrats," *Bulletin de correspondance hellénique*, 90 (1966), 465–71.

119 Kambourgolou, *Archaiologikon Deltion*, 114 (1892), 4; *Praktika* (1892), 11; I. Travlos, *Praktika* (1937), 25–41; *IG* II^2, 4570, 4574–4585.

120 Athenaeus, 13.572ef = *FGrHist* 84, fr. 9.

121 At Eryx in Sicily, according to Strabo, 6.2.6; in Cyprus, according to Herodotus, 1.199; at Comana in Pontus and Comana in Cappadocia, according to Strabo, 12.2.3 and 12.3.36; and at many other more obscure locations: for a complete overview, see Herter, 72–73; Ste. Croix, 154, and 568–69, nn. 34–40.

122 Dio Chrysostom, 37.34; Athenaeus, 13.573c. See H. Conzelmann, "Korinth und die Mädchen der Aphrodite: Studien zur Religionsgeschichte der Stadt Korinth," *Nachrichten der Akademie der Wissenschaften in Göttingen*, Philosophisch-historische Klasse (1967), 245–61.

123 Athenaeus, 8.351cd.

124 Athenaeus, 12.547d, citing Antigonus of Carystus. For varying prices, see Euripides, fr. 675 (Nauck).

125 Plato comicus, fr. 174.17.

126 Diogenes Laertius, 6.4; cf. Cercidas, fr. 5.31 (Powell).

127 *IG* I^2, 374.404–17: Ste Croix, 577, n. 22.

128 *IG* II^2, 1672–73, esp. 1672.6–8: Ste. Croix, 185–86; 577, n. 22.

129 Ste. Croix, 186.

130 Philodemus, 25 (Gow-Page) = *Palatine Anthology*, 5.126.

131 Bassus, 1 (Gow-Page) = *Palatine Anthology*, 5.125; cf. Plautus, *Cistellaria* 407 and *Poenulus* 270, for the epithet *diobolaris* applied to prostitutes.

132   Cf. Plato comicus, fr. 174.17.

133   Antipater, 53 (Gow-Page) = *Palatine Anthology*, 5.109.

134   Krenkel (1978), 53, somehow infers from this passage that four drachmae was the standard fee for boys and was fixed at that sum by city officials.

135   Athenaeus, 6.241e.

136   *Palatine Anthology*, 12.239.

137   Cf. Epicrates, fr. 9.

138   Hyperides, 3.2–3.

139   Lysias, 3.22–25.

140   Pseudo-Aeschines, *Letter* 7.3.

141   See A. W. Gomme and F. H. Sandbach, *Menander: A Commentary* (Oxford, 1973), 298, *ad* Menander, *Epitrepontes* 136.

142   Menander, *Kolax* 128–30.

143   Aulus Gellius, 1.8; Schol. *ad* Aristophanes, *Wealth* 149. Gnathaena is said to have demanded a thousand drachmae for Gnathaenion, her grand-daughter: Machon, 340 (Gow).

144   Epicrates, fr. 2/3.22. Cf. Plato comicus, fr. 174.17; Antiphanes, fr. 300; Machon, 308 (Gow); Plautus, *Poenulus* 868.

145   Philonides, fr. 5; Pollux, 7.202.

146   E.g., Phrynichus, fr. 33. Perhaps it was to such women that the term *pezos*, "infantryman," was applied: see Eupolis, fr. 169, with scholia; Plato comicus, fr. 155; Theopompus of Chios, *FGrHist* 115, fr. 213.

147   Schneider, col. 1345.

148   Clement of Alexandria, *Paedagogus* 2.116.

149   *Palatine Anthology*, 5.101. A similar exchange, which issues in a more satisfactory resolution for both parties, is portrayed by Philodemus, 4 (Gow-Page); an unsuccessful attempt at a pick-up is represented by Antiphilus, 14 (Gow-Page).

150   See Herter, 97–98.

151   Menander, *Perikeiromenê* 340.

152   This seems to be the regulation referred to by Hyperides, 4.3, who mentions flute-girls only.

153   [Hippocrates], *On the Seed/Nature of the Child* 13 (= VII, 490 Littré), translated by Lonie, 7, with my amplification.

154   See Isaeus, 3.39.

155   See Menander, *Samia* 390–97 (though Chrysis is also spoken of throughout the play as a *hetaira*). A concubine who was a slave could of course be sold to a brothel whenever her owner tired of her: see Antiphon, 1.14; Xenophon of Ephesus, 5.5.4–7.

156   On this last—disputed—point, see Cynthia B. Patterson, "Those Athenian Bastards," *Classical Antiquity*, forthcoming.

157   See Patterson (preceding note) who emphasizes this scenario.

158   See MacDowell, 89–90.

159   According to Henry, 9, 12, 17, the euphemism *hetaira* (see Plutarch, *Solon* 15.3) occurs for the first time in extant Greek documents in Herodotus, 2.134.1, where it modifies

gynê ("woman"); it occurs for the first time alone, as a noun, in Herodotus, 2.135.5, and in Aristophanes, *Peace* 440.

160 See Xenophon, *Memorabilia* 3.11, for a detailed picture of this world and its economic base.

161 Cratinus, fr. 241; cf. Plutarch, *Life of Pericles*, 24.7.

162 The Greek system of classification, distinguishing as it does between a *pornê*, *hetaira*, and *pallakê*, seems to correspond exactly to the system documented by Moodie, esp. 245, for South African townships in the twentieth century, which distinguishes between a *nongogo*, *intombi*, and *ishweshwe*. Since the South African context also features paederasty, it merits special attention for the purposes of comparison with the classical Greeks, and Moodie himself elaborates some of the analogies.

163 Anaxilas, fr. 22: Dover (1978), 21.

164 Menander, *Samia* 392–93.

165 Machon, 451 (Gow); Athenaeus, 13.584c: see Gow, 120, *ad* Machon, 340.

166 Herter, 83.

167 *OGIS* 2.674: Pomeroy (1975), 141.

6 Why is Diotima a Woman?

An earlier version of this paper was presented at a meeting of the Women's Classical Caucus in December, 1981; subsequent, progressively revised versions were read at a series of conferences (starting in January, 1986)—"Perspectives on Love, Marriage, Friendship, and Sexuality in Antiquity" at the National Humanities Center; "Bodies and Minds: Sexuality and Desire in the Ancient World" at Princeton University; "Interpreting Plato" at the University of California, Santa Cruz; "Images of Women in Ancient Greece" at Emory University—as well as at the Stanford Humanities Center, Babson College, and the Center for Literary and Cultural Studies at Harvard University. I am grateful to the organizers and audiences of these events for their interest as well as for their suggestions, many of which have been incorporated here. I wish to thank in particular Maria-Viktoria Abricka, Harry Berger, Jr., Ernestine Friedl, Jean H. Hagstrum, Judith P. Hallett, Myra Jehlen, Madeleine H. Kahn, Eva C. Keuls, David Konstan, John P. Lynch, Martha Nussbaum, Richard Parry, Cynthia B. Patterson, Richard Patterson, Ruth Perry, Sarah B. Pomeroy, Daniel L. Selden, Nicholas D. Smith, Gregory Vlastos, John J. Winkler, and Froma I. Zeitlin for much stimulating, sustained, and pertinent advice. The original impetus for this paper came from Susan Amy Gelman: I have specified the nature of my debt to her in note 10, below. An abbreviated version of this essay appears in Halperin, Winkler, and Zeitlin, 257–308.

1 Lowenstam, 89–91, 99–100, questions the validity of the refutation; Penwill, 156, questions the sincerity of Agathon's concurrence in it.

2 On Plato's conception of paederastic *orthotês*, see Kranz (1926/a), 445.

3 See Plato, *Symposium* 177d, 198d; *Lysis* 204bc; *Phaedrus* 227c, 257a; *Theages* 128b; Xenophon, *Memorabilia* 2.6.28; *Symposium* 8.2; Aeschines Socraticus, fr.11 (Dittmar). On Socratic eroticism, see Friedländer, I, 44–50; Guthrie, 390–98; Dover (1978), 153–60; Vlastos (1987), 88–93; Kahn.

4 E.g., Thomas Gould, *Platonic Love* (London, 1963), 193, n. 34: "By choosing a woman he [i.e., Plato] avoided the suggestion that the wise one was the youthful Socrates' real 'Platonic' lover." (What Plato actually wished to rule out, to be precise, was the possibility

that Socrates and his instructor in erotics had been sexual, rather than merely " 'Platonic,' " lovers.)

5 On the cults of Aphrodite Ourania and Aphrodite Pandemos at Athens, see Hug-Schöne, 41–43; Halperin, "The Democratic Body" (in this volume), Appendix 1. The association of the Athenian cult of Aphrodite Ourania with prostitution, to which Krell (1972), 444, has newly called our attention, depends on late and tenuous evidence.

6 Dover (1978), 91, summarizes Pausanias's argument; see Penwill, 145–47, for a sympathetic treatment of Pausanias's general outlook.

7 Harry Neumann, "On the Sophistry of Plato's Pausanias," *Transactions of the American Philological Association*, 95 (1964), 261–67, argues this point rather crudely; see Krüger, 95–104, esp. 99–101. Eryximachus's definition of *erôs* as a harmonious accord between opposite principles that are hateful to one another (186b and ff.) is both an elaboration, as Eryximachus himself acknowledges (186b), and a *reductio ad absurdum* of Pausanias's formulation of Uranian paederasty; Aristophanes and Agathon, by contrast, argue that *erôs* obtains between likes (192a5, 195b5), not—as Pausanias and Eryximachus had assumed—between unlikes: see Brentlinger, 9–17; Krüger, 105–06. For Plato's outlook on the traditional controversy over whether love is a relation between likes or unlikes, see Glidden.

8 Plato thus allays "our suspicion that cunning self-interest might be the mainspring of arguments for what is essentially a male homosexual foundation for philosophical activity," according to Dover (1980), 137. See Nussbaum (1979), 145; (1986), 177: "Here, then, Socrates too, takes a mistress: a priestess instead of a courtesan, a woman who prefers the intercourse of the pure mind to the pleasures of the body, who honors (or is honored by) the divine rather than the merely human"; Zeitlin (1985), 88: "In Plato's counter-drama the female as benevolent priestess has no cause of her own to protect and no conflictual interests to distract her. She is then free to lend whole-hearted support to the cause of men and to transmit to them a wisdom without tragic pain that may become entirely theirs."

9 I have been assuming throughout that the erotic doctrines enunciated by Diotima are genuinely Platonic: for a sensible discussion of the supporting evidence, see Kranz (1926/ a), 438–39. That assumption was called into question by Wilamowitz, I, 380; II, 169–76; it has been challenged more recently, if (to my mind) less persuasively, by Neumann and by Rosen, 225, who takes Diotima's speech to represent an instance of the "noble lie." The most powerful assault on Diotima's authority has been mounted by Nussbaum (1986), 165–99, esp. 197–98, who elevates Alcibiades to the rank of rival authority and claims that Plato wishes us to choose between them (Nussbaum's interpretation is followed closely—if silently—by Freeman); I have tried to argue against some aspects of that view in Halperin (1985), 183–84.

10 Singer, 79, remarks on the oddity of Plato's appeal to Diotima in the dramatic context of the *Symposium*. I wish to thank Susan Amy Gelman, my student of many years ago, for patiently insisting to me that a positive account of Diotima's gender must be given, not merely a negative one.

11 For a discussion of this imagery, its literalness, its antecedents in earlier Greek thought and expression, see James M. Edie, "Expression and Metaphor," *Philosophy and Phenomenological Research*, 23 (1963), 538–61, esp. 553–57; Morrison, 51–55; Neumann, 39; Vlastos (1981), 21n., 424; Burnyeat, 14, nn. 4, 5; Plass; Pierre Guiraud, *Sémiologie de la sexualité: Essai de glosso-analyse* (Paris, 1978), 78–83. For the "pregnancies" of Zeus as possible precedents, see the references to Hesiod's *Theogony* in note 201, below.

12 Cf. Plass, 48: " . . . the notion of pregnancy does seem in some respects rather awkward in defense of pederasty. . . ." I shall argue below, however, that in a traditional paederastic context procreative language is not only not out of place but is, on the contrary, almost inevitable.

13 *Symposium* 206c1, 7, d4, 7–8; 208e2; 209a1–2, b1, 5, c3.

14 *Symposium* 206e1.

15 *Symposium* 206c8–d1, 3, 5, 7, e5, 7–8; 207a8–9, b2, d3, 7, e4; 208a1; 209a4, b2–4, c3–4, 8, d7, e2–3; 210a7; 211a1, b3. I have followed Kranz (1926/a), 443, in treating *gennan* and *genesthai* in Diotima's vocabulary as active and passive expressions, respectively, of the same idea; but see Wilamowitz, II, 172.

16 *Symposium* 206b7, c3–4, 6, d5, e5; 209a3, b2, c3; 210c1, d5; 212a3, 5.

17 *Symposium* 208b5 (*apoblastêma*); 209c5–e4 (*paides, ekgona*).

18 *Symposium* 207b2, 5; 209c4; 212a6.

19 This notion recurs, somewhat altered, in the *Theaetetus*, esp. 148e–151d: see Burnyeat.

20 See Friedländer, III, 25; Brentlinger, 19–21.

21 I refer only to the recent controversy: Wender; Christine Pierce, "Equality: *Republic* V," *Monist*, 57.1 (1973), 1–11; Anne Dickason, "Anatomy and Destiny: The Role of Biology in Plato's Views of Women," *Philosophical Forum*, 5.1–2 (1973–74), 45–53; Sarah B. Pomeroy, "Feminism in Book V of Plato's *Republic*," *Apeiron*, 8.1 (1974), 33–35, and "Plato and the Female Physician (*Republic* 454d2)," *American Journal of Philology*, 99 (1978), 496–500; Christine Garside Allen, "Plato on Women," *Feminist Studies*, 2.2–3 (1975), 131–38; Brian Calvert, "Plato and the Equality of Women," *Phoenix*, 29 (1975), 231–43; W. W. Fortenbaugh, "On Plato's Feminism in *Republic* V," *Apeiron*, 9.2 (1975), 1–4; Geddes, 37–39; Martha Lee Osborne, "Plato's Unchanging View of Woman: A Denial that Anatomy Spells Destiny," *Philosophical Forum*, 6.4 (1975), 447–52, and "Plato's Feminism," Ph.D. diss., University of Tennessee, Knoxville (1978); Julia Annas, "Plato's *Republic* and Feminism," *Philosophy*, 51 (1976), 307–21; Saxonhouse (1976), (1984), and (1985), 37–62; Susan Moller Okin, "Philosopher Queens and Private Wives: Plato on Women and the Family," *Philosophy and Public Affairs*, 6 (1977), 345–69, reproduced in the course of a longer discussion in *Women in Western Political Thought* (Princeton, 1979), 15–70; William Jacobs, "Plato on Female Emancipation and the Traditional Family," *Apeiron*, 12 (1978), 29–31; Lynda Lange, "The Function of Equal Education in Plato's *Republic*," in *The Sexism of Social and Political Theory: Women and Reproduction from Plato to Nietzsche*, ed. Lorenne Clark and Lynda Lange (Toronto, 1979), 3–15; Harry Lesser, "Plato's Feminism," *Philosophy*, 54 (1979), 113–17; Nicholas D. Smith, "The Logic of Plato's Feminism," *Journal of Social Philosophy*, 11 (1980), 5–11, and (1983), 468–74; Giallongo, 107–34; O'Brien, 119–39; Singer, 77–81; Monique Canto, "The Politics of Women's Bodies: Reflections on Plato," in *The Female Body in Western Culture: Contemporary Perspectives*, ed. Susan Rubin Suleiman (Cambridge, MA, 1986), 339–53; Cantarella, 58–59; David Cohen, "The Legal Status and Political Role of Women in Plato's *Laws*," *Revue internationale des droits de l'antiquité*, 3d ser., 34 (1987), 27–40; Gregory Vlastos, "Was Plato a Feminist?" *Times Literary Supplement*, No. 4,485 (March 17–23, 1989), 276, 288–89; and cf. Krell (1975). For the earlier history of the question, see now Natalie Harris Bluestone, *Women and the Ideal Society: Plato's Republic and Modern Myths of Gender* (Amherst, MA, 1987), 21 ff.

22 See the informative, subtle, and judicious account by David M.Schaps, *Economic Rights of Women in Ancient Greece* (Edinburgh, 1979), who shows that Athenian women were disadvantaged by comparison with women in other parts of classical Greece. See, also,

Victor Ehrenberg, *The People of Aristophanes: A Sociology of Old Attic Comedy*, 2d rev. ed. (New York, 1962), 192–207; W. K. Lacey, *The Family in Classical Greece*, Aspects of Greek and Roman Life (Ithaca, NY, 1968), esp. 15–32, 100–76; Just; John Gould, "Law, Custom and Myth: Aspects of the Social Position of Women in Classical Athens," *Journal of Hellenic Studies*, 100 (1980), 38–59, with references to previous work on the topic; now, H. S. Versnel, "Wife and Helpmate. Women of Ancient Athens in Anthropological Perspective," in *Sexual Asymmetry: Studies in Ancient Society*, ed. Josine Blok and Peter Mason (Amsterdam, 1987), 59–86. The horrific picture recently painted by Keuls should be viewed with caution; the relatively conventional sketch by Cantarella is untrustworthy in a different way. More balanced is Sarah B. Pomeroy, *Goddesses, Whores, Wives, and Slaves: Women in Classical Antiquity* (New York, 1975), esp. 57–92. Cynthia Patterson, "*Hai Attikai*: The Other Athenians," in *Rescuing Creusa: New Methodological Approaches to Women in Antiquity*, ed. Marilyn Skinner = *Helios*, 13.2 (Fall 1986), 49–67, provides an important corrective to some of the more extreme claims advanced in the literature.

23 See, generally, *History of Animals* 538a22–b23, 608a21–b18 (authenticity disputed); *Parts of Animals* 661b27–662a6; *Generation of Animals* 732a1–11; *Politics* 1254b13–15, 1259b2–4; on the female as a "natural deformity," "monstrosity," or "infertile male," see *Generation of Animals* 723a26–30, 728a17–21, 737a27–30, 765b8–767b13, 775a4–22, 784a4–11; and see Galen, *On the Usefulness of the Parts of the Body* 14.6, who claims (14.5) to be following Aristotle.

Once again, I cite only the recent literature, beginning with the fundamental study by Robert Joly, "La biologie d'Aristote," *Revue philosophique de la France et de l'Étranger*, 158 (1968), 219–53, esp. 224–25, 228–29, 241–44; Anthony Preus, "Science and Philosophy in Aristotle's *Generation of Animals*," *Journal of the History of Biology*, 3.1 (1970), 1–52, and *Science and Philosophy in Aristotle's Biological Works* (Hildesheim, 1975), 48–107; Christine Garside, "Can a Woman Be Good in the Same Way as a Man?," *Dialogue: Canadian Philosophical Review*, 10 (1971), 534–44, esp. 534–37; Geddes, 37–39; Stephen R. L. Clark, *Aristotle's Man: Speculations upon Aristotelian Anthropology* (Oxford, 1975), 206–11 (a heavily apologetic treatment, partially retracted in "Aristotle's Woman," *History of Political Thought*, 3.2 [1982], 177–91); Horowitz (a crude assault, deftly countered by Johannes Morsink, "Was Aristotle's Biology Sexist?," *Journal of the History of Biology*, 12 [1979], 83–112, who nonetheless fails to save Aristotle from Horowitz's basic charge); W. W. Fortenbaugh, "Aristotle on Slaves and Women," in *Articles on Aristotle, 2: Ethics and Politics*, ed. Jonathan Barnes, Malcolm Schofield, and Richard Sorabji (London, 1977), 135–39; Simon Byl, *Recherches sur les grands traités biologiques d'Aristote: Sources écrites et préjugés*, Académie Royale de Belgique, Mémoires de la Classe des Lettres, 2d ser., 64.3 (Brussells, 1980); Manuli (1980), 405–08, and (1983), 162–70; Rousselle (1980), 1101–04; Peter Tumulty, "Aristotle, Feminism and Natural Law Theory," *New Scholasticism*, 55 (1981), 450–64; Saïd; Campese; Lloyd, 94–107; Giulia Sissa, "Il corpo della donna: lineamenti di una ginecologia filosofica," in Campese, Manuli, and Sissa, 81–145; Smith, 474–77; Allen; F. Sparshott, "Aristotle on Women," *Philosophical Inquiry*, 7 (1985), 177–200; Gareth B. Matthews, "Gender and Essence in Aristotle," in *Women and Philosophy*, ed. Janna L. Thompson = *Australasian Journal of Philosophy*, Supplt. to vol. 64 (June 1986), 16–25; Cantarella, 59–61.

24 I borrow this formulation from Kirsten Hastrup, "The Semantics of Biology: Virginity," in Ardener, 49–65, esp. 49.

25 See, now, Alice Jardine and Paul Smith, eds., *Men in Feminism* (New York, 1987).

26 A more nuanced understanding of Diotima's contribution to the terms of the debate in the *Symposium* is provided, along roughly similar lines, by Vlastos (1981), 3–42, who, by

contrast, does not doubt that Plato was homosexual by temperament (p. 25), but observes that Diotima's insistence on the importance of procreation as the aim of desire has the effect of structuring the erotic dynamic of Platonic love according to "a heterosexual paradigm"; he concludes, "What started as a pederastic idyl ends up in transcendental marriage" (pp. 40–42). Cf. Saxonhouse (1984), 11–22, for an analogous interpretation.

27 See Wilamowitz, I, 42–49; Kelsen; Brès, 229–32; Wender, 216–18; Vlastos (1981), 25–26; Burnyeat, 16, n. 23.

28 The evidence, such as it is, is less than compelling: see, e.g., H. Nunberg, "Homosexuality, Magic and Aggression," *International Journal of Psycho-Analysis*, 19 (1938), 1–16; D. W. Cory, *The Homosexual in America* (New York, 1951), 201; James A. Knight, "False Pregnancy in a Male," *Psychosomatic Medicine*, 22 (1960), 260–66; John Money and Geoffrey Hosta, "Negro Folklore of Male Pregnancy," *Journal of Sex Research*, 4 (1968), 34–50. The anthropological side to this story is discussed below.

29 Plass, 50–51.

30 Bennett Simon, *Mind and Madness in Ancient Greece: The Classical Roots of Modern Psychiatry* (Ithaca, NY, 1978), 308, n. 20, and 171–79. The fundamental psychoanalytic study is by Kelsen; see, also, Noel Bradley, "Primal Scene Experience in Human Evolution and its Phantasy Derivatives in Art, Proto-Science and Philosophy," *Psychoanalytic Study of Society*, 4 (1967), 34–79, esp. 52–58; Paul Plass, "Eros, Play and Death in Plato," *American Imago*, 26 (1969), 37–55; Brès; Charles Hanley, "An Unconscious Irony in Plato's *Republic*," *Psychoanalytic Quarterly*, 46 (1977), 116–47; Bohner-Cante; MacCary, 83–84, 191–95.

31 Wender, 224–27.

32 Wilamowitz, I, 379–80; earlier, Zeller (quoted by Rettig [1876], 262).

33 Bury, xxxix; earlier, K. F. Hermann, *De Socratis magistris* (Marburg, 1837), 11ff.; 17, n. 37 (cited by Rettig [1876], 262, who also inclines to this view).

34 The earliest advocate for Diotima's historicity cited by Rettig (1876), 262, is Creuzer, *Wiener Jahrbücher*, 56 (1831), 185ff.

35 Hug-Schöne, xlvii n.; Taylor, 224; Kranz (1926/b), 321; E. R. Dodds, ed., *Plato: GORGIAS* (Oxford, 1959), 12, with references to earlier work. Cf. Godel, 14, 26–27.

36 Godel, 26–27, cites the case of a lavish offering to Pythian Apollo made by Aristocrates, son of Scellias, which is casually mentioned at *Gorgias* 472ab and seemingly confirmed by *IG* I², 772—but, in fact, the inscription refers to the homonymous grandfather of Plato's Aristocrates, and Godel (or Plato) has simply confounded the two: see J. K. Davies, *Athenian Propertied Families 600–300 B.C.* (Oxford, 1971), 56–57, #1904.

37 W. Dittenberger, "Zu Plutarch," *Hermes*, 38 (1903), 313–14; Hug-Schöne, xlvii n.

38 Hug-Schöne, xlvii n.; cf. Kranz (1926/a), 437–38.

39 But, for an interpretation that defends the relevance of such details, see Nussbaum (1979), 150–52, and (1986), 177, 195; also, Saxonhouse (1984), 20–22.

40 Hug-Schöne, xlvii n.; Taylor, 224; Krüger, 142–43.

41 See Wilamowitz, I, 380n; Robin (1929), xxiii n. Further parallels are adduced by Bury, 94–95, *ad* Plato, *Symposium* 201d4.

42 See Walter Burkert, "*Goês*. Zum griechischen 'Schamanismus,' " *Rheinisches Museum für Philologie*, 105 (1962), 36–55; Marcel Detienne, *Les Maîtres de la vérité* (Paris, 1967), 129–31; Philippe Borgeaud, *Recherches sur le dieu Pan*, Bibliotheca Helvetica Romana, 17 (Rome, 1979), 160; Vernant (1982), 70, 76–79.

43 Diels, *Sitzungsber. d. Berl. Akad.* (1891), 387 ff.; Kern, "Epimenides," *Paulys Realencyclopädie der classischen Altertumswissenschaft*, ed. Georg Wissowa, vol. 6, pt. 1 (Stuttgart, 1907), cols. 173–78. I owe these references to Kranz (1926/a), 437–38.

44 Gustave Fougères, *Mantinée et l'Arcadie orientale*, Bibliothèque des Écoles françaises d'Athènes et de Rome, 78 (Paris, 1898), 325–30; Godel, 14–21.

45 This argument has been made to me in conversation by Nicholas D. Smith.

46 See Kranz (1926/a), 438–39.

47 The analogy between Diotima and Er is discussed by Robin (1929), xxiv–xxv.

48 Literary references are collected in Otto Jahn, ed., *Platonis Symposium*, 2d ed. rev. by H. Usener (Bonn, 1875), 16–18; for references to pictorial representations of Diotima, see Hug-Schöne, xlviii n. For the relief, see Gustave Fougères, "Stèle de Mantinée," *Bulletin de correspondance hellénique* (Ecole française d'Athènes), 12 (1888), pl. iv and pp. 376–80; Hans Möbius, "Diotima," *Jahrbuch der deutschen archäologischen Instituts*, 49 (1934), 45–60, esp. 58; Karl Schefold, *Die Bildnisse der antiken Dichter, Redner und Denker* (Basel, 1943), 66; Brunilde Sismondo Ridgway, *Fifth Century Styles in Greek Sculpture* (Princeton, 1981), 141–42.

49 These factors are discussed by Just, 161; Schaps; Sommerstein, esp. 418, n. 56, on Diotima (who would not, however, have been affected: see note 63, below); Jan Bremmer, "Plutarch and the Naming of Greek Women," *American Journal of Philology*, 102 (1981), 425–26. Sufficient numbers of women's names do survive to provide at least some material for the social historian: see Mark Golden, "Names and Naming at Athens: Three Studies," *Echos du Monde Classique/Classical Views*, 30, n.s. 5 (1986), 245–69, esp. 246–52. The claim by Keuls, 88–90, that some Greek women may not have been given names at all should be resisted.

50 Dover (1980), 137; citations in Kranz (1926/a), 437.

51 Rettig (1876), 263; Bury, xxxix; Dover (1980), 137, followed by Nussbaum (1986), 177 and 467, n. 28; *contra*, Taylor, 224. The suggestion by Theodor Gomperz, *Greek Thinkers*, trans. G. Berry (London, 1913), II, 396, that "the chief object of this etherealized affection" promoted in the *Symposium* was in reality Dion of Syracuse (cf. Paul Shorey, *What Plato Said* [Chicago, 1933], 45) supplies, as Bury (xxxix n.) observed, another possible explanation for the choice of Diotima's name. Lowenstam, 93, takes "Diotima" to be a substitute for and duplicate of *theophilês*, the attribute of the human being who has completed the erotic ascent, at *Symposium* 212a6 (see p. 103, n. 33, for references to the scholarly literature on the resonances of that term), adding, ". . . if one is successful in ascending the philosophical hierarchy one becomes Diotima (i.e., one could give her speech)."

52 See Judy A. Turner, *HIEREIAI: Acquisition of Female Priesthoods in Ancient Greece*, Ph.D. diss., University of California, Santa Barbara (1983).

53 Blaise Nagy, "The Naming of Athenian Girls: A Case in Point," *Classical Journal*, 74 (1978/79), 360–64.

54 I owe this line of argument, which seems entirely to have escaped scholarly discussions of Diotima's name, to the kind instruction of Sarah B. Pomeroy.

55 See Guthrie, 378, n. 1; Burnyeat, 7, 14, n. 3. Phaenarete's historical authenticity is defended by A. Raubitschek, *RE* 19.2, cols. 1562–63, and by Tomin. Some sensible remarks on this topic are provided by Tarrant, 118–20.

56 I wish to thank Nicholas D. Smith for helping me sort out the various possibilities.

57 Taylor, 224–25.

58 See Kranz (1926/a), 438. Should a fuller argument to this effect be required, Dover (1980), 10, dutifully supplies one.

59 So Hug-Schöne, xlvii n.; Kranz (1926/a), 438; Erbse, 206.

60 Charlotte L. Stough, "Forms and Explanation in the Phaedo," *Phronesis*, 21 (1976), 1–30, esp. 29–30. See, also, Friedrich Solmsen, "Parmenides and the Description of Perfect Beauty in Plato's *Symposium*," *American Journal of Philology*, 92 (1971), 62–70; Rosamond Kent Sprague, "*Symposium* 211a and Parmenides Frag. 8," *Classical Philology*, 66 (1971), 261.

61 See Harry Berger, Jr., "Plato's Flying Philosopher," *Philosophical Forum*, 13 (1982), 385–407.

62 Wilamowitz, I, 380n.

63 It might perhaps be supposed that such avoidance of detailed characterization on Plato's part merely expresses the same respect and courtesy that also operates in the law-courts and on the comic stage and that militates against the mention of a respectable woman's name: see Schaps, 330; Sommerstein. But that would be to misconstrue the Greek convention. Only those women are not mentioned who are decently secluded at home and whose names are therefore not presumed to be known by males outside the family. That is not the case with Diotima: she is a public figure, after all—someone to whom the Athenians turn at a time of public crisis, someone at least as well known as the Athenian priestesses whose names can indeed be mentioned without impropriety (Sommerstein, 395–96). Several other considerations reinforce this line of interpretation. First of all, Diotima is a foreigner, unconnected to an Athenian male by blood-tie or by marriage, so far as we know, and hence not someone whose name must be suppressed out of deference to the feelings of one's fellow-citizens. Secondly, she is for Plato's dramatic purposes a famous woman: far from attempting to conceal her name, Plato is prodigal in his use of it (201d2, e8; 202d12; 204a8, d5; 206b5; 207c5; 208b8; 212b1), though he also refers to her more obliquely by her place of origin (*hê Mantinikê gynê* or *xenê*: 201d2, 204c7, 211d1–2; cf. W. Dittenberger, "Ethnika und Verwandtes," *Hermes*, 42 [1907], 1–34, esp. 14). Finally, Sommerstein presses two further points: (1) by the time Socrates mentions Diotima she is probably dead; (2) it is likely that no other man was present on the occasions when Socrates represents himself as addressing her by name (418, n. 56). Given the freedom with which Plato treats Diotima, then, it would hardly have been disrespectful of him to tell us a little more about her.

64 See Erbse, 210–14, who argues that Xenophon's portrayal of Socrates's positive attitude to women deserves more credence than it has received; cf. Giallongo, 81–85. Kahn has now provided a thorough treatment of Socratic *erôs* in Socratic literature. Also, Krell (1975), 406.

65 See, e.g., Athenaeus, 5.220ef, 12.535c, 13.588d.

66 Most of the information in this paragraph comes from Ehlers. On this general topic, compare Friedrich Schlegel, "Über die Diotima," *Studien des klassischen Altertums*, ed. E. Behler, Kritische Friedrich-Schlegel-Ausgabe, I.1 (Paderborn, 1979), 70–115 (essay first publ. 1795).

67 Athenaeus, 5.220d; Diogenes Laertius, 6.16. Fragments are collected in Dittmar, 299–300.

68 Fr. 1 (Dittmar). The story told by Plutarch, *Pericles* 24.5–6, derives from Antisthenes's dialogue, as Athenaeus, 13.589e, testifies (unless we emend the text to read *Aeschines*, who seems after all to be Plutarch's source [cf. *Pericles* 24.4]: see note 72, below).

69 Ehlers, 30–34, esp. 31n., basing herself on Athenaeus, 5.220e, imagines a scene in which Socrates resists the blandishments of Aspasia's flute-girls; she argues, with some plausibility, that the dialogue may have depicted Aspasia as the embodiment of morally corrupting *hêdonê* (cf. Heracleides Ponticus, *apud* Athenaeus, 12.533cd); Wender, 222–23, by contrast, notes that Diogenes Laertius ascribes to Antisthenes, on the authority of Diocles, the saying that *aretê* is the same for a man as for a woman (6.12)—a passage neglected by Ehlers (but discussed by Kahn, who nonetheless follows Ehlers).

70 Athenaeus, 5.220b; Diogenes Laertius, 2.61; fragments in Dittmar, 275–83. The authenticity of Aeschines's dialogues was challenged in antiquity by Menedemus of Eretria, Idomeneus, and others: Diogenes Laertius, 2.60–63; Athenaeus, 13.611de.

71 See Ehlers, esp. 63–100.

72 Fr. 25 (Dittmar). The story in Athenaeus, 13.589e (and cf. pseudo-Lucian, *Erôtes* 30), goes back to Aeschines, as Plutarch, *Pericles* 32.3, testifies.

73 Fr. 31 (Dittmar). Reported by Cicero, *De inventione* 1.31.51–53, who is subsequently quoted by Quintilian, *Institutes* 5.11.27–29; see, also, Marius Victorinus, in *Rhetorici latini minores*, p. 240.31ff. (Halm).

74 Reported by Plutarch, *Pericles* 24.4. For Aspasia's political or rhetorical ability, and her influence on her lovers, see Schol. *ad* Plato, *Menexenus* 235e = Callias, *Pedêtai*, fr. 15 (Kock); Schol. *ad* Aristophanes, *Acharnians* 527; Didymus, *Symposium*, cited by Clement of Alexandria, *Stromateis* 4.19.122; Harpocration, *s.v.* Aspasia; Philostratus, *Letter* 73; pseudo-Lucian, *Erôtes* 30. An expanded version of the story can be found in an anonymous Greek treatise preserved only in Syriac translation (ed. Paul de Lagarde, *Analecta Syriaca* [London, 1858], 177–95; trans. J. Gildemeister and F. Bücheler, "Pseudo–Plutarchos *peri askêseôs*," *Rheinisches Museum für Philologie*, 27 [1872], 520–38): the relevant portion is translated and discussed by Ehlers, 74–77.

75 Athenaeus, 13.597a–599c, esp. 599ab = fr. 7.89–94 (Powell).

76 Athenaeus, 5.219b–e; the verses are assigned to Socrates by Bergk, *PLG*[4] 2.288. On Herodicus, see Ingemar Düring, *Herodicus the Cratetean: A Study in Antiplatonic Tradition* (Stockholm, 1941).

77 Plutarch, *Pericles* 24.3; Lucian, *De saltatione* 25; Maximus of Tyre, 24.4, 38.4b–d; Athenaeus, 5.219bc.

78 Maximus of Tyre, 24.4, 38.4b; Synesius, 1.18.59A (Petau).

79 Diodorus the Periegete, fr. 372.40 Jacoby (*FGrHist* IIIb, p. 239.6) = Schol. *ad* Plato, *Menexenus* 235e; Didymus, *Symposium*, cited by Clement of Alexandria, *Stromateis* 4.19.122; Aelius Aristides, *Oration* 46.127.15 (II, 171 Dindorf, also Schol. *ad* 46.131.2 = II, 176 Dindorf); Athenaeus, 13.569f, 589d; Themistius, *Oration* 26 (p. 396.25 Dindorf).

80 See Lucian, *Eunuch* 7; *Imagines* 17–18; Aristides, *Oration* 46.127.15 (II, 127 Dindorf with Schol. *ad loc.* = III, 468 Dindorf); Himerius, *Declamation* 1.18; Synesius, 1.18.59A; Theodoretus of Cyrrhus, *Graecarum affectionum curatio* 1.17 (p. 9.10–15 Raeder); Libanius, *Tim. or.*, decl. 12.193 (vol. 5, p. 556 Förster).

81 The tradition of an erotic connection between Socrates and Aspasia begins much later, with Hermesianax, and is satisfactorily explained, to my mind, by the scholiasts' creative extrapolation from Plato's *Symposium*, *Menexenus*, and from Aeschines's *Aspasia*. In this

I differ from Kahn, with whose excellent account I otherwise find myself in general agreement.

82 See Kranz (1926/a), 438; for similar views, see K. F. Hermann, *Disputatio de Aeschinis Socratici reliquiis* (Göttingen, 1850), 19; Gigon, *Kommentar* on Xenophon, *Memorabilia* 2.6.36; Konrad Gaiser, review of Ehlers, *Archiv für Geschichte der Philosophie*, 51 (1969), 200–209, esp. 208. (I owe these references to Charles Kahn.)

83 Cf. Ehlers, 131–36, following the interpretation of Dittmar, 40–41.

84 Dover (1980), 137, notes that "Socrates' words [about Diotima] 'she taught me *ta erôtika*' (201d5) are a slyly humorous reminder of another kind of *erôtikos logos*, in which a smirking youth tells his friends about the accomplishments of a hetaira ('Rhodopis taught me all I know . . . ')"; on the earlier tradition of *erôtikoi logoi*, cf. Hug-Schöne, x–xv; François Lasserre, "*Erôtikoi logoi*," *Museum Helveticum*, 1 (1944), 169–78. It should also go without saying that Plato would not wish to suggest that a brothel is the proper place to learn the secrets of Platonic love.

85 Cf. Rosen, 224: "It is no accident that Socrates learnt physics from a man [i.e., Anaxagoras], but politics and the erotic mysteries from women. The domain of the political-religious is essentially that of peace, associated with the womanly arts of child-rearing, housekeeping, weaving, and the like." (That politics is a womanly art would have come as a surprise to Pericles.)

86 See Wilamowitz, I, 380; II, 170–71; Morrison, 42–43.

87 See Bruce Rosenstock, "Rereading the *Republic*," *Arethusa*, 16.1–2 (1983), 219–46, esp. 221–22, on the significance of Zalmoxis and the connection with the nightlong festival of the Thracian goddess Bendis which provides the setting for the first book of the *Republic*.

88 See, generally, Friedländer, I, 126–53; Philip Merlan, "Form and Content in Plato's Philosophy," *Journal of the History of Ideas*, 8 (1947), 406–30; Ludwig Edelstein, "Platonic Anonymity," *American Journal of Philology*, 83 (1962), 1–22; Paul Plass, "Platonic Anonymity and Irony in the Platonic Dialogues," *American Journal of Philology*, 85 (1964), 254–78.

89 Friedländer, I, 148; he then goes on to discuss some of the usual interpretations: (1) By means of Diotima Plato distinguishes his own views from Socratic philosophy. (2) It is for the sake of courtesy to his host that Socrates ascribes Agathon's notions to his own former self and allows Diotima to refute them, thus avoiding having to make a personal criticism of Agathon. (3) As a good dialectician Socrates cannot permit himself to make a speech. (4) As an ignorant man Socrates cannot present himself as a guide to the transcendental Ideas. Similar views are voiced by Robin (1929), xxv–xxvii.

90 On Diotima as prophetess, see Robin (1929), xxiii–xxiv.

91 Saxonhouse (1984), 20, contends, however, that it would have been better for Athens to have suffered the plague *before* the outbreak of the Peloponnesian War and she taxes Diotima with a lack of political foresight in postponing it; applying this line of reasoning to the problem of Diotima's gender, she concludes: "The female and the philosopher— the experts in *erotike*—abstract [*sic*] from the political world. Socrates learns of love from a woman because the lovers he describes are unlike the male–focused lovers of the earlier speeches; they are apolitical."

92 But cf. *Timaeus* 70b–72d, where Plato appears to retreat from this sanguine view of mantic enthusiasm. On the mediating function of *erôs*, see Jerry Stannard, "Socratic Eros and Platonic Dialectic," *Phronesis*, 4 (1959), 120–34.

93 Friedländer, III, 15–18; Krüger, 105–19; Brentlinger, 11–12; Penwill, 147–49. Eryxima-chus is treated more sympathetically by Ludwig Edelstein, "The Rôle of Eryximachus in Plato's *Symposium*," *Transactions of the American Philological Association*, 76 (1945), 85–103, and by David Konstan, "Eryximachus' Speech in the *Symposium*," *Apeiron*, 16 (1982), 40–46, who also survey earlier work on the subject.

94 I wish to thank Richard Patterson for helpful guidance on this point. On the traditional connection between philosophical wisdom and the mystery religions in Greece, see Vernant (1982), 57–60; a rather more fanciful account can be found in Godel. Plato frequently adverts to the Eleusinian mysteries in metaphysical contexts, especially in the *Phaedo, Republic*, and *Symposium*: see Friedländer, I, 71–72, and for a list of citations, see Samuel Scolnicov, "Reason and Passion in the Platonic Soul," *Dionysius*, 2 (1978), 35–49, esp. 45, n. 24.

95 What follows is a summary of an interpretation set forth at greater length in Halperin (1985), 167–69.

96 For Plato as a "depth psychologist," see the eloquent and persuasive discussion by Glidden, 46–53; E. R. Dodds, *The Greeks and the Irrational*, Sather Classical Lectures, 25 (Berkeley, 1951), 218.

97 Fr. 897.6–7 (Nauck²) = Athenaeus, 13.561ab; the context is unknown. The fragment as a whole seems to anticipate the idea which, according to Ehlers (who neglects the fragment), originated with Aeschines—namely, that *erôs* conduces to virtue. For the connections between the erotic doctrines of Euripides and the Socratics, see Helen North, *Sophrosyne: Self-Knowledge and Self-Restraint in Greek Literature*, Cornell Studies in Classical Philology, 35 (Ithaca, NY, 1966), 73–74, qualified by Vlastos (1981), 22, n. 63.

98 Cf. Kranz (1926/a), 445–46, and (1926/b), 322, who argues that Diotima represents herself as a hierophant of the mysteries.

99 See, generally, Clinton; H. W. Parke, *Festivals of the Athenians*, Aspects of Greek and Roman Life (Ithaca, NY, 1977), 57–62; Erika Simon, *Festivals of Attica: An Archaeological Commentary*, Wisconsin Studies in Classics (Madison, 1983), 27–29, 34.

100 Lowenstam, 92, claims that the mystic vocabulary employed by Socrates's Diotima, in the presence of three persons (Alcibiades, Phaedrus, and Eryximachus) who were later to be exiled on the charge of profaning the mysteries, implies that everyone but Socrates profanes the mysteries of *erôs* in his life. For another ingenious application of the sacrilege trials to a reading of the *Symposium*, see Nussbaum (1986), 196.

101 Clinton, esp. 68–69, 86, 97–98.

102 There are, of course, other ways of tracing the cultural genealogy of Diotima as the female founder of a male institution—one thinks, for example, of Athena in the *Eumenides*: cf. Zeitlin (1984); Loraux, 119–53; Case, 320–21. It might be argued that Diotima, as a chaste priestess, plays a similar role, uniting in herself the natural (i.e., female) and the divine—but we must be careful to avoid the dangers of schematization: although Diotima, who could not decently be present at Agathon's symposium, is presumably chaste, she is not a *parthenos*, a virgin like Athena, but a *gynê*, a woman (201d2); moreover, Plato does absolutely nothing to foreground her putative chastity, in contrast to his treatment of her prophetic authority. It is also misleading to speak of Diotima as a "priestess," as is customary in the scholarly literature, thereby implying that Diotima holds some sacred office. On the contrary, Plato omits to mention any public function that Diotima regularly performs, nor does he say anywhere that she is a priestess; he merely says she has mantic expertise (*sophia*: 201d), presumably the sort of expertise that Teiresias and other male prophets also had (for references to itinerant female *manteis*, see Lloyd, 69). Perhaps there

is an analogy between Diotima and Lysistrata, whose name and authority may be intended to allude to that of her contemporary Lysimache, priestess of Athena Polias: see D. M. Lewis, "Notes on Attic Inscriptions (II), XXIII: Who Was Lysistrata?" *Annual of the British School at Athens*, 1 (1955), 1–13; Helene P. Foley, "The 'Female Intruder' Reconsidered: Women in Aristophanes' *Lysistrata* and *Ecclesiazusae*," *Classical Philology*, 77 (1982), 1–21, esp. 8; Loraux, 157–96. For an interesting treatment of some comparative material, see Elizabeth A. Clark, "Ascetic Renunciation and Feminine Advancement: A Paradox of Late Ancient Christianity," *Ascetic Piety and Women's Faith: Essays on Late Ancient Christianity*, Studies in Women and Religion, 20 (Lewiston, NY, 1986), 175–208.

103 Vlastos (1981), 56.

104 See John Patrick Lynch, "The Ancient Symposium as an Institution: Social Drinking and Educational Issues in Fifth Century Athens," *Laetaberis* (Journal of the California Classical Association), n.s. 4 (Spring 1986), 1–15, esp. 6–7, who compares the symposium to the modern institution of men's clubs and bars.

105 On sex at the symposium, especially fellatio, and its depiction on vases, see Keuls, 160–69, 180–86, 212–13, 267–73; Dover (1978), 182; Golden (1984), 313–14; Borthwick, 32.

106 To be sure, Phaedrus does deem Alcestis more heroic than Orpheus; he criticizes the latter not for being in love with a woman but for being a sissy; and his comparison of Achilles to Alcestis is not intended to promote *philia* over *erôs* but only to suggest that it is nobler to lay down your life for another when you have less incentive to do so. Nonetheless, the effect of what Phaedrus says is to dismiss both *erôs* for women and the *erôs* of women from the discussion.

107 Erbse, 201–02.

108 That is, her approval of Alcestis does not imply approval of heterosexual object-choice per se—another reminder that Plato does not consider the sameness or difference of the sexes of the sexual partners to be valid criteria for differentiating between kinds of "sexuality."

109 Kranz (1926/b), 321–22; Singer, 79; Saxonhouse (1985), 52–54; Freeman, 172–73.

110 See Jones (1991/b); Foucault (1985), 130–33.

111 I wish to thank Froma I. Zeitlin for making this aspect of Plato's strategy clear to me. Cf. Saxonhouse (1985), 62: Plato "has found in women—those who give birth, those who are different from the males, those who are closer to the private realm—a symbol that becomes useful for his critique of an Athenian society devoted to the political life of ambition, money, and war."

112 Foucault (1985), 187–225, esp. 215ff.

113 See, generally, Dover (1978), 52–53, 84–85, 103–06; further, Golden (1984); Halperin (1986); and Winkler (1989/a). In the paragraphs that follow I have summarized the thesis of Halperin (1986), which should be consulted for fuller documentation.

114 Quoted by Dover (1978), 52; see, also, Foucault (1985), 223–24.

115 Dover (1978), 85.

116 See the sources cited by Halperin (1985), 192, n. 36, and by David Armstrong and Elizabeth A. Ratchford, "Iphigenia's Veil: Aeschylus, *Agamemnon* 228–48," *Bulletin of the Institute of Classical Studies* (University of London), 32 (1985), 1–12, plates 1 and 2.

117 See Patzer, 121–22.

118 Foucault (1985), 232–33, 242–43.

119 Foucault (1985), 239–40.

120 See Thomas S. W. Lewis, "The Brothers of Ganymede," in Boyers and Steiner, 147–65, esp. 161. For *biazein* in the sense of rape, see Aristophanes, *Wealth* 1092.

121 See Friedländer, I, 49, 139–42; further, Kahn's discussion of Aeschines's *Alcibiades*. See, also, Plato, *Lysis* 222a, where the entire conversation grinds to a halt when Socrates proves the logical necessity of erotic reciprocity.

122 Halperin (1986), 76–79.

123 On the figure of the *kinaidos*, see Winkler (1989/a) and Gleason.

124 E.g., Aristotle, *Nicomachean Ethics* 1148b26–35; pseudo-Aristotle, *Problems* 4.26; Caelius Aurelianus, *On Chronic Diseases* 4.9.137.

125 Hesiod, fr. 275 (M–W); cf. Ovid, *Metamorphoses* 3.316–38.

126 On women's pleasure in intercourse, see [Hippocrates], *On the Seed* 4; Aristotle, *Generation of Animals* 727b9–10, 727b35–36, 728a9–11, 728a31–32, 739a29–35; Soranus, *Gynaecology* 1.37–38, 44; Galen, *On the Seed* 2.1; *Usefulness of the Parts* 14.9, 11. Cf., also, Aristotle, *Generation of Animals* 721b15; 723b32; 724a3; Lucretius, 4.1192–1208. Additional sources are cited by Lonie, 120–21.

127 On this point, see Rettig (1882), 424. Cf. Dover (1978), 52; also, the comment by Schnapp (1981), 110: "L'amour hétérosexuel [en Grèce] est sous le signe de la réciprocité alors que l'amour homosexuel est sous celui de la sociabilité."

128 For a possible exception, see Halperin (1986), 66n. Cf. Silvana Fasce, *Eros: la figura e il culto*, Pubblicazioni dell' Istituto di filologia classica e medievale, 49 (Genoa, 1977), 40–42, who ascribes *anterôs* to the *erômenos*, the junior partner in a paederastic relationship, whereas the term, when predicated of male subjects, normally signifies rivalry in *erôs*: see Dover (1978), 52, to whose list of citations should be added Euripides, *Rhesus* 184; Plutarch, *Moralia* 760b; Athenaeus, 540e.

129 Anterastilis is the Greek name of a prostitute in Plautus's *Poenulus*.

130 I quote the translation provided by Dover (1978), 168.

131 Aristotle, *Generation of Animals* 724a35–b6, 727b6–33, 729a9–11, a24–b21, 730a24–b33, 732a2–10, 768b15–30. Cf. Sigmund Freud, "The Economic Problem of Masochism," in Strachey, XIX, 159–70, esp. 162: masochistic fantasies "place the subject in a characteristically female situation; they signify, that is, being castrated, or copulated with, or giving birth to a baby" (and cf. Irigaray [1985/b], 34–67). Also, J. R. Willson, *Obstetrics and Gynecology* (St. Louis, 1971), 43: "The traits that compose the core of the female personality are feminine narcissism, masochism, and passivity"; James, 893: "Femininity tends to be passive and receptive, masculinity to be active, restless, anxious for repeated demonstrations of potency. . . . "; Thomas Jeffcoate, *Principles of Gynecology* (London, 1967), 726: "An important feature of the sex drive in the man is the urge to dominate the women [*sic*] and subjugate her to his will; in the women acquiescence to the masterful takes a high place" (quoted by Scully and Bart, 1048). From here it is a small step to Thomas Nagel, *Mortal Questions* (Cambridge, 1979), 50–51, who considers sadism and masochism to be perversions but upholds a distinction between male and female sexuality in terms of aggressiveness and passivity; cf. the defense of "normal sado-masochism" by Scruton, 173–79, 298–304. Similar views were routinely expressed in the marriage manuals of the 1920's and 1930's: see Jackson, 62–63.

132 Golden (1984), 313–15. See, also, Dover (1978), 102–03; Sutton, 186–89, 224–25. Possible deviations from the usual pattern are discussed by Golden (1984), 321–22, and by Keuls, 277–85, esp. 277. For further discussion, see "One Hundred Years of Homosexuality," in this volume, note 31.

133 James Redfield, "Notes on the Greek Wedding," *Arethusa*, 15 (1982), 181–201, esp. 192–98; cf. Calame (1984), xvii–xxii; Vernant (1981).

134 See Foucault (1985), 245; (1986), 148–49, 151–52, 161–64, 179–80, 181–82, 206–10, 219–26.

135 Bizarrely interpreted by L. P. Wilkinson, "Classical Approaches. IV: Homosexuality," *Encounter*, 51.3 (September 1978), 21–31, esp. 30, who concludes that the boy doesn't have an orgasm because he is below the age of puberty; Keuls, 275, seems to be under the same impression.

136 On this ideal of unity in marriage, see Lisette Goessler, *Plutarchs Gedanken über die Ehe* (Zurich, 1962); Foucault (1986), 162, who also cites Antipater, *Peri gamou, apud* Stobaeus, *Florilegium* 25.

137 The outstanding counter-example to the pattern I have been describing is provided by Petronius, 132—if, as recent editors argue, the passage in question has indeed been displaced from a paederastic context and inserted into a scene of heterosexual love-making where it did not originate: "The mere loveliness of his body called to me and drew us into love. There was the sound of a rain of kisses as our lips met, our hands were clasped and discovered all the ways of love, then our bodies were held and bound by our embrace [*iam alligata mutuo ambitu corpora*] until even our souls were made as one soul [*animarum quoque mixturam*]" (trans. Heseltine–Warmington). Richardson does not comment on this passage, which would seem to pose an obstacle to his interpretation.

138 Quoted from *The Second Sex*, trans. H. M. Parshley (New York, 1974), 465, by Stigers, 54. See, now, the elaboration of this outlook by Irigaray (1985/b), 23–33 and 205–18.

139 Unfortunately, Plato's exact meaning is not clear, because the key word, *hetairistriai*, occurs nowhere else in the classical period and its meaning is known only from the later glosses of ancient lexicographers: see Dover (1978), 172–73.

140 See Dover (1978), 163n.

141 Halperin (1985), 164–66.

142 Jones (1991/b).

143 Halperin (1985), 177–78.

144 Vlastos (1981), 41; cf. 21: "Beauty stirs us so deeply, Plato is saying, because we have the power to create and only the beauty we love can release that power."

145 See, generally, *Phaedrus* 275d–278b, where *ekgona, patêr*, and *adelphos* recur (commentary by Jacques Derrida, "La pharmacie de Platon," *La dissémination* [Paris, 1972], 69–197, esp. 84–95), although Socrates also employs agricultural imagery in speaking of literary production: cf. Page duBois, "The Homoerotics of the *Phaedrus*," *Pacific Coast Philology*, 17.1–2 (1982), 9–15, esp. 14, and duBois (1988), 177–78.

146 Burnyeat, 13, calls our attention to the "degenerate" version of this passage at *Republic* 496a, where intercourse between unworthy persons and philosophy produces (*gennan*: a2, a6) bastards and sophisms. For other instances of procreative imagery in Plato, see *Phaedrus* 275d–278b; *Theaetetus* 148e–151d, with Burnyeat's discussion.

147 For an excellent discussion of possible tensions between the accounts of erotic procreation in the *Symposium* and of intellectual midwifery in the *Theaetetus*, see Burnyeat; on the meaning of the image of midwifery itself, see Ruth Padel, "Women: Model for Possession by Greek Daemons," in *Images of Women in Antiquity*, ed. Averil Cameron and Amélie Kuhrt (Detroit, 1983), 3–19, esp. 11.

148 For a conspectus of literary sources, see Maria Grazia Bonanno, "Osservazioni sul tema della 'giusta' reciprocità amorosa da Saffo ai comici," *Quaderni urbinati di cultura classica*, 16 (1973), 110–20, and Anne [Carson] Giacomelli, "The Justice of Aphrodite in Sappho Fr. 1," *Transactions of the American Philological Association*, 110 (1980), 135–42, who discern

the same erotic dynamic in Sappho and in the male lyricists alike; for a study of Sappho's marked deviation from the dominant male pattern, see Stigers, 46–49. For some corresponding pictorial sources, see Christiane Sourvinou-Inwood, "A Series of Erotic Pursuits: Images and Meanings," *Journal of Hellenic Studies*, 107 (1987), 131–53.

149 I wish to make it clear that I do not consider there to be anything intrinsically masculine about an erotics of pursuit and capture or anything intrinsically feminine about an erotics of procreativity. The masculine and feminine paradigms of erotic feeling discussed here refer to features of the classical Greek sex/gender system, not to ideal types; I wish therefore to dissociate my own views explicitly from the frequent and typically obscurantist claims about the connection between femininity and generation—as exemplified by the following statement of Jung's: "Die Psychologie des Schöpferischen ist eigentlich weibliche Psychologie, denn das schöpferische Werk wächst aus unbewussten Tiefen empor, recht eigentlich aus dem Reiche der Mütter" (quoted by Krell [1975], 400). Compare Rochelle Paul Wortis, "The Acceptance of the Concept of Maternal Role by Behavioral Scientists: Its Effects on Women," *American Journal of Orthopsychiatry*, 41 (October 1971), 733–46; also, Callaway.

150 See Tarrant, 120. For this and for the passages that follow I am indebted to Burnyeat, 14, n. 4.

151 Fr. 199 (Kock).

152 See LSJ, s.v. *tiktô*, IV.

153 So Tarrant, 122.

154 I wish to thank Maria-Viktoria Abricka for calling my attention to this aspect of Plato's strategy.

155 Thus, Diskin Clay, "Platonic Studies and the Study of Plato," *Arion*, n.s. 2 (1975), 116–32, esp. 124–25, takes *kyein* in the *Symposium* to mean "be fecund" or "ripe"; cf. Robin (1964), 13–14.

156 *Eumenides* 658–666: the father alone qualifies as *tokeus*. See Lesky for a survey of the ancient embryological controversies; also, Joseph Needham, *A History of Embryology*, 2d ed., rev. A. Hughes (Cambridge, 1959); Geddes, 38–39; and Rankin, 141n. For a fascinating attempt to put the claims of the Aeschylean Apollo into anthropological perspective, see Delaney; also, Read, 14; O'Flaherty, 17–61, esp. 29–30.

157 Rankin, 141–42; *pace* Morrison, 54. Cf. Krell (1975).

158 Lloyd, 86–94; Detienne (1976), 80–81.

159 These reports (by Censorinus, *De die natali*, 5.4; Aëtius, 5.5.1–3) conflict in places, however, and their accuracy can be challenged; I follow Lonie, 119–20. Manuli (1980), 405, seems to accept these reports at face value; Lloyd, 87–88, provides a detailed and careful scrutiny. See, also, Joly, 78–80; Preus.

160 The Hippocratic writers seem to have agreed that women emit seed: see, esp., *On the Seed/Nature of the Child* 4–9, 12; *Regimen* 1.27–28; *Diseases of Women* 1.8, 17: discussed by Manuli (1980), 405; Rousselle (1980), 1093; Lloyd, 89–94; Lonie, 119–20. For the connection between orgasm and conception in women, see *On the Seed* 4 (implied rather than stated, *pace* Manuli [1980], 406–07: see Rousselle [1980], 1093); *History of Animals* 636b10–24, 636b36–39 (ascribing this view to women), 637b32–33: see Rousselle (1980), 1100–01, and (1988), 27–29. To be sure, the mere existence of female seed may not prove fatal to an androcentric, "monogenetic" reproductive ideology: it is necessary to establish, as Delaney, 46, n. 5, points out, that female seed is not conceived as inferior to or less generative than male seed—as Galen, for example, believed (*Usefulness of the Parts* 14.10–11); see, further, O'Flaherty, 17–61. Cf. Giallongo, 26–27, who claims that even those

writers, such as the Hippocratics, who concede the existence of female seed, agree with Aristotle and the Aeschylean Apollo in assigning the principal procreative role to the male.

161 See, generally, *Generation of Animals* 1.19–20.726a30–729a33, esp. 727b6–11, 728a31–33; also, 739a20–b19 (refuting the arguments of *History of Animals* 10, as Rousselle [1980], 1101–04, notes).

162 See Manuli (1980), 406–08; Preus; Michael Boylan, "The Galenic and Hippocratic Challenges to Aristotle's Conception Theory," *Journal of the History of Biology*, 17 (1984), 83–112; and, for the later tradition, Brown, 55–61. Soranus, *Gynaecology* 1.37, maintains the link between pleasure and conception in women, alleging even that a woman who conceives when raped must *eo ipso* have felt an unconscious, preëxistent desire; Galen, however, held that pleasure is not a necessary condition of conception (*De locis affectis* 6.5).

163 Horowitz, 183–89. Cf. Allen; Rousselle (1988), 29–32, who emphasizes the continuing influence of Aristotle in late antiquity. According to Thomas Laqueur, "Orgasm, Generation, and the Politics of Reproductive Biology," *Representations*, 14 (Spring 1986), 1–41, belief in a causal connection between orgasm and conception in women was not abandoned until the late eighteenth century.

164 See Harrison, 22–23, who notes that at Sparta the rule was the exact opposite, hence in line with the views of the Aeschylean Apollo. Cantarella, 45–46, offers some alternate interpretations of the meaning of the Athenian prohibition against the marriage of uterine siblings.

165 Vlastos (1981), 424, dismissing scholarly objections to translating *kyein* as "be pregnant," does not seem to have noticed that in certain passages of Plato's dialogue the word cannot mean "be pregnant" in any simple or straightforward sense (e.g., at 206c human beings are said to be pregnant *before* intercourse which is in turn called a *tokos*). But, despite this crucial incoherence, Plato's vocabulary—as Burnyeat, 14, n. 5, justly says—"allows no backing away from the implications of the metaphor [of pregnancy and conception]. . . ." For a fuller discussion of "pregnancy" in the *Symposium*, see Burnyeat, 8, who notes that in Plato "pregnancy is the cause, not the consequence, of love; and the birth is love's expressive manifestation."

166 See Dover (1980), 147, who notes that Diotima's description of the positive effect of beauty on the soul—the soul "melts," "relaxes"—images a female rather than a male sexual response.

167 See Kranz (1926/a), 443.

168 This clause was condemned as a gloss on *tiktein* by Ast, Rückert, Rettig, and Hug, whose editorial decisions doubtless reflect a certain uneasiness about the way *tokos* is used here; the clause was retained as genuine by Stallbaum, Cousin, and Zeller (Robin [1964], 14n.).

169 Cf. Irigaray (1985/a), 73ff., for a discussion of Freud's construction of *female* procreative desire in just these phallic terms.

170 See Kranz (1926/b), 322–23. Particularly expressive of the tone Diotima takes in talking to Socrates are the following passages: 202b10, 204b1, 207c2–4, 208c1, 209e5–210a4. One might compare the way that Jocasta's maternal identity is represented by Sophocles in the *Oedipus Rex* through her magisterial opening speech: "Why have you two raised this senseless quarrel of words? Aren't you ashamed to be pursuing private grudges when the city is as sick as it is? Why don't you come inside, Oedipus, and you, Creon, go home. . . ." For the modern analogue, cf. Ernestine Friedl, *Vasilika: A Village in Modern Greece*, Case Studies in Cultural Anthropology (New York, 1962), 78–81. By contrast, Rosen, 203, judges Diotima to be "a masculine woman, who dominates Socrates, prefers children

of the psyche to those of the body, and herself aspires to synoptic vision"; John P. Anton, "The Secret of Plato's *Symposium*," *Southern Journal of Philosophy*, 12 (1974), 277–93, esp. 282, however, takes Diotima's rebukes to Socrates to express her prophetic anticipation of what Anton considers his erotic and educational failure with Alcibiades.

171 See Jones (1991/b).

172 See Colin Murray Turbayne, "Plato's 'Fantastic' Appendix: The Procreation Model of the *Timaeus*," *Paideia*, 5 (1976), 125–40.

173 Cf. *Symposium* 203c3–4: *tiktein epithymei hêmôn hê physis*; is there a pun on *physis* here, which also means (female) genitalia? (See Winkler [1989/d], 217–20.)

174 Manuli (1983), 189.

175 Rousselle (1980), 1092, 1098; Manuli (1980), 393–94, describes the topic addressed by Hippocratic gynaecology as women's "genitality" rather than "sexuality" and discusses the physicians' isolation of and concentration on the reproductive function in women (pp. 393–403); so, also, Manuli (1983), 152.

176 Rousselle (1980), 1095, ascribes a belief in the therapeutic value of sexual intercourse and pregnancy to the female patients as well as to the Hippocratic doctors; see, also, Manuli (1980), 400–01, and (1983), 157–58; Lloyd, 84–85, for contrasting treatments of this issue. On the ancient practice of prescribing for women drugs made from animal parts associated with male potency, see Lloyd, 83; note that the plant "cyclamen," which often figures in Hippocratic prescriptions for a variety of gynaecological complaints, is said by Theophrastus (*History of Plants* 9.9.3) to be useful in *philtra*, presumably love-potions: Lloyd, 129, 133.

177 Cf. G. E. R. Lloyd, *Polarity and Analogy: Two Types of Argumentation in Early Greek Thought* (Cambridge, 1966), 15–85; Vernant (1974), 149–50; duBois (1988), 39–85.

178 D. M. Balme, trans., *Aristotle's DE PARTIBUS ANIMALIUM I and DE GENERATIONE ANIMALIUM I (with passages from II.1–3)*, Clarendon Aristotle Series (Oxford, 1972), 23. Cf. Aeschylus, fr. 44 (Radt); Plato, *Menexenus* 237e–238a, with the cautionary remarks of Loraux, 89n.

179 See Menander, *Perikeiromenê* 435–36/1013–14, *Dyscolus* 842–43, *Misoumenos* 444–45, *Samia* 726–27, Fragmentum dubium (p. 300 Sandbach), fr. 720 (Kock).

180 Detienne (1977), 78–81; Vernant (1981); Burkert (1985), 242–46. See, generally, Allaire Chandor Brumfield, *The Attic Festivals of Demeter and their relation to the Agricultural Year*, Monographs in Classical Studies (Salem, NH: The Ayer Company, 1981), 236–39, on the connection between the festivals of Demeter, agriculture, and women. For a reconstruction of the meaning of the Thesmophoria to the Greek women who were its sole participants, interpreting it (in opposition to Detienne) not as a triumph over but as a celebration of women's fertility, see Winkler (1989/c). On the female body as arable land or furrow, see Theognis, 582; Aeschylus, *Seven against Thebes* 754; Pindar, *Pythian* 4.254–57; Sophocles, *Antigone* 569, *Trachiniae* 31–33, *Oedipus Rex* 1211, 1257, 1485, 1497–8; Euripides, *Medea* 1281, *Ion* 1095, *Orestes* 553, *Phoenissae* 18, 22; Plato, *Cratylus* 406b, *Laws* 839a; Plutarch, *Moralia* 144b; pseudo-Aristotle, *Economics* 3.2; Soranus, *Gynaecology* 1.35ff.; Artemidorus, *Oneirocritica* 1.51, 2.24: discussion by Vernant (1974), 140–41; duBois (1988), 67–81. On marriage as taming, see Calame (1977), I, 411–20; Seaford; now, Carson.

181 See the opinion of Empedocles quoted by Aristotle, *Generation of Animals* 723a25, 764a3–b3; [Hippocrates], *Regimen* 1.27, 34; Galen, *On the Seed* 2.5; *Usefulness of the Parts* 7.22, 14.6–7, who claims (14.5) to be following Hippocrates and Aristotle; Aristotle, *Generation of Animals* 726b30–727a1, 728a17–21, 765b2–766b26, 775a14–21; *Parts of Animals* 648a9–15; cf. 650b19–651a19; *Problems* 4.25.879a33–34; cf. 4.28.88a12–20 (cited by Carson); Artemidorus, *Oneirocritica* 3.16; Clement of Alexandria, *Paedagogus* 3.19.2 (discussed by

Gleason). See Lesky, 31–38/1255–62; Joly, 80–81; Saïd, 113–15; James Longrigg, "Galen on Empedocles (Fragment 67)," *Philologus*, 108 (1964), 297–300; May, I, 382n.; Lloyd, 90–91; Jones (1991/a). The homology between women and earth in the ancient medical writers is discussed further by Hanson; the coldness and wetness of women is treated by Carson.

Since, as I have stated above, Greek notions of women were not stable or consistent but variable according to the context of masculine interest, women's bodies can also be thought of as hotter than men's if it is to men's advantage that they be so: see Parmenides, quoted by Aristotle, *Parts of Animals* 648a29–30; the anonymous writers (identified as the Hippocratics by Hanson) to whom Aristotle refers at *Generation of Animals* 4.1.765b; and the author of [Hippocrates], *Diseases of Women* 1.1, who claims that women are moister but warmer. Hanson maintains that the Hippocratics generally considered women warmer, and cites *Epidemics* 1.13 (case 14), 3.17 (cases 7 and 12) as evidence; so, also, Manuli (1983), 159. For other instances of the same outlook, one might mention the various Greek expressions that represent women's bodies as stoves in which phalluses and babies are cooked: see Jeffery Henderson, *The Maculate Muse: Obscene Language in Attic Comedy* (New Haven, 1975), 47–48; duBois (1988), 110–29.

182 E.g., [Hippocrates], *On the Seed* 4: see Foucault (1985), 128–30. A similar view was expressed by Marie Stopes, the modern British sexologist, who claimed that women's bodies required the periodic infusion of male secretions in order to escape being physiologically "starved": see Jackson, 66.

183 Willard R. Cooke, *Essentials of Gynecology* (Philadelphia, 1943), 59–60, quoted by Scully and Bart, 1046.

184 James, 893, quoted by Callaway, 169 (italics mine).

185 Scully and Bart, 1048.

186 Langdon Parsons and Sheldon C. Sommers, *Gynecology* (Philadelphia, 1962), 501–02, quoted by Scully and Bart, 1047 (italics mine). For a critique of this tradition as it surfaces in psychoanalysis, see Irigaray (1985/b), 34–67.

187 Detienne (1977). Cf. J. Hillman, *The Myth of Analysis* (Evanston, 1972), 224–25: ". . . we encounter a long and incredible history of theoretical misadventures and observational errors in male science regarding the physiology of reproduction. These fantastic theories and fantastic observations are not misapprehensions, the usual and necessary mistakes on the road to scientific progress; they are recurrent deprecations of the feminine phrased in the unimpeachable, objective language of the science of the period. The mythic factor recurs disguised in the sophisticated new evidence of the age" (quoted by Zeitlin [1984], 180); cf. Anne Fausto-Sterling, *Myths of Gender: Biological Theories about Women and Men* (New York, 1985). For a discussion of Greek science as the "literate representation of Greek folklore," see Lloyd, 201–17; also, Robert Joly, *Le Niveau de la science hippocratique. Contribution à la psychologie de l'histoire des sciences* (Paris, 1966).

188 E.g., Augustine, *De nuptiis et concupiscentia* 1.4.17, 1.27.24. See Paula Fredriksen, "Augustine and his Analysts: The Possibility of a Psychohistory," *Soundings*, 61.2 (1978), 206–27, esp. 216–17; Brown, 61–67.

189 Aristotle, *Generation of Animals* 727b6–12, 728a31–33, 739a29–31; Galen, *De locis affectis* 6.5. See Manuli (1980), 405–08; Rousselle (1980), 1101–04, 1111–12.

190 Bettelheim, 100–08; J. S. La Fontaine, "Ritualisation of Women's Life-Crises in Bugisu," in *The Interpretation of Ritual: Essays in Honour of A. I. Richards*, ed. La Fontaine (London, 1972), 159–86, esp. 180; J. van Baal, "The Role of Women as Care-Givers," *Reciprocity and the Position of Women: Anthropological Papers* (Assen, 1975), 97–123, esp. 116–18.

191 For a general survey, see P. G. Rivière, "The Couvade: A Problem Reborn," *Man*, n.s.
9 (1974), 423–35; Rancour-Laferriere, 362–64, with plentiful references to the medical
and scholarly literatures, to which should be added Joel Richman, W. O. Goldthorp, and
Christine Simmons, "Fathers in Labour," *New Society* (October 16, 1975), 143–45.

192 Callaway, 170; Kittay (note 196, below), 114–15.

193 See, esp., Herdt (1981). On male initiation rites featuring pseudo-procreative imagery
(but not necessarily sexual contacts between men and boys), see Read; Robert Murphy,
"Social Structure and Sex Antagonism," *Southwestern Journal of Anthropology*, 15.1 (1959),
81–96; Bettelheim, 113–21; M. J. Meggitt, "Male-Female Relationships in the Highlands
of Australian New Guinea," *American Anthropologist*, 66.2 (1964), 204–24; M. Allen, *Male
Cults and Secret Initiations in Melanesia* (Melbourne, 1967); Hogbin; L. R. Hiatt, "Secret
Pseudo-Procreation Rites Among the Australian Aborigines," in *Anthropology in Oceania:
Essays Presented to Ian Hogbin*, ed. Hiatt and Chandra Jayawardena (Scranton, PA, 1971),
77–88; Langness; Marilyn Strathern, *Women in Between: Female Roles in a Male World*
(London, 1972).

194 On male menstruation (not necessarily linked with paederasty), see Read, 15; Bettelheim,
105–08; Hogbin, 87–89, 91, 114–21; Langness, 203; Anna S. Meigs, "Male Pregnancy
and the Reduction of Sexual Opposition in a New Guinea Highlands Society," *Ethnology*,
25 (1976), 393–407, esp. 397–400; Herdt (1981), 185, 190–94, 244–46; La Fontaine, 127–
29; Gregor, 186–94; Chris Knight, "Menstrual Synchrony and the Australian Rainbow
Snake," in *Blood Magic: The Anthropology of Menstruation*, ed. Thomas Buckley and
Alma Gottlieb (Berkeley, 1988), 232–55, with further references to the anthropological
literature.

195 Herdt (1981), 211, 234–35.

196 For a frank avowal to this effect by the Kunapipi, see Paula Weideger, *Menstruation and
Menopause* (New York, 1976), 105. For some of the earlier literature on male "envy," see
Margaret Mead, *Male and Female: A Study of the Sexes in a Changing World* (New York,
1949), 102–04; Bettelheim; Ruth W. Lidz and Theodore Lidz, "Male Menstruation: A
Ritual Alternative to the Oedipal Transition," *International Journal of Psycho-Analysis*, 58
(1977), 17–31; Eva Feder Kittay, "Womb Envy: An Explanatory Concept," in *Mothering:
Essays in Feminist Theory*, ed. Joyce Trebilcot (Totowa, NJ, 1984), 94–128, esp. 108–12;
Rancour-Laferriere, 369–84, esp. 370–71, with references to the psychoanalytic literature.
For a somewhat analogous approach to Greek material, which however avoids the
simplistic literalism of "envy" models, see Zeitlin (1984), 177–81, and "Cultic Models of
the Female: Rites of Dionysus and Demeter," *Arethusa*, 15 (1982), 129–57, esp.147–48,
comparing Platonic philosophy, understood as a drive for hidden realities, to the male
fascination with feminine secrets, with what a woman conceals; cf. Nussbaum (1986),
189–90, for a similar argument. My own interpretation follows, instead, the somewhat
different lead provided by Zeitlin (1985), esp. 65–66, 84–88, picking up from the point
where she leaves off.

197 Keesing, 23, summarizing this aspect of the New Guinea ethnographies, has written,
"Women's physical control over reproductive processes and emotional control over their
sons must be overcome by politics, secrecy, ideology, and dramatized male power." See,
also, Langness.

198 Adam (1985/a), 22–23.

199 See "Two Views of Greek Love," in this volume, note 18.

200 J. J. Bachofen, *Das Mutterrecht*, ed. K. Meuli (Basel, 1948), II, 629–30.

201 E.g., Euripides, *Medea* 573–75; *Hippolytus* 616–24: see Vernant (1974), 132–38; Loraux,
76. Note, also, Zeus's womb (*nêdys*) in Hesiod, *Theogony* 487, 890, 899 (cf. 460).

202 E.g., Aristotle, *Generation of Animals* 741b4–5: see Horowitz, 194–95; Manuli (1980), 406–08; Detienne (1976). Compare O'Flaherty, 28–29, 37–38.

203 See Zeitlin (1984), for the definitive study of this theme in Aeschylus; also, Arthur, 111–12.

204 Cf. O'Brien (1981), 127–33, esp. 132: "Plato is struggling with the biologically based realities of male reproductive consciousness. The products of female reproductive labour—species integration and genetic continuity—are deprived of their unity of understanding and action precisely because this unity is not immediately accessible to men. It must be mediated. The experiential moments of female reproductive consciousness, confirmed in actual labour, are thus denigrated and dehumanized, given a low value while they are quite frankly imitated in a 'higher' sphere, the creation of concepts in a male intercourse of spirit and thought"; duBois (1988), 169–83, esp. 169: "I believe that Plato's appropriation of the reproductive metaphors of Greek culture used to describe the place of women and his use of this metaphorical network to authorize the male philosopher are linked to a metaphorical project—to the task of a monistic metaphysics, the positing of a one—father, sun, god—who is the source and origin of the good."

205 Irigaray (1985/b), 156.

206 For this and much of what follows, I owe a great deal to the work and conversation of Madeleine H. Kahn.

207 Julia Kristeva, *Le texte du roman* (The Hague, 1970), 160. I owe this reference to Miller, 49.

208 For the most extensive meditation on this topic, see Irigaray (1985/a), who analyzes both Freudian psychoanalysis and Platonic metaphysics in these terms but fails unaccountably to discuss Diotima (Irigaray is followed by duBois [1988], 169–83, who concentrates on the *Phaedrus* and similarly neglects Diotima); that omission is partially (if perfunctorily) rectified by Freeman.

209 Miller, 49.

210 Helene P. Foley, "Women in Greece," in Grant and Kitzinger, 1301–17, esp. 1301–02; compare the statement quoted by Woolf (1957 [1929]), 45n., from F. L. Lucas, *Tragedy*, 114–15: "It remains a strange and almost inexplicable fact that in Athena's city, where women were kept in almost Oriental suppression as odalisques or drudges, the stage should yet have produced figures like Clytemnestra. . . . [T]he paradox of this world where in real life a respectable woman could hardly show her face alone in the street, and yet on the stage woman equals or surpasses man, has never been satisfactorily explained." Lucas goes on, in the passage Woolf cites, to note that "in modern tragedy the same predominance exists." Woolf conducts her own survey of literature; her conclusion, if accurate, suggests that this paradox of social oppression and poetic license may not be so distinctive to Greek culture as Foley imagines: "if woman had no existence save in the fiction written by men, one would imagine her a person of the utmost importance; very various; heroic and mean; splendid and sordid; infinitely beautiful and hideous in the extreme; as great as a man, some think even greater. But this woman is in fiction. In fact . . . she was locked up, beaten and flung about the room. A very queer, composite being thus emerges. Imaginatively she is of the highest importance; practically she is completely insignificant. She pervades poetry from cover to cover; she is all but absent from history. She dominates the lives of kings and conquerors in fiction; in fact she was the slave of any boy whose parents forced a ring upon her finger. Some of the most inspired words, some of the most profound thoughts in literature fall from her lips; in real life she could hardly read, could scarcely spell, and was the property of her husband" (pp. 45–46).

211 See Case, 318: "the suppression of actual women in the classical world created the invention of a representation of the gender 'Woman' within the culture. This 'Woman' appeared on the stage, in the myths, and in the plastic arts, representing the patriarchal values attached to the gender of 'Woman' while suppressing the experiences, stories, feelings, and fantasies of actual women."

212 See Zeitlin (1981), 177–78. For a close parallel that does not depend on gender-crossing, see Robert C. Toll, *Blacking Up: The Minstrel Show in Nineteenth-Century America* (New York, 1974).

213 For some different accounts of Socratic transvestitism, see Bohner-Cante, 69–81; John Brenkman, "The Other and the One: Psychoanalysis, Reading, the *Symposium*," in *Literature and Psychoanalysis: The Question of Reading—Otherwise*, ed. Shoshana Felman (Baltimore, 1982), 396–456, esp. 426, 448–50; Page duBois, "Phallocentrism and its Subversion in Plato's *Phaedrus*," *Arethusa*, 18 (1985), 91–103, amplified in duBois (1988), 174–83; Freeman, 172; Stanley Rosen, "Platonic Hermeneutics: On the Interpretation of a Platonic Dialogue," in *Proceedings of the Boston Area Colloquium in Ancient Philosophy: Volume I (1985)*, ed. John J. Cleary (Lanham, MD, 1986), 271–88, esp. 285. On transvestitism in Greek culture, see Zeitlin (1981), 177–81, and (1985), 65–66, with further references on p. 89, n. 9; duBois (1988), 176–77; Nicole Loraux, "Herakles: The Super-Male and the Feminine," and Françoise Frontisi-Ducroux and François Lissarrague, "From Ambiguity to Ambivalence: A Dionysiac Excursion through the 'Anakreontic' Vases," both translated by Robert Lamberton in Halperin, Winkler, and Zeitlin.

214 The issue, of course, is considerably more complex than I have made it out to be: in a culture, for example, in which both women and men "menstruate," might not menstruation mean something quite different from what it means when it is associated with a gender-specific physiology? In such a culture, in other words, might not "menstruation" simply refer to (e.g.) a process of purification which both men and women periodically undergo, albeit in different ways? See Gilbert Lewis, *Day of Shining Red: An Essay on Understanding Ritual* (Cambridge, 1980), esp. 111–12; La Fontaine, 129. For an analysis of the relation between (female) menstruation and (male) nose-bleeding in the ancient medical writers—an analysis that coincides on many points with the results of anthropological work in Melanesia—see Jones (1991/a) and, for the mediaeval analogue, see Bynum (1986), 421–22, 436.

215 Maximus of Tyre, 24.4, remarked that Socrates fashioned *Erôs* in his own image—but in the image of himself as it had appeared on the comic stage (see, in addition to Aristophanes's *Clouds*, Eupolis, fr. 352; Ameipsias, fr. 9 [Kock]).

216 Note the use of *homologein* and its compounds to express the unbroken continuity of assumptions spanning the two conversations: 199b9, d9; 200b6, d6, e7; 201b1, b9 (thus far Agathon); 201e (Socrates's justification for replacing himself with Diotima); 202b3, b6, c1, d1, d4 (Diotima takes over).

217 It was on these grounds that Wilamowitz, II, 170–76, esp. 174, suspecting that Plato was having a bit of fun with his reader, refused to accept the early portions of Diotima's speech as Platonic doctrine; other scholars have confined their skepticism to Diotima's historicity: Bury, xxxix, maintains, "It is only for purposes of literary art that Diotima here supplants the Platonic Socrates: she is presented, by a fiction, as his instructor, whereas in fact she merely gives utterance to his own thoughts"; similarly, Robin (1929), xxv–xxvii, and Friedländer, I, 148–50 and III, 25, argue that Diotima is the creation not of Plato but of the Platonic Socrates: she is an ironic mask behind which the Platonic Socrates conceals himself (Friedländer's interpretation has been followed recently by Lowenstam, esp. 86). For another discussion of how Plato sometimes allows Socrates to

undermine his own narratorial reliability, see Harry Berger, Jr., "Facing Sophists: Socrates' Charismatic Bondage in *Protagoras*," *Representations*, 5 (1984), 66–91, esp.72–74.

218 See Lowenstam, 98, on this "confusion of roles"; cf. Saxonhouse (1985), 54, who emphasizes Socrates's identification with *Penia*.

219 On the magical qualities associated with Socrates's person in Socratic literature, see Dorothy Tarrant, "The Touch of Socrates," *Classical Quarterly*, n.s. 8 (1958), 95–98. On the imagery of filling and emptying in the *Symposium*, see Lowenstam, 88–89, 96–97; Bruce Rosenstock, "Socrates' New Music: The *Symposium* and the *Phaedo*" (unpublished ms.) For interpretations of the Alcibiades episode as an illustration of the myth of *Poros* and *Penia*, see O'Brien, 128–129; Lowenstam, 98–100.

220 Compare Lowenstam, 100.

221 See my paper, "Plato and the Erotics of Narrativity," in *Methodological Approaches to Plato and His Dialogues*, ed. James Klagge and Nicholas D. Smith, forthcoming.

222 Woolf (1957 [1929]), 26. "What could be the reason, then, of this curious disparity, I wondered," Woolf continues. "Why are women . . . so much more interesting to men than men are to women?" (p. 27; see, generally, pp. 26–37).

223 Freud, "Femininity," *New Lectures on Psycho–Analysis*, trans. James Strachey, in Strachey, XXII, 112–35 (quotation, with Strachey's italics, on p. 113). See Irigaray (1985/a), 13ff., esp. 13: "It is a matter, then, for you, men, to speak among yourselves, men, about woman who is not at all interested by the reception or production of a discourse concerning *the riddle*, the *logogriphe* which she represents to you. The mystery which *is* woman thus will constitute *the aim, the object*, and *the sport* of a masculine discourse, of a debate among men which will not pose the question to her, which should not concern her. About which she should know essentially nothing." (I quote here the translation provided by Timothy Murray in *Theatre Journal*, 37 [1985], 272.)

224 See, e.g., *P. Oxy.* 3656; Diogenes Laertius, 3.46: discussion by Alice Swift Riginos, *Platonica: The Anecdotes concerning the Life and Writings of Plato* (Leiden, 1976), 183–84. (I wish to thank Mary Lefkowitz for providing me with these references.)

225 Note that "sexual difference" is typically put into the singular, as if there were only one difference between the sexes that really counted. . . .

226 See Teresa de Lauretis, "Sexual Indifference and Lesbian Representation," *Theatre Journal*, 40 (1988), 155–77, who derives this concept from Luce Irigaray, esp. Irigaray (1985/b), 86: in Western discourses on female sexuality (psychoanalytic discourse is the case in point here) "*the feminine occurs only within models and laws devised by male subjects*. Which implies that there are not really two sexes, but only one. A single practice and representation of the sexual." See, also, Irigaray (1985/a), 28: Freud, defining "sexual differences [note Irigaray's plural] as a function of the a priori of the same," has "recourse, to support this demonstration, to the age-old processes [of classical philosophy]: analogy, comparison, symmetry, dichotomic oppositions, and so on"; he thereby exposes "sexual 'indifference' " as a condition of traditional metaphysical coherence. Irigaray also renders this concept by her punning coinage *hom(m)osexualité*—a concept best illustrated by the textual practice of the conservative British philosopher Roger Scruton, esp. x, who, in his discussion of (hetero)sexual desire, retains the masculine pronoun for both the subject and object of desire, on the ground that "it is stylistically correct." Here we see the paradoxical implications of what Scruton calls "traditional practice" plainly exposed: by regularly treating the ungendered subject as male and thus excluding women, it creates a unitary, universalizing discourse whose uniquely masculine terms, for all their ostensible involvement in heterosexist paradigms, produce an unintended homoerotic effect—pre-

cisely the conjunction that Irigaray's coinage is designed to represent. See Jones (1991/a), who makes a similar argument about Hippocratic medicine.

227 See Glenn W. Most, "Seming and Being: Sign and Metaphor in Aristotle," in *Creativity and the Imagination: Case Studies from the Classical Age to the Twentieth Century*, ed. Mark Amsler, Studies in Science and Culture, 3 (Newark, 1985), 11–33.

228 Cf. Monique Wittig, "The Straight Mind," *Feminist Issues*, 1.1 (Summer 1980), 103–11, who, having argued that " 'man' and 'woman' are political concepts of opposition, and the copula which dialectically unites them is, at the same time, the one which abolishes them" (p. 108), concludes that " 'woman' has meaning only in heterosexual systems of thought and heterosexual economic systems. Lesbians are not women" (p. 110); Rubin (1975), 178–80.

229 I wish to thank Daniel L. Selden for supplying me with the formulations contained in the last two paragraphs.

Bibliography
of frequently cited works

Adam, Barry D. 1985/a. "Age, Structure, and Sexuality: Reflections on the Anthropological Evidence on Homosexual Relations": 19–33 in Blackwood.

Adam, Barry D. 1985/b. "Structural Foundations of the Gay World." *Comparative Studies in Society and History*, 27:658–71.

Allen, Prudence. 1985. *The Concept of Woman: The Aristotelian Revolution 750 B.C. to A.D. 1250* (Montreal).

Ardener, Shirley, ed. 1978. *Defining Females: The Nature of Women in Society*. The Oxford Women's Series (London).

Ariès, Philippe, and Béjin, André, eds. 1985. *Western Sexuality: Practice and Precept in Past and Present Times*. Trans. Anthony Forster (Oxford).

Arthur, Marilyn B. 1983. "The Dream of a World without Women: Poetics and the Circles of Order in the *Theogony* Prooemium." *Arethusa*, 16.1–2:97–116.

Beaver, Harold. 1981/82. "Homosexual Signs (*In Memory of Roland Barthes*)." *Critical Inquiry*, 8:99–119.

Bethe, E. 1907. "Die dorische Knabenliebe: ihre Ethik und ihre Idee." *Rheinisches Museum für Philologie*, 62:438–75.

Bettelheim, Bruno. 1962. *Symbolic Wounds: Puberty Rites and the Envious Male*. Rev. ed. (New York).

Beye, Charles Rowan. 1984. "Repeated Similes in the Homeric Poems": 7–13 in *Studies Presented to Sterling Dow on His Eightieth Birthday*. Greek, Roman, and Byzantine Monograph 10 (Durham, NC).

Blackwood, Evelyn, ed. 1985. *Anthropology and Homosexual Behavior* = *Journal of Homosexuality*, 11.3–4.

Bohner-Cante, Marie-Hélène [Hanna Glyphe]. 1981. *Platonisme et sexualité. Genèse de la métaphysique platonicienne* (Toulouse).

Borthwick, E. K. 1977. "Starting a Hare: A Note on Machon, fr. 15 (Gow)." *Bulletin of the Institute of Classical Studies* (University of London), 24:31–36.

Boswell, John. 1980. *Christianity, Social Tolerance, and Homosexuality: Gay People in Western Europe from the Beginning of the Christian Era to the Fourteenth Century* (Chicago).

Boswell, John. 1982–83. "Revolutions, Universals and Sexual Categories": 89–113 in Boyers and Steiner.

Boswell, John. 1989. "Gay History" [Review of Greenberg]. *The Atlantic*, February: 74–78.

Bothmer, Dietrich von. 1986. "An Archaic Red-Figure Kylix." *J. Paul Getty Museum Journal*, 14:5–20.

Boyers, Robert, and Steiner, George, eds. 1982–83. *Homosexuality: Sacrilege, Vision, Politics = Salmagundi*, 58–59.

Brandt, Paul [pseud. "Hans Licht"]. 1932. *Sexual Life in Ancient Greece*. Trans. J. H. Freese. Ed. Lawrence H. Dawson (London).

Bray, Alan. 1982. *Homosexuality in Renaissance England* (London: Gay Men's Press).

Bremmer, Jan. 1980. "An Enigmatic Indo-European Rite: Paederasty." *Arethusa*, 13:279–98.

Brentlinger, John A. 1970. "The Cycle of Becoming in the *Symposium*": 1–31 in *The Symposium of Plato*. Trans. Suzy Q. Groden (University of Massachusetts Press).

Brès, Yvon. 1968. *La psychologie de Platon* (Paris).

Brisson, Luc. 1973. "Bisexualité et médiation en Grèce ancienne." *Nouvelle revue de psychanalyse*, 7:27–48.

Brown, Peter. 1983. "Sexuality and Society in the Fifth Century A.D.: Augustine and Julian of Eclanum": 49–70 in *Tria corda: Scritti in onore di Arnaldo Momigliano*. Ed. E. Gabba (Como).

Buffière, Félix. 1980. *Eros adolescent: la pédérastie dans la Grèce antique* (Paris).

Bullough, Vern L. 1979. *Homosexuality: A History* (New York).

Burkert, Walter. 1984. *Die orientalisierende Epoche in der griechischen Religion und Literatur*. Sitzungsberichte der Heidelberger Akademie der Wissenschaften, Philosophisch-historische Klasse, 1984.1 (Heidelberg).

Burkert, Walter. 1985. *Greek Religion*. Trans. John Raffan (Cambridge, MA).

Burnyeat, M. F. 1977. "Socratic Midwifery, Platonic Inspiration." *Bulletin of the Institute of Classical Studies* (University of London), 24:7–16.

Bury, R. G., ed. 1932. *The Symposium of Plato*. 2d ed. (Cambridge).

Bynum, Caroline Walker. 1986. "The Body of Christ in the Later Middle Ages: A Reply to Leo Steinberg." *Renaissance Quarterly*, 39:399–439.

Bynum, Caroline Walker. 1987. *Holy Feast and Holy Fast: The Religious Significance of Food to Medieval Women* (Berkeley).

Calame, Claude. 1977. *Les choeurs de jeunes filles en Grèce archaïque*. Filologia e critica, 20–21 (Rome). Two volumes.

Calame, Claude. 1984. "Eros inventore e organizzatore della società greca antica": ix–xl in *L'amore in Grecia*. Ed. Calame. 3d ed. (Rome).

Callaway, Helen. 1978. " 'The Most Essentially Female Function of All': Giving Birth": 163–85 in Ardener.

Campese, Silvia. 1983. "Madre Materia: Donne, casa, città nell' antropologia di Aristotele": 13–79 in Campese, Manuli, and Sissa.

Campese, Silvia, Manuli, Paola, and Sissa, Giulia. 1983. *Madre materia: Sociologia e biologia della donna greca* (Turin).

Cantarella, Eva. 1987. *Pandora's Daughters: The Role and Status of Women in Greek and Roman Antiquity*. Trans. Maureen B. Fant (Baltimore).

Caplan, Pat, ed. 1987. *The Cultural Construction of Sexuality* (London).

Carson, Anne. 1989. "Putting Her in Her Place: Woman, Dirt, and Desire": 135–69 in Halperin, Winkler, and Zeitlin.

Cartledge, Paul. 1981. "The Politics of Spartan Pederasty." *Proceedings of the Cambridge Philological Society*, n.s. 27:17–36.

Case, Sue-Ellen. 1985. "Classic Drag: The Greek Creation of Female Parts." *Theatre Journal*, 37:317–27.

Chauncey, George, Jr. 1982–83. "From Sexual Inversion to Homosexuality: Medicine and the Changing Conceptualization of Female Deviance": 114–46 in Boyers and Steiner.

Chauncey, George, Jr. 1985/86. "Christian Brotherhood or Sexual Perversion? Homosexual Identities and the Construction of Sexual Boundaries in the World War One Era." *Journal of Social History*, 19:189–211.

Clarke, W. M. 1978. "Achilles and Patroclus in Love." *Hermes*, 106:381–96.

Clinton, Kevin. 1974. *The Sacred Officials of the Eleusinian Mysteries*. Transactions of the American Philosophical Society, 64.3 (Philadelphia).

Cohen, David. 1984. "The Athenian Law of Adultery." *Revue internationale des droits de l'antiquité*, 3d ser., 31:147–65.

Cole, Susan Guettel. 1984. "Greek Sanctions against Sexual Assault." *Classical Philology*, 79:97–113.

Cole, Susan Guettel. 1991. "*Gynaixi ou themis*: Male and Female in the Greek *Leges Sacrae*." *Helios*, 17.2:forthcoming.

Davidson, Arnold I. 1986/87. "How to Do the History of Psychoanalysis: A Reading of Freud's *Three Essays on the Theory of Sexuality*": 252–77 in *The Trial(s) of Psychoanalysis*. Ed. Françoise Meltzer. *Critical Inquiry*, 13.

Davidson, Arnold I. 1987/88. "Sex and the Emergence of Sexuality." *Critical Inquiry*, 14:16–48.

Davidson, Arnold I. Forthcoming. "Closing Up the Corpses: Diseases of Sexuality and the Emergence of the Psychiatric Style of Reasoning": forthcoming in *Meaning and Method: Essays in Honour of Hilary Putnam*. Ed. George Boolos (Cambridge).

Delaney, Carol. 1987. "Seeds of Honor, Fields of Shame": 35–48 in Gilmore (1987/a).

De Martino, Gianni, and Schmitt, Arno. 1985. *Kleine Schriften zu zwischenmännlicher Sexualität und Erotik in der muslimischen Gesellschaft* (Berlin: author).

Detienne, Marcel. 1976. "Potagerie de femmes ou comment engendrer seule." *Traverses*, 5–6:75–81.

Detienne, Marcel. 1977. *The Gardens of Adonis: Spices in Greek Mythology*. Trans. Janet Lloyd (Atlantic Highlands, NJ).

Devereux, George. 1968. "Greek Pseudo-Homosexuality and the 'Greek Miracle.' " *Symbolae Osloenses*, 42:69–92.

Dittmar, Heinrich. 1912. *Aischines von Shpettos: Studien zur Literaturgeschichte der Sokratiker*. Philologische Untersuchungen, 21 (Berlin).

Dover, K. J. 1973. "Classical Greek Attitudes to Sexual Behaviour." *Arethusa*, 6:59–73.

Dover, K. J. 1974. *Greek Popular Morality: In the Time of Plato and Aristotle* (Oxford).

Dover, K. J. 1978. *Greek Homosexuality* (London).

Dover, Kenneth, ed. 1980. *Plato: Symposium*. Cambridge Greek and Latin Classics (Cambridge).

Dover, K. J. 1988. "Greek Homosexuality and Initiation": 115–34 in *The Greeks and their Legacy = Collected Papers, Volume II: Prose Literature, History, Society, Transmission, Influence* (Oxford).

Drabkin, I. E., ed. and trans. 1950. *Caelius Aurelianus: ON ACUTE DISEASES and ON CHRONIC DISEASES* (Chicago).

Dreyfus, Hubert L., and Rabinow, Paul. 1983. *Michel Foucault: Beyond Structuralism and Hermeneutics*. 2d ed. (Chicago).

duBois, Page. 1984. "Sexual Difference: Ancient and Modern." *Pacific Coast Philology*, 19.1–2:43–49.

duBois, Page. 1988. *Sowing the Body: Psychoanalysis and Ancient Representations of Women* (Chicago).

Durand, Jean-Louis, and Schnapp, Alain. 1984. "Boucherie sacrificielle et chasses initiatiques": 48–66 in *La cité des images*. Ed. anon. (Paris).

Dynes, Wayne. 1985. *Homolexis: A Historical and Cultural Lexicon of Homosexuality*. Gai Saber Monograph No. 4 (New York: Gay Academic Union).

Edmunds, Lowell. 1988. "Foucault and Theognis." *Classical and Modern Literature*, 8.2:79–91.

Ehlers, Barbara. 1966. *Eine vorplatonische Deutung des sokratischen Eros. Der Dialog Aspasia des Sokratikers Aischines*. Zetemata, 41 (Munich).

Ellis, Havelock. 1922. *Sexual Inversion = Studies in the Psychology of Sex*, Vol. II. 3d ed. (Philadelphia).

Epstein, Steven. 1987. "Gay Politics, Ethnic Identity: The Limits of Social Constructionism." *Socialist Review*, nos. 93/94 = 17.3–4:9–54.

Erbse, Hartmut. 1966. "Sokrates und die Frauen." *Gymnasium*, 73:201–20.

Féray, Jean-Claude. 1981. "Une histoire critique du mot homosexualité." *Arcadie*, 28, nos. 325–328:11–21, 115–24, 171–81, 246–58.

Flynn, Thomas R. 1985. "Truth and Subjectivation in the Later Foucault." *Journal of Philosophy*, 82:531–40.

Foley, Helene P., ed. 1981. *Reflections of Women in Antiquity* (New York).

Forsyth, Neil. 1987. *The Old Enemy: Satan and the Combat Myth* (Princeton).

Foucault, Michel. 1972. *The Archaeology of Knowledge and The Discourse on Language*. Trans. A. M. Sheridan Smith (New York).

Foucault, Michel. 1977. "Nietzsche, Genealogy, History": 139–64 in *Language, Counter-Memory, Practice: Selected Essays and Interviews*. Trans. Donald F. Bouchard and Sherry Simon. Ed. Donald F. Bouchard (Ithaca, NY).

Foucault, Michel. 1978. *The History of Sexuality. Volume I: An Introduction*. Trans. Robert Hurley (New York).

Foucault, Michel. 1980/a. "Introduction": vii–xvii in *Herculine Barbin, Being the Recently Discovered Memoirs of a Nineteenth-Century French Hermaphrodite*. Trans. Richard McDougall (New York).

Foucault, Michel. 1980/b. *Power/Knowledge: Selected Interviews and Other Writings 1972–77*. Ed. Colin Gordon. Trans. Colin Gordon, Leo Marshall, John Mepham, and Kate Soper (Brighton, Sussex: Harvester Press).

Foucault, Michel. 1983. "On the Genealogy of Ethics: An Overview of Work in Progress": 229–52 in Dreyfus and Rabinow.

Foucault, Michel. 1984. "Preface to *The History of Sexuality*, Volume II." Trans. William Smock: 333–39 in *The Foucault Reader*. Ed. Paul Rabinow (New York).

Foucault, Michel. 1985. *The Use of Pleasure*. The History of Sexuality, Volume Two. Trans. Robert Hurley (New York).

Foucault, Michel. 1986. *The Care of the Self.* The History of Sexuality, Volume Three. Trans. Robert Hurley (New York).

Foucault, Michel, and Sennett, Richard. 1981. "Sexuality and Solitude." *London Review of Books*, 3.9:3, 5–7.

Freeman, Barbara. 1986. "Irigaray at *The Symposium*: Speaking Otherwise": 170–77 in *Sexual Difference*. Ed. Robert Young = *Oxford Literary Review*, 8.1–2.

Friedländer, Paul. 1969. *Plato.* Trans. Hans Meyerhoff. Bollingen Series, 59. Volume I: *An Introduction.* 2d ed.; Volume III: *The Dialogues. Second and Third Periods* (Princeton).

Gagnon, John H., and Simon, William. 1973. *Sexual Conduct: The Social Sources of Human Sexuality* (Chicago).

Geddes, Anne. 1975. "The Philosophic Notion of Women in Antiquity." *Antichthon*, 9:35–40.

Giallongo, Angela. 1981. *L'immagine della donna nella cultura greca* (Rimini).

Gilmore, David D., ed. 1987/a. *Honor and Shame and the Unity of the Mediterranean.* Special Publication of the American Anthropological Association, 22 (Washington).

Gilmore, David D. 1987/b. "Introduction: The Shame of Dishonor": 2–21 in Gilmore (1987/ a).

Gleason, Maud W. 1989. "The Semiotics of Gender: Physiognomy and Self-Fashioning in the Second Century C.E.": 389–415 in Halperin, Winkler, and Zeitlin.

Glidden, David K. 1981. "The *Lysis* on Loving One's Own." *Classical Quarterly*, 31:39–59.

Godel, R. 1954. "Socrate et Diotime." *Bulletin de l'Association Guillaume Budé*, 4th ser., No. 4:3–30.

Godelier, Maurice. 1976. "Le sexe comme fondement ultime de l'ordre social et cosmique chez les Baruya de Nouvelle-Guinée. Mythe et réalité": 268–306 in *Sexualité et pouvoir.* Ed. Armando Verdiglione (Paris).

Godelier, Maurice. 1981. "The Origins of Male Domination." *New Left Review*, 127:3–17.

Golden, Mark. 1984. "Slavery and Homosexuality at Athens." *Phoenix*, 38:308–24.

Golden, Mark. 1985. "*Pais*, 'Child' and 'Slave.' " *L'Antiquité classique*, 54:91–104.

Gordon, R. L., ed. 1981. *Myth, Religion and Society* (Cambridge).

Gow, A. S. F., ed. 1965. *Machon: The Fragments* (Cambridge).

Gow, A. S. F., and Page, D. L., eds. 1965, 1968. *The Greek Anthology: Hellenistic Epigrams* and *The Garland of Philip and some contemporary epigrams* (Cambridge). Two volumes each.

Grant, Michael, and Kitzinger, Rachel, eds. 1988. *Civilization of the Ancient Mediterranean: Greece and Rome* (New York).

Greenberg, David F. 1988. *The Construction of Homosexuality* (Chicago).

Greenblatt, Stephen. 1986. "Fiction and Friction": 30–52, 329–32 in Heller, Sosna, and Wellbery.

Gregor, Thomas. 1985. *Anxious Pleasures: The Sexual Lives of an Amazonian People* (Chicago).

Gresseth, Gerald K. 1975. "The Gilgamesh Epic and Homer." *Classical Journal*, 70.4 (April–May):1–18.

Guthrie, W. K. C. 1969. *A History of Greek Philosophy, 3: The Fifth-Century Enlightenment* (Cambridge).

Hackforth, R., trans. 1952. *Plato's Phaedrus* (Cambridge).

Hägg, Robin, ed. 1983. *The Greek Renaissance of the Eighth Century B.C.: Tradition and Innovation*

(Proceedings of the Second International Symposium at the Swedish Institute in Athens, 1–5 June, 1981). Skrifter utgivna av Svenska Institutet i Athen, 4; 30 (Stockholm).

Halperin, David M. 1983. *Before Pastoral: Theocritus and the Ancient Tradition of Bucolic Poetry* (New Haven).

Halperin, David M. 1985. "Platonic *Erôs* and What Men Call Love." *Ancient Philosophy*, 5:161–204.

Halperin, David M. 1986. "Plato and Erotic Reciprocity." *Classical Antiquity*, 5:60–80.

Halperin, David M., Winkler, John J., and Zeitlin, Froma I., eds. 1989. *Before Sexuality: The Construction of Erotic Experience in the Ancient Greek World* (Princeton).

Hammond, Dorothy, and Jablow, Alta. 1987. "Gilgamesh and the Sundance Kid: The Myth of Male Friendship": 241–58 in *The Making of Masculinities: The New Men's Studies*. Ed. Harry Brod (Boston).

Hansen, Mogens Herman. 1976. Apagoge, Endeixis *and* Ephegesis *against* Kakourgoi, Atimoi *and* Pheugontes: *A Study in the Athenian Administration of Justice in the Fourth Century B.C.* Odense University Classical Studies, 8.

Hanson, Ann Ellis. 1989. "The Medical Writers' Woman": 309–38 in Halperin, Winkler, and Zeitlin.

Harrison, A. R. W. 1968. *The Law of Athens, 1: The Family and Property* (Oxford).

Held, George F. 1983. "Parallels between *The Gilgamesh Epic* and Plato's *Symposium*." *Journal of Near Eastern Studies*, 42:133–41.

Heller, Thomas C., Sosna, Morton, and Wellbery, David E., eds. 1986. *Reconstructing Individualism: Autonomy, Individuality, and the Self in Western Thought*. With Arnold I. Davidson, Ann Swidler, and Ian Watt (Stanford).

Henderson, Jeffrey. 1988. "Greek Attitudes Toward Sex": 1249–63 in Grant and Kitzinger.

Henriques, Julian, Hollway, Wendy, Urwin, Cathy, Couze, Venn, and Walkerdine, Valerie. 1984. *Changing the Subject: Psychology, Social Regulation and Subjectivity* (London).

Henry, Madeleine Mary. 1985. *Menander's Courtesans and the Greek Comic Tradition*. Studien zur klassischen Philologie, 20 (Frankfurt).

Herdt, Gilbert H. 1981. *Guardians of the Flutes: Idioms of Masculinity* (New York).

Herdt, Gilbert H., ed. 1982. *Rituals of Manhood: Male Initiation in Papua New Guinea* (Berkeley).

Herdt, Gilbert H., ed. 1984. *Ritualized Homosexuality in Melanesia* (Berkeley).

Herter, Hans. 1960. "Soziologie der antiken Prostitution im Lichte der heidnischen und christlichen Schriftum." *Jahrbuch für Antike und Christentum*, 3:70–111.

Herzer, Manfred. 1985. "Kertbeny and the Nameless Love." *Journal of Homosexuality*, 12.1:1–26.

Heseltine, Michael. 1969. *Petronius*. Rev. E. H. Warmington. Loeb Classical Library (Cambridge, MA).

Hocquenghem, Guy. 1978. *Homosexual Desire*. Trans. Daniella Dangoor (London).

Hogbin, Ian. 1970. *The Island of Menstruating Men: Religion in Wogeo, New Guinea* (Scranton, PA).

Horowitz, Maryanne Cline. 1976. "Aristotle and Woman." *Journal of the History of Biology*, 9:183–213.

Housman, A. E. 1931. "Praefanda." *Hermes*, 66:402–12.

Hug, Arnold, and Schöne, Hermann, eds. 1909. *Symposion.* 3d ed. Platons ausgewählte Schriften, ed. Christian Cron and Julius Deuschle, 5 (Leipzig).

Irigaray, Luce. 1985/a. *Speculum of the Other Woman.* Trans. Gillian C. Gill (Ithaca, NY).

Irigaray, Luce. 1985/b. *This Sex Which Is Not One.* Trans. Catherine Porter, with Carolyn Burke (Ithaca, NY).

Irwin, Terence, trans. 1985. *Aristotle: Nicomachean Ethics* (Indianapolis: Hackett).

Jackson, Margaret. 1987. " 'Facts of Life' or the Eroticization of Women's Oppression? Sexology and the Social Construction of Heterosexuality": 52–81 in Caplan.

Jacobsen, Thorkild. 1929/30. "How Did Gilgameš Oppress Uruk?" *Acta Orientalia,* 8:62–74.

Jacobsen, Thorkild. 1976. *The Treasures of Darkness: A History of Mesopotamian Religion* (New Haven).

James, G. W. B. 1963. "Psychology and Gynaecology": II, 885–96 in *British Obstetric and Gynaecological Practice.* Ed. Aleck Bourne and Sir Andrew Claye. 3d ed. (London).

Jocelyn, H. D. 1980. "A Greek Indecency and its Students." *Proceedings of the Cambridge Philological Society,* n.s. 26:12–66.

Joly, Robert. 1960. *Recherches sur le traité pseudo-hippocratique du Régime.* Bibliothèque de la Faculté de Philosophie et Lettres de l'Université de Liège, 156 (Paris).

Jones, Lesley Ann. 1991/a. "Andrology in the Greek Medical Writers." *Helios,* 17.2:forthcoming.

Jones, Lesley Ann. 1991/b. "The Politics of Pleasure: Female Sexual Response in Greek Medical Writings." *Helios,* 17.2:forthcoming.

Just, Roger. 1975. "Conceptions of Women in Classical Athens." *Journal of the Anthropological Society of Oxford,* 6.3:153–70.

Kahn, Charles. Unpublished. "*Sokratikoi logoi* as background for the interpretation of Platonic dialogues" (mss.).

Kay, N. M. 1985. *Martial Book XI: A Commentary* (London).

Keesing, Roger M. 1982. "Introduction": 1–43 in Herdt (1982).

Kelsen, Hans. 1942. "Platonic Love." Trans. George B. Wilbur. *American Imago,* 3:3–110.

Kennedy, Hubert. 1988. *Ulrichs: The Life and Works of Karl Heinrich Ulrichs, Pioneer of the Modern Gay Movement* (Boston: Alyson).

Keuls, Eva C. 1985. *The Reign of the Phallus: Sexual Politics in Ancient Athens* (New York).

Kilmer, Anne Draffkorn. 1982. "A Note on an Overlooked Word-Play in the Akkadian Gilgamesh": 128–32 in *ZIKIR ŠUMIM: Assyriological Studies Presented to F. R. Kraus on the Occasion of his Seventieth Birthday.* Ed. G. van Driel, Th. J. H. Krispijn, M. Stol, and K. R. Veenhof (Leiden).

Klein, Fritz, and Wolf, Timothy J., eds. 1985. *Bisexualities: Theory and Research = Journal of Homosexuality,* 11.1–2.

Kock, Theodor. 1880–88. *Comicorum Atticorum Fragmenta* (Leipzig). Three volumes.

Koehl, Robert B. 1986. "The Chieftain Cup and a Minoan Rite of Passage." *Journal of Hellenic Studies,* 106:99–110.

Kranz, Walther. 1926/a. "Diotima von Mantineia." *Hermes,* 61:437–47.

Kranz, Walther. 1926/b. "Diotima." *Die Antike,* 2:313–27.

Krell, David F. 1972. "Socrates' Body." *Southern Journal of Philosophy,* 10.4:443–51.

Krell, David Farrell. 1975. "Female Parts in *Timaeus.*" *Arion,* n.s. 2:400–21.

Krenkel, Werner A. 1978. "Männliche Prostitution in der Antike." *Das Altertum,* 24:49–55.

Krenkel, Werner A. 1979. "Pueri meritorii." *Wissenschaftliche Zeitschrift der Wilhelm-Pieck-Universität Rostock,* 28:179–89.

Krüger, Gerhard. 1983. *Einsicht und Leidenschaft: Das Wesen des platonischen Denkens.* 5th ed. (Frankfurt).

La Fontaine, Jean. 1985. *Initiation* (Harmondsworth).

Langness, L. L. 1974. "Ritual, Power, and Male Dominance." *Ethos,* 2:189–212.

Laqueur, Thomas. 1986. "Orgasm, Generation, and the Politics of Reproductive Biology": 1–41 in *Sexuality and the Social Body in the Nineteenth Century.* Ed. Catherine Gallagher and Thomas Laqueur. *Representations,* 14.

Lefkowitz, Mary. 1985. "Sex and Civilization." *Partisan Review,* 52:460–66.

Lesky, Erna. 1951. *Die Zeugungs- und Vererbungslehren der Antike und ihr Nachwirken* = 1225–1425 in Akademie der Wissenschaften und der Literatur in Mainz, Abhandlungen der geistes- und sozialwissenschaftlichen Klasse, Jahrgang 1950, No. 19 (Wiesbaden).

Lloyd, G. E. R. 1983. *Science, Folklore and Ideology: Studies in the Life Sciences in Ancient Greece* (Cambridge).

Lonie, Iain M. 1981. *The Hippocratic Treatises "On Generation" "On the Nature of the Child" "Diseases IV".* Ars Medica: Texte und Untersuchungen zur Quellenkunde der Alten Medizin, 2.7 (Berlin).

Loraux, Nicole. 1981. *Les enfants d'Athéna: Idées athéniennes sur la citoyenneté et la division des sexes* (Paris).

Lowenstam, Steven. 1985. "Paradoxes in Plato's Symposium." *Ramus,* 14:85–104.

MacCary, W. Thomas. 1982. *Childlike Achilles: Ontogeny and Phylogeny in the ILIAD* (New York).

MacDowell, Douglas M. 1978. *The Law in Classical Athens.* Aspects of Greek and Roman Life (Ithaca, NY).

Macleod, M. D., trans. 1967. *Lucian.* Vol. 8. Loeb Classical Library (Cambridge, MA).

MacMullen, Ramsay. 1983. "Roman Attitudes to Greek Love." *Historia,* 32:484–502.

Manuli, Paola. 1980. "Fisiologia e patologia del femminile negli scritti ippocratici dell' antica ginecologia greca": 393–408 in *Hippocratica: Actes du Colloque hippocratique de Paris (4–9 septembre 1978).* Ed. M. D. Grmek. Colloques internationaux du Centre National de la Recherche Scientifique, 583 (Paris).

Manuli, Paola. 1983. "Donne mascoline, femmine sterili, vergini perpetue: La ginecologia greca tra Ippocrate e Sorano": 147–92 in Campese, Manuli, and Sissa.

Marmor, Judd, ed. 1980. *Homosexual Behavior: A Modern Reappraisal* (New York).

Marshall, John. 1981. "Pansies, Perverts and Macho Men: Changing Conceptions of Male Homosexuality": 133–54 in Plummer.

May, Margaret Tallmadge, trans. 1968. *Galen: On the Usefulness of the Parts of the Body* (Ithaca, NY).

McIntosh, Mary. 1968/69. "The Homosexual Role." *Social Problems,* 16:182–92.

Miller, Nancy K. 1981. " 'I's' in Drag: The Sex of Recollection." *The Eighteenth Century: Theory and Interpretation,* 22.1 (Winter):47–57.

Moodie, T. Dunbar. 1987/88. "Migrancy and Male Sexuality on the South African Gold Mines." *Journal of Southern African Studies,* 14:228–56.

Morrison, J. S. 1964. "Four Notes on Plato's *Symposium*." *Classical Quarterly*, 14:42–55.

Nagy, Gregory. 1979. *The Best of the Achaeans: Concepts of the Hero in Archaic Greek Poetry* (Baltimore).

Nauck, August, ed. 1926. *Tragicorum Graecorum Fragmenta.* 2d ed. (Leipzig).

Neu, Jerome. 1987. "Freud and Perversion": I, 153–84 in Shelp.

Neumann, Harry. 1965. "Diotima's Concept of Love." *American Journal of Philology*, 86:33–59.

Nussbaum, Martha. 1979. "The Speech of Alcibiades: A Reading of Plato's *Symposium*." *Philosophy and Literature*, 3:131–72.

Nussbaum, Martha C. 1985. "Affections of the Greeks." *New York Times Book Review* (10 November), 13–14.

Nussbaum, Martha C. 1986. *The Fragility of Goodness: Luck and Ethics in Greek Tragedy and Philosophy* (Cambridge).

O'Brien, Mary. 1981. *The Politics of Reproduction* (Boston).

O'Flaherty, Wendy Doniger. 1980. *Women, Androgynes, and Other Mythical Beasts* (Chicago).

Osborne, Robin. 1985. "The Erection and Mutilation of the Hermai." *Proceedings of the Cambridge Philological Society*, n.s. 31:47–73.

Padgug, Robert A. 1979. "Sexual Matters: On Conceptualizing Sexuality in History." *Radical History Review*, 20:3–23.

Parker, Robert. 1983. *Miasma: Pollution and Purification in Early Greek Religion* (Oxford).

Patzer, Harald. 1982. *Die griechische Knabenliebe*. Sitzungsberichte der Wissenschaftlichen Gesellschaft an der Johann Wolfgang Goethe-Universität Frankfurt am Main, 19.1 (Wiesbaden).

Payer, Pierre J. 1984. *Sex and the Penitentials: The Development of a Sexual Code 550–1150* (Toronto).

Pearce, Frank, and Roberts, Andrew. 1973. "The Social Regulation of Sexual Behaviour and the Development of Industrial Capitalism in Britain": 51–72 in *Contemporary Social Problems in Britain*. Ed. Roy Bailey and Jock Young (Westmead: Saxon House).

Penwill, J. L. 1978. "Men in Love: Aspects of Plato's *Symposium*." *Ramus*, 7:143–75.

Peradotto, John, and Sullivan, J. P., eds. 1984. *Women in the Ancient World: The ARETHUSA Papers.* SUNY Series in Classical Studies (Albany).

Petersen, William L. 1986. "Can *ARSENOKOITAI* Be Translated by 'Homosexuals'?" *Vigiliae Christianae*, 40:187–91.

Plass, Paul C. 1978. "Plato's 'Pregnant' Lover." *Symbolae Osloenses*, 53:47–55.

Plummer, Kenneth, ed. 1981. *The Making of the Modern Homosexual* (London: Hutchinson).

Pomeroy, Sarah B. 1984. *Women in Hellenistic Egypt from Alexander to Cleopatra* (New York).

Powell, John U., ed. 1925. *Collectanea Alexandrina: Reliquiae minores Poetarum Graecorum Aetatis Ptolemaicae 323–146 B.C.* (Oxford).

Preus, Anthony. 1977. "Galen's Criticism of Aristotle's Conception Theory." *Journal of the History of Biology*, 10:65–85.

Rancour-Laferriere, Daniel. 1985. *Signs of the Flesh: An Essay on the Evolution of Hominid Sexuality*. Approaches to Semiotics, 71 (Berlin: de Gruyter).

Rankin, H. D. 1963. "On *ADIAPLASTA ZOIA*: (Plato, Timaeus 91 d 3)." *Philologus*, 107:138–45.

Read, K. E. 1952. "Nama Cult of the Central Highlands, New Guinea." *Oceania*, 23.1:1–25.

Redfield, James M. 1975. *Nature and Culture in the* Iliad*: The Tragedy of Hector* (Chicago).

Rettig, Georg Ferd. 1876. *Platons Symposion* (Halle).

Rettig, G. F. 1882. "Knabenliebe und Frauenliebe in Platons Symposion." *Philologus*, 41:414–44.

Richardson, T. Wade. 1984. "Homosexuality in the *Satyricon*." *Classica et Mediaevalia*, 35:105–27.

Robin, Léon, ed. 1929. *Le Banquet*. Platon: Oeuvres complètes, 4.2 (Paris).

Robin, Léon. 1964. *La théorie platonicienne de l'amour*. 3d ed. (Paris).

Robinson, T. M. 1981. [Review of Dover (1978).] *Phoenix*, 35:160–63.

Rosen, Stanley. 1987. *Plato's Symposium*. 2d ed. (New Haven).

Rousselle, Aline. 1980. "Observation féminine et idéologie masculine: le corps de la femme d'après les médecins grecs." *Annales (E.S.C.)*, 35:1089–1115.

Rousselle, Aline. 1986. "Gestes et signes de la famille dans l'Empire romain": I, 231–69 in *Histoire de la famille*. Ed. André Burguière, Christiane Klapisch-Zuber, Martine Segalen, and Françoise Zonabend (Paris).

Rousselle, Aline. 1988. *Porneia: On Desire and the Body in Antiquity*. Trans. Felicia Pheasant (Oxford).

Rubin, Gayle. 1975. "The Traffic in Women: Notes on the 'Political Economy' of Sex": 157–210 in *Toward an Anthropology of Women*. Ed. Rayna R. Reiter (New York).

Rubin, Gayle. 1984. "Thinking Sex: Notes for a Radical Theory of the Politics of Sexuality": 267–319 in *Pleasure and Danger: Exploring Female Sexuality*. Ed. Carole S. Vance (Boston).

Saïd, Suzanne. 1983. "Féminin, femme et femelle dans les grands traités biologiques d'Aristote": 93–123 in *La femme dans les sociétés antiques*. Ed. Edmond Lévy (Strasbourg).

Salzman, Leon. 1980. "Latent Homosexuality": 312–24 in Marmor.

Sartre, Maurice. 1985. "L'homosexualité dans la Grèce ancienne." *L'Histoire*, 76 (March):10–17.

Saxonhouse, Arlene W. 1976. "The Philosopher and the Female in the Political Thought of Plato." *Political Theory*, 4.2:195–212.

Saxonhouse, Arlene W. 1984. "Eros and the Female in Greek Political Thought: An Interpretation of Plato's *Symposium*." *Political Theory*, 12:5–27.

Saxonhouse, Arlene W. 1985. *Women in the History of Political Thought: Ancient Greece to Machiavelli* (New York).

Schaps, David. 1977. "The Woman Least Mentioned: Etiquette and Women's Names." *Classical Quarterly*, 27:323–30.

Schnapp, Alain. 1981. "Une autre image de l'homosexualité en Grèce ancienne." *Le Débat*, 10:107–17.

Schnapp, Alain. 1984. "Eros en chasse": 67–83 in *La cité des images*. Ed. anon. (Paris).

Schneider, K. 1913. "Hetairai": cols. 1331–72 in *Paulys Real-Encyclopädie der classischen Altertumswissenschaft*, 8.2. Ed. Georg Wissowa (Stuttgart).

Schrijvers, P. H. 1985. *Eine medizinische Erklärung der männlichen Homosexualität aus der Antike (Caelius Aurelianus DE MORBIS CHRONICIS IV 9)* (Amsterdam: B. R. Grüner).

Scruton, Roger. 1986. *Sexual Desire: A Moral Philosophy of the Erotic* (New York).

Scully, Diana, and Bart, Pauline. 1973. "A Funny Thing Happened on the Way to the Orifice: Women in Gynecology Textbooks." *American Journal of Sociology*, 78:1045–50.

Seaford, Richard. 1988. "The Eleventh Ode of Bacchylides: Hera, Artemis, and the Absence of Dionysos." *Journal of Hellenic Studies*, 108:118–36.

Sergent, Bernard. 1986. *Homosexuality in Greek Myth*. Trans. Arthur Goldhammer (Boston).

Shelp, Earl E., ed. 1987. *Sexuality and Medicine*. Philosophy and Medicine, 22–23 (Dordrecht: D. Reidel). Two volumes.

Singer, Irving. 1984. *The Nature of Love, 1: Plato to Luther*. 2d ed. (Chicago).

Sinos, Dale S. 1980. *Achilles, Patroklos and the Meaning of* Philos. Innsbrucker Beiträge zur Sprachwissenschaft, 29 (Innsbruck).

Smith, Nicholas D. 1983. "Plato and Aristotle on the Nature of Women." *Journal of the History of Philosophy*, 21.4:467–78.

Snitow, Ann, Stansell, Christine, and Thompson, Sharon. 1983. *Powers of Desire: The Politics of Sexuality*. New Feminist Library (New York).

Sommerstein, Alan H. 1980. "The Naming of Women in Greek and Roman Comedy." *Quaderni di Storia*, 11:393–418.

Ste. Croix, G. E. M. de. 1981. *The Class Struggle in the Ancient Greek World from the Archaic Age to the Arab Conquests* (London).

Stigers, Eva Stehle. 1981. "Sappho's Private World": 45–61 in Foley.

Strachey, James, ed. 1953–74. *The Standard Edition of the Complete Psychological Works of Sigmund Freud* (London). Twenty-four volumes.

Sutton, Robert F., Jr. 1981. *The Interaction between Men and Women Portrayed on Attic Red-Figure Pottery*. Ph.D. diss., University of North Carolina, Chapel Hill.

Tarán, Sonya Lida. 1985. "*EISI TRIKHES*: An Erotic Motif in the *Greek Anthology*." *Journal of Hellenic Studies*, 105:90–107.

Tarrant, Harold. 1988. "Midwifery and the *Clouds*." *Classical Quarterly*, 38:116–22.

Taylor, A. E. 1960. *Plato: The Man and his Work*. 7th ed. (London).

Tigay, Jeffrey H. 1982. *The Evolution of the Gilgamesh Epic* (Philadelphia).

Tomin, Julius. 1987. "Socratic Midwifery." *Classical Quarterly*, 37:97–102.

Tripp, C. A. 1975. *The Homosexual Matrix* (New York).

Trumbach, Randolph. 1977. "London's Sodomites: Homosexual Behavior and Western Culture in the 18th Century." *Journal of Social History*, 11:1–33.

Ungaretti, John R. 1982. "De-Moralizing Morality: Where Dover's *Greek Homosexuality* Leaves Us." *Journal of Homosexuality*, 8.1:1–17.

Vanggaard, Thorkil. 1972. *Phallós: A Symbol and its History in the Male World* (New York).

Vernant, Jean-Pierre. 1974. "Hestia-Hermès. Sur l'expression religieuse de l'espace et du mouvement chez les Grecs": I, 124–70 in *Mythe et Pensée chez les Grecs*. 4th ed. (Paris).

Vernant, Jean-Pierre. 1981. "Entre bêtes et dieux. Des jardins d'Adonis à la mythologie des aromates": 141–76 in *Mythe et société en Grèce ancienne* (Paris).

Vernant, Jean-Pierre. 1982. *The Origins of Greek Thought* (Ithaca, NY).

Veyne, Paul. 1978. "La famille et l'amour sous le Haut-Empire romain." *Annales (E.S.C.)*, 33:35–63.

Veyne, Paul. 1985. "Homosexuality in Ancient Rome": 26–35 in Ariès and Béjin.

Vlastos, Gregory. 1981. *Platonic Studies*. 2d ed. (Princeton).

Vlastos, Gregory. 1987. "Socratic Irony." *Classical Quarterly*, 37:79–96.

Walcot, Peter. 1978. "Herodotus on Rape." *Arethusa*, 11.1–2:137–47.

Weeks, Jeffrey. 1977. *Coming Out: Homosexual Politics in Britain, from the Nineteenth Century to the Present* (London).

Weeks, Jeffrey. 1980. "Capitalism and the Organisation of Sex": 11–20 in *Homosexuality: Power & Politics*. Ed. Gay Left Collective (London).

Weeks, Jeffrey. 1981/a. "Discourse, Desire and Sexual Deviance: Some Problems in a History of Homosexuality": 76–111 in Plummer.

Weeks, Jeffrey. 1981/b. *Sex, Politics and Society: The Regulation of Sexuality since 1800* (London).

Wender, Dorothea. 1984 [1973]. "Plato: Misogynist, Paedophile, and Feminist": 213–28 in Peradotto and Sullivan.

Wilamowitz-Moellendorff, Ulrich von. 1920. *Platon*. 2d ed. (Berlin). Two volumes.

Williams, F. E. 1936. *Papuans of the Trans-Fly* (Oxford).

Winkler, John J. 1989/a. "Laying Down the Law: The Oversight of Men's Sexual Behavior in Classical Athens": 45–70 in Winkler (1989/d).

Winkler, John J. 1989/b. "Unnatural Acts: Erotic Protocols in Artemidoros' *Dream Analysis*": 17–44 in Winkler (1989/d).

Winkler, John J. 1989/c. "The Laughter of the Oppressed: Demeter and the Gardens of Adonis": 188–209 in Winkler (1989/d).

Winkler, John J. 1989/d. *The Constraints of Desire: The Anthropology of Sex and Gender in Ancient Greece* (New York).

Wion, Frida. 1970. "L'amour grec." *Bulletin de l'Association Guillaume Budé*, 4th ser.:249–58.

Wood, Ellen Meiksins. 1988. *Peasant-Citizen and Slave: The Foundations of Athenian Democracy* (London).

Woolf, Virginia. 1957 [1929]. *A Room of One's Own* (New York).

Wright, David F. 1984. "Homosexuals or Prostitutes? The Meaning of *ARSENOKOITAI* (I Cor. 6:9, I Tim. 1:10)." *Vigiliae Christianae*, 38:125–53.

Zeitlin, Froma I. 1981. "Travesties of Gender and Genre in Aristophanes' *Thesmophoriazousae*": 169–217 in Foley.

Zeitlin, Froma I. 1984. "The Dynamics of Misogyny: Myth and Mythmaking in the *Oresteia*": 159–94 in Peradotto and Sullivan.

Zeitlin, Froma I. 1985. "Playing the Other: Theater, Theatricality, and the Feminine in Greek Drama." *Representations*, 11:63–94.

Addendum

While this book was already in press, I had the good fortune to read several sections of an important work in progress on *Homosexuality and the Athenian Democracy* by Professor Keith DeVries of the University of Pennsylvania. In the course of a wide-ranging discussion of many issues connected with his topic, DeVries documents the depiction on Attic pottery (black-figure, mostly, with particular attention to the work of a painter termed The Affecter) of reciprocal erotic contacts between adult males—scenes whose significance had hitherto been neglected or insufficiently appreciated by historians of ancient Greek sexual behavior. DeVries also catalogues instances of the portrayal on Greek vases of a reversal of conventional erotic roles between man and boy. This testimony, though relatively scanty and in need of careful interpretation, makes me inclined to qualify or to moderate even further some of the already tentative general claims about the nature of Greek paederasty advanced here and there throughout these essays (on pp. 47, 130–31, and 160–61, for example) and it absolutely requires me to correct the impression, with which I left the reader on pages 47 and 160–61 (Chapter 1, note 31) and which I had myself been under until I read DeVries's study, that my conclusions were based on a complete review of the pictorial evidence.

Index

A Note on the Author

DAVID M. HALPERIN is Professor of Literature in the School of Humanities and Social Sciences at the Massachusetts Institute of Technology. He has published widely on Greek and Latin bucolic poetry, on the relations between ancient Greece and the Near East, and on a variety of topics in literary history, comparative literature, Greek philosophy, Soviet literature, and the history of sexuality; his work has appeared in *Critical Inquiry, The Yale Review, The South Atlantic Quarterly, The Virginia Quarterly, Diacritics, Partisan Review, Ancient Philosophy, Classical Antiquity, American Journal of Philology, Classical Journal, Transactions of the American Philological Association,* and in many different collections. In addition, he is the author of *Before Pastoral: Theocritus and the Ancient Tradition of Bucolic Poetry* (Yale University Press, 1983) and is co-editor, with John J. Winkler and Froma I. Zeitlin, of *Before Sexuality: The Construction of Erotic Experience in the Ancient Greek World* (Princeton University Press, 1989). He has been a Fellow of the American Academy in Rome, the National Humanities Center, and the Stanford Humanities Center.